MW00826466

Praise for *The Sense of Mystery*

"Next to his major works in fundamental theology (*De Revelatione*) and in philosophical theology (*God: His Existence and Nature*), this arguably is Garrigou-Lagrange's most important theological contribution at the intersection of fundamental and dogmatic theology. Though considerably shorter, this book displays in focus and in substance a striking similarity to Matthias Josef Scheeben's classic *The Mysteries of Christianity*. *The Sense of Mystery* considers the reality of the divine mystery, the way it informs the fundamental relationship between nature and grace, and, by way of the latter, shapes the central topics of dogmatic theology.

At a time when analytic hyper-rationalism, perspectivalist historicism, and pastoral intuitivism vie for the pole position in contemporary systematic theology, theologians and students thereof ignore at their own peril this welcome exercise in theological perspicuity and epistemic humility. The sacred monster of Thomism turns out to be a practitioner of theological sanity helping us understand what is theologically at stake in the face of the contemporary alternatives. *Tolle, lege*—Take and read!"

—REINHARD HÜTTER
Ordinary Professor of Fundamental and Dogmatic Theology
School of Theology and Religious Studies
The Catholic University of America
Washington, DC

"'Faith and reason are like two wings on which the human spirit rises to the contemplation of truth' (*Fides et Ratio*, Introduction). Thus, Pope St. John Paul II. His theological mentor composed this volume to explain why logic and mystery both serve revealed truth. All should welcome this English translation."

—ROMANUS CESSARIO, O.P.
Saint John's Seminary
Brighton, Massachusetts

"Is Garrigou-Lagrange also among the theologians of mystery? The answer is emphatically yes. We are in Matthew Minerd's debt for producing such a fine translation with annotations that nicely contextualize Garrigou-Lagrange's insights. It is past time to add Garrigou-Lagrange (and his sources) to the reading list of all who seek true *ressourcement* of the entire Catholic tradition. If liberal theology is to be opposed in the twenty-first century Church, we will need both the neo-scholastics and the *nouvelle theologie*, whose insights can now be gleaned without condemning the one or the other. May the publication of this book signal an end to the circular firing squad of those who should be allies in the struggle against Catholic Troeltschian theology."

—MATTHEW LEVERING
James N. and Mary D. Perry Jr. Chair of Theology
Mundelein Seminary
Mundelein, Illinois

"In 1998, Pope John Paul II published *Fides et Ratio*, one of his seminal encyclicals, which examines the relationship of faith and reason thematically in light of the notion of three forms of wisdom: philosophical, theological, and mystical wisdom. This thematic approach has its precedent especially in this influential work of Garrigou-Lagrange, *Le Sens du Mystere*, now translated into English. This book explores questions of skepticism and metaphysical realism, knowledge of the existence of God, the supernatural life of faith, theology and its relation to the mystical life. A landmark book that should be widely read . . ."

—THOMAS JOSEPH WHITE, O.P.
Dominican House of Studies
Washington, DC

The Sense of Mystery

The Sense of Mystery

CLARITY AND OBSCURITY
IN THE INTELLECTUAL LIFE

Fr. Réginald Garrigou-Lagrange, O.P.
Translated by Matthew K. Minerd

EMMAUS
ACADEMIC

www.emmausacademic.com
Steubenville, Ohio

EMMAUS
A C A D E M I C

Steubenville, Ohio
www.emmausacademic.com
A Division of The St. Paul Center for Biblical Theology
Editor-in-Chief: Scott Hahn
1468 Parkview Circle
Steubenville, Ohio 43952

Original French edition, *Le Sens du Mystère et le Clair-Obscur Intellectuel, Nature et Surnaturel*
published by Desclée de Brouwer in 1934.

Library of Congress Cataloging-in-Publication Data
Names: Garrigou-Lagrange, Reginald, 1877-1964, author.
Title: The sense of mystery: clarity and obscurity in the intellectual life
  / Fr. Reginald Garrigou-Lagrange, O.P. ; translated by Matthew K. Minerd.
Other titles: Sens du mystere et le clair-obscur intellectuel. English
Description: English [edition]. | Steubenville : Emmaus Academic, 2017. |
  Identifiers: LCCN 2017045158 (print) | LCCN 2017047663 (ebook) | ISBN
  9781947792340 (ebook) | ISBN 9781947792326 (hardcover) | ISBN
  9781947792333 (pbk.)
Subjects: LCSH: Thomas, Aquinas, Saint, 1225?-1274. | Knowledge, Theory of.
Classification: LCC B765.T54 (ebook) | LCC B765.T54 G3413 2017 (print) | DDC
  230/.2--dc23
LC record available at https://lccn.loc.gov/2017045158

Cover image: *Interior of the Cathedral, Pisa* (1859) by David Roberts.
The Berger Collection, Denver, Colorado / Wikimedia Commons.

Cover design and layout by Margaret Ryland

"*Each one of our acts contains a mystery; if the act is morally good and salutary, it is the mystery of grace; if it is evil, it is the mystery of the divine permission of evil for the sake of a higher good.*"

Contents

Foreword

Réginald Garrigou-Lagrange, O.P. (1877–1964): Theologian, Thomist, Contemplative

Cajetan Cuddy, O.P.
Couvent Saint-Albert-le-Grand
Fribourg, Switzerland
14 September 2017
The Exaltation of the Cross

"Having purified your souls by your obedience to the truth for a sincere love of the brethren, love one another earnestly from the heart."　　　　　　　　　　　　　　　(1 Peter 1:22)

"By wisdom a house is built, and by understanding it is established."　　　　　　　　　　　　　　　(Proverbs 24:3)

"What have you that you did not receive?"
　　　　　　　　　　　　　　　(1 Corinthians 4:7)

*　*　*

RENEWED INTEREST IN THE WORKS of the Dominican priest Réginald Garrigou-Lagrange continues to gain momentum. The publication of this translation of his 1934 *Le Sens du mystère et le clair-obscur intellectuel* signals a noteworthy moment in the contemporary rediscovery of the late "Fr. Garrigou." Earlier, in 2013, an independent publication of Garrigou-Lagrange's essay *The Essence and Topicality of*

Thomism appeared.[1] In 2015, a new edition of his forgotten book on the Christian life came back into print.[2] And now, in 2017, Catholic philosophers and theologians have English access to this book, *The Sense of Mystery*. Additionally, new or revised translations of his articles can be found in academic journals.[3] Two book-length studies of Fr. Garrigou's life and thought are available in English.[4] Finally, digital books and essays about his life and work lie scattered across the virtual world.[5] From even a cursory list of recent publications in Garrigouvian texts and studies, one observes that the life and legacy of Réginald Garrigou-Lagrange today enjoys a renaissance.[6]

Why Garrigou-Lagrange?

Garrigou-Lagrange proved an unavoidable figure during the early twentieth century. His contemporaries read and considered his works, though not always with appreciation. Still, the influence Garrigou-Lagrange exercised on Catholic thought during his own period ensured that he, at the very least, would not be relegated to mere footnote-existence in subsequent analyses of Catholic intellectual history.

One, however, may legitimately ask, why Garrigou-Lagrange today? Can Fr. Garrigou claim a pertinence for the contemporary practice of

---

[1] Réginald Garrigou-Lagrange, O.P., *The Essence and Topicality of Thomism*, trans. Alan Aversa (2013).

[2] Réginald Garrigou-Lagrange, O.P., *Knowing the Love of God: Lessons from a Spiritual Master* (DeKalb, IL: Lighthouse Catholic Media, 2015). This book originally appeared under the title *The Last Writings of Reginald Garrigou-Lagrange*, trans. Raymond Smith, O.P., and Rod Gorton (New York: New City Press, 1969).

[3] For a recent example, see Réginald Garrigou-Lagrange, O.P., "Where is the New Theology Leading Us?" *Josephinum Journal of Theology* 18, no. 1 (2011): 63–78.

[4] Richard Peddicord, O.P., *The Sacred Monster of Thomism: An Introduction to the Life and Legacy of Reginald Garrigou-Lagrange, O.P.* (South Bend, IN: St. Augustine's Press, 2005); Aidan Nichols, O.P., *Reason with Piety: Garrigou-Lagrange in the Service of Catholic Thought* (Ave Maria, FL: Sapientia Press, 2008).

[5] Jude Chua Soo Meng and Thomas Crean, O.P., eds., *Reginald Garrigou-Lagrange, O.P.: Teacher of Thomism* (http://educationaltheoria.files.wordpress.com/2014/02/garrigou-teacher-thomism.pdf).

[6] It appears that Aidan Nichols first coined the adjective "Garrigouvian" (see Nichols, *Reason with Piety*, 93).

Catholic philosophy and theology? Because he—like all past influential figures—belonged to a particular era, the question of pertinence emerges. Although a master of distinction, Garrigou was not a subtle doctor. Readers always know what Garrigou-Lagrange thinks about the questions and topics that he engages. Intellectual clarity and literary transparency permeate the pages that still bear his authorship. The questions and controversies of the early twentieth century certainly influenced his writings. But today? What enduring value do his books and articles hold for the twenty-first century thinker?[7] Further, one wonders what accounts for the renewed interest in his life and work.

In order to answer these questions, I offer three reflections about Réginald Garrigou-Lagrange. These reflections help to explain why his legacy transcends the specific questions Catholic thought took up in the early twentieth century. They also help to explain the present-day renewal of interest in this influential Dominican.

1. A Theologian: Service to the Depositum Fidei

In the opening sentence of the 1992 Apostolic Constitution *Fidei Depositum*, "On the Publication of the *Catechism of the Catholic Church* Prepared Following the Second Vatican Ecumenical Council," St. John Paul II states: "Guarding the deposit of faith is the mission which the Lord has entrusted to his Church and which she fulfills in every age."[8] The preservation of the *depositum fidei* lies at the heart of the Church's very identity and mission. The Church did not and does not generate this sacred deposit herself. She received the deposit of faith from Our Lord. Jesus himself confided for all ages this *depositum fidei* to his One, Holy, Catholic, and Apostolic Church. "Sacred tradition and Sacred Scripture form one sacred deposit of the word of God, committed to the Church."[9] The Church does not create truth. She treasures and

---

[7] For a bibliography of Garrigou-Lagrange's books, articles, and reviews, see Benedetto Zorcolo, O.P., "Bibliografia del P. Garrigou-Lagrange," *Angelicum* 42 (1965): 200–72.

[8] John Paul II, Apostolic Constitution On the Publication of the Catechism of the Catholic Church *Fidei Depositum* (October 11, 1992), §I.

[9] Second Vatican Council, Dogmatic Constitution On Divine Revelation *Dei Verbum* (November 18, 1965), §10.

guards the precious gift that Jesus conferred on her for the salvation of the world.[10]

Consequently, the Church understands the "vocation of the theologian" in reference to her own charge over the sacred deposit. The Instruction *Donum Veritatis* expounds upon the theologian's mission "to pursue in a particular way an ever deeper understanding of the Word of God found in the inspired Scriptures and handed on by the living Tradition of the Church."[11] Herein lies the theological pattern of "faith seeking understanding."[12] The theologian always fulfills his sacred function "in communion with the Magisterium which has been charged with the responsibility of preserving the deposit of faith."[13] The true vocation of the theologian finds its intelligibility only in reference to the Church's mission of preserving this sacred deposit. Theologians faithfully serve the Magisterium and its mission of life and unity in the truth.[14] St. Irenaeus beautifully expresses the priorities of the authentic teacher of Catholic truth: "We guard with care the faith that we have received from the Church, for without ceasing, under the action of God's Spirit, this deposit of great price, as in an excellent vessel, is constantly being renewed and causes the very vessel that contains it to be renewed."[15]

References to or emphases on the sacred deposit of faith may strike some contemporary readers as rather cold or impersonal, that is, some-

---

[10] See First Vatican Council, Dogmatic Constitution On The Catholic Faith *Dei Filius* (April 24, 1870), c. 4.

[11] Congregation for the Doctrine of the Faith, Instruction On the Ecclesial Vocation of the Theologian *Donum Veritatis* (May 24, 1990), §6.

[12] "The Catechism emphasizes the exposition of doctrine. It seeks to help deepen understanding of faith. In this way it is oriented towards the maturing of that faith, its putting down roots in personal life, and its shining forth in personal conduct"(CCC 23).

[13] *Donum Veritatis*, §6.

[14] Romanus Cessario, O.P., explains: "Theologians enjoy the responsibility of helping the Church safeguard the deposit of faith (*depositum fidei*), so that the bonds of unity in the apostolic faith will continue to grow extensively and develop coherently" (*Introduction to Moral Theology*, rev. ed. [Washington, DC: The Catholic University of America Press, 2013], xiv).

[15] As quoted in CCC 175. See also the profoundly moving words of St. Gregory of Nazianzus ("the Theologian") in reference to the Christian obligation to "guard" the "great deposit of faith" (CCC 256).

thing akin to a collection of abstract facts or theses-like articles that can inform minds but, perhaps, fail to enliven hearts. Even though this visceral reaction might be excusable in those unfamiliar with the dynamics of Catholic theology, it compels such readers to examine the opening lines of the *Catechism of the Catholic Church*. As St. John Paul II began his apostolic constitution on the Catechism by invoking the *fidei depositum*, so the Catechism begins with the most essential and shaping reality whose truth Jesus committed to his Church: "God, infinitely perfect and blessed in himself, in a plan of sheer goodness freely created man to make him share in his own blessed life."[16] God stands as the initiating word—the shaping subject, the formal object— of the Catechism's opening sentence. God always comes first. The sacred truth Jesus entrusted to the Church unfolds, invariably and ulti- mately, the truth about God. The God of power and might is other, certainly. Nonetheless, he does not remain at a distance. In fact, "at every time and in every place, God draws close to man" so that human persons might become "his adopted children and thus heirs of his blessed life."[17] This truth—this very personal "Good News"—consti- tutes the "treasure, received from the apostles" and "faithfully guarded by their successors."[18]

Réginald Garrigou-Lagrange was a Catholic theologian, and his thought received shape from this theocentric orientation. God stood at the center of his vocation and mission. His theology grew out of his consecration to the Bride of Christ and to the sacred deposit entrusted to her: "Theology is a commentary ever drawing attention to the word of God which it comments on."[19] Fr. Garrigou eschewed all forms of intellectual solipsism. He cautioned against the "deformation of the theologian's profession" which emerges when a theologian "digresses too much and is too much given to argumentation," as if the formula- tion of new ideas and erudite discussions were the end of his profession. Unlike the "hunters who find greater delight in the sport of hunting

---

[16] CCC 1.

[17] Ibid.

[18] CCC 3.

[19] Réginald Garrigou-Lagrange, O.P., *Reality: A Synthesis of Thomistic Thought*, trans. Rev. Patrick Cummins, O.S.B. (St. Louis, MO: B. Herder Book Co., 1950), 70.

than in the game they take," the Catholic theologian never pursues a mere "mode of demonstrating the truth" but rather "the actual discovery of the truth itself." Alarmingly, temptations for things other than the truth can present themselves "even when they [theologians] are investigating things most sublime."[20] In other words, ideas—even ideas about the noblest realities—are not the end of theology. God himself remains the end. "Theology, like the Baptist, forgets itself in the cry: Behold the Lamb of God, who takes away the sin of the world."[21] Because they joyfully conform to the obeisant pattern of their sacred science, Catholic theologians do not resent the *depositum fidei*. Theologians can never forsake the real object of their holy discipline.

Garrigou-Lagrange received his vocation to theology from the Church, not from the academy. The grace of the *depositum fidei* shaped his vocation in a way that the priorities of academia never did and never could. "Theology accepts the *depositum fidei*, and studies its documents, Scripture and tradition, under the guidance of the teaching Church . . . theology defends revealed truths by showing either that they are contained in the deposit of faith, or that they contain no manifest impossibility."[22] Theology grows out of the call to contemplate, to serve, and to preserve the *depositum fidei*—and this deposit only resides in Christ's Church. Fr. Garrigou stood unwavering in his commitment to the deposit Jesus confided to his bride. And his example can inspire those who claim the theologian's vocation to renounce the tragic alternatives to such devotion. A theologian who replaces consecration to the *depositum fidei* with allegiances to the professional academy inevitably forfeits the sacred truth that belongs to him by vocational birthright. Fr. Garrigou cautioned theologians against the danger of "particularism," the result of an "excessive influence of certain ideas prevalent at some period of time or in some region, ideas which after thirty years will appear antiquated."[23] He continues:

---

[20] Réginald Garrigou-Lagrange, O.P., *The One God: A Commentary on the First Part of St. Thomas' Theological Summa*, trans. Dom Bede Rose, O.S.B. (St. Louis, MO: B. Herder Book Co., 1943), 26.

[21] Garrigou-Lagrange, *Reality*, 70.

[22] Ibid., 64.

[23] Garrigou-Lagrange, *The One God*, 33.

Some years ago ideas of this or that particular philosophy prevailed, which now no longer find favorable acceptance. It is so in every generation. There is a succession of opinions and events that arouse one's admiration; they pass with the fashion of the world, while the words of God remain, by which the just man must live.[24]

Although the truth may fall out of favor among some, it never loses its relevance to all. Garrigou-Lagrange understood that the living dynamism of Catholic theology finds its principle in the Eternal Word. His legacy illustrates the liberating purification that comes from standing in "obedience to the truth" (1 Peter 1:22). This obedience does not resemble the dim subservience of the voluntarist. On the contrary, the theologian obeys the truth because the theologian loves the truth. Admittedly, divine truth eludes easy explanation, but the fruits of its contemplation excel those of all other possible objects. Garrigou puts it this way: "The study of sacred theology, which sometimes is hard and arduous, though fruitful, thus disposes our minds for the light of contemplation and of life, which is, as it were, an introduction and a beginning of eternal life in us."[25]

The truth of reality never ceases to govern the theologian's craft. "The Angelic Doctor never cherished method for its own sake, but for the purpose of finding out the truth and transmitting it to posterity, especially divine truth to which he especially directed his attention."[26] Sacred truth abides as a gift to the creature. The *depositum fidei* ensures that the *donum veritatis* will never suffer extinction. Fr. Garrigou-Lagrange cherished the truth, and he never took leave of his service to the sacred deposit. He exemplified the theological life that St. John Paul II describes in *Fidei Depositum*.[27] And, as a result, Garrigou-La-

---

[24] Ibid.

[25] Ibid., 37.

[26] Ibid., 26.

[27] For a consideration of Garrigou-Lagrange's influence on John Paul II, see Cajetan Cuddy, O.P., and Romanus Cessario, O.P., "Witness to Faith: George Weigel, Blessed John Paul II, and the Theological Life," *Nova et Vetera* 10, no. 1 (2012): 1–13.

grange experienced the liberating excellence of the truth.[28] He knew the reality that he loved.

2. A Thomist: "Intellectual Monasticism"

Réginald Garrigou-Lagrange was a theologian. He was also a Thomist. These identities found synergistic union in his writings as they had in his fellow Thomists who have served the Church for more than seven hundred years. Fr. Garrigou revered the teaching of St. Thomas and the legacy of the Thomist tradition for the same reason that he treasured the vocation of the theologian. Thomism was not something incidental to his calling. The Thomist tradition shaped the mode of his service to the Church. Like the theologian's vocation, one best understands Thomas and the Thomist tradition in reference to ecclesial service.[29] And like Thomas and the other Thomists, Garrigou-Lagrange served the Church by championing something rare and precious: the order of wisdom.

In his commentary on the *prima pars* of Aquinas's *Summa Theologiae*, Garrigou-Lagrange pauses to highlight the macrostructure of the Angelic Doctor's theological project:

> In the *Summa* [*Theologiae*] of the Angelic Doctor all questions are considered as they refer to God, who is the proper object of theology, rather than as they refer to man and his liberty. This point of view may be called therefore theocentric but not anthropocentric, as the psychological tendency is of modern times.[30]

---

[28] "The truth which sets us free is a gift of Jesus Christ (see Jn 8:32). Man's nature calls him to seek the truth while ignorance keeps him in a condition of servitude. Indeed, man could not be truly free were no light shed upon the central questions of his existence including, in particular, where he comes from and where he is going. When God gives Himself to man as a friend, man becomes free" (*Donum Veritatis*, §1).

[29] For a consideration of the Thomist tradition's perpetual service to the Church, see Romanus Cessario, O.P., and Cajetan Cuddy, O.P., *Thomas and the Thomists: The Achievement of Thomas Aquinas and His Interpreters* (Minneapolis, MN: Fortress Press, 2017).

[30] Garrigou-Lagrange, *The One God*, 38.

The teaching of Aquinas and of his followers grew out of vocations in service to the *depositum fidei*. Neither Thomas nor the Thomists considered their work to be a mere record of intellectual divertissements. Rather, they understood their projects as expressions of their consecration to the truth—a truth that is real, perennial, liberating, and salvific. Here St. Thomas stands as a striking image of his spiritual father, St. Dominic. Those who knew St. Dominic remembered him as a man who spoke "only to God or about God." St. Dominic was a theocentric man, and his theocentricism led him to found a religious order consecrated to the truth.[31]

St. Thomas received this theocentric orientation in full measure. It permeated and shaped his own life and work—a life and work unparalleled in sanctified intellectual capacity and productivity. As his spiritual father only spoke to God or about God, so Thomas structured all of his theology around him who is pure act and Trinity of Divine Persons. This theocentricism manifests itself in the very structure of his *magnum opus*. St. Thomas's theology begins with God, and it is ordered to God. "All things are treated in the *sacra doctrina* under the aspect of God: either because they are God himself or because they have an order to God as their principle and end. Hence, it follows that God, truly, is the subject of this science."[32] Thus, as St. Dominic gave to the world a religious *form of life* consecrated to the God of truth, so St. Thomas gave to the world a theological *form of thought* consecrated to the truth of God.[33] The latter follows as the intellectual consequence of the spiritual former.

Certainly, not all Thomists have been, nor need be, Dominican friars. Historical record attests to the many and varied members of the Thomist tradition who have emerged from clerical, religious, and lay

---

[31] For more information about St. Dominic and those conformed to his image, see the following books by Guy Bedouelle, O.P.: *Saint Dominic: The Grace of the Word* (San Francisco: Ignatius Press, 1995); *In the Image of Saint Dominic: Nine Portraits of Dominican Life* (San Francisco: Ignatius Press, 1994).

[32] *ST* I, q. 1, a. 7. Translation original.

[33] Romanus Cessario, O.P., reflects upon the Dominican *forma vitae* in his essay: "The Grace Saint Dominic Brings to the World: A Fresh Look at Dominican Spirituality," in *Theology and Sanctity*, Romanus Cessario, O.P., ed. Cajetan Cuddy, O.P. (Ave Maria, FL: Sapientia Press, 2014), 1–17.

vocations.[34] Nevertheless, all included within the Thomistic school participate in the form of thought that Aquinas bequeathed to his disciples. And this form of thought bears the theocentric imprint of St. Dominic's way of life. In light of this analysis, one might suggest that "Thomism" can be described as "intellectual monasticism." As Dominic's theocentric form shaped all elements of Aquinas's life—his time, his activity, and even the architecture of the Dominican priories in which he lived—so this theocentric order shaped all aspects of Aquinas's thought. Monastic and religious structure marked Aquinas's life from an early age. And his teaching discloses an analogously monastic configuration. In the Dominican priory, God stands at the center of life. In the Thomist tradition, God stands at the center of thought. The abstract "architecture" of Aquinas's intellectual project resembles the concrete design of the Dominican *couvent*.

Interest in the monastic life persists even in a secular age like our own.[35] Genuine monastic inclination does not include the desire to escape reality but rather the desire to realize wise order in reality. Order facilitates shape, structure, and freedom. Wisdom and order go together: *"Sapientis est ordinare"* ("It belongs to the wise man to order").[36] The order of St. Benedict's monasticism shaped western civilization.[37] The order of St. Dominic's religious observance gave shape to the core of civilization: the city.[38] The order of St. Thomas's intellectual monasticism gives shape to the core of the human person: the rational soul, the intellect. These shaping influences did not cease with the death of these saints. Garrigou reminds his readers: "the influence of the founders of religious orders perdures even in heaven so that their orders may continue in being." And "St. Thomas's influence also per-

---

[34] For a listing of some of the key figures in the Thomist tradition, see David Berger and Jörgen Vijgen, ed., *Thomistenlexikon* (Bonn: Verlag Nova et Vetera, 2006).

[35] For example, see Rod Dreher, *The Benedict Option: A Strategy for Christians in a Post-Christian Nation* (New York: Sentinel, 2017).

[36] Thomas Aquinas, *Sententia libri Ethicorum*, 1.1.

[37] For further elaboration, see Thomas E. Woods, Jr., *How the Catholic Church Built Western Civilization* (Washington, DC: Regnery, 2005).

[38] For an analysis of the Dominican presence in urban settings, see William A. Hinnebusch, O.P., *The History of the Dominican Order*, 2 vols. (New York: Alba House, 1966–1973).

dures that the true spirit of his doctrine may be conserved."[39] Only a wise man can construct an edifice that will endure: "By wisdom a house is built, and by understanding it is established" (Proverbs 24:3). The sage order of St. Dominic and St. Thomas shaped the life and thought of Réginald Garrigou-Lagrange. "The more we have studied this *Theological Summa*, the more we have seen the beauty of its structure."[40] Indeed, Garrigou-Lagrange never tired of reminding his readers that God's unique and exclusive identity as "self-subsisting Being" serves as "the golden key of the whole doctrinal edifice, which is constructed by the Angelic Doctor."[41] St. Thomas built his speculative architecture on this fundamental truth. Fr. Garrigou observes:

> The perfection of this edifice is in great part due to the consummate skill with which he [Aquinas] effects the divisions between the treatises or the questions or the articles or the arguments. These divisions, of course, are not extrinsic but intrinsic, arranged in accordance with the formal point of view of the whole to be divided, and effected by means of members that are truly opposites to each other, so that the divisions are adequate, with subordinate subdivisions; yet all is done with discretion and not by descending to the least details. Thus by a gradual process the light of the principles reaches to the ultimate conclusions.[42]

Just as each moment and place in a monastery possesses a specific purpose and occupies a specific location that orders the monk to a deeper union with God, so each article and distinction in the *Summa* enjoys a specific purpose and location that orders the believer toward a deeper understanding of divine truth. The theocentric life of St. Dominic engenders the form of the religious buildings his sons inhabit.

---

[39] Réginald Garrigou-Lagrange, O.P., *The Trinity and God the Creator: A Commentary on St. Thomas' Theological Summa, Ia, 1. 27–119*, trans. Frederic C. Eckhoff (St. Louis, MO: B. Herder Book Co., 1952), 445.

[40] Garrigou-Lagrange, *The One God*, 26.

[41] Ibid., 25.

[42] Ibid., 26.

By the same token, the theocentric thought of St. Thomas engenders the form of the intellectual edifice his followers have adopted. For the same sapiential reason, the Church rejoices both in the graces of monasticism and Thomism: "it belongs to the wise man to order."

Like Thomas and the other Thomists, Fr. Garrigou remained vigilant in his conviction that the order of wisdom can shape the minds and hearts of people and civilizations at all times and in all seasons. Neither his religious life nor his commitment to the teaching of St. Thomas Aquinas facilitated an escape from reality. Each served his vocation as a theologian. Garrigou was a religious and a Thomist. He understood that only "by wisdom a house is built" (Proverbs 24:3).

3. A Contemplative: The First Principles of Being

Famously, in the *Summa Theologiae*, Aquinas says: "As it is better to illuminate rather than to shine only, so it is better to hand on to others what has been contemplated rather than to contemplate only."[43] This passage captures St. Thomas's person and work: he was a contemplative whose labor reflects this identity. The proper activities of the contemplative are subject to numerous misunderstandings, however. Today "contemplation" sometimes carries connotations of something spiritually elusive or even esoterically hidden. One benefit that befalls those who study *The Sense of Mystery* concerns contemplation. In a word, Réginald Garrigou-Lagrange explains the reality that underlies contemplation.

In his introduction to *The Sense of Mystery*, Garrigou-Lagrange makes the following observation with such concision that readers can easily miss its profundity: "St. Thomas has fear neither for logic nor for mystery."[44] Both find happy (though proper) union on natural and supernatural levels. As mystery permeates the natural order as well as the supernatural order, so reason serves the contemplation of grace as

---

[43] "Sicut enim maius est illuminare quam lucere solum, ita maius est contemplata aliis tradere quam solum contemplari" (*ST* II-II, q. 188, a. 6). Translation original. The customary translation of "contemplata" as "the fruits of one's contemplation" does not fully capture the meaning of the Latin.

[44] Réginald Garrigou-Lagrange, O.P., *The Sense of Mystery*, trans. Matthew Minerd (Steubenville, OH: Emmaus Academic, 2017), xxxix-xl.

well as of nature. The Catholic theologian rejects all misguided efforts: 1) to set logic and mystery as mutually excluding antinomies, 2) to limit reason's pertinence exclusively to the order of nature, and 3) to restrict mystery's presence solely to the order of grace (and glory). A failure to properly distinguish or to unite reason and faith frustrates the fulfillment of the theologian's vocation.[45] The true contemplative avoids the frustrations inherent in the hubris of rationalism as well as the dissatisfaction that always accompanies the sentimentalism of fideism.[46] Mystery—both natural and supernatural—invites the inquiry of reason. Garrigou-Lagrange observes that Aquinas's "logical lucidity leads him to see in nature those mysteries that speak in their own particular ways of the Creator." At the same time, the presence of real mysteries in the order of nature does not in any way denigrate the transcendent profundity of the mysteries of the faith. As our author writes, "Likewise, this same lucidity aids him in putting into strong relief other secrets of a far superior order—those of grace and of the intimate life of God, which would remain unknown were it not for Divine Revelation."[47]

Fr. Garrigou immediately proceeds to identify two fundamental first principles that illuminate the mysteries of reality—both natural and supernatural: 1) the real distinction between being and nonbeing, and, consequently, 2) the real distinction between act and potency.[48] One cannot overestimate the importance of these first principles. Elsewhere, he explains that "the definition of potency determines the Thomistic synthesis" and tradition. "When potency is conceived as really distinct from all act, even the least perfect, then we have the Thomistic position."[49] The real distinction between potency and act serves as the distinguishing and unifying principle of the Thomist philosophical and theological tradition. The tradition's commitment to these first principles of being also explains why Thomists are effective

---

[45] For further explanation of these themes, see Romanus Cessario, O.P., *"Duplex Ordo Cognitionis,"* in *Reason and the Reasons of Faith*, ed. Paul J. Griffiths and Reinhard Hütter (New York: T&T Clark, 2005), 327–338.

[46] See *Fides et Ratio*, §55.

[47] Garrigou-Lagrange, *The Sense of Mystery*, xl.

[48] Ibid.

[49] Garrigou-Lagrange, *Reality*, 37.

in their service of the *depositum fidei*. These first principles equip the theologian with realist tools for articulating the truth and the coherence of the articles contained in the deposit of faith.[50] No point exists at which these principles cease to apply. The real distinction between potency and act enjoys privileged citizenship on all metaphysical planes (natural and supernatural). Always and everywhere, potency and act remain truly distinct. It applies to the lowliest being and even to God himself. Only God is pure act. The utter absence of any potency in God alone confirms the speculative utility of the real distinction. Every other being (from the highest angel to the smallest particle) exists as a composite of act and potency—and all other beings receive their proportionate actuality from him who is *actus purus*.[51] In a word, the first principles of being ensure the realism of contemplation. "What have you," St. Paul inquires, "that you did not receive?" (1 Corinthians 4:7). The actuality of all created being—natural and supernatural—comes forth as the gift of God.

Because they aim to become contemplative realists, members of the Thomist tradition recognize the necessary and profound harmony that exists between theological reflection and the spiritual life. This theme permeates the writings of Garrigou-Lagrange:

> Theological study and the interior life should be *united*; we must, indeed, make a distinction between the two, but we must never separate them or confuse one with the other. Otherwise theological science, through a confusion with piety, would lose its objectivity and immutability, and the interior life might perhaps be reduced to the theses on spirituality. Sacred theology would thus unhappily be reduced . . . to an intellectual expression of subjective religious experience. On the other

---

[50] For a concise illustration of this point, see Romanus Cessario, O.P., and Cajetan Cuddy, O.P., "Mercy in Aquinas: Help from the Commentatorial Tradition," *The Thomist* 80, no. 3 (2016): 329–339.

[51] For a recent and profound consideration of the real distinction between potency and act and its universal implications, see Steven A. Long, *Analogia Entis: On the Analogy of Being, Metaphysics, and the Act of Faith* (Notre Dame, IN: University of Notre Dame Press, 2011).

hand, our interior life would become too intellectual; it would become a theory of the interior life and would lose its realism, its serious depth and fecundity.[52]

The details of Fr. Garrigou's analysis in this paragraph warrant close attention. He cautions against any separation of theological inquiry from the interior life. The two must always receive proper distinction and proper union. When theological study and the interior life lack proper integration, both suffer. Theological study suffers a deprivation of "objectivity and immutability." The interior life suffers the loss of its proper "realism" and so becomes a mere "theory." Both errors constitute a step away from the real and objective truth of God. Garrigou-Lagrange thus urges all Catholic theologians to pursue contemplative realism. Ideas, even good ideas, about God remain insufficient. God alone suffices. True theological science—like its proper subject and object—enjoys an objectivity and immutability that transcends place and time. A healthy spiritual life yearns for the real God—not ideas about God. It is never content to subsist on a mere "thesis existence." Nonetheless, the truth about God which he graciously confides to his Church abides as truly knowable. Theological agnosticism—even of an erudite sort—that never comes to rest in the truth God has revealed about himself always remains inimical to the contemplative realist. A self-reflexive intellectualism finds no place in the soul of the Thomist theologian.

The first principles of being serve the contemplative not because of their conceptual elegance but because of their inextricable foundation in objective reality. A commitment to these fundamental principles is a sign of the theologian's consecration to the truth. The human intellect can understand the truth about anything that is real—human nature, angels, sacraments, grace, divine mercy, heavenly glory—only in reference to the proper principles: potency and act, essence and existence. These principles underlie all of reality—even revealed, supernatural reality. And a commitment to these principles helps to ensure that

---

[52] Réginald Garrigou-Lagrange, O.P., *The Priesthood and Perfection*, trans. E. Hayden, O.P. (Westminster, MD: The Newman Press, 1955), 13. Emphasis original.

the theologian's contemplation does not lose real contact with real truth and true being. A contemplative realist never forgets the absolute necessity of grace nor despairs before the disintegration of nature. Why? God is real. Grace is real. Mercy is real. And the real God brings real salvation to a fallen humanity.

Garrigou-Lagrange understood that reality enjoys no actuality that it does not receive. He embodied the contemplative realist who labored to communicate to others—even to us—the saving reality he contemplated. His legacy finds it crowning merit in his contemplative realism.

Conclusion

Why Réginald Garrigou-Lagrange today? The answer appears simple: he was a theologian, a Thomist, and a contemplative. These three facets of his intellectual physiognomy remain as vital to the Church's well-being in the twenty-first century as they were for the Church of the twentieth century (and before). Because each facet terminates in the truth, they stand as compenetrating features of Garrigou's legacy. Although one may distinguish his theological vocation from his Thomistic commitments and from his contemplative realism, one can never separate them. In fact, a reader can recognize their mutually-sustaining influence on virtually every page Garrigou ever wrote.

I conclude with one final observation: each of Fr. Garrigou's books bears a dedication to the Blessed Virgin Mary. Facile readers might interpret this gesture as a touching vestige of the Marian piety that characterized the French School of Spirituality. References to authors of the French School certainly appear in Garrigou's writings. However, upon further reflection, something profound emerges. The realism of his Marian piety reaches, to invoke an earlier Thomist, the "frontiers of the Divinity" itself. Fr. Garrigou explains what this means in an autobiographical vignette:

> As a young student . . . I was so engrossed in the many and varied questions of critica and metaphysics that I was in danger of losing my simplicity and elevation of mind and bal-

anced judgment. It was then I realized that I needed a spiritual mother with unlimited kindness and wisdom.[53]

Fr. Réginald Garrigou-Lagrange consecrated himself and his work to the Holy Mother of God. Theologians, Thomists, and contemplatives alike require Mary's spiritual maternity. For only in Mary does one really learn what it means to live in obedience to the truth: "Behold, I am the handmaid of the Lord; let it be to me according to your word" (Luke 1:38). Mary's consecration to the truth was such that she conceived the Eternal Word in her womb. All those who seek the grace of the word must seek the assistance of the Blessed Virgin. She remains for all generations the Holy Mother of God: "the Virgin Mary is called 'the Mother of God' because she is the mother of Jesus, who *is* God."[54] Her being and identity are only understood in light of her predestination to the divine maternity. "By one and the same decree the Father predestined Jesus to natural divine sonship and Mary for the divine maternity."[55] The metaphysics of Mary's maternity causes angelic intellects to bow in reverence before the wisdom of God. Garrigou-Lagrange was no different.

> Since the value or worth of a relation depends on the term which it regards and which specifies it . . . the dignity of the divine maternity is measured by considering the term to which it is immediately referred. Now this term is of the hypostatic order, and therefore surpasses the whole order of grace and glory. *By her divine maternity Mary is related really to the Word made flesh.* The relation so set up has the uncreated Person of the Incarnate Word as its term, for Mary is the Mother of Jesus, Who is God. . . . It is He and not His humanity that is the Son of Mary. Hence Mary, reaching, as Cajetan says, even to the frontiers of the Divinity, belongs terminally to the hypostatic

---

[53] Réginald Garrigou-Lagrange, O.P., *The Priest in Union with Christ*, trans. Rev. G.W. Shelton (Westminster, MD: The Newman Press, 1954), 94.

[54] *The Sense of Mystery*, 68. Emphasis original.

[55] Réginald Garrigou-Lagrange, O.P., *The Mother of the Saviour and Our Interior Life*, trans. Bernard J. Kelly, C.S.Sp. (St. Louis, MO: B. Herder Book Co., 1948), 24.

order, to the order of the personal union of the Humanity of Jesus to the Uncreated Word.[56]

Mary conceived the Eternal Word himself in her sacred womb. She was shaped by the wisdom of God who ordained that she should be a holy dwelling place for the Son (see Revelation 21:3). Finally, the reality of her identity reaches "even to the frontiers of the Divinity."

Our Lady makes a summary statement easy to formulate. The legacy of Fr. Réginald Garrigou-Lagrange, O.P., retains a lasting value. It reminds the world that the theologian, the Thomist, and the contemplative each receive their identity through a real relation to the Eternal Word—in Mary.

---

[56] Ibid., 31–32. Emphasis added.

Translator's Introduction

W E SOMETIMES STUMBLE BACKWARDS into projects. Such was the case with this translation of Fr. Réginald Garrigou-Lagrange's *Le Sens du mystère et le clair-obscur intellectuel*. Over the years, I have seen various French Thomists cite this work. Thus, for some time, I had intended to read the text. When I finally did so, I was richly rewarded. Being a philosopher by training, I was lucky to have waited to read *Le sens du mystère*, for it was only by way of Providential happenings that I had picked up the conceptual vocabulary needed for a deep appreciation of the profound points made by Fr. Garrigou-Lagrange in this book.

Throughout the latter part of the twentieth century, Fr. Garrigou-Lagrange's particular tradition of Thomism waned in popularity. Though numerous examples could be cited, one need consider only the words of Fr. Louis Bouyer, who, in his *The Invisible Father*, expresses himself in a kind of diatribe against the scholastic notion of virtual revelation (a topic to be covered in the body of Fr. Garrigou-Lagrange's text). Indeed, after referring to this position as "'John of St. Thomist' theology,"[1] Fr. Bouyer soon continues:

---

[1] Louis Bouyer, *The Invisible Father: Approaches to the Mystery of the Divinity*, trans. Hugh Gilbert (Edinburgh: T&T Clarke, 1999), 249. I do not intend to engage here in a direct discussion of Fr. Bouyer's words. They are merely called upon as a testament to a particularly bold statement of the anti-Commentatorial outlook that one often finds today. It should be noted, however, that he cites only Fr. Garrigou-Lagrange's *Dieu, son existence et sa nature*, which, properly speaking, is written as a kind of natural theology illuminated by Christian revelation. There are numerous philosophical difficulties involved in this kind of undertaking, but the most important thing to note is

Traveling on such a road—and this has been the mentality, more or less of Baroque Thomism, not to mention modern Neo-Thomism—one inevitably comes to prolong this now bloodless religious philosophy into a correspondingly depreciative theology of revelation. Such a theology ceases to be able to vivify by the vision of faith, and at the same time refine and reform our merely human concepts, and it increasingly tends to yield to the disastrous policy of clearing out the Word of God of everything that cannot be circumscribed by or reduced to pre-formed concepts constructed without reference to the Word.

It is therefore not surprising if such so-called Thomism gives the impression that the philosophical-theological thought of St. Thomas is nothing but a gigantic and futile exercise in tautology which, while claiming to explain and develop the statements of the faith, in fact eviscerates and disjoins them. And it is worth emphasizing that if this can happen in the case of so distinguished a mind and so worthy a man of the spirit as Fr. Garrigou-Lagrange, then how much worse it will be when this kind of philosophy and theology is taken up by some college rector whose chief concern is to bring out the "errors" of his colleagues, and either has no interior life or never dreams (quite rightly!) of nourishing it on his theology![2]

Fr. Bouyer's words provide a striking expression of a general milieu in contemporary Catholic thought. Indeed, the sentiment even holds for a significant domain of Thomistic scholarship, one having numerous adherents—sometimes for good reasons, sometimes for reasons that can be perplexing. I have had personal experience with people having this sentiment against the tradition of the Dominican commentators. It seems that some people argue by way of *reductio ad Ioannem*, rejecting a given position merely because it was articulated by John Poinsot (a.k.a. John of St. Thomas). The frustrations under-

---

that the text *is not* primarily concerned with matters pertaining to supernatural theology. There are many other works (the current text included) that gravely challenge the strong claims made in Fr. Bouyer's remark.

[2]   Ibid., 250.

lying this reaction are well explained by Jürgen Mettepenningen: "The *new theologians* valued scholasticism, but wanted to replace 'John of St. Thomism'—an expression of Louis Bouyer, referring to the Thomistic system represented par excellence by John of St. Thomas—with a more genuine 'Thomism.'"[3]

While aware of the limitations of the tradition of the Dominican commentators, I have always been perplexed at this level of animosity for a particular tradition of commentators who, in general, are such keen lights illuminating the principles of St. Thomas's thought. Maritain expressed these issues with nuance:

> [In an essay on wounded nature and knowledge:]
> This reading [of St. Thomas's metaphysics, especially in the two *Summae*,] must be particularly attentive when there is a question of the great Commentators, especially of Cajetan, who in spite of his genius (or because of the special characteristics of this genius), was more subject to the influence of the *Philosophus*, and was unable, as St. Thomas did so admirably, to free himself from Aristotle's notionalism.[4]

> [In a letter to Jerzy Kalinowski and Stefan Swiezawski:]
> You know that my position with regard to the great Commentators is not the same as Gilson's. They are far from being infallible and have often hardened our differences. I gladly recognize the serious deficiencies of Cajetan. But it remains that these great minds (and especially John of St. Thomas—from whom on occasion though I do not hesitate to separate myself) are like very precious optical instruments which enable us to *see much more clearly* certain depths of St. Thomas's thought (even though other depths are given short shrift by them).[5]

---

[3] Jürgen Mettepenningen, *Nouvelle Théologie: New Theology, Inheritor of Modernism, Precursor of Vatican II* (London: T&T Clark, 2010), 82.

[4] Jacques Maritain, "Reflections on Wounded Nature," in *Untrammeled Approaches*, trans. Bernard Doering (Notre Dame, IN: University of Notre Dame Press, 1997), 236.

[5] Jacques Maritain, "Letter on Philosophy at the Time of the Council," in *Untrammeled Approaches*, 67.

[In his late-life reflections in *The Peasant of the Garonne*:]
The loss of potential due to this ever-alert intuitivity is the underlying cause of the baneful deterioration which has taken place in the direction of notionalism and fixation upon abstract essences (hence, a metaphysics unmindful of the intuition of being) for which Gilson is doubtless right in regarding Cajetan as particularly responsible. (It is not without a certain ruefulness that I admit this since, in other respects, I am an admirer of this incomparable reasoner; he was, alas, a partisan of Aristotle in the very sense St. Thomas was not, and yet for all that, a theologian of extraordinary power.) But the Commentator with whom I fell in love—without being afraid to depart from him whenever I have to—isn't Cajetan, it's John of Saint Thomas, who, despite his interminable sentences and his charming fondness for logical technicalities, was himself basically an intuitive.[6]

Of course, there is much that can be said regarding the need to return to St. Thomas's own words—something that Fr. Garrigou-La-grange does time and again. The illuminated clarity of the *Summa theologiae* forever refreshes the intellect. It is understandable that one may fear the canonization of the baroque commentator—especially if this risks leading one to spurn the luminous words of the Saint!

Nonetheless, time did, in fact, pass after Aquinas's day, and many debates arose among the various *scholae* of Scholasticism. It seems that not a single point was left untouched among the riotous disputations from the fourteenth century onward. Thus, we have the intellectual sparring among the various factions—the Scotists, the Thomists, the Albertists, the various flavors of "nominalists," and others. And things would continue to develop as well! With the passage of time, we add to the debates not only Catholics such as the Suarezians and Molinists; we also add the voices of Protestant authors, as well as condemned Catholic positions such as those of Michael Baius and Cornelius Jansen. We

---

[6]   See Jacques Maritain, *The Peasant of the Garonne*, trans. Michael Cuddihy and Elizabeth Hughes (New York: Holt, Rinehart and Winston, 1968), 149.

would be remiss if we did not at least listen to the latter-day Thomists of high repute who strove to uphold St. Thomas's thought in the midst of so many controversies. Even where they force this or that point too emphatically (or, even, in a flatly wrong manner), these guides help to illuminate the heights and depths of the Angelic Doctor's thought. We do not recreate all thought anew in a kind of Cartesian rejection of all that comes before our own day.

Fr. Garrigou-Lagrange's approach to the thought of St. Thomas led him to such commentators as John Capreolus, Thomas da Vio Cajetan, Francesco Silvestri (a.k.a. Sylvester of Ferrara), John of St. Thomas, the Carmelites of Salamanca, Charles René Billuart, and Vincenzo Gotti (among others). Certainly, there are other traditions of Thomism, even within the Dominican order.[7] Given Fr. Garrigou-Lagrange's close (though *not* uncritical, as we will see) adherence to his particular commentatorial tradition, what does he have to say to us today, given our Patristic and historical sensitivities? Granted, there have been studies praising the merits of Fr. Garrigou-Lagrange's thought, such as Fr. Richard Peddicord's *The Sacred Monster of Thomism: An Introduction to the Life and Legacy of Reginald Garrigou-Lagrange, O.P.,*[8] and Fr. Aidan Nichols's *Reason with Piety: Garrigou-Lagrange in the Service of Catholic Thought.*[9] However, can the Old Lion of Roman Thomism speak to us today?

The reader can already guess that I will say, "Yes," and I encourage the skeptic to approach Fr. Garrigou-Lagrange's text with an open mind and an open heart. Let us remember that, even though he and Maritain had an unfortunate falling out, the latter could write of Fr. Garrigou-Lagrange the touching words:

---

[7] One of the great proponents of this point has been Michael Tavuzzi. For his excellent studies, see Michael Tavuzzi, *Prierias: The Life and Works of Silvestro Mazzolini Da Prierio (1456–1527)* (Durham, NC: Duke University Press, 1997); Tavuzzi, "Hervaeus Natalis and the Philosophical Logic of the Thomism of the Renaissance," *Doctor Communis* 45 (1992): 134–52.

[8] Richard Peddicord, *The Sacred Monster of Thomism: An Introduction to the Life and Legacy of Reginald Garrigou-Lagrange, O.P.* (South Bend, IN: St. Augustine's Press, 2004).

[9] Aidan Nichols, *Reason with Piety: Garrigou-Lagrange in the Service of Catholic Thought* (Ave Maria, FL: Sapientia Press, 2008).

I transcribe my notes of 1937 without attenuating anything in them; I insist only on remarking that our differences in political matters never diminished the affection and the gratitude which Raïssa and I had for him. (And he for his part, even when he found fault with me, did what he could to defend me.) This great theologian, who was little versed in the things of the world, had an admirably candid heart, which God finally purified by a long and very painful physical trial, a cross of complete annihilation, which, according to the testimony of the faithful friend who assisted him in his last days, he had expected and which he accepted in advance. I pray to him now with the saints in Heaven.[10]

Today, Fr. Garrigou-Lagrange is sometimes disdained for not undertaking an in-depth historical study of the matters at hand. This is, of course, a limitation, but as a wise theologian recently stated, while it is quite edifying to know the Victorine theology of the Trinity, it is also quite important to know *just what is the truth of the matter*. Having a great number of historical studies is not a bad thing. However, we also need to have someone who teaches us how conclusions are connected to principles; that is, we need a teacher who appreciates the scientific, demonstrative illation involved in theological science. Fr. Garrigou-Lagrange is such a master. Theology is more than a mere collection of opinions. It is indeed a science and a wisdom, though with its own particular methods.

This text is like a long reflection on several major principles, circling over them to see the way that they illuminate various philosophical and theological conclusions. Its chapters are an invitation to look upon mysteries that shine with a light too bright for us as we turn our gaze beyond the human intellect's proper object (i.e., the quiddities of sensible beings) and, especially, as we focus our attention on the majestic heights of what has been revealed to us by supernatural faith, vigorously striven after by us with a supernatural hope, and grasped

---

[10] Jacques Maritain, *Notebooks*, trans. Joseph W. Evans (Albany, NY: Magi Books, 1984), 168–69.

by us in the supernatural charity that empowers the human will with a love that is truly divine.

As a final point, I would like to note one translational detail for the reader who may not be familiar with French. The French *clair-obscur* could be given the literal translation "bright-dark" or "clear-obscure". The word is properly translated "chiaroscuro," the style of painting utilizing light and darkness in a self-aware manner, utilizing the contrasts for artistic effect. One can readily see the play on words in the literal sense of the French. A chiaroscuro, with its interplay of light and dark, gives a vision at once clear and obscure—like a mystery. Given that Fr. Garrigou-Lagrange makes explicit reference to this style of painting in the final chapter of the first section of the text, I have chosen to retain the term "chiaroscuro" throughout the text. The reader should be aware, however, of the play on words that is implicit in the original French. You will sense it at times in Fr. Garrigou-Lagrange's prose.

On the whole, all lengthy citations of Scripture are taken from the Revised Standard Version. On occasion, it made sense to translate directly from the text at hand, especially when the sense of the Vulgate's Latin was presupposed in an explanation being presented. All citations from Denzinger are taken from Ignatius Press's forty-third edition of the text. Unless noted, all of Fr. Garrigou-Lagrange's Latin texts have been translated into English except where the sense is obvious from the context. Also, on a number of occasions, I have filled out the details of Fr. Garrigou-Lagrange's citations, which are regularly partial. Finally, where available, I provide citations of the English translations of Fr. Garrigou-Lagrange's works when he cites himself.

Throughout my translation, I have included some pedagogical footnotes (marked "Tr. note"), in which I have tried to provide the reader with remarks concerning points that may well be opaque, often citing the works of Thomists in the same tradition as that of Fr. Garrigou-Lagrange. In particular, Maritain and Yves Simon remain important sources for understanding this tradition of Thomism. While their popularity, like that of many others, waned in the second half of the twentieth century, their philosophical writings are still relatively well known and provide lengthier treatments of certain topics discussed by Fr. Garrigou-Lagrange.

In similar fashion to my translator's notes, any material appearing in square brackets in the main text represents my own insertion of helpful detail into Fr. Garrigou-Lagrange's text. Italics, in addition to use for emphasis, are also used for Fr. Garrigou-Lagrange sometimes paraphrasing of statements in Scripture or by the Fathers and Doctors rather than quoting directly, the latter of which will always be in quotation marks. Finally, whenever words or phrases appear in all capital letters, this is for absolute emphasis and done under the influence of the same practice in the notes and commentary of Fr. Austin Woodbury, a close student of Fr. Garrigou-Lagrange whose teaching and discourse style was strikingly similar to that of his mentor according to those who had been at the Angelicum with Fr. Garrigou-Lagrange.

No work comes about without the involvement of many hands. Special thanks go to Andrew Jones and Chris Erickson for shepherding this project throughout its process of publication. Being relatively new to this process, I was in need of able guides and gladly had their kind help. Much gratitude is owed to Benjamin Heidgerken for his keen reading of the translation, providing corrections for which I owe him a genuine debt. Even more do I owe a great debt to the editorial staff at Emmaus Academic, without whose superb editing this volume would have been a shadow of its finished form. Likewise, I express gratitude to Scott Hahn, Matthew Levering, and Fr. Thomas Joseph White, O.P., for their interest in this project. Finally, a word of appreciation is owed to my wife, Courtney, who encouraged this project long before we had any thought of finding a publisher. And let us, together, give thanks to God Almighty for the grace to begin this project and bring it to completion.

This translation is dedicated to the memory of Fr. Sebastian Samay, O.S.B.

Author's Introduction

AFTER THIRTY YEARS OF EXPLAINING the works of St. Thomas to students of theology—especially his commentary on the *Metaphysics* of Aristotle and nearly all of the treatises of the *Summa theologiae*—we came up with the idea of highlighting in the text before you that which is clear and that which retains the character of mystery in the traditional and Thomistic solution concerning the great problems pertaining (1) to our knowledge in general, (2) to our knowledge of God (whether naturally or supernaturally attained), and (3) to questions pertaining to grace.[1]

We are justified in saying that St. Thomas has fear neither for logic

---

[1] We have treated this last problem at length in the articles on Predestination, Providence, and Divine Premotion in the *Dictionnaire de théologie catholique*.

　　We do not know if we will be able to finish a treatise on grace; we set forth here at least the beginnings of such a treatise in our treatment of the principle of predilection (see part II, ch. 6).

　　[Tr. note: Fr. Garrigou-Lagrange's *De gratia* was not published until 1946 as *De Gratia: Commentarius in Summam Theologiae S. Thomae, I-IIae, q. 109–114* (Turin: Berruti, 1946). His volume on Predestination was published originally as *La prédestination des Saints et la grâce: Doctrine de S. Thomas comparé aux autres systèmes théologiques* (Paris: Desclée de Brouwer & Cie, 1936). His volume on Providence was published as *La providence et la confiance en Dieu: Fidélité et abandon* (Paris: Desclée de Brouwer & Cie, 1932). The reader can consult the following English editions of these works: Réginald Garrigou-Lagrange, *Grace: Commentary on the Summa Theologica of St. Thomas Ia-IIae, q. 109–114*, trans. The Dominican Nuns of Corpus Christi Monastery (St. Louis, MO: B. Herder, 1952); Garrigou-Lagrange, *Predestination*, trans. Bede Rose (St. Louis, MO: B. Herder, 1939); Garrigou-Lagrange, *Providence*, trans. Bede Rose (St. Louis, MO: B. Herder, 1954).]

nor for mystery. Indeed, logical lucidity leads him to see in nature those mysteries that speak in their own particular ways of the Creator. Likewise, this same lucidity aids him in putting into strong relief other secrets of a far superior order—those of grace and of the intimate life of God, which would remain unknown were it not for Divine Revelation.

One naturally comes to stress (as we have done in the past) the eminent luminosity of this great master's doctrine. However, it is not a useless venture to draw attention from time to time to the sense of mystery that he likewise possessed to an eminent degree. This is what we shall do here.

Far from ignoring the element of inexpressibility found in things, the lucid genius of St. Thomas finds it even in the very nature of matter—in pure potency. Matter, which can become air, water, earth, plant, or animal, in St. Thomas's eyes is a simple *real capacity*, susceptible to being indefinitely determined in thousands upon thousands of manners. It is a real capacity that is distinct at one and the same time *from act* (i.e., the determination that it receives, no matter how insignificant such determination may be) *and from nonbeing*, as well as from negation, privation, and *the simple possibility* required for creation *ex nihilo*.

Pure potency (or, real, receptive capacity)—a kind of middle between being in act (however impoverished it may be) and pure nonbeing—is already something very hidden.

St. Thomas also finds mystery in things whenever it is necessary to pass from one order of nature to another order that is much more elevated—for example, when it is necessary to define the notion of life in such a way that it can be applied *analogically* (but, nevertheless, in a *sense that is proper* and without falling into mere metaphor) both to the blade of grass and to God. Likewise, when, on the chain [*échelle*] of beings beginning with sensation, the notion of *knowledge* is defined in such a manner that it too can be applied *analogically* (but, again in a *proper and not merely metaphorical* sense) to the lowliest of tactile sensation and to the very Uncreated Knowledge that God has of Himself and of all that is not Him.

If St. Thomas saw and delimited clearly these secrets that are found in the orders of plant life as well as sense life, all the more did he likewise see the mysteries pertaining to the intellectual and spiritual life, known by us *in speculo sensibilium* (in the mirror of sensible realities), in particular the mystery of the relations found between nature and grace (i.e., of the relations of the nature of every created spirit with *the intimate life of God*). It is above all about this that we will speak in this work.

Generally, one does not note often enough that, to this sense of mystery, which is found so manifestly in the Angelic Doctor, as in St. Augustine, there corresponds on the side of the object a chiaroscuro[2] that is of such a nature as to profoundly captivate the intellect.

The idea of an intellectual chiaroscuro comes naturally to the mind of a disciple of St. Thomas when he sees his master—who is, admittedly, so fond of clarity—declaring, nevertheless, everything that remains ineffable in reality—from matter to God.

Nothing is clearer for the senses than is the visible and tangible sensation. However, under these phenomena, there is something very obscure for our intellect—matter. From this matter, we abstract the intelligible that we know; however, precisely because of this fact, matter remains like a residue that is refractory (in some manner, so to speak) to intelligibility. The profound reason for this fact is that matter is indeterminate in itself and is capable of becoming all sensible things. Now, that which is so undetermined of itself (i.e., is potential and purely in potency) escapes knowledge, which comes to rest only upon that which is determined or is in act: "*Unumquodque est cognoscibile secundum quod in actu*. [Each thing is knowable insofar as it is in act.]"[3] "*Materia secundum se neque esse habet, neque cognoscibilis est*. [Matter, of itself, neither has existence nor is knowable.]"[4] Under the sensible

---

2   [Tr. note: As noted in the translator's introduction, chiaroscuro is the style of painting utilizing light and darkness in a self-aware manner, utilizing the contrasts for artistic effect and emphasis. The reader will most likely be familiar with the use made of this style by Caravaggio and Rembrandt.]

3   *Summa theologiae* [hereafter, *ST*] I, q. 12, a. 1.

4   St. Thomas expresses himself in this manner when he asks whether God has an idea of matter. He responds in *ST* I, q. 15, a. 3, ad 3: "According to some accounts, Plato held that matter was not created. Therefore, he did not hold that there is an idea of matter but an idea was a kind of co-cause with matter. However, since we hold that matter is created by God (not, however, without form) there is indeed an Idea of matter in God, though not apart from the Idea of the composite—for of itself, matter can neither have existence nor be knowable."

clarity of phenomena, of the visible and of the tangible, there remains
the obscurity of matter, which, on account of its lack of determination,
its poverty, and its lack of fixed consistency, remains elusive for the
intellect.

Similarly, nothing is empirically clearer than is the difference that
separates two animal species, such as the eagle and the lion, or two
plant species, such as the oak and the fir. However, how are we to
define these species except in a manner that is descriptive or empirical?
How are we to render them intelligible? Only their generic characteristics—"corporeal substance," "living," "endowed or not endowed with
sensation"—come to the level of intelligibility. However, the *specific
difference* of the oak, the fir, the eagle, or the lion remains hidden to
us. It is impossible to have a distinct intellectual knowledge of them
from which we could deduce from their natures the properties of these
natures as we do in the case of, for example, the circle or the triangle.
And why is this the case? It is so because their *specific* (i.e., substantial)
form remains, so to speak, *buried and immersed in matter*. And, thus,
the human idea of the eagle or the lion is like a mountain with a clear
summit but with a base that remains in the shadows. The eagle and the
lion are clearly intelligible for us inasmuch as they are beings, inasmuch
as they are substances, corporeal substances endowed with life and
with sensation. However, that which formally constitutes the eagle as
an eagle or the lion as a lion remains very obscure for our intellect, and
we hardly surpass a descriptive and empirical definition. St. Thomas
also noted this fact often, namely that *the specific differences of sensible
beings are often unnamed.*[5] There is a dearth of names because there is a
dearth of distinct ideas.

Without a doubt, there is one sensible being of which we know distinctly the specific difference—it is man because this specific difference

---

[5] *ST* I, q. 29, a. 1, ad 3: "Because substantial differences are not known to us, or even are
not named, it is necessary at times to use accidental differences in place of substantial
differences. For example, as though we were to say: fire is a body that is simple, hot,
and dry. This is so because proper accidents are effects of substantial forms and manifest them."

This affirmation is frequent in the works of St. Thomas, as is shown in the general
index of his works for the word *differentia*, nos. 18 and 19.

is no longer buried in matter but, instead, dominates it, emerging above materiality. It is the *rationality* or mode (not of animality but of *intellectuality*) that is intelligible, for it is essentially relative to being, the first intelligible object: "*Obiectum intellectus est ens.*" The object of the intellect is intelligible being, as the object of vision is color and the object of hearing is sound. Therefore, the human intellect, relative to being, is intelligible to itself. Man, who does not succeed in defining intellectually the eagle or the lion, is able to define himself intellectually—the rational animal—and to deduce from this definition his properties—free, susceptible to morality, endowed with speech, and so on.

However, there is in man an element that yet escapes intelligibility in some manner: matter, which, in him, is the principle of individuation.[6] Whence does it happen that two men, even two as perfectly similar as twins, as indiscernible as two drops of water, are nevertheless *two* and not one? It comes from the fact that human nature is found—in one and the other—in two distinct parts of matter, as the nature of water is found in two distinct parts that constitute two drops of water, which do not occupy the same location in space. *Matter, capable of such and such quantity (susceptible also to growth) as opposed to such and such another quantity,*[7] makes it possible that this human embryo is distinct from another, and that this child is distinct from his twin brother. At least when these two infants are seen at the same time, one sees that they are two and not one. In each one, matter is the principle of a host of individual differentiations that elude us at first glance but come to light ever more forcefully if one enters into the intimate depths of these two twins, noting the different ways that they react under the influence of causes that are identical. *These individual differences,* just like their root principle, cannot become fully intelligible for us. This point merely expresses the meaning of the scholastic adage: *individuum est ineffabile.* The individual human is ineffable, though certainly not in the same manner as God, who is above the limits of intelligibility, but rather because individuality comes from matter, which, by its very poverty, is at the inferior frontiers of being and of the intel-

---

[6] See *ST* I, q. 3, a. 3; q. 29, a. 1, ad 3; q. 75, aa. 4 and 5; III, q. 77, a. 2.

[7] As formulated by Cajetan: "Materia capax huiusce quantitatis ita quod non illius."

ligible realm. From another perspective, *individuality* is far different from ontological *personality* (the root of psychological and moral personality), for personality is that by which each rational being is a *first subject of independent attribution* in his being and his action: "*Per se separatim existens, et per se separatim operans*. [Essentially existing and acting independently.]" In Jesus Christ, as in us, individuality comes from matter. For this reason, Jesus was born in such-and-such a point in space, at such an hour in time, whereas His personality is nothing other than that of the Word made flesh. It is what permitted Him to say, "I am the Way, the Truth, and the Life."

*   *   *

If the human individual, on account of the matter that contributes to his constitution, is ineffable, he is no less mysterious in that which concerns *the life of the spirit*, though for a totally different reason. We come to know the nature of our own spirit only *in the mirror of sensible things*. Why is this? It is because the *proper object of our intellect* (specifically distinct from that of the angels and that of God) is the *least [dernier] of intelligible things*—the intelligible being of sensible things.[8] And then, despite the evidence of the first rational principles as the laws of being and of the intellect, despite the evidence following upon the *cogito ergo sum*, the very nature of our spirit remains quite mysterious for us indeed—until the instant when our soul, being separated from its body, will look upon itself without intermediary [*immédiatement*], just as the angel looks upon himself.

In the course of this life, we know the nature of spirit in a *negative* manner, in calling the spiritual "immaterial," and in a manner that is *relative* to sensible things—as when we say that the life of the spirit is superior to that of plant life or sense life, or as when we say, by analogy with the world of bodies (existing with the dimensions of space), that a person has a lofty, deep, [and] expansive spirit or an incisive intellect. Here again, we find together both rays of light as well as shadows.

---

[8]   See *ST* I, q. 76, a. 4. See also *ST* I, q. 12, a. 4.

* * *

In the life of the spirit, *all that which is relative to love*, says St. Thomas, *is particularly mysterious* and *often unnamed*.⁹ This is so because the intellect knows less that which is found in another faculty than that which is in it, and because love *tends toward the good*, which is in the things and not in mind [*espirit*]. This tendency, like all that still remains undetermined, is not wholly intelligible. We find there, once more, an even more captivating chiaroscuro.

* * *

Finally, if it is clear that there must be a First Cause of the universe, a Cause Who exists of Itself, which is Being Itself, Wisdom Itself, alone capable of ordering the universe, it is still the case that the inward depths of God remain extremely hidden. The assertion often came to the quill of St. Thomas: "*Nescimus de Deo quid est.* [Concerning God, we do not know what He is (i.e., in His Essence).]" By our natural powers, we can know God only through the reflection of His Perfections in creatures. *His inward life* (or, *the Deity* as such) cannot be participated in by created (or creatable) nature, but only by sanctifying grace, which alone can fundamentally dispose us for seeing God immediately as He sees Himself and loving Him as He loves Himself.

Hence, while materialism has a horizontal view of things (making more elevated realities descend to the level of matter), true wisdom has a vertical view of things and distinguishes ever more clearly the two obscurities of which we have spoken—the one from below that originates in matter (as well as in error and evil) and the one from on high, which is that of the very inward and intimate life of God.

* * *

Moreover, St. Thomas—a man whose mind so obviously desires clarity—often says, *fides est de non visis*:¹⁰ the object of faith is *not seen*;

---

⁹ See *ST* I, q. 37, a. 1.
¹⁰ See *ST* II-II, q. 1, aa. 4 and 5.

it remains *obscure*, even though we know it with certitude by means of Divine testimony confirmed by evident and sometimes dazzling signs. St. Thomas adds that one and the same thing cannot (at one and the same time and in the same respect) *be known and believed* by the same intellect—that is, it cannot be *seen* and *not seen*.

It follows that *the arguments of suitability* relative to the existence (and even to the possibility) of supernatural mysteries such as the Holy Trinity, the Redemptive Incarnation, and eternal life *are not demonstrative*—in spite of the light (often quite great) that they contain. It is not that they are of an order inferior to demonstration. On the contrary, they pertain to a sphere that is superior to what is demonstrable. In these arguments, there remains an element of obscurity. One can always deepen them without touching the depth (nay, rather, the summit) at which they aim, and we thus tend toward a *superior clarity* that we often take to be that of a demonstration. It is an order of clarity that is far more elevated—it is *the essentially supernatural clarity* of the Beatific Vision.

These arguments of suitability are like unto a polygon inscribed within the circumference of a circle. One can forever multiply the sides of the polygon without ever reaching a state of identity with the circumference, though the polygon will increasingly approximate that circumference.

These arguments of suitability are inferior to demonstration as regards their rigor, but they are superior to it as regards their object; they penetrate a superior sphere where one can only enter by the way of probability—that is, of a sublime probability.

A detailed study concerning these questions and the problems connected to it would bring theologians of our time to a definition of "probable" that is somewhat forgotten and to the radical distinction that must be made between *two forms of the probable* that one sometimes tends to confound under one and the same denomination of "probability," whereas, to speak clearly, there is, on the one hand, the *probably true* and, on the other hand, the *probably false*. These matters will be taken up below in part I, chapter 4.

The disciple of St. Thomas is thus led to distinguish constantly the superior sort of obscurity found in Divine mysteries and the inferior sort of obscurity that arises from matter, error, moral evil, or the mysteries of iniquity.

Finally, such a disciple must remark that his master is particularly attentive to distinguish in each of his articles *true clarity* from *false clarity*, such as that found in objections that are sometimes quite specious. The objection, which is born of a superficial view of the real, is often easier to understand than St. Thomas's response, which is sometimes quite elevated and not within the reach of all.

In order to grasp the meaning and range of St. Thomas's thought concerning these problems, we will say briefly what is, according to him, the nature of metaphysical wisdom, as well as the nature of the two kinds of supernatural wisdom (i.e., theology and the [Spirit's] gift of wisdom). As regards the object of first philosophy, we will insist upon the metaphysics of the *verb "to be,"* upon its difference from the *verb "to have,"* and upon their relation with the substantive noun, as well as with the adjective and the adverb. That is, we will speak of the metaphysics that is found hidden in grammar or in everyday language, a metaphysics at once rudimentary but very reliable and rich in its virtual power.[11]

We will then speak of the philosophical spirit and of the sense of mystery. We will speak of that which corresponds objectively to this sense—namely, of the intellectual chiaroscuro—insisting on the distinction between the *two obscurities* about which we spoke earlier and the distinction between the *two clarities* that are no less different from one another.

We will pause in particular on the chiaroscuro that is found in the two great problems pertaining to the relation between nature and grace:

1. *Is the existence of the order of supernatural truth and supernatural life demonstrable?* We will respond, "Yes," for by our natural powers of reason, it is certain that the *intimate life of God, the Deity*, remains hidden from us and can be known by us only by

---

[11] [Tr. note: "Virtual" is here being used to call to mind the way an effect is pre-contained in its cause, though without implying *any* intermediary between potency and act. It is "within the power (*virtus*)" of the cause.]

means of Divine Revelation—"nescimus de Deo quid sit," as
St. Thomas himself says.

2. *Is the possibility of the Beatific Vision rigorously demonstrable?* To
this, we will respond, "No," for this would be to demonstrate
by reason alone the possibility of an *essentially supernatural
mystery*—namely, that of eternal life, the possibility of sanctifying grace, and of the light of glory. All of these are of an
order far superior to that of miracles or to naturally knowable,
miraculous divine interventions.

We will then consider the doctrine of St. Thomas, as explicated
by Thomas de Vio Cajetan, concerning the eminence of *the Deity* in
its relations with the Divine Attributes that can be demonstrated by
natural reason and with the Divine Persons who can be known only by
revelation.

In order to determine better the sense of mystery, one ought to
have (especially the theologian), we will study the profound distinction that separates the *supernaturality of miracles* from that much loftier
supernaturality of infused faith and of grace. We will see what this sense
of mystery is in a St. Augustine and a St. Thomas with regard to the
problem of *the Divine Predilection* and of the possible salvation of all.[12]
We will close by speaking of the chiaroscuro found in the life of the
soul and will see, in some particularly striking examples, the practical
application of the principles enunciated here.

As was quite well shown by Jacques Maritain in *The Degrees of
Knowledge*, the great Doctors of the Church had *the sense of mystery* in a
high degree.[13] We can say of them what a Christian thinker once wrote
concerning true grandeur:

The superior man responds to premonitions unknown to
humanity. . . . He reveals to men the part of themselves that

---

[12] On this subject, it is important to explain why certain summits of truth can appear to
    some to be so close to grave errors.

[13] [Tr. note: Though uncited, I suspect he is referring above all to Jacques Maritain, *The
    Degrees of Knowledge*, trans. Gerald B. Phelan (Notre Dame, IN: University of Notre
    Dame Press, 1995), 263–328.]

they do not know. He descends to our depths more profoundly than we have the habit of descending. He gives word to our thoughts. He is more intimate with us than we are with ourselves. He irritates us and gladdens us, like a man who wakes us in order to see with him the rising of the sun.

In thus wrenching us from our homes, in order to bring us within his domains, he brings us inquietude and at the same time gives us a superior peace. . . .

The superior man, incessantly tormented, torn apart by the opposition of the ideal and the real, senses human grandeur better than any other; and better than any other, he also senses human misery. . . . He feels more strongly called toward the ideal splendor that is our final end. . . . He illuminates in us the love of being and awakes in us an awareness of our nothingness. He is superior to the actions that he performs. His thought is superior to his work, . . . which he always finds to be unfinished.[14]

He always aspires to a most elevated contemplation and love, which he will only find *in patria*.

---

[14] Ernest Hello, *L'homme: la vie—la science—l'art*, 7th ed. (Paris: Perrin, 1903), 1.8 (pp. 66–67).

Part I

THE SENSE OF MYSTERY

In order to study what ought to be the sense of mystery for the philosopher and for the theologian, we will speak of four topics in this first part of this text:

1. Metaphysical wisdom and the two forms of supernatural wisdom
2. The verb "to be"—its profound sense and its scope
3. The philosophical spirit and the sense of mystery
4. The intellectual chiaroscuro in the twofold philosophical and theological domain

Chapter 1

Metaphysical Wisdom and the Two Supernatural Wisdoms

T HE SENSE OF MYSTERY is found manifestly in artists of genius, in great scientists and scholars, in philosophers who are worthy of the name of "philosopher," in true theologians, and, above all, in the great contemplatives. Here, we will consider what ought to be the sense of mystery in the case of the philosopher and the theologian. To this end, it is important that, from the very beginning of our discussions, we have a correct idea of the nature of metaphysical wisdom in comparison to the superior wisdom of theology and to the wisdom that is the [Spirit's] gift of wisdom that, along with that of understanding [*intelligence*], is the principle of infused contemplation. As our guide, we will follow St. Thomas, who discussed his ideas concerning metaphysical wisdom in his commentary on the first two chapters of the first book of Aristotle's *Metaphysics*, his ideas on the nature of theology in the first question of the *Summa theologiae*, and his ideas concerning the gift of wisdom in the *Summa theologiae* [hereafter, *ST*] II-II, q. 45.

Metaphysical Wisdom—First Philosophy

At the beginning of his *Metaphysics*, Aristotle searches for the definition of wisdom. He follows his usual manner, taking as his point of departure the nominal (or, common) definition that expresses the sense of this word. From this, he arrives at a real definition by means of an ascending, comparative induction and by a descending progressive division of the various modes of knowledge.[1]

He begins with the supposition of this very elementary, vague [*confuse*] nominal definition: *wisdom is something excellent in the order of knowledge*. Without this very vague notion, we could not give any sense to the word, nor could we distinguish it in the slightest way from that which is the sense of other terms that are more or less similar to it, such as the notions of science, art, experience, and prudence.

In order to give precision to this notion, which is still so very vague, Aristotle remarks: a*ll men naturally desire to know that which is*, even independently from the concrete, practical utility that may be derived from such knowledge. For example, they love to see a beautiful panoramic view, to discover new regions in the heights of a mountain, to contemplate the starry sky; and the loftier the order of knowledge, all the more do they love it for itself, independently of every concrete usefulness that follows from such knowledge. This is the innate love *for truth*, which is not only a useful good or a delightful good (like gold or the fruits of the earth) but is a fitting [*honnête*] good,[2] one that has

---

[1] Indeed, he compares the thing that is being defined, vaguely understood, with things that are similar and dissimilar—here, wisdom with other modes of knowledge, whether they are quite close in nature to wisdom or are distant from it. These modes have to be divided in a rigorous manner: (1) Non-rational knowledge (i.e., sense knowledge) and (2) rational knowledge, which itself will be subdivided.

[2] [Tr. note: The expression *bien honnête"* is here standing in for *bonum honestum*, which is sometimes translated as the "moral good," though the latter is a rough translation at best. The expression is difficult to translate in any context, but the general sense is that the *bonum honestum* is good for its own sake, as Fr. Garrigou-Lagrange indicates. I have chosen to translate it as the "fitting good" so as to harmonize the language here with that of Fr. Garrigou-Lagrange's student Fr. Austin Woodbury, S.M. (1899–1979). For years, Fr. Woodbury ran the Aquinas Academy in Sydney, Australia, and his unpublished works represent one of the most comprehensive accounts of the Thomist school. His texts owe a great deal to Fr. Garrigou-Lagrange, as well as to F.-X. Maquart and Jacques Maritain, among others. A brief biography of Woodbury can be found in the volumes prepared by Mr. Andrew Wood, who has been devoted for years to the curation and future publication of Fr. Woodbury's works. See Austin Woodbury, *Basic Morals*, ed. Andrew Wood (Sydney, AU: Donum Dei Press, 2016), iii–xlvi. The centrality of the fitting good is not stressed in the basic course found in *Basic Morals*. However, it is emphasized repeatedly in his full ethics text, as can be found in Austin Woodbury, *Ethics* (The John N. Deely and Anthony F. Russell Collection, Latimer Family Library, St. Vincent College Library, Latrobe, PA).]

a value in itself, independent of the utility and delight that can be derived from it. This leads one to think that not only the truth but also *knowledge of the truth* (above all, knowledge of the highest truths) *has a value in itself*, independent of every usefulness that may follow upon it. This realization stands in contradiction to what has been said by the sophists and many others with them.

The Degrees of Knowledge

However, it is important to distinguish well the various degrees of knowledge. Even at the lowest such degree, the level of sensation, there is already something very remarkable: "The knower differs from the non-knowing being (such as a plant) in the fact that the knower is, in a certain manner, able to become other beings";[3] *anima fit et est quodammodo omnia;*[4] the human soul becomes, in a certain manner, the beings that it knows, by the representation that it has of it. While the plant under the influence of the sun *becomes hot* after being cold, the animal endowed with vision *sees the sun*. It receives not only the heat that it does indeed appropriate to itself, which becomes its own; it also receives the representative likeness of the sun *without appropriating it to itself* and in such a manner that it remains the likeness of another being, "Cognoscens quoddamodo fit aliud a se [The knower becomes, in a certain manner, something that is other than itself]." This fact assumes that the knower has a certain kind of immateriality, one that does not exist in the case of the plant. This notion of knowledge—already verified in sensation (even in the sense of touch)—will be able to be applied in an analogical and proper sense to God Himself. Knowledge is not a genus; it rises above genera; it is an analogical notion that expresses an absolute perfection (*perfectio simpliciter simplex*).

Above sensation, there is *sense memory*. Without this, wild beasts would never return to their lairs, nor the bird to its nest, nor the horse to its master's house. By means of this sense memory, the *instinct* of animals is perfected in the sense that, little by little, it is accompa-

---

[3] See *Summa theologiae* [hereafter, *ST*] I, q. 14, a. 1.
[4] See Aristotle, *De anima* 3.8.431b20–21. See, also, lec. 13 of St. Thomas on this passage.

nied by *an empirical prudence* evident in any old fox.[5] Aristotle and St. Thomas speak of these lesser degrees of knowledge in order to determine in what way properly human knowledge is superior to such lesser forms of knowledge.

*   *   *

Human knowledge does not reach only to sensible beings insofar as they are sensible. It is not limited to phenomena. Instead, it reaches that which is intelligible in sensible things. That is to say, human reason does not seize only facts. It seizes also the *raisons d'être*[6] of facts—it seizes the *why*, τὸ διότι. Where does this knowledge come from? It comes from that which differentiates the *intellect* from the external and internal senses (even the most elevated of these); it comes from that which the intellect has for its first object—neither color, nor sound, nor physical resistance, nor physical extension, nor the internal state of consciousness, but *being* or the *intelligible real*.

This appears from the fact that the three operations of our intellect (conception, judgment, and reasoning) are all related, not only to color, nor to sound alone, nor to internal events of consciousness, but to intelligible being. Indeed, every conception or notion presupposes that most universal notion—*being*. Every judgment presupposes *the verb "to be."* To say, "Peter runs," is to say, "Peter is running." Every demonstrative reasoning expresses either the *raison d'être* for the thing

---

[5] [Tr. note: i.e., the estimative sense of the animals in question.]

[6] [Tr. note: I have chosen to maintain the literal French. Sometimes (e.g., Fr. Bede Rose's admirable English translation of Fr. Garrigou-Lagrange's *Dieu*), *principe de raison d'être* is understandably translated as "principle of sufficient reason." The literal meaning, "reason for being," is more evocative in its implications, as will become evident in what follows. It also avoids confusing Fr. Garrigou-Lagrange's thought with the rationalist tradition for which the principle of sufficient reason played a mighty role. However, this English expression ("reason for being") is somewhat forced. Hence, I have chosen to maintain the literal French. This choice is supported by the fact that, when Fr. Garrigou-Lagrange writes the expression in Latin, he renders it as *principium rationis essendi*. See Réginald Garrigou-Lagrange, "De Investigatione definitionum secundum Aristotelem et S. Thomam. Ex posteriorum Analyt. L. II, C. 12–14; L. 13–19 Commentarii S. Thomae," *Acta Pont. Academiae Romanae S. Thomae Aq. et Religionis Catholicae* 2 (1935): 195.]

that is so demonstrated (if it is a demonstration *a priori*) or the *raison d'être* for the affirmation of the existence of something (if it is a demonstration *a posteriori*).[7]

Since the intellect has being for its object, it searches out the *raisons d'être* of facts and of things. Does the child cease in multiplying his or her question, "Why?"

> Child: Why does the bird fly?
> Parent: In order to search out nourishment—that is its end. Because it has wings—that is the cause without which it could not fly.
> Child: But why does it have wings?
> Parent: Because it is the nature of a bird to have wings.
> Child: Why does it die?
> Parent: Because it is a material being, and every material being is corruptible.

These multiple and various *raisons d'être*—the final, efficient, formal, and material causes—are accessible, as such, only to reason. They are accessible neither to sense nor to imagination. Only the intellect, which

---

[7] [Tr. note: The senses of *a posteriori* and *a priori* here are not the same as what is received from Kant's *Critique of Pure Reason*. Although Kant is the inheritor of much medieval, renaissance, and baroque Scholasticism, his sense of the terms is quite different from the developed Scholastic position within the Thomist school. Although Fr. Garrigou-Lagrange may be using the terms a little bit loosely, he was well aware of how these terms were used by Thomist logicians in his day. Indeed, he approved of Édouard Hugon's *Cursus Philosophicus Thomisticae*, vol. 1, *Logica* (Paris: Lethielleux, 1927). In this text, see p. 384: "Demonstration *a priori* does not coincide with demonstration *propter quid*, nor does demonstration *a posteriori* coincide with demonstration *quia*. Demonstration *a priori* proceeds through causes of any sort, whether proximate or remote; however, demonstration *propter quid* . . . through proper, immediate, and adequate causes. Hence, every demonstration *propter quid* is *a priori*; however, not every demonstration *a priori* is *propter quid*. Demonstration *a posteriori* is only through an effect; however, demonstration *quia* is through an effect or [lit. *et*] through remote causes. Therefore, every *a posteriori* demonstration is *quia*, while it is not the case that every *quia* demonstration is *a posteriori*" (my translation). Although the immediate context justifies reading "et" as "or," see also his remarks from p. 383: "Demonstration *quia*, taking the word 'quia' not as causal (i.e., meaning "because") but as it means 'that the thing is,' proceeds either through a sign and effect or through remote, common, and inadequate causes."]

has intelligible being for its object, can know *the end* as such (and the end is the *raison d'être* of the means). The imagination will never seize upon finality as such—the *raisons d'être* of things are inaccessible to it.[8]

The Image and the Idea

It is this fact that shows the profound difference—indeed, an immense distance without measure—between the *image*[9] and the idea, no matter how vague the latter may be. A dog can possess an image of a clock. Indeed, it can have even a composite image of various clocks of different sizes and colors, an image in which the resemblances are accentuated and differences eliminated. Indeed, to such a composite image, the parrot may add the name "clock" and repeat what it has heard said: "The clock chimes." However, it does not understand *why* it chimes; it does not grasp the *raison d'être* of its movement. It cannot know the end or the efficient cause of this movement.

In contrast, the small child realizes quite quickly not only that "clock" is an object providing physical resistance, color, and sound, but also that it is *a machine made to indicate the solar time* (a *raison d'être* of finality), for its regular movement is in conformity to the apparent

---

[8]   When we ask a philosophy student why only the intellect, and not the imagination, can know *finality* or *the end* as such (i.e., *sub ratione finis*), it is not rare to have the student respond, "Because the imagination can neither abstract nor know relations; only the intellect knows them and can abstract."

    However, what does it abstract first of all? *Intelligible being.* (In fact, it is because the intellect knows it that we attribute to it the power of abstracting, not only *the common sensibles*, like extension and distance, but *the intelligible*.) And, it is because it alone can know intelligible being that only the intellect also can know *the end*, which is the *raison d'être* of the means. The animal knows in a sensate fashion the thing that is the end; however, it knows in no way *finality* as such. Likewise, it knows sensibly the thing that offers physical resistance to it, but it in no way knows *efficiency* (i.e., the causality that the thing exercises upon it).

[9]   [Tr. note: This is being used in the broad sense for the kinds of phantasms produced by the internal senses. (Strictly speaking, they are produced only as a means for such sense knowledge. They are the foundation of the formal signs of the sensible order, leading to cognition of their respective objects. Thus, the production is akin to that involved in the intellectual production of the concept in human knowledge—the productivity is virtual; it occurs indeed, but only as the ontological ground for the relation of the knower to the known.)]

motion of the sun.[10] Thus, the child is not slow to grasp *what* a clock *is*; he is not slow in being able *to define* it in an *intelligible* manner that even the most perfect animal will never grasp. Likewise, he does not delay in conceiving, at least in a vague manner, that the solar time is part of a *day*, the day a part of the *year*, itself definable in relation to the motion of the sun. Little by little, he comes to have an idea of *time* before coming to define it philosophically as "the measure of movement according to before and after." Likewise, he distinguishes the present, the past, and the future, all in relation to what *is*—this little word whose meaning is accessible only to the intellect.

And while the animal grasps a *sensible being* only by means of its *phenomena* (color, sound, taste, etc.), the child, by means of his intellect, grasps it from the outset as a *being*. Little by little, he grasps it as *a being that remains one and the same* under the multiple, variable phenomena. That is to say, he grasps it as a *substance*. Although the child knows, by means of his sense of taste, the sweetness of milk (*ens dulce* **ut dulce**), this same little one also knows by his intellect the reality of milk (*ens dulce* **ut ens reale**).[11]

True Science

It goes without saying that this profound distinction between the image and the idea is indispensable if we are going to have a true awareness of what separates human *science* from the animal's *purely empirical knowledge*. At the very beginning of Aristotle's *Metaphysics*, we find

---

[10] Thus, the idea that enables one to know *what* a clock *is* is *universal*. Every clock *must* be a machine whose regular movement is conformed to that of the sun so that it can indicate the solar time.

[11] This is why Aristotle and, after him, St. Thomas say to us that the *intelligible being* of sensible things is a *per accidens sensible*, known immediately by intelligence, before all reasoning, by the simple presentation of a sensible object. See St. Thomas's commentary on *De anima* 2.13: "Immediately, at the occurrence of sense experience it is apprehended by the intellect."

   Nominalist empiricism speaks as though our intellect knows only the sensible *phenomena* and their experimental laws and not *intelligible being* and its *absolutely necessary laws*. However, in sensible being, our intellect grasps immediately intelligible being, which is an *absolute perfection*, something attributable analogically to God, while color and sound cannot be attributed to Him.

the Philosopher proposing a refutation of the empiricism that is again found in modern positivism. For such an outlook, the notion of being is nothing other than the most confused of all images that is accompanied by a *name*—it is a radical form of nominalism. Thus, from this perspective, being is not the first idea that renders reality and its phenomena to be *intelligible*; it is not what makes possible *judgment*, which has for its "soul" the verb *to be*; it is not what makes possible human reasoning, which explains the *raisons d'être* of things and of our affirmations concerning things.

Thus, it follows that science differs from purely empirical knowledge precisely in that it alone can assign the "why." It alone can assign the *raisons d'être* of things and phenomena so that they are rendered intelligible: *Scientia est cognitio rerum per causas* [Science is the knowledge of things through causes].[12] Science does not have for its first end the practical utility that can be derived from knowledge (for example, controlling nature by utilizing its forces). Science seeks to know things and their *raisons d'être* so as to come to discover, above all, their supreme *raison d'être*. Consequently, the primordial laws of intelligible being (in as much as it differs from phenomena, sounds, colors, etc.) will be the first principles of intellectual knowledge. For example: One thing cannot both be and not be at one and the same time and in the same respect.

This is a kind of *necessity*, known by the intellect and inaccessible to our senses as well as to the experience, which can know only the contingent and the singular. Well before Leibnitz, Plato and Aristotle had seen that empiricism is refuted in light of the *evident necessity of the principles* of contradiction, causality, and so on. In these principles, we also see the foundation of the proof of the spirituality and immortality of the soul.[13]

---

[12] See Aristotle, *Posterior analytics* 1.1. See also St. Thomas's commentary on this text, lec. 4. Thus, science (or, knowledge through causes) is superior to simple knowledge of *experimental laws*, which are like general facts or the statement of the constant relations found among phenomena.

[13] See *ST* I, q. 75, a. 5: "Everything that is received into something is received in that thing according to the manner appropriate to that receiver. Now, the intellective soul knows a given thing *according to its absolute nature*—for example, it knows a stone inasmuch as it is a stone, absolutely speaking (and not only as it is this or that stone).

If such is the difference existing between true science and merely empirical knowledge, how are we to conceive of wisdom? How ought we to define it? It is to this question that Aristotle devotes the second chapter of the first book of the *Metaphysics*.

The Characteristics of Wisdom and Their Raison d'être

In order to consider this problem aright, it is necessary to seek inductively the *notes* (or, the defining characteristics) of the wise man according to universal testimony. Then, it will be necessary to render these notes intelligible by assigning to them their *raison d'être*.

Now, as the vaguest notion of wisdom already noted in our discussions heretofore is the notion of being something excellent in the order of knowledge, it is not surprising that one commonly says about the wise man:

1. that he knows more than others *all* that which is accessible to our knowledge and is worth the effort of being known;
2. that he likewise knows even *the most difficult things*;
3. that he knows them *with a greater degree of certitude* than does the common man and that he does not change his judgment after speaking to his most recent interlocutor;
4. that he can *assign causes* or *raisons d'être* to facts and things and, hence, can then teach;
5. that he *loves knowledge of the truth for its own sake* and not for the material usefulness or honors that might ensue from such knowledge, that he is magnanimous, disinterested, and that he often dies a poor man;
6. and that he is able to *order* things in a fitting manner—whether in the theoretical order or in the practical order, and that wisdom thus understands the subordination of the sciences but is not itself subordinated to any of them. *Sapientis est ordinare* [It is the office of the wise man to order things].

. . . Therefore, the intellective soul is an absolute form and not something that is composed from matter and form."

This is a descriptive definition that already helps to indicate the *object* of wisdom (all things, even the most difficult), *its manner of knowing* (with certitude by means of causes), *its end* (knowledge of the truth for its own sake), and *its effects* (ordering the other sciences, as well as human action).

One might object that the enumeration provided by these six notes of wisdom is perhaps not complete. However, it is not necessary that it be utterly complete. It suffices that we observe inductively the most notable characteristics of wisdom. This is akin to when we define, for example, a circle. To do so, it suffices that we know the length of the radius, which generates the circle by revolving around one of its ends.

* * *

What is the *raison d'être* of these notes; that is, what is the rationale that can render them intelligible?

First, why is it commonly said that the wise man knows *all* that which is able to be known? If by "know" we mean knowledge by means of causes, the wise man knows that which is knowable inasmuch as he knows *the first and most universal causes*, for he who knows the universal knows (at least in a certain fashion) all of that which falls within the scope of that universal. By affirming this in *Metaphysics* 1.2, Aristotle poses a principle from which St. Thomas will deduce[14] that God alone can create (i.e., to produce something from nothing—*ex nihilo*). That which is the most universal effect (i.e., the being of all things—considered from the perspective of *being*) can result only from a cause that is most universal—namely, from God. God alone, who is Being Itself, can provide the rationale for *all the being* in anything whatsoever, even the being of the matter that enters into its constitution.

The causes that are inferior to the Supreme Cause can only alter a preexisting subject. God alone can create.

Aristotle did not explicitly deduce this conclusion, but it derives necessarily from the principles that are here formed by him, though he

---

[14] See *ST* I, q. 45, a. 5.

does not seem to have suspected [*soupçonné*] the sovereign freedom of the Creator's act.[15]

On the second point, why is it said that the wise man knows the most difficult things among those that are accessible to us? It is said for the same reason—it is because he knows the first and most universal causes, which are the most difficult to know, for they are far above the level of sensible things, which are the first things that we know. These supreme causes are *highly intelligible in themselves*—they are the principle and end of all things, and everything is illuminated by them. However, they are *difficult for us to know* because they are far removed from our senses, which are the starting point for our knowledge.[16] Also, because of the difficulty of metaphysical wisdom, it is accessible to us only after the study of the other philosophical sciences—after logic and the philosophy of nature.[17]

On the third point, why is it said that the wise man knows what he knows with *a greater degree of certitude* than other men? Once again, for the same reason—because he knows the first and most universal causes, which enable him to *assign the ultimate reasons of things*, reasons that can be connected to the first notions and first principles that are

---

[15] On this point, see what St. Thomas says in his commentary on *Metaphysics* 6.1, lec. 1, concerning one of the loftier texts of Aristotle concerning the First Cause of beings: "From the preceding remarks on this passage, we can see manifestly the falsity of the opinion held by those who state that Aristotle thought that God was not the cause of the substance of the heavens but only of its motion."

[16] St. Thomas says the same in *ST* I, q. 2, a. 1: "Considered in itself, the proposition, 'God exists,' is known in and of itself, for the predicate is the same as the subject; . . . however, from our perspective as knowers, it is not known in and of itself."

We see well that, if God exists, He exists of Himself—but does He, in fact, exist? Our *abstract notion* of God, which abstracts from the act of existence, does not permit us to affirm existence before we assure ourselves that the world requires a Cause that is superior to it. [Tr. note: Fr. Garrigou-Lagrange is referring here to the distinction between abstractive and intuitive cognition. The Thomistic sense of this will be discussed later below.]

[17] As St. Thomas says in his commentary on *Metaphysics* 1.2, lec. 2: "Although this science, which is called wisdom, holds *the first place as regards its dignity*, it still is the *last thing in the order of teaching*." [Tr. note: See Réginald Garrigou-Lagrange, "Dans Quel Ordre Proposer Les Sciences Philosophiques," *Revue thomiste* 40 (1924): 18–34. This article was incorporated into Fr. Garrigou-Lagrange's *Le réalisme du principe du finalité*, a translation of which is scheduled to be published by Emmaus Academic.]

the source of all certitude. If one grasps the profound sense of the principle of causality—*all of that which comes to exist requires a cause*—one will see that, in the final analysis, it is required that there be a *Cause* that is not caused, that does not *come into existence* but that exists of Itself and is Pure Act. Likewise, if one grasps the profound sense of the principle of finality—*every agent acts for an end that is proportioned to it*—one will thus be led to see that there is a subordination of agents and ends *and* that the Supreme Agent ought to act for the Supreme End of the universe. Finally, if one admits, with Anaxagoras, that *order cannot be explained without an ordering intelligence*, it is necessary to admit as well that the order of the universe presupposes an Ultimate Intelligence who is Eternally Subsistent Thought Itself.

As regards the fourth point, why can one say that the wise man, more than anyone else, is able *to teach*? One can say this because teaching is nothing else than giving others scientific knowledge of things—that is, giving them knowledge through causes. Therefore, since the wise man knows the ultimate causes, he is able to teach more so than anyone else. Thus, wisdom is the most doctrinal form of science—*illa scientia est magis doctrix vel doctrinalis, quae magis considerat causis.*[18]

Here, we find ourselves far from what a nominalist empiricist or a positivist says. According to such doctrines, metaphysics is far from being the ultimate science. Indeed, it is not even the least of the sciences but, instead, is only a collection of unverifiable hypotheses.

However, positivism is the negation of all philosophy, for it holds that our knowledge does not rise above internal and external experiences, which amounts to confusing the intellect with the sense powers—at least with the most elevated of the internal senses (with imagination and sense memory)—and confusing the intelligible with the sensible, confusing being with phenomena. Positivism declares that the proofs of the existence of God are *not scientific* because they are *not verifiable by experience.* Thankfully they are not! If they were verifiable by the senses, God—like sensible beings—would fall within the grasp of our experience and would no longer be God—the Supreme Cause and Last End.

Fifthly, why is it said that *wisdom* is *loved* by the wise man more

---

[18] See St. Thomas's commentary on *Metaphysics* 1.2, lec. 2.

than every other kind of knowledge and that it is loved *for its own sake*, independently of the material usefulness that might be derived from it? It is so loved because the man who loves truth for its own sake loves, above all, the Ultimate Truth, who is found in knowing the highest causes, and who is the eminent Source of intelligibility and of all intellectual and moral life.

Sixthly and finally, why is it said that it belongs to the wise man *to order* things in a fitting manner, whether in the domain of theory or in that of practical knowledge? As always, it is for the same reason—because he knows the loftiest causes, the Last End, which is the principle of all order because everything ought to be subordinated to it. Speaking of the supernatural order of grace, St. Paul writes, "The spiritual man judges all things, and he himself is judged by no one" (1 Cor 2:15).

What Does Wisdom Receive from the Other Sciences, as well as from Experience?

Perhaps one could object, along with nominalist empiricism and subjectivist idealism, as follows:

> By the very confession of Aristotle, metaphysics is not the first of the sciences according to the order of learning. Therefore, according to this order, *it presupposes other sciences* and, from them, it receives necessary notions. Thus, it is subordinated to them. It receives from logic notions such as the notions of demonstration, of principles that are demonstrative in nature, and of induction. From the philosophy of nature, it receives the notion of becoming. From psychology, it receives the very notions of concepts, intellection, and sensation. Since it receives from other sciences these notions that are absolutely necessary for it, metaphysics is subordinate to these sciences. Thus, it cannot be a true wisdom.

To this, it is necessary to respond, in accordance with Aristotle: Metaphysics receives from these sciences *the matter that it considers,* but it receives from them neither *its very principles, nor its first notions.* On the contrary, it is in light of these absolutely primordial notions—relative to intelligible being in all of its universality—that it illuminates from on high the inferior notions that it borrows from the other sciences. And therefore, it is not subordinate to them. On the contrary, it judges them from on high.

Metaphysics finds its first principles—those of contradiction, causality, and finality—by deepening the first intellectual apprehension of *intelligible being,* which is the first object of the human intellect, known from the outset by it from its first contact with sensible things, grasped by the senses.

As regards these principles—these very first, necessary, and absolutely universal principles, which are presupposed by all of the other sciences—metaphysics analyzes them, formulates them rigorously, and defends them against those who deny them.[19] Thus, metaphysics remains superior to all of the other disciplines, even to those that furnish it with the matter used for its consideration—the matter that it judges from on high with a superior intellectual light.

*   *   *

One could perhaps insist further:

> However, according to Aristotle, in opposition to Plato, *our intellectual knowledge depends upon the senses*—not accidentally as an occasion for intellectual knowledge, but *necessarily.* Therefore, it cannot be *more certain* than sensation. Thus, metaphysics cannot be more certain than experience and the so-called experimental sciences.

To this, again, it is necessary to respond, in accordance with Aristotle and St. Thomas. Our intellectual knowledge does depend *necessarily* on the senses—in a way that is *material and extrinsic,* not *formal*

---

[19] See Aristotle, *Metaphysics* 4.3 and 4.4. See also, St. Thomas's commentary on *Metaphysics* 4, lec. 5–7.

and intrinsic. As is well explained by St. Thomas in *ST* I, q. 84, a. 6: "Sense knowledge cannot be the total and perfect cause of intellectual knowledge, *sed magis quoddammodo est materia causae*—rather, it is, in a certain manner, the matter for the cause."[20]

In what sense should we take this? We should understand it as meaning that the intelligible is only in potency in sensible things and that it becomes intelligible only in act under the intellectual light, which Aristotle termed "the agent intellect." Only under this light does the intelligible appear to the intellect capable of knowledge; it appears to it in an intellectual light that is far superior to sensible light.

---

[20] [Tr. note: In order to be a bit more precise on this point, it is possible to say that, from the perspective of a robust Thomistic theory of knowledge, the phantasms produced by the internal senses provide the *objective instrumental cause* involved in the process of intellectual illumination undertaken by the intellect insofar as it is in act (i.e., the "agent intellect") vis-à-vis the phantasms (in which the intelligibility merely exists potentially). Following John of St. Thomas, we can refer to the phantasm as a *kind of* matter out of which intellectual knowledge will proceed, so long as we consider this only from the perspective of its *objective* or *specificative* role. Technically, in a state of separation from the body, the soul itself suffices for being the principle self-knowledge, for as an immaterial form, it is *actually intelligible*. Hence, it can function as *species impressa*, just as the substance of the angel can function as the *species impressa* of its own self-knowledge.

Returning to our main point, however, the "kind of" (or *quoddammodo*) is very important, qualifying the sense of "material causality." Indeed, Fr. Garrigou-Lagrange's French translation (which matches the English of the passage translated above) actually represents the matter better than the very popular 1920s English translation of the *Summa*, which reads "material cause" instead of "matter for the cause." The latter translation stands up well to other passages from St. Thomas, as can be seen especially in the texts gathered in John Peifer's work, cited below in this note. The relationship between intellect and phantasm is *not* a relationship of *form* and *matter*. It is a relationship of *higher agent* and *objective instrument*. This is precisely the sense that John of St. Thomas gives to this text in *Cursus philosophicus thomisticus*, ed. Beatus Reiser, vol. 3 (*Naturalis philosophiae*, vol. 2) (Turin: Marietti, 1930), pt. IV of *Naturalis philosophiae*, q. 10, a. 2 (306B37–309B33, esp. 308B20–38).

Fr. Garrigou-Lagrange does not deal with this issue at length in his text (though it certainly is behind his clarifying remarks). Though he is not afraid at times to differ from the conclusions of John of St. Thomas, he also has much respect for the great baroque Thomist. These lofty and difficult topics are discussed with great lucidity in Yves Simon, *An Introduction to the Metaphysics of Knowledge*, trans. Vukan Kuic and Richard J. Thompson (New York: Fordham University Press, 1990), 113–27. Also, a similarly excellent and lucid presentation can be found in John Frederick Peifer, *The Concept in Thomism* (New York: Bookman Associates, 1952), 119–31.]

That is why St. Thomas writes in *ST* I, q. 84, a. 5: "As one says that we see colors in the sun (or, by means of it), it is necessary to say that the human soul knows in an intellectual manner all things *in the Eternal Reasons* for it knows by means of its participation in these. The natural light of the intellect, which is in us, is, in fact, a kind of participated likeness of the Uncreated Light, which contains the Eternal Reasons of things."

Thus, our intellect can abstract *ab hic et nunc* ["from the here and now"] the nature of things and consider them *sub specie aeternitatis* ["from an eternal point of view"]. Thus, the nature of the lion or the lily is for our intellect what the lion or the lily would be said to be from all eternity— τὸ τί ἦν εἶναι, *quod quid erat esse*, "that which it was to be"; it has a kind of timelessness that is nearly inexpressible.[21]

However, besides the natural light of the intellect, we need ideas abstracted (by this very light) from sensible things.

In this way, the METAPHYSICAL CERTITUDE of the *real value of first principles* such as that of contradiction, causality, and so on (i.e., of their value as laws not only of the mind [*espirit*] but also of being) is FORMALLY AND INTRINSICALLY FOUNDED upon the *intellectual evidence* of these principles in the natural light of the intellect and not upon the necessarily prerequisite sensation. However, this metaphysical certitude is also MATERIALLY AND EXTRINSICALLY FOUNDED on *sensation and its object*. Indeed, this is the meaning of the profound remark of St. Thomas in *ST* I, q. 84, a. 6: "Sense knowledge cannot be the total and perfect cause of intellectual knowledge, but is rather something like the matter for the cause." The form for the cause (*forma causae*) is the natural light of the intellect in which we know intelligible being as we know colors in the light of the sun.[22]

If, on the contrary, the intellectual certitude of the first principles were founded *formally and intrinsically* on *sensation*, the nominalist empiricism of positivists would be true. The intellect would not be able to judge from on high the value of the sensation that it uses. On the con-

---

[21] [Tr. note: Strictly speaking, the issue of the role of seeing things *sub specie aeterni-tatis* requires careful and detailed treatment. See Armand Maurer, "St. Thomas and Eternal Truths," *Mediaeval Studies* 32 (1970): 91–107].

[22] [Tr. note: See, again, the important clarifying remarks above in note 20.]

trary, it judges their value in the light of the first principles—as when it is said that a sensation of nothing sensed (*vera sensatio sine reali sensato* [a true sensation without something real that is sensed]) is impossible,[23] and similarly a sensation without a cause and without finality.

Thus, the intellect can judge sensation and experience from on high because it does not arrive only at the abstract sensible (e.g., abstract color, abstract sound, abstract extension) but, instead, arrives at *intelligible being,* abstracted from sensible things—intelligible, being that, as such, is in no way sensible and can be grasped neither by the senses nor by the imagination. Likewise, the latter is incapable of grasping *efficient causality* as such or *finality,* for even though it arrives at color or sound, it cannot arrive at *being* and the *raisons d'être* of things.

Therefore, it remains that metaphysical wisdom is in no way subordinate to the sciences that it utilizes. It is superior to them and judges them from on high. This is why it can even *use* them—in the exact sense of the word "to use." Indeed, only the superior uses the inferior, and *not vice versa.*

Thus, metaphysics can judge the other sciences and cannot itself be judged by any other—*et ipsa a nemine judicatur* [and this one, i.e., metaphysics or the metaphysician, is judged by nobody]—in the natural order.

---

[23] The text of St. Thomas in *ST* III, q. 76, a. 8, as is shown by John of St. Thomas, is not contrary to this assertion. It states that, if God produces a subjective alteration in the sense without there being a corresponding real object, it would be *as though a man were expressly seen.* It seems to be a sensation, but there is not a genuine sensation. See: *ST* I, q. 51, a. 2; III, q. 57, a. 6, ad 3. [Tr. note: For a more detailed treatment on this point, see Simon, *An Introduction to the Metaphysics of Knowledge,* 89–91n9. The topic of precisely understanding the nature of sensation has been repeatedly emphasized by John Deely in, e.g., *Intentionality and Semiotics: A Story of Mutual Fecundation* (Scranton, PA: University of Scranton Press, 2007), 159–63. One should see also Réginald Garrigou-Lagrange, "Non potest esse genuina sensatio sine reali sensato," *Studia Anselmiana* 7–8 (1938): 189–201. This was translated by Thomas DePauw and Edward M. Macierowski as Réginald Garrigou-Lagrange, "There Cannot be Genuine Sensation without a Real Sensed Thing," *Studia Gilsoniana* 4:2 (April–June 2015): 165–79.]

The Real Definition of Wisdom

We are thus led to the definition of wisdom, not only a nominal definition, but indeed the real definition: *It is the science of things through their Supreme Cause*; in other words: the science capable of making known *the ultimate reasons for things*. In the twelfth book of the *Metaphysics*, Aristotle shows that God is the end of the universe, and in the third chapter of the first book, he gives a great eulogy for Anaxagoras, who appeared like a sage among drunk men when he said that the universe requires an ultimate Intelligence that had organized it.

We have now the foundational character that renders intelligible the diverse notes gathered in the descriptive definition of the sage, a definition that responds to the meaning that one commonly gives to this term in order to distinguish it from any other.

It follows that the proper or formal object of metaphysics is *intelligible being insofar as it is being*—and not insofar as it is mobile and changing. Its proper object is *the real insofar as it is real*. Here, the intelligible real is *abstract*, not only from individual matter (as when one considers not *this* water but water in general, or substantial change in general, etc.).[24] It is abstract *from all matter*,[25] such that one can attrib-

---

[24] The *philosophy of nature*, as Aristotle says at the beginning of his *Physics*, has for its object *ens mobile, ut mobile*, sensible and mobile being—at the *first degree of abstraction* (see *Metaphysics* 6.1). That is to say, it considers being not by abstracting from all matter but, instead, only from *individual sensible matter*. For example, it considers not *this or that* local movement but, instead, considers local movement, qualitative movement (or change), the movement (or change) found in growth, the substantial change of things. It searches into the innermost causes of these things (e.g., prime matter and substantial form) and even into the Supreme Cause—the *first mover*, whose existence Aristotle proves in the final book of his *Physics*. The sciences that are subordinated to the philosophy of nature—such as mechanics, hydrostatics, acoustics, optics, etc., explain sense phenomena but do so by means of proximate causes, not their first causes (i.e., prime matter, substantial form, and the first mover of the universe).

[25] [Tr. note: The immediate concern of the metaphysician is not with notions pertaining to positively immaterial beings such as the angels and God. It is more exact to say that metaphysics is concerned with notions that are *not limited* to materiality. This is a kind of immateriality that could be termed "negative"—not material. Much has been made of this point by contemporary Thomists. Just as an example, see the extensive work of Msgr. John Wippel in "Metaphysics and *Separatio* According to Thomas Aquinas," *The Review of Metaphysics* 31 (1978): 431–70, and "Thomas Aquinas and Avicenna on the Relationship between First Philosophy and the Other Theoretical

ute *being* to spirit and even analogically to God, the First Being.

While other sciences consider being under a particular aspect— physics under the aspect of mobile being, mathematics under the aspect of quantitative being or quantity—metaphysics must consider being *as being*, as well as the first principles of being. The other sciences make use of these principles without treating of them expressly. This domain ought not to remain unexplored. Metaphysics, therefore, must undertake a treatment of the real insofar as it is real.

These matters must be so if metaphysics is indeed knowledge of things by their supreme cause. In fact, as Aristotle shows in the first chapter of the fourth book of the *Metaphysics*, *each general cause* (i.e., not each individual cause) by which a *general effect* is explained (like vegetative life on the surface of the earth) *corresponds of itself to* THE NATURE *of this effect*. If *this living being*, the father of another being, is the cause of the coming into existence of *this other*, he does not account

---

Sciences: A Note on Thomas's *Commentary on Boethius's De Trinitate*, q. 5, art. 1, ad 9," *The Thomist* 37 (1973): 133–54. Similar concerns (though for different reasons) animated the so-called River Forest tradition of Thomism. It is also represented in an older set of concerns regarding the proper subject of metaphysics, a topic that received much ink among Thomists of various inflections and persuasions. For some recent work on this, see Philip Neri Reese, "Dominic of Flanders, O.P. (d. 1479) on the Nature of the Science of Metaphysics" (PhL thesis, Catholic University of America, 2015).

These same points were not missed in Garrigou-Lagrange's day and, arguably, not by him. As one form of confirmation, see the remarks of his disciple on many matters, Jacques Maritain, *The Degrees of Knowledge*, trans. Gerald B. Phelan (Notre Dame, IN: University of Notre Dame Press, 1995), 233n19, 453; and *Existence and the Existent*, trans. Gerald B. Phelan and Lewis Galantiere (New York: Pantheon, 1948), 32n15.

There are some of the school of Gilson (but others, including those following the work of Msgr. Wippel) who may react poorly to Fr. Garrigou-Lagrange stating that it is "abstract." However, Fr. Garrigou-Lagrange is not referring here directly to the first operation of the intellect, whose psychological activity is rightly called abstraction that leads to conceptualization of the quiddities of things. Indeed, Fr. Garrigou-Lagrange's position regarding the centrality of proper proportionality among the types of analogy *requires* him to include *all three* acts of the intellect to explain how we come to know being in its full analogical scope. This will become more evident as we progress through this text. For a defense of the claim that metaphysics can deal with being taken in the abstract (without thereby falling into some kind of conceptualism or essentialism), see John C. Cahalan, "The Problem of Thing and Object in Maritain," *The Thomist* 59, no. 1 (1995): 31–36.]

for the *life* that is contingently in him, as in his son.[26] It is necessary that there be a *general and superior cause* of the existence of the *vegetative life* that is found on the surface of the earth. Likewise, there must be an eminent cause for the existence of *sense life*, and likewise an even higher cause of *intellectual life*. Finally, there must be a Supreme Cause of the *being* of things that come into existence—a cause of their *being as being*, ὂν ᾗ ὂν.

Now, we have seen that metaphysics is knowledge of all things by their supreme cause.[27] Therefore, it has for its proper and formal object being insofar as it is the being of things, and metaphysics explains it by its ultimate causes (i.e., its efficient and final causes). Aristotle concluded: "Therefore, metaphysics must search out the first causes of being insofar as it is the being of things."[28] Thus, he formulates anew the principle from which St. Thomas deduced that *God alone can create*,[29] for the most universal effect (the being of all things) can only be produced by the most universal Cause.

*   *   *

We have thus arrived at the end of our hunt for the definition—*venatio definitionis*. From a very vague [*confus*] concept of wisdom—that is, as something excellent in the order of knowledge—we have come now to a distinct concept. It is the same concept under two different aspects, just as one and the same being is first an infant and then grows into a man.

The passage from a vague concept (expressed by the *nominal defi-*

---

[26] See *ST* I, q. 104, a. 1.

[27] [Tr. note: Fr. Garrigou-Lagrange is a bit inconsistent with his capitalization. Here "supreme cause" is uncapitalized. The matter is ambiguous, for, according to Fr. Garrigou-Lagrange's outlook, articulated here and in other works, metaphysics understands all things under the light of the principle of non-contradiction (or, of identity), seeing all things in light of the First Cause of Being, the Pure Self-Subsistent Act of Existing *only at the terminus of its inquiries*. It is only in a qualified sense that metaphysics knows all things through their First and Supreme Cause. In this, it differs greatly from acquired supernatural theology, which *does* know all things in relation to God understood in His essentially supernatural Being, as will be articulated below.]

[28] See *Metaphysics* 4.1.

[29] See *ST* I, q. 45, a. 5.

nition) to a distinct concept (expressed by the *real definition*) is made by an *ascending comparative induction*. That is to say, the passage is effected by comparing the vaguely [*confusément*] known thing to be defined with similar and dissimilar things—in our particular case, with the lowest and the highest modes of knowledge. This ascending comparative induction joins with *the descending division of diverse modes of knowledge*: sense knowledge versus rational knowledge; rational knowledge through proximate causes versus rational knowledge through the highest of causes. It is only the last that deserves to be called *wisdom*, at least so long as we wish to preserve the true sense of the word, which itself was already indicated by the nominal definition.

At the end of this *venatio definitionis realis*, of this hunt for the definition (as Aristotle says in providing the rules for such a chase),[30] *the vague concept*, which was THE GUIDING PRINCIPLE of the ascending and descending search, is itself recognized in the *distinct concept*, as a man who is half asleep recognizes himself when, fully awake, he looks at himself in a mirror. Thus, the search for the definition is the work of understanding [*intelligence*]—more a work of νοῦς than it is a work of discursive reason.[31]

---

[30] See Aristotle, *Posterior analytics* 2.3–7. Also, see St. Thomas's accompanying commentary on these chapters.

[31] There is much that could be said about this subject, as much in theology as in philosophy. We cannot here pay heed to this capitally important subject. We can only note what seems to us to be the principal point.

It is understanding, νοῦς, that progressively passes from the first *vague* [*confuse*] intellectual apprehension (before any judgment or reasoning) to *distinct* intellectual apprehension. To accomplish this, it uses as its *instruments* (in a sense inferior to it) ascending comparative induction and descending division. However, these are only instruments for it, and the real definition attained by this process exceeds these instruments.

Various works published in recent years concerning the Aristotelian method of research for the *definition* (i.e., treating *Posterior analytics* 2) do not reflect on what is most important in this research, that is, *its guiding principle*—which is superior to discursive reason and which is nothing other than νοῦς and its *vague* [*confuse*] intellectual apprehension of the thing to be defined. This apprehension is expressed in the *quid nominis*, which contains in a vague manner [*confusément*] the *quid rei*.

The intellect would not search for the real definition if it had not in some sense already have found it.

[Tr. note: This problem, which Aristotle addresses in the *Posterior analytics* clearly from the perspective of Plato's *Meno*, is of pivotal importance. It is related to similar

This example of the search for definitions shows well the method by which Aristotle establishes definitions for the soul, man, the different virtues (such as prudence, justice, courage, temperance), that of art (*recta ratio factibilium*, right reason of things to be made),[32] and many others. Thus, Aristotle has given precision to Socrates's own method expressed in his personal concern, above all, with defining well that about which we are having a discussion, with first determining the meaning that we give to the terms that we commonly use (and without which language and thought would be impossible). Thus, he reduced the sophists to using words in a determinate sense (or, failing that, to maintain a profound silence).[33]

It follows from the definition given for wisdom that it has, like the truth that it knows, a value in and of itself, independent of the practical usefulness that may be derived from it and from all material profit. If one says that it is "useless", this is because it is *above usefulness* and not because it is beneath it in dignity. Now, that which is above the useful and the delightful is the *true and fitting* [good], which merits being loved for its own sake, independent from the advantages or enjoyment that one may find in it. Moreover, as Aristotle adds, wisdom, which is the highest and most honorable knowledge, is something more divine than human:[34] "We can, with all due reason, find that the possession of this science is above the level of humanity, for man's nature is enslaved

---

issues raised at the end of the ninth book of the *Metaphysics*. On this topic, the reader will benefit much from the more recent reflections of Robert Sokolowski in "Making Distinctions," in *Pictures, Quotations, and Distinctions: Fourteen Essays in Phenomenology* (Notre Dame, IN: University of Notre Dame Press, 1992), 55–91. This same theme is stressed by Fr. Garrigou-Lagrange in the text cited in note 6 of the previous chapter.]

[32] [Tr. note: I am correcting here what appears to be an error in the original. It reads *recta ratio agibilium*—right reason regarding things to be done. This is the classic definition of prudence, not art. This must have slipped past Fr. Garrigou-Lagrange and his editors. To this end, the reader would benefit from reading Jacques Maritain, *Creative Intuition in Art and Poetry* (Cleveland, OH: Meridian, 1955), 32. Similar conversations can be found in the opening chapters of Maritain, *Art and Scholasticism*, trans. John O'Connor (Tacoma, WA: Cluny Media, 2016).]

[33] [Tr. note: This is what Aristotle shows in his discussion of the Principle of Non-Contradiction in *Metaphysics* 4.]

[34] See *Metaphysics* 1.2.

in a thousand ways.[35] In the words of Simonides, 'There is none other than God who can enjoy this privilege of wisdom.' But man would fail himself if he did not seek this high knowledge to the degree that he can come to possess it. . . . And the least degree that he would possess of it would be superior to all the other sciences."[36]

Aristotle shows well in book IV of the *Metaphysics* that metaphysics differs specifically from both mathematics and the philosophy of nature by its *manner of defining* and, thereby, its manner of *demonstrating*—for demonstration rests upon definitions. This is so because metaphysics abstracts from all matter, *abstrahit ab omni materia*. In sensible reality, it considers those foundational characteristics themselves of a supra-sensible order.

The philosophy of nature abstracts from only the individual matter. It is not concerned with *this or that* substantial change, but with *substantial change, generation, and corruption as such*. It is not concerned with *this or that* plant or *this or that* animal, but with *vegetative life, sensitive life, and their four causes*—formal, material, efficient, and final. It is the first degree of abstraction.

Mathematics abstracts from sensible qualities and from movement. Thereby it abstracts from the efficient and final cause as well. It does so in order to consider only *quantity* as continuous or discrete: figures and numbers and their properties. This is the second degree of abstraction, in which physico-mathematical sciences participate.[37]

---

[35] *Prius est vivere (etiam materialiter) deinde philosophiari.* Id est prius vivere etiam materialiter, non in ordine intentionis sed in ordine executionis. [One must first live (even merely materially live) and only then philosophize. However, it is a priority in the order of execution, not in the order of intention.] The life of the body is subordinate to that of the intellect, but the life of the body must be first assured.

[36] In what follows this quotation, Aristotle remarks against the poet Simonides that God does not at all envy the wisdom (otherwise so imperfect) of man. In fact, the envious are sad from the fact that they desire that which exceeds them and that they are saddened at the felicity of others. Now, God cannot be sad or desire that which exceeds Him. He is above envy.

[37] [Tr. note: To get one's bearings on questions concerning the second degree of abstraction from a Thomist perspective, see Armand Maurer, "Thomists and Thomas Aquinas on the Foundation of Mathematics," *The Review of Metaphysics* 47, no. 1 (1993): 43–61. Maurer's position will not in all ways be congenial to that of Fr. Garrigou-Lagrange, but the article is a good resource for citations. Likewise, it should be

Metaphysics proceeds according to the third degree of abstraction. It abstracts *from all matter* and considers in sensible things the intelligible characteristics that are most universal and the absolutely necessary principles that are found in the supra-sensible order: *intelligible being*, unity, truth, goodness, beauty, substance, quality, and causality. In brief—the intelligible is known by abstraction from matter, and therefore, the intelligible is superior by abstraction from all matter. From this results a superior certitude involving the most necessary laws of the real.[38]

By this, one sees that, in order to discover the efficient and Final Cause of the very being of sensible things and of man, we must not proceed—like Spinoza—through metaphysics with a mathematical method, a method that abstracts from the efficient and final cause. We likewise must not wish to reduce ontology to psychology—intelligible being to the Cartesian *cogito*; nor must we reduce intelligible being to a force that is aware of itself, like Leibniz's monads. On the contrary, we must conceive of the *cogito* (and of thought in general) in relation to intelligible being; we must define *force* and *action* in relation to the being that can act and the being that can be produced (*operari sequitur esse*—operation follows upon existence). In the light of the first principles of reason and of being, metaphysics rises to the First Cause, which does not need to be moved in order to act—for, *this Cause is Its very own Action* (*est suum agere*), and this implies that It is *Being Itself* (*est suum esse*). *Operari sequitur esse, et modus operandi modum essendi: Ego sum qui sum* [Operation follows upon existence and the mode of operation upon the mode of existence: I Am Who Am].[39]

---

remembered that the physico-mathematical sciences are formally mathematical and materially physical—and, that they are more physical than they are mathematical. An accessible study can be found in Jacques Maritain, *The Philosophy of Nature*, trans. Imelda C. Byrne (New York: Philosophical Library, 1951).]

[38] See St. Thomas, *De Trinitate*, q. 5, a. 1.

[39] See *ST* I, q. 3, a. 4.

The Two Supernatural Wisdoms

We can understand the nature of metaphysical wisdom more fully by comparing it to two wisdoms of a superior order that can themselves judge metaphysics from on high, *ex alto*. That is, we will speak of theology and the [Spirit's] gift of wisdom.

Theology: Its Object, Its Light, and Its Rooting in Infused Faith

Theology is a wisdom of the supernatural order, for it necessarily presupposes *infused faith*, which could be likened to the roots of theology. This is so because theology has for its ends: (1) The conceptual explication or analysis of *revealed truths* (or, *truths of faith*) in order to understand them better in contrast to the deformations found in heretical understandings; (2) the deduction of *other truths* that are virtually[40] contained in revealed truths—such truths are properly called "theological conclusions," the fruit of a reasoning that

---

[40] [Tr. note: The term "virtually" here means "precontained in the ability/power of the cause." From the primary principles of faith, we can conclude many other things. These latter things are not *formally* or directly revealed. They are, however, true conclusions derived from the principles of faith. Thus, they are in the power (*virtus*) of revelation itself. Whence, we speak of "virtual revelation." Fr. Garrigou-Lagrange continues to explain the point, but it is necessary that we understand why the strange-seeming old term "virtually" is being maintained! Our formal motive for holding something that is virtually revealed (i.e., explicitly exposited in theological *sapientia*) is not the same as our formal motive in holding something directly through the theological virtue of faith. See Réginald Garrigou-Lagrange, *The One God*, trans. Bede Rose (St. Louis, MO: B. Herder, 1946), 43–56.

On this topic, St. Augustine's Press is scheduled to publish John of St. Thomas, *On Sacred Science: Cursus Theologicus I, Question 1, Disputation 2*, ed. Victor M. Salas, trans. John P. Doyle (South Bend, IN: St. Augustine's Press, 2017). Also, see Emmanuel Doronzo's accessible *Introduction to Theology* (Middleburg, VA: Notre Dame Institute Press, 1973). Also, for a good summary of relevant discussions of these matters, see Doronzo, *The Channels of Revelation* (Middleburg, VA: Notre Dame Institute Press, 1974), 52–59. Doronzo was Fr. Garrigou-Lagrange's student at the Angelicum, a professor at the Catholic University of America in Washington, DC, and author of a series of scholarly texts on the sacraments and theology in general, as well as several popularized but profound theology texts.]

is not merely explanatory but objectively inferential.[41]

The distinction between *revealed truths* and *other truths* deduced from revelation is the key to the problem of the evolution of dogma—wherein it is incredibly important to avoid confusing that which the Church condemns infallibly as erroneous with that which she condemns as being heretical. It is only in this latter case that the contradictory proposition is a dogma of faith.[42]

---

[41] [Tr. note: a proper *scientific* syllogism is objectively illative, inferring a truth (i.e., the conclusion) from two premises. As regards the distinction between an explicative and an illative syllogism, see the remarks of Fr. Austin Woodbury, S.M., in *Logic*, The John N. Deely and Anthony Russell Collection, Latimer Family Library, St. Vincent College, Latrobe, PA, pp. 239–41 (nos. 299–300):

> In every syllogism properly so-called, from one truth is inferred ANOTHER TRUTH. Therefore, whenever by a syllogism there is not inferred a NEW TRUTH, this is a syllogism improperly so-called. The syllogism improperly so-called is twofold, to wit: the expository syllogism and the explicative syllogism. . . . From the expository syllogism must be distinguished the explicative syllogism; whereof, this is an example: "Man is mortal. But a rational animal is a man. Therefore, a rational animal is mortal."
>
> Here, [the middle term] is universal, and therefore there is a true illation. Nevertheless, it is not a syllogism properly so-called, because it does NOT infer in the conclusion another truth, i.e. a judgment other than in the premises. For here, the conclusion expresses the same truth but explicates it BY OTHER CONCEPTS. For these two propositions, "man is mortal," and, "rational animal is mortal," express the same truth, but the latter expresses it by more distinct concepts than the former. Wherefore, to this is rightly given the name of EXPLICATIVE syllogism.
>
> In the explicative syllogism, the conclusion is IDENTICAL AS REGARDS ITSELF (*quoad se*) with the major but NOT AS REGARDS US (*non quoad nos*); and therefore, there is a formal illation, but not an objective illation. [He cites here R.-M. Schultes, *Introductio ad historiam dogmatum* (Paris: Lethielleux, 1922).]
>
> OBSERVE that the major [premise] and the conclusion of an explicative syllogism are in THE SAME MODE OF SAYING "PER SE"; otherwise, there would be had, not an explicative syllogism but a syllogism PROPERLY SO-CALLED. In the example given above, both these propositions are IN THE SECOND MODE of saying "per se." But the case is otherwise with this syllogism: "A rational animal is capable of science. But man is a rational animal. Therefore, man is capable of science." Here, the major [premise] is in the FOURTH mode of saying "per se"; otherwise, the syllogism would be employed to no purpose. But the conclusion is in the SECOND manner of saying "per se." Wherefore this is a syllogism properly so-called.]

[42] The passage from the *quid nominis* [nominal definition] to the *quid rei* [real definition], from a vague [*confus*] concept (often expressed first in a concrete manner) to a

The work of *conceptual analysis* (which is the most important part of the theological treatises on the Trinity, the Incarnation, the Sacraments, grace, etc.) and that *of deducing* theological conclusions is a human work undertaken on the data of revelation (or, revealed data). In this sense, we follow St. Thomas in saying that theology *acquiritur studio humano* [is acquired by human study] and that it is *not* an *infused habitus*[43] or an infused science.

---

distinct concept (expressed in a more abstract and precise manner), is a capital point in the question of the *evolution of dogma*. Such an "evolution" is a passage from the vague to the distinct, from the implicit to the explicit, *in the expression of one and the same truth*. For example: The mystery of the Trinity or of the Incarnation, or that of the real presence of the body of Christ in the Eucharist.

As to theological conclusions (properly speaking)—that is, to conclusions arrived at by objectively inferential reasoning and not conclusions that are only explanatory—such conclusions are *other truths* that are only *virtually revealed*. When the Council of Nicaea defined that the Word is consubstantial with the Father, it did not define a theological conclusion. Instead, it brought to precision this revealed truth: *Et Deus erat Verbum*; "And the Word was God" (John 1:1).

It has been contended recently that, if it was revealed only that God is *Being Itself* and *Wisdom Itself*, all of the conclusions that could be deduced rigorously from such revelation (such as, "God is free") could be proposed by the Church as revealed and as dogmas of faith. In order to defend this thesis, one would necessarily be led to hold that these conclusions are *the same truth* as the revealed principles from which they are derived. See Francisco Marín-Sola, *L'evolution homogene du dogme catholique*, vol. 2 (Fribourg, CH: Imprimerie et librairie de l'oeuvre de Saint-paul, 1924), 333: "Two propositions (concerning God) of really identical *predicates* have a *meaning* that is really identical."

In other words, such a position comes down to saying: As the Divine Attributes are not really distinct, the proposition "God is intelligent" has *the same sense* as "God is free" or "God is just," or "God is merciful." Now, this is the nominalist thesis according to which the divine names are synonyms just like Tullius and Cicero. Compare such a claim to *ST* I, q. 13, a. 4 ("Utrum nomina divina sint synonyma [Whether the divine names are synonyms]). From the aforementioned perspective, one could say, "God punishes by His mercy and pardons by His justice."

[Tr. note: The topic of doctrinal development is taken up at length by Fr. Garrigou-Lagrange in a number of works. It is thematically presented in *Le sens commun: la philosophie de l'être et les formules dogmatiques*, 4th ed. (Paris: Desclée de Brouwer & Cie, 1936), 274–397. A translation of this book is scheduled to be published by Emmaus Academic in the near future.]

[43] [Tr. note: I am retaining the word *habitus* on the good council of Yves Simon, who long considered this matter, ultimately concluding that it is better to retain the Latin so as to avoid a confusion with *habit* or subjective potency. On this, insightful remarks can be found in Yves Simon, *The Definition of Moral Virtue*, ed. Vukan Kuic (New York: Fordham University Press, 1986), 47–68.]

However, from the fact that it has its *roots* in infused faith, theology is a wisdom of the supernatural order. It has for its *proper object* not being insofar as it is the being of things, or even God as being—First Being and Author of our nature. Instead, it has for its object *God as God*—God in *His Deity* or His intimate life, naturally unknowable, God as known by Divine Revelation, God the *Author of grace* and of glory, or of eternal beatitude, an essentially supernatural object. Indeed, this is what St. Thomas says in *ST* I, q. 1, a. 6:[44]

> *Sacred doctrine most especially determines matters pertaining to God* in a manner according to that which is the highest cause. This is so because sacred doctrine not only determines matters about God according to what can be known through created realities. The philosophers know of such things, as is said in Romans 1:19, "That which is known of God is manifest in them." But sacred doctrine also determines matters pertaining to God *according to that which is known of Himself by Himself alone* and by others *by means of communicated revelation.* Whence, sacred doctrine is most highly called wisdom.

Theology attains this object (God and His Deity, in His intimate life, *obscurely known* by faith before being clearly known by Vision) under the light of revelation called "virtual" because, after having conceptually analyzed revealed truths, it deduces other truths that are virtually contained in the revealed truths.

From this, it follows that one can have an adequate idea concerning the elevation of theology—the science of faith, or of that which is given in revelation—only if one has an adequate idea of *infused faith* and its *essentially supernatural, eminent certitude.* It is a certitude that, despite the obscurity of the object believed, is superior in itself to metaphysical certitude.[45]

We said above that the *metaphysical certitude* of the real value of the first principles of contradiction, causality, and so on is *founded formally*

---

[44] [Tr. note: The text incorrectly reads a. 10 here. Elsewhere, he cites it correctly.]

[45] See *ST* II-II, q. 4, a. 8: *Utrum fides sit certior scientia et aliis virtutibus intellectualibus* [Whether faith is more certain than science and the other intellectual virtues].

and intrinsically upon the intellectual evidence of these principles and that it is *founded materially and extrinsically* upon sensation.

Here, as St. Thomas explains well,[46] *the essentially supernatural certitude* of infused faith in the mysteries of the Trinity and the Redemptive Incarnation *is founded formally and intrinsically* upon the authority of God the Revealer, upon the First Revealing Truth to whom infused faith adheres as its formal motive. Infused faith is founded *materially and extrinsically* upon Divine Revelation's signs, which are the miracles, the fulfilled prophecies, the marvelous life of the Church, and so on.

As vision grasps by one and the same act both color and the light that renders color to be actually visible, as natural understanding grasps by one and the same act a principle and the light that shows the truth to it, so too does *infused faith adhere supernaturally* by one and the same act *to the revealed mysteries* and *to God who reveals them,* as proposed by the Church. In St. Thomas's words, "*Credere Deo* (revelanti) et *Deum* (revelatum) est *unus et idem actus.* [*To believe God* (as revealing) and *to believe in God* (as revealed) is *one and the same act.*]"[47]

This is what makes infused faith, despite the obscurity of its object, more certain *in itself* than the natural adherence of the intellect to the first [naturally known] principles:

> Something is called *more certain* (in itself) when it has *causes that are more certain.* In this manner of speaking, *faith is more certain than the aforementioned three things* (namely, metaphysical wisdom, science, and the understanding of first principles), BECAUSE FAITH IS FOUNDED UPON THE DIVINE TRUTH, whereas the aforementioned three are founded upon human reason.[48]

Infused faith, due to the obscurity of its object, does not attain it in a manner that is as connatural and satisfying, as [when] natural understanding attains evident principles. Nonetheless, in spite of this

---

[46] See ibid. See also, *ST* II-II, q. 1, aa. 1, 3, and 4; q. 2, aa. 1 and 2. See also, below, part II, ch. 5: "The Supernaturality of Faith."

[47] *ST* II-II, q. 2, a. 2, corp. and ad 1.

[48] See *ST* II-II, q. 4, a. 8.

fact, infused faith's formal motive—the First, Revealing Truth to whom it adheres supernaturally and infallibly—produces a certitude higher than all natural certitude.

This is why theology, which has its roots in infused faith, while being less certain than said faith itself, is more certain than metaphysics. Thus, theology can *judge metaphysics from on high by making use of it*—as the superior uses (*utitur*) the inferior [i.e., metaphysical wisdom]. At the very least, it judges that a given metaphysical proposition is not opposed in any way to reveal truths but that, on the contrary, it is in conformity with them. In this sense, St. Thomas writes in *ST* I, q. 1, a. 6, ad 2:[49]

> The proper nature of the knowledge achieved in this science (i.e., theology) is that it is *by revelation* and not, however, that it is through natural reason. And therefore, it does not pertain to theology to prove the principles of other sciences but, instead, only *to judge concerning them*; for anything found in the other sciences that is *opposed* to the truth of this science, is completely condemned as being *false*.[50]

Infused faith is far superior to theology, "quae acquiritur studio humano [which is acquired by human study]." However, infused faith communicates something of its certitude to the science that is derived from it and that is, consequently, a wisdom superior to metaphysical wisdom.

The Comfort Offered to Metaphysics by Divine Revelation

As we see in Christian philosophy, metaphysics can be greatly strengthened from on high by means of Divine Revelation.[51]

Metaphysical wisdom, even for things of its own order, receives a

---

[49] [Tr. note: Fr. Garrigou-Lagrange incorrectly has *ST* I, q. 1, a. 2.]

[50] *ST* I, q. 1, a. 2.

[51] Jacques Maritain has admirably shown this in his book *The Degrees of Knowledge*, above all in a chapter of utmost value relating to the topic of "Augustinian wisdom" (*The Degrees of Knowledge*, 310–28).

kind of *comforting* (objective and subjective)[52] from infused faith and from theology. In this way, the demonstrative certitude of the existence of God is strengthened for a philosopher if he becomes a Christian. Infused faith *confirms from on high* the philosopher's *natural adherence* to the proofs he already knew.

St. Thomas often speaks of this form of comforting. For example, see *ST* II-II, q. 1, a. 5, ad 4,[53] and q. 2, a. 9, ad 3; and *Quodlibet* II, q. 4, a. 1.[54]

This kind of comforting is particularly manifest in the case of the idea of *free creation ex nihilo*. Metaphysical wisdom can arrive at this notion, but it was not arrived at even by the Greeks—the people best endowed for philosophical speculation. Instead, in the first line of *Genesis*, it is revealed, "In the beginning God created the heavens and the earth." There is the mark of Divine Intelligence upon the Bible from the first words of the first book.

Aristotle well affirmed with certitude in the twelfth book of his *Metaphysics* that *God, Pure Act,* is *the Final Cause of the universe*—every agent acts for an end, for a good, and tends toward the supreme good, known or unknown. In the third chapter of the first book of the same work, he expressed great praise for Anaxagoras because he proclaimed the necessity of there being a First Intelligence that ordered the world. Aristotle never denied that God is *the first mover in the order of efficient causality* and even in a certain way the *cause of beings*. He even suggests this point, in particular in the sixth book of the *Metaphysics*: "All the first causes necessarily are eternal, but, *above all, the causes that are immobile and separate from matter*, for they are *the causes of visible things*."[55] Upon this text, St. Thomas noted:

> Now, from this, we can see manifestly the falsity of the opinion
> held by those who state that Aristotle thought that God was

---

[52] [Tr. note: See Jacques Maritain, *An Essay on Christian Philosophy*, trans. Edward H. Flannery (New York: Philosophical Library, 1955).]

[53] [Tr. note: The text reads "ad 7." It appears that he is referring to "ad 4."]

[54] [Tr. note: The text states "*Quodlibet* II, 6." He appears to be referring to the sixth overall article in *Quodlibet* II.]

[55] Aristotle, *Metaphysics* 6.1.1026a17.

not the cause of the substance of the heavens but only of its motion.[56]

But Aristotle did not raise himself to the explicit idea of *free creation ex nihilo*—indeed, not even to the idea of *creation ab aeterno* [from eternity]. There were two difficulties that, in Aristotle, have no answer: (1) How can a being, even a grain of sand, be produced, not by a transformation of a preexisting matter but *completely and entirely, from nothing*? (2) How can the purely immobile Act—which if It acts as an efficient cause upon the world appears to act *always in the same manner*—produce the world *freely* by a *free act* that could have not been in it (and of such a kind that It would have been able not to create or to create another world than this one)?

These questions, which do not have a response in Aristotle, find an answer in the *Summa theologiae* of St. Thomas—see *ST* I, q. 19, aa. 3, 4, 5, and 8; q. 22, aa. 1–3; q. 45, aa. 1–5; q. 46, aa. 1–3; and q. 104, aa.1–4. One sees there the superiority of Christian philosophy. The same point could be made as regards the certitude to be had about the immortality of the soul.

The Spirit's Gift of Wisdom and Quasi-experiential Knowledge of God

But there is yet another wisdom, which is superior to the acquired wisdom that we call theology. It is *infused wisdom* or the [Spirit's] gift of wisdom—the wisdom of the saints.

St. Thomas says very clearly: "As it pertains to the wise man to judge, there are two distinct wisdoms according to two manners of judging."[57] In fact, it happens that a man can *judge by way of inclination* (*per modum inclinationis*), as when someone who has a virtue (e.g., chastity) judges well the object of this virtue because he is inclined to it. In this sense, Aristotle has said, that "the virtuous man is the measure

---

[56] See Aquinas, commentary on *Metaphysics* 6.1, lec. 1.

[57] *ST* I, q. 1, a. 6, ad 3.

and rule of human acts";[58] he has a right judgment of them. But there is another manner of judging. It is that of someone who instructs in the things pertaining to *moral science.* Such a person can make a judgment concerning the acts of a given virtue, even if he does not possess it.[59]

As St. Thomas states in *ST* I, q. 1, a. 6, ad 3:

> On the subject of divine things, the first manner of *judging* (i.e., *by inclination or sympathy*) pertains to the wisdom that is a gift of the Holy Spirit, according to the saying of St. Paul in I Cor. 2:15, 'The spiritual man judges all things and is not himself judged by anyone.' Likewise, [Pseudo-]Dionysius in *The Divine Names* 2.9 says of Hierotheus that he knows Divine things, not only by means of study, but also by a divine impression—ου μόνον μαθών, αλλά και παθών τα Θεία, *non solum discens, sed et patiens divina.*[60] The second manner of judging pertains to the theological science which is acquired through study even though its principles are known through revelation.

The first manner is through connaturality or sympathy, the second is *secundum perfectum usum rationis*—according to a perfect use of reason.

In explicitly treating the [Spirit's] gift of wisdom in *ST* II-II, q. 45, aa. 1 and 2, St. Thomas adds precision to this teaching. In article 1, he speaks above all about the *special inspiration of the Holy Spirit* from which this infused knowledge proceeds, an inspiration to which the gift of wisdom renders us docile. In the second article, he speaks above all of the *sympathy* or *connaturality for Divine things*, founded upon infused charity. This connaturality *makes use* of the special inspiration of the Holy Spirit in order to show us how the Lord is good—*gustate et videte quoniam suavis est Dominus* [taste and see that the Lord is good] (Ps 34:8). From the fact that the Holy Spirit inspires in us a wholly filial affection for God, an infused love, the mysteries revealed by Him

---

[58] See Aristotle, *Nicomachean Ethics* 10.5.

[59] [Tr. note: i.e., the virtues are operative habits enabling one to do certain actions. However, the speculatively practical knowledge pertaining to ethical science does not incline one to act in this or that set of circumstances. Only the moral virtues do this.]

[60] By a kind of sympathy: καὶ ἐχ τῆς πρὸς αὐτὰ συμπαθείας.

appear to us not only as being *true* because they are revealed but also as being *goods* and sovereignly *conformed* to our aspirations, above all to the supernatural aspirations that grace arouses in us. Thus did the disciples say on the road to Emmaus, "Is it not true that our hearts burned within us when he spoke to us on the way and explained the Scriptures to us?" (Luke 24:32).

From the fact that we *now love* the revealed mysteries of the Incarnation and Redemption, there is now in us *a relation of conformity* of these mysteries to our intimate dispositions or, rather, from our dispositions to the mysteries. Therefore, under the special inspiration of the Holy Spirit, these mysteries appear to us not only as *believable* because they are revealed but also as *sovereignly loveable* and worthy of a love that ought to become ever purer and ever stronger.[61] By this, infused wisdom *even tastes that which is of greater obscurity* in these mysteries and that cannot be expressed, for this very thing is the Divine and Sovereign Good; it is what is most ineffable and *most intimate in the intimate life of God*. It is what led St. Teresa of Ávila to say, "I especially have more devotion or love for the mysteries of the faith that are more obscure." She knew that this obscurity differs absolutely from that of absurdity or incoherence—and that it comes from a light that is too strong for our weak eyes.

---

[61] See Cajetan in *In ST* I-II, q. 58, a. 5, no. 10: "*By means of an appetite affected toward something*, for example vengeance, from this very fact that it is affected toward that other thing two things happen simultaneously. *In the very person there occurs the very affect* directed toward vengeance, and in the vengeance *there arises a relation of agreement to such an appetite*. Thus it happens that the vengeance begins to exist, and agrees with such an appetite, which before this was not in agreement—not because of a change in the vengeance but because of a change in the appetite. *However, with the vengeance consonant with the appetite, it arises in the intellect that reason judges it to be in agreement.*"

That which is said here about vengeance ought to be said also about the object of chastity and even more so about that of charity.

John of St. Thomas, discussing *ST* I-II, q. 68, aa. 1 and 2 (*Cursus Theologicus, De Donis Spiritus Sancti*, disp. 18, a. 4, no. 11), profoundly explains this knowledge through connaturality and says, "Sic amor transit in conditione objecti. [Thus does love pass over into the condition of an object.]" The object appears all the more loveable the more that we love it. See also John of St. Thomas's treatment of *ST* I, q. 43, a. 3, concerning the dwelling of the Holy Trinity in us like a quasi-experientially knowable object.

* * *

The splendor of this infused wisdom in these great contemplatives is incomparable. One has most justly said concerning them:

> There is a certain inferior wisdom, which dares to usurp the name of wisdom because it is limited in such a manner that it does not see that which it lacks. The narrowness of its horizon gives itself the horrid gift of being content with itself.
>
> Mysticism is the other wisdom—that which is from on high—that sees far enough to be aware of its own short view. The grandeur of contemplation is a mirror without defect where it sees its own insufficiency. The immensity of the places of its habitation gives it the magnificent gift of sacred contempt for itself.
>
> With this contempt is its grandeur increased, and with its grandeur its goodness is increased.
>
> The lofty majesty of the contemplations ablaze in someone like Rusbrock have greater fecundity than earth-bound wombs, gentler than the breathing of a sleeping infant. A characteristic unique to Christian and Catholic splendor is that *practice follows it*, as the shadow follows the body.
>
> The more the mystery is inscrutable, the higher is the contemplation, the more profound too is the gaze of the contemplative so as to grasp human miseries in their abyss—merciful so as to encourage, mild so as to comfort, ardent so as to love, tender so as to bring relief.[62]

It is a living image of intimate reconciliation of the Divine perfections—wisdom, justice, and mercy.

---

[62] Ernest Hello, introduction in Jan van Rusbrock, *Rusbrock l'admirable: oevres choisies*, ed. and trans. Ernest Hello (Paris: Librairie Poussielgue Frères, 1869), ix–x.

*   *   *

Thus, one sees the notable difference between the three wisdoms of which we have spoken. And just as theological wisdom, which has its roots in infused faith, strengthens from on high the metaphysical wisdom of which it makes use, so too does *the gift of wisdom*, the principle of *infused contemplation*, strengthen theological wisdom from on high—as one sees above all in the great doctors of the Church, notably in ones such as St. Augustine and St. Thomas. It is *with love* and under the special inspiration of the Holy Spirit that they speak of the mystery of the Trinity and that of the Redemptive Incarnation. They speak about these matters like things that are the life of their soul—indeed, the life of their life. And, especially in reading particular pages written by them—in particular their *Commentary* [sic] *on the Gospel of St. John*—one senses that they have not only *an abstract knowledge* of the living God (a knowledge that is given by the study of sound philosophy and, in a superior order, the study of theology) but also *a quasi-experiential knowledge*[63] (that of the gift of a wisdom, which grows in them with the love of God).[64]

More than the philosophers of antiquity, they have had *certitude* concerning Divine things; and more than the philosophers of antiquity have they had *the sense of mystery* that, as we will see, grows along with certitude instead of decreasing and destroying it.

---

[63] See St. Thomas, *In I Sent.*, d. 14, q. 2, a. 2, ad 3: "Cognitio ista est quasi experimentalis [such knowledge is quasi-experiential]." This is said of this affective knowledge of God given by the Holy Spirit. See also *ST* I, q. 43, a. 3, corp., ad 1, and ad 2. *In Rom* 8, lec. 4, on these words of St. Paul in Rom 8:14–16: "The Spirit gives testimony to our spirit that we are sons of God."

[64] We have spoken at length elsewhere about this quasi-experiential knowledge of God. See Réginald Garrigou-Lagrange, *The Love of God and the Cross of Jesus*, vol. 1, trans. Sr. Jeanne Marie (St. Louis, MO: B. Herder, 1948), 154–73.

The Role of Rectified Will in Two Other Species of Certitude

We find two other important cases involving the rectified will when we consider two other species of certitude—namely, that of prudence and that of hope.

It is appropriate for us to say some words about these in order to see what St. Thomas has thought of the so-called *spirit de finesse* (or, "intuitive mind") that Pascal loved to oppose to the so-called "mathematical [*géométrique*][65] mind."

How does it happen that certain people who have little formal instruction but great virtue can have *a sound and very just judgment* in moral matters in the same situations in which many people who have studied moral theology would hesitate and would end up giving a choice between two solutions that are sometimes very convoluted? How does it happen that, in another order, certain Christians have a hope that is so firm and so certain (in spite of the objections that are presented to their minds) while a number of those who have speculatively studied the mystery of salvation say to themselves, "*Am I predestined?* And if I cannot respond to this question, how can *my hope* be sure? How can it be assured, if I am not certain of my salvation?"

St. Thomas has considered these two difficulties well and gives them nearly the same response, which shows us the importance of knowledge through sympathy in the spiritual life.

---

[65] [Tr. note: lit. "Geometric," a word of no small importance in early modern thought if we think merely of the pretenses of Spinoza to construct a metaphysics *more geometrico*. The method of clear reasoning involved in geometry inspired a whole movement within modern philosophy—a movement not least of all embodied by Descartes. An excellent overview of these matters can be found in Zvi Biener, "The Unity of Science in Early-Modern Philosophy: Subalternation, Metaphysics and the Geometrical Manner in Scholasticism, Galileo and Descartes" (PhD diss., University of Pittsburgh, 2008).

Many translate Pascal's *géométrique* as "mathematical." I am following this for the sake of clarity for the reader. Likewise, "intuitive" is chosen, though the word does not capture the exact meaning.]

The Certitude of Prudence

In the course of asking himself whether prudence is a *true intellectual virtue*, one that is superior to opinion, St. Thomas presents himself with this potential objection:

> An intellectual virtue is always the principle of a true judgment; never does a false judgment proceed from it. Now, it does not appear that this is the case for prudence, for it is almost impossible for a man to avoid every error in the practical judgment that ought to direct our actions, which are contingent things in the midst of variable circumstances. Also, it is said in the book of Wisdom 9:14 that, "The thoughts of mortals are fearful and that our prudence is uncertain in foresight." Therefore, it does not seem that prudence truly ought to be an intellectual virtue (that surpasses opinion or the domain of the probable).[66]

Likewise, how can one judge without error the *appropriate golden mean* to take *here and now* in firmness, mildness, humility, and patience with regard to people who are greatly different from one another—in regard to superiors, equals, and inferiors?

To such objections, St. Thomas responds:

> The truth of the practical intellect (or, the *practico-practical intellect*, i.e., of prudence)[67] is understood in a different sense than

---

[66] *ST* I-II, q. 57, a. 5, obj. 3. [Tr. note: The final expression in parentheses is added by Fr. Garrigou-Lagrange.]

[67] [Tr. note: This qualification is important and is added by Fr. Garrigou-Lagrange. When quotes from St. Thomas have parentheses in them, the text contained therein are explanatory remarks by Fr. Garrigou-Lagrange. Here, he is noting that, within the domain of practical knowledge, there is a great degree of variability all the while remaining practical in character. The prudential command, which directs action, is practical knowledge *par excellence*. However, there can be other degrees of practical knowledge. The most obvious instance is that of moral philosophy, which considers practical *matters* in a speculative *manner*. Moral philosophy is not a form of speculative science *tout court*, for it deals with *human actions*, not physical actions. However, it deals with them in such a manner that it lays out the *reasons for acting* in light of *first principles*. Hence, it is scientific in character. Its goal is *speculative knowledge of practical matters*. It can, therefore, be called, *speculatively practical*. On this point, see

the truth of the speculative intellect, as the Philosopher says in *Nicomachean Ethics* 6.2. In fact, *the truth of the speculative intellect* is constituted by *conformity with the extramental thing (per conformitatem ad rem)*. And because the intellect can be conformed in an *infallible manner* only to *necessary objects* and not to *contingent* objects (above all the future events which it is necessary to foresee with prudence), for this reason the speculative intellectual virtues (i.e., wisdom, the *habitus* of first principles, and the various sciences) are not concerned with contingent (and particular) objects but with necessary (and universal) truths.

In contrast to this, the truth of the practical intellect (or, practico-practical truth—that is to say, prudence, as distinct from moral science) is constituted *by conformity to rectified appetite*, or to right intention—*per conformitatem ad appetitum rectum*. This conformity ought not to have a place in the order of necessary matters but only in regard to contingent matters, which depend upon us, as do human acts.[68]

Thus, with regard to the morality of an act that one will posit, one can have a kind of *practical certitude*, even when there coexists with it an *invincible ignorance* or an *involuntary speculative error*. Thus, someone can judge prudently with a true *practical* certitude that he can take a beverage that is offered to him even though this beverage might have been poisoned (a matter that is humanly unforeseeable).

The danger of subjectivism is removed because we presuppose that *the right intention* of the will itself has a rectitude founded in the order of the necessary and the universal, *per conformitatem ad rem*; for, the *truth* of the first moral principles (*synderesis*) and the moral

---

appendix VII of Maritain's *The Degrees of Knowledge*. The works of Yves Simon may also be consulted to great profit: *A Critique of Moral Knowledge*, trans. Ralph McInerny (New York: Fordham University Press, 2002); *Practical Knowledge*, ed. Robert J. Mulvaney (New York: Fordham University Press, 1991).

There are also speculatively practical judgments rendered in the process of prudential reasoning, though the sense is not quite the same as the very clear case of the distinction between the prudential command (purely practically-practical) and moral philosophy (speculative practical). See Woodbury, *Ethics*, nos. 90, 214, 226, and 317.]

[68] *ST* I-II, q. 57, a. 5, ad 3.

science that derives from them consists in conformity to the *object*.

The speculative rectitude of the first moral principles, as well as the universal and necessary conclusions of moral science, cannot descend directly by way of reasoning all the way to the *contingent singular* that is our human act to be ruled.[69] This contingent singular contains—precisely because of its very singularity and contingence—something of the ineffable, something of the mysterious. How *are we to determine without error* concerning this contingent reality what ought to be the *golden mean* to maintain *here and now* and, at times, to maintain simultaneously in firmness and mildness, in magnanimity and humility, with persons who are very different and in difficult circumstances where there is much that is indeed imponderable?

It is possible only by means of an appetite rectified *by conformity to right appetite*. That is to say, it is possible only by rectitude of the will and sensibility—a rectitude assured by the moral virtues, without which prudence cannot exist.

Thus, St. Thomas often notes (following upon Aristotle) that *the virtuous person* (even if he is not well studied in moral science) judges soundly by means of inclination—*iudicat per modum inclinationis*—concerning what is to be done in conformity with virtue. He who is chaste judges well what is in conformity with this virtue; similarly, he who at the same time is humble and mild, firm and magnanimous, judges appropriately the golden mean to maintain *here and now* in these different virtues that it is sometimes necessary to exercise at this same moment.

Here, we have indeed a case of knowledge through a kind of sympathy, for from the fact that the will and the sensibility are *rectified* by these moral virtues, there is a *relation of conformity* between the virtuous man and *the golden mean* to maintain in these various acts. It is this that makes the virtuous man—with a kind of tact or, perhaps, flair—discern quickly what might go beyond the measure of due action, either by excess or by defect. The virtuous man discerns the wrong notes on the keyboard of the virtues and, by means of a great *discretion*, comes to avoid all confusion between frankness and roughness or boastfulness,

---

[69] [Tr. note: The sense is that the human act and the human will are ultimately *measured* (or, "ruled") by the principles known through synderesis, and ultimately upon the Divine Law, which is the same as God's own being.]

between mildness and weakness, firmness and rigidity, magnanimity and pride. There are nuances that speculative knowledge cannot determine (at least in concrete matters), while knowledge by means of such sympathy grasps them quickly, indeed sometimes immediately.

This reminds us of Pascal's distinction between the so-called "intuitive mind" and the so-called "mathematical mind." He says:

> The reason why the mathematicians are not intuitive [*fins*] is that they do not see that which is in front of them and that, being accustomed to the clear, cut-and-dry principles of mathematics[70] and to reasoning only after having first understood and handled their principles, *they become lost in matters of intuition* where principles do not allow themselves to be handled in such a manner. One hardly sees such principles; one feels them rather than sees them. One has infinite troubles to make them felt by those who do not by themselves feel them. These are such delicate and numerous things that one must have a sense that is adequately delicate and clear in order to feel them and *to judge rightly and justly according to this feeling* . . . It is necessary *all of the sudden to see something at a single glance,* and not by means of the progress of reasoning, at least to a certain degree. Thus, it is rare that mathematicians are intuitive and that the intuitive are mathematicians. . . . The intuitive, who are only intuitive, cannot have the patience needed for descending unto the first principles of speculative things. They do it tacitly, naturally, and without art.[71]

One could not better describe this knowledge through sympathy.[72]

---

[70] In order to speak thus of the mathematician/geometer, it had to be a geometer well detached from his science and who feels himself to be superior to it.

[71] See Blaise Pascal, *Pensées* in *Pensées and Other Writings,* ed. Anthony Levi and trans. Honor Levi (London: Oxford University Press, 2008), 150–51. [Tr. note: This is retranslated here. However, given the variability in editions of the *Pensées* and the fact that Fr. Garrigou-Lagrange does not cite his edition, I have chosen to cite the pagination from the aforementioned English edition.]

[72] [Tr. note: On this topic, see: Réginald Garrigou-Lagrange, "La prudence dans l'organisme des vertus," *Revue thomiste* 31, n.s. 9 (1926): 411–26; Garrigou-Lagrange,

The Certitude of Hope

Just as St. Thomas has undertaken a metaphysical study of the proper character of prudence's certitude (i.e., by means of conformity to a rectified will), so too he has studied the similar issue of what constitutes the certitude pertaining to the theological virtue of hope. Here, we see an even more striking example of the will's role as regards a very special kind of certitude in matters pertaining to the order of action.

St. Thomas studies this problem[73] by posing a twofold difficulty to himself. It does not seem that hope can be certain, for it is not in the intellect, but in the will. Moreover, lacking a special revelation, nobody here below can be certain that he is in a state of grace or that he will ultimately be saved; many are lost, even after having hoped. Therefore, if one who hopes *is not certain about his salvation*, how can he have a *certain hope*?

To these difficulties, St. Thomas responds:

> Certitude is found *essentially* in the faculty of knowledge—i.e., in the intellect. However, it is also found *by participation* in all that is infallibly moved toward its end by the intellect. Thus, we say that *nature* (i.e., the nature of beings that are inferior to us) *acts with certitude* inasmuch as the Divine Intellect infallibly moves each of the beings of nature toward its end. (Thus, the bee infallibly makes its hive as it must.)
>
> Likewise, one says that the moral virtues act more certainly than does art inasmuch as they are moved as by a kind of second nature to their acts by reason, or, prudence. (Thus,

---

"Du caractère métaphysique de la Théologie morale de saint Thomas, en particulier dans ses rapports avec la prudence et la conscience," *Revue thomiste* 30, n.s. 8 (1925): 341–55. A translation of the latter article is scheduled for publication in the English edition of *Nova et Vetera* in 2017. It is also presented in an altered form in Fr. Garrigou-Lagrange's *Le réalisme du principe de finalité*, which is scheduled to be released in translation by Emmaus Academic, as is a separately published translation of the first article.]

[73]   See *ST* II-II, q. 18, a. 4 ("Utrum spes viatorum habeat certitudinem" [Whether hope of wayfarers has certitude]).

justice is never the principle of an act of injustice, nor the virtue of courage the principle of an act of cowardice.)[74]

For the same reason, *hope tends with certainty toward its end* by a participation in the certitude of faith, which is in the intellect, and which proposes its object to it. Although we do not know with certitude concerning our salvation—that would require a special revelation—our hope is certain with a CERTITUDE OF TENDENCY. This kind of certitude is not a kind of speculative certitude like that of faith in revealed mysteries. Instead, it is a *practical certitude*, a certitude of *tendency, which,* under the light of faith, *is infallibly oriented in the true direction of the end to be attained.* Thus is one's trust in the infinitely helping God and in His Divine promises certain; for hope principally rests not upon grace that has been received but, instead, upon the *all-powerful Divine help* and upon the mercy of God in which we believe infallibly.

And the more that hope (enlivened by charity) grows, the more does the practical certitude proper to it increase. It is found in the will, but the intellect is not without its own judgment regarding *this relation of conformity* that increases each day—a conformity between the hope that is strengthened and the all-powerful and merciful God who inspires such hope.

*   *   *

Thus, one sees that the *intellectualism* of St. Thomas—in the case of man as well as in the case of God—grants a *large place to the will and to freedom,*[75] and above all to the Divine Freedom: God has created by a

---

[74] [Tr. note: Fr. Garrigou-Lagrange is implicitly opposing this to the arts, which can be the principle of "bad" artistic acts. The master organist knows how to make a good mistake so as to teach a student, and the best logician has a great mastery of sophisms, even using them for the sake of showing forth his great learning. See *ST* I-II, q. 57, a. 3.]

[75] [Tr. note: On this, the reader would *greatly* benefit from reading Maritain, *Existence and the Existent,* 47–61. Also, see Réginald Garrigou-Lagrange, *God: His Existence and His Nature: A Thomistic Solution of Certain Agnostic Antinomies,* vol. 2, trans. Bede Rose (St. Louis, MO: B. Herder, 1949), 306–38 and 370–72. Fr. Garrigou-Lagrange cites this text when discussing related matters.]

sovereignly free act, and, as Bossuet remarks, God is neither greater nor better because He has created the universe. Neither Plato nor Aristotle saw this. Despite the fact that there is a kind of appropriateness to the fact that God created, there would have been no impropriety had God created nothing at all; and there is no more perfection after creation than before.[76] In addition, St. Thomas, himself habituated to recognizing the motives that are not infallibly determining for the *free election to action* (or, to *choice*), is not afraid to affirm that, in God, there are acts of pure *good pleasure*—for which He does not need to have a reason that is antecedent to choice.[77] For example, it is by a sovereignly free good pleasure that God chose the Virgin Mary rather than any other virgin to be the mother of his Son at such a moment rather than at another time, in such a place rather than in another place, and in such people rather than in another people.

Likewise, the intellectualism of St. Thomas grants a large place to the will and freedom of man, even up to this *knowledge by way of sympathy* that we have discussed, especially in that of *prudence*, which presupposes the moral virtues, and in that of the *gift of wisdom*, which presupposes the theological virtue of charity and which grows in us with our free generosity and merit—that is to say, with the love of God and love of souls in God.

---

[76] [Tr. note: A point of capital importance in a generally Christian outlook. One can find fine reflections on this point in Robert Sokolowski, *The God of Faith and Reason: Foundations of Christian Theology* (Washington, DC: Catholic University of America Press, 1995), 1–30.]

[77] See *ST* I, q. 23, a. 5, ad 3. [Tr. note: Of course, as Thomas says in this response, the "reason" for such choices is found in the goodness of God. This topic will be taken up again much later, though the reader would do well to read Thomas's complete response to get the sense to Fr. Garrigou-Lagrange's point here.]

Chapter 2

The Verb "To Be"—Its Sense and Its Scope

I N O R D E R T O G R A S P what ought to be the sense of mystery in metaphysics and in theology, let us first insist on what is *clear* in these two sciences. We will do so by a metaphysical analysis of the verb "to be."

In the previous chapter, we saw how we ought to understand the oft-repeated expression of Aristotle and St. Thomas: "Obiectum intellectus est ens (The object of the intellect is *intelligible being*)." This is true for any intellect; however, if we are concerned with the *most inferior [dernier] kind of intellect* (i.e., the human intellect), it is necessary for us to say that the human intellect has for its proper object *the most inferior of intelligibles* (i.e., the *intelligible being of sensible things*). This is why the human intellect needs to be united to the senses in order to reach that sort of intelligible being. This is also why, in its current state, the human intellect does not naturally know spiritual realities except in the mirror of sensible things. Hence, in this state, the human intellect defines the *spiritual* in a negative matter, naming it "immaterial"—a sign that this intellect knows first of all that which is in matter. In contrast, for a pure spirit, it is material reality instead that is known negatively—it is "nonspiritual."

In addition, we have seen that the object of metaphysics is *being, inasmuch as it is the being* of things—being that has been abstracted from all matter and susceptible to being attributed to created spirits and analogically to God. However, metaphysics considers it *in speculo sensibilium* [in the mirror of material realities]. Hence, it differs essen-

47

tially from the intellectual intuition that the angel has of itself, as well as from the immediate vision of the Divine Essence that the blessed experience.

One may ask how the proposition "the object of the intellect (in general) is intelligible being" is established. To this inquiry, we can respond that it is a self-evident proposition—at least for anyone who truly grasps the meaning of the subject and of the predicate.

However, in order to grasp the meaning of each, it is necessary for us to observe inductively that our intellect has three operations—*conception* (or first apprehension), *judgment,* and *reasoning.* Hence, we must note that, in each of these intellectual operations, the intellect first grasps intelligible being and the *raisons d'être* of things. Indeed, the *conception* or notion of anything presupposes *the utterly fundamental notion of being;* without it, it is impossible to conceive of unity, truth, goodness, beauty, substance, life, quality, quantity, action, and so on. As regards *judgment,* the verb is like the very soul of the judgment. As we will come to see, every verb is reduced to the verb "to be." To say "Peter runs" is to say "Peter is running." Finally, reasoning expresses the *raison d'être*—whether it be of something demonstrated (if it be an *a priori* demonstration) or the affirmation of the existence of a given reality (if it be an *a posteriori*[1] demonstration). As regards philosophical induction, it is a matter of methodically passing from a vague [*confuse*] conception to a distinct one—and we have seen that every conception presupposes the conception of intelligible being.

From such remarks, one can see inductively, by passing precisely from the vague to the distinct, that it is true to say that *the object of the intellect is intelligible being.* It is not merely phenomena and their relatively constant relationships as expressed by experimental laws. Far above such laws there are the *first principles of reason* and *of being*—like that of contradiction, without which all thought, judgment, and reasoning would be impossible.

---

[1] [Tr. note: See remarks above in note 7 of the previous chapter.]

Metaphysical Reflection upon Forms of Language

However, these fundamental assertions receive a new confirmation by the philosophical study of the *verb* "to be"—that is, by the metaphysical reflection on what grammar can tell us about it, above all if we compare the two fundamental verbs "to be" and "to have" to each other and if we seek their profound meaning and their relations with the noun, the adjective, and the adverb.

There is an infinite distance between these two propositions: "I have truth and life," and, "I am the truth and the life." It is already a great thing to be able to say, "*I have* truth and life"; I am certain of possessing them and am able to transmit them. However, he alone could say, "I am the truth and the life," who was God Himself (John 14:6).[2]

Likewise, St. Thomas says, "*Solus Deus EST suum esse*."[3] Only God is His existence; He alone is Being Itself and was able to say, "I am that I am ," or, "He who is."[4] In contrast, every other being *has* existence; it is true to say, "Peter IS NOT his existence." That is true before our mind's own consideration of the matter. Just as the verb "to be" expresses the real identity of the subject and predicate, as when one says, "God *is* Being Itself," the negation "is not" denies this real identity, as when one says, "Peter *is not* his existence, but he only *has* existence." *In solo Deo essentia et esse sunt idem.* [Only in God are essence and existence one and the same.] There is an abyss that separates *being* and *having*.

To the eyes of the theologian, the treatise on the Trinity likewise can be summarized thus: The Father *is* God; the Son *is* God; the Holy Spirit *is* God.[5] However, the Father *is not* the Son, for no one begets

---

[2] The entire doctrine of the Incarnation of the Word (or, the Hypostatic Union) rests upon the deep sense of the verb "to be" in this proposition: *Hic homo est Deus* (This man is God). See *Summa theologiae* [hereafter, *ST*] III, q. 16, a. 2.

[3] See *ST* I, q. 3, a. 4: "Not only is God His own essence; He is also His own existence." *Summa contra gentiles* [hereafter, *SCG*] II, ch. 52; IV, ch. 11.

[4] Exod 3:14: "Deus ad Moysen, 'Ego sum qui sum. . . . Dices fillis Israel, "Qui est misit me ad vos"'" [God said to Moses, "I am who I am. . . . You will say to the children of Israel, 'He who is sends me to you'"].

[5] See *ST* I, q. 28, a. 2; q. 39, a. 1.

Himself, and the Father and the Son *are not* the Holy Spirit.[6]

Likewise, again, the entire doctrine of transubstantiation is contained in the true sense of the verb "to be" in this proposition: "Hoc *est* enim corpus meum. [Indeed, this is my body.]"[7]

*   *   *

This profound difference between the verbs "to be" and "to have"—and also that of the affirmation "it is" and the negation "it is not"—invites the philosopher to reflect upon the forms of language and upon the treasures that are hidden in the rules of grammar commonly admitted by all for the correct expression of a *judgment*.

The most interesting aspect of grammar for philosophy is morphology, which shows the variations in form undergone by words in order to express various modifications of thought. Philosophy also ought to be particularly interested in comparative grammar, which studies a whole group of languages and which, placing each idiom in its historical place, surrounded by its dialects and the associated languages that explain it, considers it in its development and its transformations.

However, above all else, the metaphysician ought to study attentively the *verb*, which expresses the state of something or its action. The metaphysician ought to consider what distinguishes the two species of verbs: (1) *active*/transitive verbs that are susceptible to becoming passive and reflexive and (2) *neutral*/intransitive verbs (with which the impersonal verbs are associated).

Finally, in these two broad categories, it is necessary to consider the two verbs that have the greatest importance: "to be" and "to have." "To be" is a neutral verb that is at the basis of all the other verbs and, therefore, at the basis of all judgments. It corresponds to the very object of

---

[6]   See *ST* I, q. 28, a. 3; q. 40, a. 2. Council of Florence, *Cantate Domino*: "These three Persons are one God, not three gods, because there is one substance of the three, one essence, one nature, one Godhead, one immensity, one eternity, and everything [in them] *is* one where there is no opposition of relationship" (Denzinger, no. 1330). Thus, analogically in the case of an equilateral triangle, each of the three angles *is* the entire surface of the triangle with which it is identified and, nonetheless, each of these three angles *is not* one of the two others.

[7]   See *ST* III, q. 75, aa. 1 and 2.

the intellect inasmuch as it is distinguished from the senses; only an intellectual [*intelligent*] being can grasp the sense of this little word—*is*.

The verb "to have" is an active verb, and in French [and English], as in numerous other modern languages, it serves (along with the verb *to be*) a role in the conjugation of other verbs and enters into the formation of certain tenses. From this perspective, they are called "auxiliary verbs."

Verbs are found in all languages, for it is the indispensable element of every proposition—the linking of our ideas. In particular, the verb "to be"—the basis of all the others—is the soul of judgment and, consequently, of discourse.

*   *   *

We could make a philosophical study—or a pseudo-philosophical study—of the rules of grammar from a nominalist point of view, a conceptualist point of view, or even from that of traditional realism.[8]

Radical nominalism reduces the concept to a composite image accompanied by a common name. Thus, it cannot elevate itself to the level of intelligible being.

Subjectivist conceptualism reduces the concept of being (and our other concepts) to a subjective form in our mind. The real value of this subjective concept remains, at least, doubtful.

For traditional realism, the *notion of being* has a real value, and the *first principles* implied in this notion are the *laws of being* and not only the laws of the mind. Therefore, it is under the intellectual light of the notion of being and of the first principles that realism undertakes a philosophical study of the rules of grammar. Far from being enslaved to

---

[8] [Tr. note: Although Étienne Gilson was no great lover of Garrigou-Lagrange, the reader would benefit from his late life reflections on language in *Linguistics and Philosophy: An Essay on the Philosophical Constants of Language*, trans. John Lyon (Notre Dame, IN: University of Notre Dame Press, 1988). Also, for a perspective informed by Thomism, one can consult Mortimer J. Adler, *Some Questions about Language: A Theory of Human Discourse and Its Objects* (Chicago: Open Court, 1991). John Deely's work on this project injected John of St. Thomas into Adler's approach, although Deely ultimately withdrew his name because of insoluble differences with Adler regarding the text.]

these rules like nominalism, such realism dominates them and discovers the treasures that are hidden in them.

This manner of investigation is one that often was undertaken by Aristotle. In particular, consider the first and fifth chapters of the *Categories*, which treats notions [i.e., undivided conceptions]. Likewise, at the beginning of the *Perihermenias* (i.e., the *De interpretatione*) in the text's first four chapters, which discuss propositions—that is, the expressions of judgments. Finally, in the fifth book of the *Metaphysics*, where he explains and justifies the division of the categories of being by examining the *diverse modes of attribution* or the use of the verb *to be*.[9]

*   *   *

Every proposition is composed of at least two terms—the subject and the predicate—reunited by the copula, which is reduced to the verb "to be." However, it happens that a proposition is sometimes expressed as a single word. For instance, consider the Latin *sum* or *amo*—"I am," and, "I love." Nevertheless, the sense of these is: *ego sum existens* and *ego sum amans*—"I am existing," and, "I am loving."

The verb, as its etymology indicates (*verbum* [word]), is the word *par excellence*. It is the essential term in the proposition. The proposition can be reduced to it; for example: resist, speak, act.

The persons—I, you, he—these either show us who undertakes the action that is expressed by the verb or show us that to which is attributed a given state, which it signifies.

The mood is the manner by which the verb presents the state or action that it expresses: the indicative, conditional, imperative, subjunctive, infinitive.

The tense is the form taken by the verb in order to mark the moment when the thing being discussed was done. Consequently, the present, past, and future are the three principle tenses. Although the noun (God, man, virtue) abstracts from time, the verb (with the exception of the infinitive) expresses the time that measures the given state or action: I am, I was, I will be, I write, I wrote, I will write.

---

[9] See Aristotle, *Metaphysics* 5.7.

Thus, the persons, moods, and tenses teach us *by whom, how,* and *when* the action is done, or with regard to the attribution of a given state, they teach us *to whom, how,* and *when* the given state is attributed to someone or something.

*   *   *

This grammatical structure of every proposition corresponds to *the very structure of judgment* that the proposition expresses, and the true judgment itself corresponds to *reality*—that is, to the existence of things, either to their nature or their condition [état], their action or their passion.

To express his realism, Aristotle likes to say, "The terms are signs of the concepts, and the concepts are likenesses of things."[10] Whether affirmative or negative, the proposition is the very expression of the judgment. And, if it is true that the verb is the soul of the judgment, and that every judgment is reduced to the verb "to be,"[11] consequently we find a kind of rudimentary ontology or metaphysics in the judgments that are recognized as true by all men—a kind of *intellectual view of the real, of intelligible being.* However, it is, so to speak, petrified in language. If we consider this language only in a superficial or solely grammatical way, in a nominalist manner, we will not suspect the treasures that it contains. Likewise, we will not suspect the intellectual life that is found in it like something hidden and recorded in it. It is necessary that we retrieve the *spirit under the letter.*

To know the profound sense of the verb "to be" would be to understand already the manner in which it is applied analogically to *that which exists through Itself* for all eternity, and to *that which exists through another,* and in a contingent way, to that which *exists in itself* (substance) or *in another* (accident).[12] To know the profound sense of this

---

[10] See Aristotle, *On Interpretation* 1.1.

[11] E.g., "I act" = "I am acting."

[12] [Tr. note: Thus, to be clear, he is first distinguishing between (1) Uncreated Being (=God) and (2) created being. Then, within (2), he is distinguishing between (a) substance and (b) accident. Technically, some special provisions would need to be made for the case of relation, which essentially has an *esse ad.* However, so long as we consider only the categories of real being as categories, it is both *esse in* and *esse ad.*]

verb would be to know how being is applied to *the actually real* and to the *possibly real*, then to the *past* and to the *future*. Likewise, it would be to know the definition of the *absolute future* (e.g., Peter *will be* faithful to his mother) or that of the *conditional future* (even if he were placed in the most unfortunate of circumstances, Peter *would be* faithful to his mother, even to the point of martyrdom). Now, this would be to know already the essential teachings of general metaphysics or ontology and much more indeed, for the absolute future and the conditional future cannot be defined without relation to the eternal decrees of God.[13]

If the first man, before the Fall knew (in the natural order) only these general truths, he would have known something very profound—the essential structure of human affirmation—certainly more important than that which characterizes this or that species of plant or animal. Metaphysical knowledge of the sense of the personal pronouns—of *I, you, him*—is nothing other than knowledge of what formally constitutes the person.[14]

---

[13] See *ST* I, q. 14, a. 13; q. 19, a. 8. See also *ST* I, q. 16, a. 7, ad 3: That which exists now was *future from all eternity* only because an eternal cause must produce it and only the first cause is eternal. [Tr. note: The text is a paraphrase by Fr. Garrigou-Lagrange.] See also St. Thomas, *In I Perihermenias*, lec. 13.

[14] See *ST* III, q. 4, a. 2, and nos. 6–9 of Cajetan's commentary on this. The foundation of personality is *that by which* every reasonable being is a *first subject of attribution* that can say "I" or "me" and to which one attributes all that pertains to the person while that personality itself is not attributable to anyone else. Thus Peter and Paul are persons. Thus, as one says as a matter of course, "Peter *is* a man; Peter *is* existing (or, exists); Peter is conscious of himself; Peter is free." In each of these affirmative judgments, the verb *to be* expresses the real identity of the subject of the proposition and the attribute in question. Indeed, to say "Peter *is* a man" is to say "Peter is the very being which is a man"—and likewise for the other examples.

How can we safeguard this real identity of the subject and the attribute in each of these propositions? In order to do that, it is necessary that there be in Peter something that is one under the diversity of qualities that are attributed to him. There must be something identical and real that formally constitutes the *first subject of attribution* of all of that which pertains to him—of human nature, of existence, of self-consciousness, of freedom, etc. This is the very foundation of personality. We have treated this topic elsewhere as regards the personality of Christ. See Réginald Garrigou-Lagrange, *Our Savior and His Love for Us*, trans. A. Bouchard (St. Louis, MO: B. Herder, 1958), 78–91.

*   *   *

Above all, it is important to grasp the *diverse senses of the verb "to be"* in relation to *the nature of things* and in relation to *their existence*—to their extramental existence and to that which they can have in our mind. Then, we must note with Aristotle that the various modes of attribution (or nuances of the verb "to be") correspond *to the categories of the mind and of being*: substance and accident (quantity, quality, action, passion, relation, etc.).

The Diverse Senses of the Verb "To Be" in Relation to the Nature or to the Existence of Things

Judgment is true if it affirms that which is and if it denies that which is not. In this sense, Christ himself expresses it, "Est est, non non"—"Let your yes be your yes, and your no be your no" (see Matt 5:37). And, St. Paul adds, "The Son of God, Jesus Christ, whom we preached among you, was not Yes and No; but in him it is always Yes" (2 Cor 1:19). Likewise, the prophet Isaiah: "Woe to those who call evil good and good evil, who put darkness for light and light for darkness, who put bitter for sweet and sweet for bitter!" (Isa 5:20). *Est est, non non.* In the intellectual chiaroscuro[15] [lit. *clair-obscur*, clear-obscure] to deny what is clear on account of what is obscure would be to replace mystery with absurdity, to confound being and nonbeing, the good and the bad, spirit and matter.

This is why metaphysical wisdom must consider the real value of the principle of contradiction[16]—*being is not nonbeing*; this itself is a negative formula of the principle of identity: *being is being, nonbeing is*

---

[15] [Tr. note: As noted in the translator's introduction, chiaroscuro is the style of painting utilizing light and darkness in a self-aware manner, utilizing the contrasts for artistic effect. The reader most likely is familiar with its use by Caravaggio and Rembrandt.]

[16] [Tr. note: Although Fr. Garrigou-Lagrange tends to prefer "the principle of contradiction," he is not completely consistent in his various works. Occasionally, he will call it "the principle of non-contradiction."]

nonbeing. As we say: "The good is good, the evil is evil, they are necessarily distinct; the flesh is flesh, the spirit is spirit, God is God, the
creature is a creature. It is an aberration to confuse them." All of the
sciences presuppose the truth of the principles of contradiction and
identity, though they do not expressly treat of their value. If metaphysical wisdom is the science of being as being, it belongs to it to treat
openly concerning the value of this principle. It does so by showing
that to deny the value of the principle of contradiction would lead to
the destruction of all thought, all language, all substance, even of all
opinion and action.[17] Every affirmation, even one that is only probable,
would be destroyed in being posed. By this, every desire and all action
would likewise become impossible.

*   *   *

Consequently, it belongs to metaphysical wisdom to treat of *truth,*
which is formally in our mind's judgment, and of the relation of conformity between the true judgment and things.

In wishing to present Aristotle and St. Thomas's thought concerning this point, Fr. Sertillanges has written a few years ago, "*Truth is not
a relation of us to things.* It is a relation from ourselves to ourselves, in
a correspondence of adequation with things. . . . The relation of truth
is a purely interior relation. The Thomist definition of truth does not
prejudge the Kantian question in any way. . . . Even when the essences
represent only a work of the mind on the mysterious noumenon,[18] this
judgment, 'Man is a rational animal,' would not be less true, taken in
its own place."[19]

Beyond this, it is still necessary that, in "the mysterious noume-

---

[17] See Aristotle, *Metaphysics* 4.3–5, and St. Thomas's commentary on this.

[18] [Tr. note: The "noumenal" refers to the so-called unknown "thing in itself," as
opposed to its phenomenal presentation to the knower. This distinction plays an
important role in Kant's mature epistemology. Clearly, Fr. Garrigou-Lagrange does
not pose the question in such Kantian terms.]

[19] See A. D. Sertillanges, *Saint Thomas Aquinas,* vol. 2 (Paris: Félix Alcan, 1920),
182–83. [Tr. note: See Fr. Garrigou-Lagrange's critical remarks on this passage in
*God: His Existence and His Nature: A Thomistic Solution of Certain Agnostic Antino-
mies,* vol. 2, trans. Bede Rose (St. Louis, MO: B. Herder, 1949), 232–34.]

non," there be *a real and essential* distinction between God, man, and beings inferior to man. Otherwise, how would it be true to say, "Man is a rational animal at one and the same time distinct from God and nonrational animals"?

*   *   *

While it is *sometimes* true that the relation of truth is one that is purely interior, as when I say, "*Cogito*—I think," it does not follow that truth in general ought to be defined likewise in this way. Also, from the fact that a true judgment is *not always* a judgment of existence, even when it pertains to extramental things (taken in their nature [i.e., and not as regards their actual existence]), it does not follow that one can define truth in general as being a purely interior relation. This would be to forget that *truth*, which is formally in the mind's judgment, is said *analogically* (and not univocally) depending on whether it pertains to the Uncreated Intellect or to a created intellect. Likewise, it is said analogically depending on whether it pertains to the conformity of our judgment with *the nature* of extramental things or with their *existence* or, again, with *that which exists in our own mind*. St. Thomas often says, "The (true) judgment of the intellect pertains to the thing according to the way that it is."[20] And the word "is" is said analogically of the nature of things and of their existence—whether outside of the mind or in it. We must not confuse the last members to which the analogy is applied with the analogical notion taken in general. In this way, one

---

[20] See St. Thomas, *De veritate*, q. 1, a. 9. See also, *In I Perihermenias*, lec. 9: "Truth is in the intellect inasmuch as it judges *to be* that which is and *not to be* that which is not." See also *ST* I, q. 16, a. 3 ("The truth that is in the intellect is convertible with being as that which manifests is with that which is manifested"), and I, q. 85, a. 1 ("Truth is analogically said just as being").

[Tr. note: Solely from the perspective of logic (and not the fuller metaphysical considerations being undertaken here), the reader would benefit well from the remarks made by Maritain regarding the manifold ways existence is involved in judgments. On this, see his insightful remarks in Jacques Maritain, *Formal Logic*, trans. Imelda Choquette (London: Sheed and Ward, 1946), 60–72, 226–33. These brief expositions bear witness to the robust strength of a fully developed logic within a wholly Thomistic vocabulary—one that benefitted well from its long disputations with Scotist and Nominalist logicians.]

would confuse being in general with the least of beings or even with its accidents.[21]

If it pertains *to that which is in my intellect,* I can make a judgment *of existence* (*cogito*—I now have this or that thought) or a judgment on *the nature* of my thought or of this or that reasoning. As regards the latter, we may speak of the true *real laws of thought*—either from the perspective of experimental psychological laws or of those concerning the profound nature of intellection. Likewise, we can speak truly with regard to the *logical laws* of thought—for example, the rules of the syllogism—as the consistency of thought with itself.[22]

If it pertains to *the existence of extramental things,* I can make a judgment of existence that affirms an existing positive quality or, also, a negation or privation. For example: "Peter has good sight," or, on the contrary, "Peter is blind [i.e., is deprived of sight]."

If it pertains to *the nature of extramental things,* we can also make a judgment either regarding a positive perfection or regarding a privation. An example of such a judgment concerning a positive perfection

---

[21] [Tr. note: The reader would benefit immensely from considering the reflections on analogy undertaken in Yves R. Simon, "On Order in Analogical Sets," in *Philosopher at Work: Essays by Yves R. Simon,* ed. Anthony O. Simon (Lanham, MD: Rowman & Littlefield, 1999), 135–71. Though Simon's opinion of Fr. Garrigou-Lagrange did not remain steady throughout his life, this essay carries forward the tradition on analogy inherited from the same school of thought. It is a *sine qua non* for those who wish to affirm the primacy of proper proportionality in analogical predication without becoming lost in the numerous battles occurring in contemporary literature on these matters.]

[22] [Tr. note: Fr. Garrigou-Lagrange is here distinguishing between the *real* "psychology and metaphysics of knowledge" and the discussions undertaken in logic. According to the traditional Thomist doctrine, this pertains to the domain of beings known as *ens rationis,* more particularly to the *relationes rationis* (mind-dependent relations) formed naturally by the intellect in the process of its cognition. See M. -D. Philipe, "Originalité de 'l'ens rationis' dans la philosophie de Saint Thomas," *Angelicum* 52, no. 1 (1975): 91–124. This topic was the subject of a lengthy set of disputations by Hervaeus Natalis (ca. 1250–1323). Though not written from an explicitly "Thomistic" perspective, his work contains many points that are quite related to what one will find in later Thomists (both those who would agree with his outlook and those who did not). See Hervaeus Natalis, *A Treatise of Master Hervaeus Natalis (D. 1323), the Doctor Perspicacissimus, on Second Intentions,* ed. and trans. John P. Doyle (Milwaukee, WI: Marquette University Press, 2008). See also Michael P. Tavuzzi, "Hervaeus Natalis and the Philosophical Logic of the Thomism of the Renaissance," *Doctor Communis* 45, no. 2 (1992): 132–52.]

would be: "Sight is a valuable quality for animals." An example of such a judgment concerning a privation would be: "Blindness is an evil." If someone asks us, "Is blindness an evil?," we respond, "Yes, it is." However, we do not affirm anything regarding the *existence* of this evil; in so answering, we speak only of its nature. Likewise, when we consider the nature of man, abstracting from factual existence, we say, "Man *is* a rational animal," just as we affirm, "In every triangle, the three angles are equal to two right angles." This judgment remains true even if no triangle were to exist, since this proposition abstracts from existence; however, it does speak of *the nature* of an extramental thing. Likewise again, we could say, "A square circle not only is subjectively *inconceivable*; it also is *really impossible* for it to exist outside of the intellect." To say that it is REALLY IMPOSSIBLE is to say much more than solely to affirm that *it is unthinkable.*

*   *   *

Therefore, in the intellectual chiaroscuro, where rays of light and shadows mingle together, it is important not to forget that *the light of truth* is taken in *various senses*, analogically or *proportionally similar* in relation to the nature of things or to their existence, whether extramental or in our intellect, in the form of a likeness or of an idea.[23]

Also, it is necessary that we do not confuse direct ideas that have a direct relationship with things (i.e., *first intentions*, such as the idea of man or lion) and ideas that are, in some manner, reflex ideas, the fruit of our reflection on our direct ideas, to classify the latter such that we come to speak (for instance) of genera and species (i.e., *second intentions*).[24] From this point of view, the true judgments that pertain to our reflex ideas (e.g., concerning the rightness of the laws of the syllogism,

---

[23] See Aquinas, *In I Sent.*, d. 19, q. 5, a. 1, where this proposition is explained at length: "Truth has its foundation in the thing, but its notion is completed by the action of the intellect, namely when the thing is apprehended with regard to its mode of existence."

[24] See ibid. [Tr. note: This pertains not to a reflection on the psychological apparatus in question (pertaining to the natural philosophy and metaphysics of cognition) but, instead, to reflexive awareness of the *relationes rationis* involved in our thought—i.e., a kind of "logical reflection." At the time of Aquinas's writing, these topics were not in the foreground, so it is easy to miss the point in his brief words to this end.]

subjectively taken) are notably different from the true judgments pertaining to the nature of extramental things (i.e., when abstracted from their existence). There is between them the same difference[25] as when I say, "A square circle is not only *subjectively inconceivable*, it is REALLY IMPOSSIBLE outside of the intellect; it is obvious that even the All Powerful God would not be able to actualize such a being in reality, even by a miracle." One sees in this indestructible evidence the value of our intellect, which thus grasps not only the subjective laws of the mind but also *the absolutely necessary laws of being* with an absolute certitude.

Finally, if it concerns not only the created intellect [*esprit*] and its various kinds of judgments but also the Uncreated Intellect [*esprit*], then *the truth* of the Divine Intellect [*intelligence*] is not only a *conformity* with the Divine Being but also an *identity*; for the Divine Being *of itself* (by its very nature) not only is intelligible in act but also is always actually known by Himself. While the nature of a plant or an animal is only *intelligible in potency*, and while the nature of a created spirit (especially as soon as it is separated from the body[26]) is *intelligible in act*, the Nature of God is of itself *intellecta in actu*, actually known. The Nature of God is Being Itself, always actually known; indeed, it is eternally subsistent Thought Itself—not an elusive point but a pure, intellectual flash like that of a man of genius, yet always immutable, measured by the unique instant of immobile eternity.[27] Furthermore, anterior to

---

[25] [Tr. note: To clarify his point, this parallel focuses primarily on the impossibility of extramental existence, not conceivability. Like the square circle, no second intention can exist extramentally. Unlike the square circle, however, second intentions are conceivable in their own way, for we can discuss the laws of logic.]

[26] [Tr. note: The original French is a little ambiguous here. The language itself reads as it is rendered above, making it seem like he is talking only about human souls. However, it is technically not the case that the human soul is *intelligible in act* in the state of union with the body, given that the spiritual soul is not directly known through itself but is known only through reflection upon its spiritual acts of intellection and willing. Only the essences of separated souls and the angels are intelligible in act in a primordial sense. On this topic, see Réginald Garrigou-Lagrange, "Utrum mens seipsam per essentiam cognoscat, an per aliquam speciem," *Angelicum* 5 (1928): 37–54, a translation of which is anticipated in a future volume by Emmaus Academic.]

[27] See *ST* I, q. 10, a. 1: "Utrum convenienter definiatur *aeternitas: interminabilis vitae TOTA SIMUL et perfecta possessio* [Whether eternity is suitably defined as 'a completely simultaneously-whole and perfect possession of interminable life']."

every decree of His Will, God knows all that is possible [*les possibles*], but He knows future contingents only in His decree, whether they be positive decrees (if it pertains to being and good) or permissive (if it pertains to moral evil).[28]

It is clear that, in all of these examples, the notion of truth is not univocal but, instead, *analogical*; it does not have one meaning but, instead, has *several meanings* that are *proportionally similar* and that always remain, nonetheless, proper in their meaning and not merely metaphorical. If it is only by a metaphor that we say that God is *angry*, it is in a *proper* sense that we say that God is true, that He is Truth Itself, and it is also in a proper sense that we say that our judgment is *true* when it conforms with the nature or with the existence of the things that are judged.

One can reduce what we have said about these matters to the following schema:

---

[28] See *ST* I, q. 19, aa. 4, 8; q. 14, a. 13. As St. Thomas says in *ST* II-II, q. 171, a. 3: "Certain things in themselves are not knowable, such as future contingents whose truth is not determined." Their truth, whether it pertains to absolute or to conditional future contingents, is determined only by an eternal decree of God that remains hidden from us.

[Tr. note: For Fr. Garrigou-Lagrange's treatment of these matters, see his *Predestination*, trans. Bede Rose (St. Louis, MO: B. Herder, 1939); and *Providence*, trans. Bede Rose (St. Louis, MO: B. Herder, 1954). On this thorny topic, the reader can profit from consulting the work of Maritain, who saw his position as deferentially correcting certain aspects of Garrigou-Lagrange's thought, though maintaining the overall outlines that inspired the traditional Dominican position in the *De auxiliis* controversy. See Jacques Maritain, *God and the Permission of Evil*, trans. Joseph Evans (Milwaukee, MI: Bruce, 1966). For a study on the debate during Garrigou-Lagrange's lifetime (from a more openly disagreeing perspective), see Michael D. Torre, *Do Not Resist the Spirit's Call: Francisco Marín-Sola on Sufficient Grace* (Washington, DC: Catholic University of America Press, 2013). As can be seen between the lines (and in footnotes), Fr. Garrigou-Lagrange did not agree with Fr. Marín-Sola on certain questions concerning the nature of theology. They were also involved in disagreements on grace, predestination, and the problem of evil. Torre's text documents these matters well.]

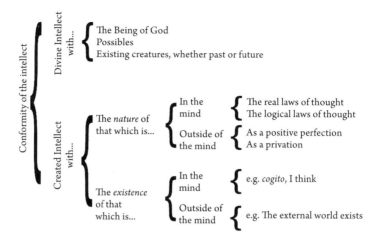

Quite obviously, these are diverse nuances of the clear in the midst of many obscurities resulting from that which is both *above* and *below* the frontiers of intelligibility accessible to us. In this, we see the *diverse meanings* of the *verb "to be"* (without falling into metaphor), depending on whether we are speaking of that which *is* in our intellect or that which *is* in things and, also, whether it concerns the nature of things or their existence.

However, it is necessary to press further and to consider the diverse nuances of the verb "to be" in relation to the diverse modalities of being, which we call the categories.

The Diverse Meanings of the Verb "To Be" and the Diverse Categories of the Real

The diverse categories of the mind [*espirit*] such as substance, quantity, quality, action, relation, and so on can be considered either from a logical point of view, a psychological point of view, or from the point of view of metaphysics (i.e., in relation to the real itself).

Aristotle presents the first [i.e., logical] point of view in the first book of the *Categories* and the third [i.e., metaphysical] in the seventh chapter of the fifth book of his *Metaphysics*.

What Aristotle states in this latter text takes on very different value depending on whether one is a realist, a nominalist, or a conceptualist. Aristotle himself obviously speaks as a realist, drawing here on the real value of the principle of contradiction, which he had defended earlier in the *Metaphysics* in book IV.[29]

See how he expresses himself in analyzing precisely the diverse nuances (or acceptations) of the verb "to be" in relation to reality and to its different categories. He shows that the *diverse modes of attribution* correspond to *diverse modalities of being* inasmuch as the attribution or affirmation is in conformity with the real:

> Thus, *among the attributes* (which we affirm of things) some express *the very nature* or *essence* of the thing (e.g., the stone is an inanimate substance, Socrates is a man), some express *its quality* (e.g., Socrates is virtuous), others *its quantity* (e.g., Socrates is large), others *its relation* (e.g., Socrates is the son of this person), others its *action* (e.g., Socrates writes), others *its passion* (e.g., Socrates is warmed or illuminated), others *the place* (e.g., Socrates is in Athens), and finally, *time* (e.g., Socrates is forty years old). In each of these attributions, we affirm this or that mode of being. For there is not the least difference between "this man is recovering" and "this man recovers" or between "this man is walking or cutting" and "this man walks or cuts." The same may be observed in the other categories.[30]

Some historians of philosophy have noted that this correct remark perhaps had been made for the first time by Aristotle and that the grammarians then took it up. Whatever might be the case, it amounts to saying that, at the foundation, there is a single verb, the substantive verb, the verb "to be." All of the other verbs presuppose this one and

---

[29] [Tr. note: Here, Fr. Garrigou-Lagrange refers to books IV and V by parenthetically noting that they can also be numbered III and IV, likely acknowledging the questionable status of the second book of the *Metaphysics*.]

[30] Aristotle, *Metaphysics* 5.7. In other texts, Aristotle gives a more complete list of the categories. See Aristotle, *Categories* 1b25–27; and *Topics* 1.9.103b20–23.

add to it a modality—that of quantity, quality, action, passivity, relation, and also time and place.

We are not looking to see if, in this enumeration of the categories, the latter ones ought to be reduced to that of relation.[31] What is certain is that we have here, from a realist point of view, a metaphysical reflection upon the various senses of the verb "to be" in its relation with the noun (e.g., man, animal), with the adjective (e.g., virtuous), and with adverbs of time or place. The *noun* or *substantive* (which serves to designate persons, animals, and things) expresses their nature or substance (e.g., Socrates, man, horse, paper). The pronoun—I, you, him—takes the place of the noun. The *adjective* is added to the noun in order to indicate a quality (e.g., a black horse, a virtuous man). The *adverb* serves to modify the signification of the verb, adjective, or another adverb (e.g., "this horse runs quickly, very quickly, and it is very beautiful"); it especially indicates the time and the place (e.g., "tomorrow I must go far").

Such is the structure of human language in various tongues. It expresses the structure of judgment, the soul of which is the verb, which reduces foundationally to the verb "to be."

St. Thomas, in his commentary on this chapter of the *Metaphysics*, makes numerous remarks relative to this fundamental verb. After seeing what he says, one is aware that it would be erroneous to think that the Aristotelian division of the categories is only a grammatical deduction obtained by the comparison of vocables (i.e., of the verb, noun, adjective, and adverb).[32]

In fact, Aristotle has done three things here, following his usual method:

---

[31] [Tr. note: The advanced reader will benefit from John of St. Thomas's treatment of this question (i.e., whether action, passion, place where, position, time when, and "vesture" are absolute categories, relations, or extrinsic denominations); see *Cursus philosophicus thomisticus*, vol. 1, *Ars logica*, ed. Beatus Reiser (Turin, IT: Marietti, 1930), pt. II, q. 19, a. 1: "Utrum haec praedicamenta sint formae absolutae vel relativae vel denominationes extrinsicae" (621A40–625B4).]

[32] However, this is what was thought by Trendelenburg, Grote, and Emile Boutroux. See Boutroux's entry "Aristotle" in *Grande Encyclopédie*, ed. Ferdinand-Camille Dreyfus and André Berthelot, vol. 3 (Paris: H. Lamirault, 1886), 933–54.

1. *He considers vocables.* This is only the point of departure for the investigation (a useful point of departure). As he says at the beginning of *On Interpretation*, "Terms are signs of concepts, and these are likenesses of things." However, Aristotle does not stop at this grammatical consideration.

2. *He considers above all else the verb "to be"* in diverse species of judgments, remarking expressly that the *diverse modes of being* correspond to *diverse modes of attribution* or affirmation relative to being (i.e., to the real). Aristotle certainly does not here lose sight of what he often has said elsewhere—namely, that the object of the intellect is not the sensible phenomenon but, instead, is intelligible being. Likewise, he does not lose sight of the fact that the soul of every judgment is the verb "to be." Indeed, in this chapter of the *Metaphysics*, he says, "This man walks = this man is walking."

3. *He considers that being in general is not a genus* (for a genus is understood only in one sense or by one meaning), *but, instead, is an analogue* that is understood in various senses, though proportionally similar. The Stagirite [i.e., Aristotle] has this point present to his mind, for in his book on the *Categories* (or, the predicaments), in the introduction devoted to the notions anterior to the Categories (i.e., the *antepraedicamenta*), he discusses *univocal, equivocal, and analogous* names and says, throughout his works, that being is not an equivocal notion but an analogical one.[33] Indeed, *a genus* (like animality) has a unique signification ("animal" = a body endowed with sense life) and is diversified by *extrinsic differences* (i.e., the specific differences of man, lion, dog—differences that are not of animality [as such] but, instead, are extrinsic to it). On the contrary, *being* (like every analogous term) *has multiple senses* ("substance" = to be through oneself; "accident" = to be in another) and *the modalities* that differentiate them *are intrin-*

---

[33] See Aristotle, *Posterior analytics* 2.13–14; *Metaphysics* 3.3, 10.1, 12.4; and *Nicomachean ethics* 1.6. It is true, however, that Aristotle does at times call the analogue *an equivocal—not by mere chance but by intention.*

sic to them,[34] for they are also of being. While rationality (the specific difference of man) is not something of animality [as such], *substantiality* (i.e., the modality proper to substance, as opposed to accident) *is also something of being* and is a mode of being; for nothing of that which is is outside of being. The notion of being does not contain the notion of substance explicitly, but it does contain it in a manner that is actual and implicit.[35] Nothing of that which is is outside of being.

Therefore, in order to distinguish the categories (or modalities) of being, Aristotle is not content merely with undertaking a comparison of vocables. Instead, he has considered above all the diverse senses of the verb "to be," keeping in mind that the object of the intellect precisely is intelligible being, which is not a genus susceptible to extrinsic differences. Being can be diversified only by *modes of being* (which, again, are of being) that correspond to *diverse modes of attribution*, since attribution (or, affirmation) expresses being under its various aspects.

To say "man is a rational animal" is to say what man is *substantially*. To say that this or that man is virtuous is to say what he is *qualitatively*. To say that he is large is to say what he is *quantitatively*. To say that he is the father of someone else is to say what he is *relatively*. To say that he is writing is to say in what way he is *acting* (in this or that particular way). So too for the other categories.

Thus, the diverse modalities of being are something akin to its nuances. They are to being a little like what the seven colors of the rainbow are to light.[36]

---

[34] See Aristotle, *Metaphysics* 3.3, and St. Thomas's commentary on this passage.

[35] [Tr. note: That is, if we speak of abstraction in regard to analogical notions, we must note that it is an imperfect abstraction from the analogates. On this point, see Simon, "On Order in Analogical Sets."]

[36] Moreover, as St. Thomas shows in *In V Met.* 7, lec. 9, if the attribute *belongs to the essence* of the first subject of attribution, it is a *substantial* attribute (e.g., Socrates is a man). Otherwise, *it does not pertain to its essence*; then, it is an *accident*. It can be an *absolute* accident that inheres in the subject on account of its form (i.e., quality) or on account of its matter (i.e., quantity). Likewise, it can be an accident *relative* to another being (e.g., paternity) or a denomination relative to the effect of an action, to time, place, etc. Being is not divided immediately into the ten categories. Instead,

What Identity is Expressed by the Verb "To Be"

We can be certain that there is a logical distinction (or a "distinction of reason") between the subject of an affirmative proposition and its predicate. However, does not the verb "to be," which reunites these two, express their *real identity*? For example, is this not the case when we say, "Peter *is* a man," or, "Peter *is* existing," or, "Peter *is* large," or, "Peter *is* virtuous," or, "Peter *is* acting," or, "Peter *is* undergoing [something]," and so on? Yes! These judgments express the real identity of the subject and the predicate—Peter is the same being who is man, who is existing, who is large, and so on. It is *the same subject* that *is* all of this in various ways.

However, we do not say, "Peter is his existence." Indeed, we even say, "*Solus Deus est suum esse*," God alone is His existence.[37] God alone is Being itself, for in Him alone is existence an *essential attribute*. Peter IS NOT his existence. HE only HAS existence, which, for him, is a *contingent attribute*. And, one cannot repeat enough that here there is an infinite distance between the verb "to be" and the verb "to have."

Likewise, although Peter *is* man, he *is not* his humanity. The latter (all while being for him an essential attribute and not a contingent one) is only *his essential part*. And the part—even an essential part—*is not* the whole; it is not really identical with the whole that contains at the same time something else. In this, there is a real, inadequate distinction; the part is not really adequate with regard to the whole. There is an even greater distinction between *Peter* and *his existence*, which is a contingent attribute for him, not an essential one.

The proposition "Peter *is not* his existence" (by which fact his case is different from that of God's) is true *before* our mind's consideration. Likewise, the proposition "God *is* His existence" is true in the same manner. Now, if in this latter proposition, the verb "to be" affirms the real identity of the subject and the predicate, is it not necessary to say that, in the first proposition, the negation ("is not") denies this real identity and, therefore, affirms a real distinction—a distinction *ante-*

---

the division is made first into two members, which are then subdivided. It is not of great importance that the latter subdivision contains some difficulties. This does not invalidate the preceding divisions. [Tr. note: See notes 12 and 31 above.]

[37] See *ST* I, q. 3, a. 4; q. 50, a. 2, ad 3.

rior to the mind's consideration? Yes. In other words, it affirms with St. Thomas that *in Petro aliud est essentia et aliud esse* [in Peter, essence is one "thing" (loosely using the term "thing") and existence another].[38]

Likewise, *aliud est persona Petri* (per propriam personalitatem iam constituta) *et aliud esse* [the person of Peter (through his own personality now constituted) is one "thing" and his existence is another]; for *esse* (i.e., existence) is only a contingent attribute for Peter, totally distinct from his essence. And for every created person, *aliud est quod est* (i.e., the supposit) *et esse* [what is (i.e., the supposit) and existence are diverse].[39] It is only in God that essence and existence are identical.[40]

If this proposition "Petrus non est suum esse (Peter is not his existence)" is true, if it is true before our mind's consideration, is it not necessary to say that, prior to this consideration, there is a distinction (and therefore real distinction) between the essence of Peter and his existence? *He has* existence instead of *being* his existence. Only the Savior can say, "*I am* the truth and the life," which presupposes that he can say: "I am Being Itself. *Ego sum qui sum* (Exod 3:14)." This was a very clear affirmation of His Divinity. Therefore, the Virgin Mary is called "the Mother of God" because she is the mother of Jesus, who *is* God.

The verb "to be" expresses the real identity of the subject and predicate in the proposition "Hic homo Christus *est* Deus [This man, Christ, *is* God]." This real identity is that of the *unique person*, of the unique first subject of attribution to which pertains the human nature and the Divine Nature: "*Ego sum via* (ut homo), *veritas et vita* (ut Deus) [I am the way (as human), the truth, and the life (as God)]"

---

[38] See ibid. See also *SCG* IV, ch. 52.

[39] [Tr. note: To understand Fr. Garrigou-Lagrange aright, one should consider well the distinction between supposit, nature, and existence, for instance, in *Christ the Savior*, trans. Bede Rose (St. Louis, MO: Herder, 1950), 139–72. One may also profitably consult Jacques Maritain, *Degrees of Knowledge*, trans. Gerald B. Phelan (Notre Dame, IN: University of Notre Dame Press, 1995), 454–68. An accessible pedagogical introduction to this issue can be found in R. P. Phillips, *Modern Thomistic Philosophy: An Explanation for Students*, vol. 2, *Metaphysics* (Westminster, MD: Newman Press, 1962), 213–22.]

[40] When we say, "In Peter, animality *is not* rationality," there is not a real distinction between animality and rationality. Why? Because these are two formalities reduced *to the very concept* of humanity, while *existence* (being a *contingent* predicate of every created being) cannot be an essential predicate of any created nature.

(John 14:6).[41] Thus, again is the sacramental formula verified: "Hoc *est* enim corpus meum [Indeed, this *is* my body]."[42]

Such is the profound meaning of the verb "to be." It contains at one and the same time something that is clear (based on the evidence of numerous judgments) and something obscure following on the nature of the more or less distant extremes that it reunites (e.g., Christ is God) and following upon the superficial or profound knowledge that we have of them. Moreover, these extremes, in a sense, can exceed the limits of the kind of intelligibility naturally accessible to us, exceeding them either from on high (from the perspective of God) or from below (from the perspective of matter or contingency, whose determination escapes us—as happens for the future contingents). We will come to this latter point below.

Finally, let us note that the identity expressed by the verb "to be" varies depending on the domain where it is applied. It does not always designate an identity of supposit (*suppositum*) or of person. Sometimes it expresses the identity of nature (e.g., man according to his nature is a rational animal; man by his very nature has the property of *being* free, sociable, etc.). Furthermore, we conceive even privations in the manner of positive qualities in speaking of their nature—"Blindness *is* an evil."

Finally, the verb "to be"—because it expresses the truth of the real laws of thought (e.g., human thought *is* always united to an image[43]) or the logical laws of thought (e.g., the rules of the syllogism *are* true)—expresses an identity of the same order as that of the subject of the proposition; that is to say, whether it is real (though mental) or whether it is of the order of logic.[44]

The variety of such applications is as extended as is the analogy of being.

---

[41] See *ST* III, q. 16, a. 2, and St. Thomas's commentary on this verse of the Gospel of John [14:16].

[42] See *ST* III, q. 75, aa. 1–3. St. Thomas shows that this formula can be understood only by means of transubstantiation and that it excludes the annihilation of the substance of the bread.

[43] [Tr. note: See footnote 20 in chapter 1 of this part.]

[44] [Tr. note: Again, notice how Fr. Garrigou-Lagrange is distinguishing between the "real" psychological qualities and logical *relationes rationis*.]

Being in Act and Being in Potency

Finally, as Aristotle remarks, "Being can sometimes mean being in potency, at other times being in act. . . . Indeed, we say that Hermes *is* in the stone (from which one can make his statue), . . . and we call 'wheat' that which is not yet fully mature."[45]

In a certain sense, the oak *is* in the seed that the acorn contains. It is not there actually; it is there in potency, as the statue is in the currently unformed marble that can be used by the sculptor. Thus, prime matter, which enters into the composition of all bodies, is *potentially* air, earth, water, silver, plant, animal, and so on. It is all of these in potency, for it *can* become them. But of itself, it has none of these determinations that it is susceptible to receiving; as Aristotle says, "It is neither a this, nor a quality, nor a quantity." It is only a *real capacity* for all of the perfections that it can receive.

It is a passive potency, which cannot be actuated except by an active power—as the clay is modeled by the sculptor.

The passive potency, a real capacity susceptible to being actualized, is like a *mysterious middle* between *being in act* (though it be so impoverished) and *pure nothingness*. The pure potency that is the first (or, prime) matter is more than nonbeing, more even than the *simple nonrepugnance* (or, *real possibility*) that is a prerequisite for creation *ex nihilo*.[46] However, it is less than every act, no matter how imperfect. It is simple potency in comparison to the specific form of the most elementary bodies and of the most insignificant [*plus pauvre*] of atoms. Likewise, the essence or nature of every being susceptible to existing— for example, of an angel—is only a *real potency* in relation to the act of existence that it receives and limits. For, the angel has gratuitously received existence; its nature, of itself, has *no right to exist*.

One knows that Aristotelianism—above all, as it was understood and perfected by St. Thomas—resolves all of the great philosophical

---

[45] See Aristotle, *Metaphysics* 5.7.

[46] [Tr. note: A square circle, being only a spoken expression but actually impossible mathematically, can never exist in any form. It lacks the prerequisite nonrepugnance for existence.]

problems by the division of being into potency and act.[47] And as we have written elsewhere,[48] this philosophy of being, like common sense itself, is both clear and obscure at one and the same time. *It is clear with regard to the place that it gives to act, obscure with regard to the place that it gives to potency*: "Unumquodque cognoscitur secundum quod est actu, non autem secundum quod est in potentia [Everything is known according to how it is in act, not however according to how it is in potency]." Need we be surprised at this obscurity? At its base, it is this relative absence of determination and intelligibility that allows there to be a place for Divine and human freedom. It makes conceivable the existence of the created order in addition to that of the Uncreated Godhead—the finite in addition to the Infinite, the multiple and changing in addition to the One and the Immutable. *God alone is intelligible in all that He is—because He is Being Itself, Pure Actuality.*

The world, on the contrary, to the degree that there is multiplicity and becoming in it, contains something obscure in itself—*a nonbeing which is*, as Plato said in speaking of matter.[49] All sensible beings are *composed of potency and act* (as Aristotle said more precisely). Every created being, even the angel, is composed of potency of act, of real essence and existence, of operative potency and action (as St. Thomas adds to the point).[50] God alone is His Existence and His Action; *solus Deus est suum esse et suum agere.*

---

[47] In fact, it is by this distinction that the Aristotelians resolve the *problem of being and becoming* discussed by Heraclitus and Parmenides, the problem of the *multiplicity of beings* (act is multiplied by the potency that receives it), the problem of *the multiplicity of individuals* in one and the same species (form is multiplied by matter), the problem of the *union of the soul and the body*, the problem of the relation of *sensation with the sensible*, the problem of the relation of *intellect with the intelligible*, the problem of the relation of *freedom* with *reason* that deliberates, the problem of the *continuous* that is divisible but not divided to infinity, and finally, the problem of the relation of God and the world and those things that derive from it. See *Le sens commun*, cited in the next note.

[48] Garrigou-Lagrange, *Le sens commun: La philosophie de l'être et les formules dogmatiques*, 3rd ed. (Paris: Nouvelle Librairie Nationale, 1922), 153. [Tr. note: A translation of the fourth edition of *Le sens commun* is scheduled to be published by Emmaus Academic in the near future.]

[49] [Tr. note: The theme haunts Plato in many places throughout his works. However, for a very forceful example of him addressing this, see his *Sophist* and *Timeaeus*.]

[50] See *ST* I, q. 54, aa. 1–3.

However obscure the notion of *potency* or *real capacity* (i.e., that which is not already determined and is distinct from the determination that it receives) might be, it only makes explicit a common sense viewpoint that says to us that the seed contained in the acorn *really can* become an oak. Likewise, it makes explicit the common sense view that the sleeping architect, without actually building anything, does have the *real ability* to build. This notion of real potency also responds to the Christian sense: the sinner who in no way accomplishes the Divine precept CAN, *however, really here and now accomplish it*, for God never commands the impossible. Sufficient grace does not yet lead one (like efficacious grace) actually to accomplish the precept, though it gives the real and practical *ability* to accomplish it *here and now*. And, if the sinner does not resist this sufficient grace, God will give him efficacious grace, which was offered in the sufficient grace like a fruit in the flower. If the flower is not destroyed, the fruit itself will be given.

In these matters, there certainly is a chiaroscuro, where the shade is no less accentuated than the clarity. However, it is a simple corollary to that other chiaroscuro enunciated by God in Exodus 3:14 and that St. Augustine explains in this way: "*Ego sum qui sum* tanquam in eius comparatione ea quae mutabilia facta sunt, *non sint* [I am He Who Is such that in comparison to Me, those things that have been created as changeable beings *are not*]."[51] Our Lord said likewise to St. Catherine of Siena (and it reveals to us the profound sense and scope of the verb "to be"): "I am He who is; you are she who is not."[52] The creature: that which of itself *is not* and which would not exist except through a free, creative, and conserving *fiat*; and, all the while, after creation there is neither more being, nor more life, nor more wisdom, nor more love. *Post creationem* sunt plura entia, sed *non est plus entis*, nec plus sapientae, nec plus amoris.

---

[51] See Augustine, *City of God* 8.11.
[52] See Bl. Raymond of Capua's *The Life of St. Catherine of Siena.*

Chapter 3

The Philosophical Spirit and the Sense of Mystery

M UCH HAS BEEN WRITTEN in recent days concerning the spirit of Christian philosophy, in such diverse senses that, on the one hand, some would bring it quite close to being apologetics and, on the other hand, other thinkers would define it without sufficiently affirming the positive conformity that it ought to have with Christian faith and with theology.[1]

The manner in which this delicate problem has been treated by many shows that it supposes another problem that we wish to address here as "the philosophical spirit and the sense of mystery." This pertains

---

[1] [Tr. note: A history of the debate is chronicled in *Reason Fulfilled by Revelation: The 1930s Christian Philosophy Debates in France*, ed. Gregory Sadler (Washington, DC: Catholic University of America Press, 2011). The classic historical/thematic study of Christian philosophy arguably remains (at least in its magnificent scope and outline) Étienne Gilson, *The Spirit of Medieval Philosophy*, trans. A. H. C. Downes (Notre Dame, IN: University of Notre Dame, 1990). Many of Gilson's works revisit these themes, but recall that he and Fr. Garrigou-Lagrange were not in full agreement on various matters. Arguably of greatest theoretical import is Jacques Maritain's *Essay on Christian Philosophy*, trans. Edward H. Flannery (New York: Philosophical Library, 1955). Maritain notes at the start of this text (which covers some very important matters with clarity and profundity) the concord of *both* Fr. Garrigou-Lagrange and Étienne Gilson with his position. Below, Fr. Garrigou-Lagrange will explicitly accept Maritain's positions, and he defends Maritain in "De Relationibus inter philosophiam et Religionem," *Acta secundi congressus Thomistici internationalis* (1936): 379–405, and "L'instabilité dans l'état de péché mortel des vertus morales acquises," *Revue thomiste* 43 (1937): 255–62. Translation of these articles are anticipated in a future volume by Emmaus Academic.]

to the philosophical spirit in general in such a way that it is manifest not only in Christian philosophers but also in a Plato or in an Aristotle. Thus, it also pertains to the sense of mystery that is already found in the order of natural things far beneath those of grace.

Often, people ask what differentiates the philosophical spirit not only from common knowledge but also from knowledge obtained by the cultivation of sciences that are inferior to philosophy (e.g., the experimental sciences and mathematical sciences). In other words, in what does the acquired *habitus* of wisdom, of which Aristotle[2] and St. Thomas[3] speak, differ from the spirit of the positive sciences and the spirit of geometry?

It is clear that it differs from them above all and essentially by its formal object and by the point of view under which it considers its object. While the positive sciences, which establish the laws of phenomena, consider the *real* as *sensible* (i.e., as an object of external or internal experience), and while mathematics considers the *real* as *quantitative*, first philosophy (i.e., metaphysics) considers the *real* as *real* (i.e., being insofar as it is being).[4]

However, from this there derive other important differences relative to the very spirit of each particular science and to that of the philosophical spirit. It is upon this point that we will focus in this chapter. One of these differences is brought to light by a principle formulated with clarity by Aristotle that it is important to recall here.

---

[2]   See Aristotle, *Metaphysics* 1.2.

[3]   See *Summa theologiae* [hereafter, *ST*] I-II, q. 57, a. 2.

[4]   In order to simplify matters, we will not speak here of the philosophy of nature, which (according to Aristotle and St. Thomas) is specifically distinct from metaphysics inasmuch as the philosophy of nature has for its object not being insofar as it is being, but *ens mobile, ut mobile* [mobile being], known not only according to its phenomenal laws but according to its first causes.

The Order of Sense Knowledge Is Inverse to the Order of Intellectual Knowledge

Aristotle[5] and St. Thomas[6] often note that *sense knowledge grasps the singular before the universal*, which it only perceives accidentally. The senses know Peter and Paul by their sensible qualities; however, they cannot be elevated to knowledge of man qua man, which they do not grasp except insofar as Peter and Paul are men. *On the contrary, our intellectual knowledge grasps the universal before the singular.* Our intellect knows Peter and Paul only inasmuch as it knows man first, at least in a vague manner.

Now, the sciences that are inferior to philosophy, such as the positive and mathematical sciences, in certain respects, resemble sense knowledge inasmuch as they have objects that are less universal than philosophy's object (above all, the object of first philosophy or metaphysics). These sciences first grasp their proper objects at least vaguely, whereas first philosophy first grasps its most universal object—the real as real or the intelligible being of sensible things insofar as it is being.[7] At first very vague, this intellectual knowledge passes unnoticed; however, it nonetheless exists, and without it, no other knowledge would be possible afterwards.

Then, it passes from being vague to being distinct—from being in potency to being in act.[8]

From this fact are derived numerous truths that are important to mention, as much as regards the parts of philosophy as, also, regards the relations of philosophy with the particular sciences.

Notably, it follows that *our intellect* knows directly and vaguely the *intelligible being* of sensible things before it makes a reflexive[9] judg-

---

[5] See Aristotle, *Metaphysics* 1.1–2 and 5.1, and *Physics* 1.1.

[6] See *ST* I, q. 85, aa. 3 and 8.

[7] Here, we are concerned with man's philosophical knowledge, which (following the nature of his intellect) is first turned toward sensible things. We are not concerned with the philosophical life that might be said of the angels, who first perceive spiritual realities.

[8] As Aristotle notes in Physics 1.1, infants at first call all men "Daddy," for their intellect does not yet distinguish men from one another.

[9] [Tr. note: "Reflexive" awareness and "reflexion" here refer to the kind of second-

ment concerning the value of sensation and its own unique character, although sensation is required (in us humans) for all intellectual knowledge. Likewise, our intellect grasps directly and vaguely the intelligible being of sensible things before judging by reflexion that these ideas come from the senses by means of abstraction. The intellect instinctually is a realist; it is the *faculty of the real* before being occupied with *beings of reason*,[10] which are objects of reflexive knowledge.[11] Therefore, it carries in it the sense of mystery hidden under the phenomena and within the *real*, which is rich in a different way than is the *being of reason* on which logic speculates.

Also, it follows from the principle enunciated that every philosophical mind [*espirit*] will proceed from the outset to what is *more universal and more real*[12] in things so as to sound it to its depths, while the geometric mind will stop itself at quantity and the spirit of the positive sciences will concern itself immediately with the phenomena as such and with their laws (without taking much interest in the most

---

ary knowledge that the human person has of his or her acts by "turning back" upon himself or herself. I am maintaining the awkward spelling of "reflexion" to stress this distinction. I have chosen not to translate "*réflexe*" by "reflex" out of fear of confusion to the reader. However, it should be noted that the Thomist school traditionally made clear distinctions between direct and reflex concepts, and Fr. Garrigou-Lagrange is almost certainly referring to this distinction when writing of "*un jugement réflexe.*" The reader would likely benefit greatly from reading the overview on this topic provided in John of St. Thomas, *The Material Logic of John of St. Thomas: Basic Treatises*, trans. Yves R. Simon, John J. Glanville, and G. Donald Hollenhorst (Chicago: University of Chicago Press, 1955), q. 23, a. 3 (pp. 421–29). This article is also translated in both editions of John N. Deely's volume of John of St. Thomas's treatise on signs: *Tractatus de Signis: The Semiotic of John Poinsot*, ed. and trans. John N. Deely and Ralph Austin Powell, 2nd ed. (South Bend, IN: St. Augustine's Press, 2013), 324–33.]

10   [Tr. note: I.e., *Entia rationis*, which include, among other things, the *relationes rationis* that are studied in logic. They are beings that exist only as objects of knowledge and have no entitative existence, even if they presuppose entitative existence so that they may exist, in the language of the Thomist school, "objectively."]

11   [Tr. note: Thus we know logical relations/*relationes rationis* (e.g., the relations of *genus*, *syllogism*, etc.) only in a reflexive manner.]

12   What is more universal in things is what is more real, in the sense that they are the immutable laws of being insofar as it is being, laws that all the others presuppose. And to these *universal characteristics* of things (*universalia in praedicando*) correspond the *most universal causes* (*universalia in causando*), for the most universal effects are connected to the most universal causes; thus is it that God the Creator is the cause of being insofar as it is being, of all that exists outside of Him. See *ST* I, q. 45, a. 5.

universal, great problems or in the real as real). Even more, the non-philosophical spirit will make no room for *the real, the object of ontology,* between the *physical* (the object of the positive sciences) and *the logical;* it will instinctively turn the object of metaphysics into being of reason. Such is the case for nominalists and conceptualists.

From this, there is derived another consequence that Aristotle noted regarding the senses, and that is also applied, with every proportion retained, to the sciences that have a limited object: *the senses know the composed before the simple, while the inverse is true for the intellect.*[13] For example, the senses grasp first *this* musician-man, while the intellect can know *this* musician-man only if it first knows man and musician in general. For the same reason, as is noted by St. Thomas, our intellect knows animal in general before knowing man, which it defines as being "a rational animal."[14] Also, as we have said, it knows being in general before it knows animal, which it defines as a corporeal being endowed with life that is not merely vegetative but also capable of sensation.

From this, it follows, as Aristotle himself said, that the senses know first the *properties of the composed* (by way of sensible notes) before knowing the *properties of the simple* (in the same way). For example, they know the properties of extended, resistant surface before knowing those of the line and the point. In contrast, the intellect knows the properties of the line before those of the surface, which is defined by the line. Thus, consequently, the intellect knows vaguely the properties of being (such as unity and truth) before knowing those of the line or the point.

The Philosophical Spirit and Common Knowledge

From this difference between the senses and the intellect, we can derive a multitude of corollaries relative to the subject with which we are currently occupied. We will insist on one of them, one that enables us to

---

[13] See Aristotle, *Metaphysics* 5.1.

[14] See *ST* I, q. 85, a. 3.

conceive better the nature of the philosophical spirit, as well as what distinguishes it from every other spirit. The philosophical spirit, proceeding immediately according to the order of intellectual knowledge (as opposed to that of sense knowledge), from the very beginning of its inquiry, seeks *to connect, in an explicit and distinct manner, all things to the most universal, simple, first principles.* That is, the philosophical spirit wishes to connect all things to the most general laws of being and of the real. Thus, it is quickly led to see the *mysteries* of the natural order where the common outlook sees no mystery; indeed, it sees them where even the inferior sciences do not suspect there to be such mysteries. It is from this sort of perspective that, for example, in the least case of local motion, the philosophical spirit sees all of the sudden something incredibly profound and mysterious—something that, in the final analysis, will be explained only in terms of the invisible intervention of God, the First Mover. Similarly, in the least of sensations, the philosophical spirit sees immediately the abyss separating sense life from all that is inferior to it. From this fact, there arises the great difficulty of explaining how sensation is produced under the influence of any exterior object that is far inferior in itself to the vital and psychological order proper to that of sensation.[15] Idealism is born from the great difficulty of answering this question.

In contrast, common knowledge (and even that of the experimental sciences) sees nothing profound nor anything mysterious in the least local motion or in the least of sensations, for instead of starting from the simplest notions and the most universal principles, these forms of knowledge start from concrete and complex facts and do not seek to link them to first principles and the ultimate causes (except in a very vague manner that has nothing of a truly scientific character). They do

---

[15] [Tr. note: The topic will be taken up again below. There is much to be said about this issue. For an outline of the issue, see Yves Simon, *An Introduction to the Metaphysics of Knowledge*, trans. Vukan Kuic and Richard J. Thompson (New York: Fordham University Press, 1990), 104–6n23. In Fr. Garrigou-Lagrange, see the chapter entitled "Le mystère de la connaissance et sa finalité" in *Le réalisme du principe de finalité* (Paris: Desclée de Brouwer, 1932), 176–208. For a dissenting voice, see George P. Klubertanz, "De Potentia, 5.8: A Note on the Thomist Theory of Sensation," *Modern Schoolman* 26, no. 4 (1949): 323–31. A translation of Fr. Garrigou-Lagrange's *Le réalisme du principe de finalité* is scheduled to be published by Emmaus Academic.]

not link them to first principles and ultimate causes in an explicit and distinct manner, as does the philosopher. The sciences that are inferior to philosophy, failing to achieve distinct knowledge of the principles of things, forever retain to some degree the common way of proceeding; they never see any mystery, any profundity, in the same place where the philosopher is astonished with that wonderment that is, as Aristotle has said, the very beginning of science.[16]

This shows the superiority of philosophy; however, it also shows its weakness, which is, rather, the weakness of the philosopher, who often is *hasty* in his systematization. In this haste, the philosopher sometimes (not without some contempt for common sense) restrains or limits reality unduly, as seen in such philosophical doctrines as those of Parmenides, of Heraclitus, of the Pythagoreans, of the Atomists, of Descartes, of Malebranche, and of the idealists. It was this state of affairs that led Leibniz to say that philosophical systems are generally true in what they affirm and false in what they deny.

Here, common sense, which has been thus despised, takes its revenge. It says to the philosopher, "There are more things on earth and in the heavens than in all of your philosophy." Common sense (or, natural reason) comes thus in its own manner to correct the narrowness of many philosophical systems, for common sense (in what is at least its own true patrimony) does not limit reality unduly, and if it does not pretend to arrive at an explicit and distinct knowledge of things, it does affirm in a vague [*confuse*] manner the existence of the First Cause, the Last End, no less than it affirms the existence of facts (i.e., of the objects of our experience). If these affirmations remain vague, at least common sense does not deny what must be absolutely maintained.

Two examples will clearly show the truth of what we have said: that of the least of sensations and that of local movement.

---

[16] We will speak below concerning the difficulty raised by the principle of inertia, according to which a body placed in motion even by the smallest of motions conserves *this motion forever* so long as it is not stopped by any obstacle (e.g., air resistance). Is there still something *new* in that which is called *the state of movement* of this body? If yes, how can it be that this new something is ever produced without *a new influx*? How is it that the principle of inertia thus formulated is reconciled with the principle of efficient causality and with that of finality: every agent acts for an end, an end that is determined?

The Mystery of Sensation

Sensation does not present any sort of mystery for common awareness. It is not astonished at all that, as constantly happens, material objects in the world can produce an impression upon our senses, producing in them a likeness of themselves, a representation that permits us to perceive them. Already, when one wishes to explain this fact, as experimental psychology seeks to do, numerous difficulties arise, such as those spoken of regarding the alleged errors of the senses: for example, the stick plunged into the water appears to be broken even though it is not. The philosopher appears, he sees all of the sudden that there is something very profound in the least of sensations, and he is astonished with that wonderment that is the beginning of science—in the elevated sense of that word "science," of the science that searches not only for the constant laws or relations of phenomena but also, instead, for causes and that does not stop until it arrives at the ultimate cause.

The philosopher speaks to us in the following manner: This sensation, which is constantly produced, is something very mysterious. If, in fact, according to the universal principles that shed light upon all things, *the agent ought to be superior* (or, at least equal) *to that upon which it acts,* if the more cannot come from the less, how is it that an inanimate exterior body (of the order of brute matter) can produce in our senses a likeness of itself, *far superior to it,* a representative likeness that not only is *physical* like the impression of a signet upon wax but also is *vital*—and vital not merely in a vegetative manner but vital according to the order of sense life, *the order of the animal soul,* which is not a body (even though it is intrinsically dependent upon the organism that it vivifies and does not survive it)? If the agent must be superior to what it acts upon, if the more cannot come from the less, how then does an external body (e.g., a block of stone) produce in my senses, even under the influx of light, a likeness of itself of an order already so elevated, a likeness of the vital and psychological order (far superior to the image produced in a mirror, which cannot see, or on the polished surface of a plant, or, again, in the eye of a blind man deprived of vision, or in the open eye of a corpse). What is at the foundation of this *representative likeness* that is produced in the living eye and that renders *sight capable of seeing* one thing as opposed to another, this block of stone rather than some other thing?

Does the block of stone produce this representation of the vital or psychological order? Does the light of the sun? Are the senses only passive when they receive it?

The difficulty would certainly be insoluble if sensation were an act of the soul alone and not of the animated organ. But, even in admitting that it is the act of the *animated organ*, as Aristotle has said quite well, how can we explain the difference between it and an impression that is simply *physical* (such as that of the ring in wax or of this same ring reflected by a mirror or by the eye of dead man who a second earlier had been able to see)? In short, how can we explain the production of *the vital and psychological impression* by which *the being who sees an object*, following the expression of St. Thomas as well as that of Aristotle, "QUODAMMODO FIT ALIUD A SE [in a certain manner becomes something other than itself],"[17] in such a manner that it becomes *not other* but *something other than itself—the perceived object*? The plant, under the influence of the sun, goes from being cold to being hot, but it does not become the sun in any way. In contrast, the animal that *sees* the sun becomes (in a mysterious fashion, called intentional or representative) the very sun which it sees. Thus, the well-known expression of Aristotle: "Anima *fit* quodammodo omnia [The soul becomes, in a certain manner, all things]." While matter *does not become* form, but instead only receives, appropriates, and individualizes it, the knower (in a certain manner) becomes *the other being* that it knows by means of the representation that it receives. There is an abyss between material reception, which appropriates the form received, and the already immaterial reception that does not appropriate the form received. There is an immeasurable distance between the impression that the sun makes upon the plant and that which it makes upon the eye that sees it.

If there is already an abyss between brute matter and vegetative life, the same could be said for what separates vegetative life from sense life.

---

[17] See *ST* I, q. 14, a. 1. [Tr. note: see also Réginald Garrigou-Lagrange, "Cognoscens quodammodo fit vel est aliud a se," *Revue néo-scolastique de philosophie* 25 (1923): 420–30. A translation of this article is anticipated in a future volume by Emmaus Academic.]

The former could be perfected forever in its own order without ever attaining the least degree of the latter.

To the philosopher's eyes, there is something very profound and very mysterious in the production of the least sensation, though the common outlook and even that of simply experimental science scarcely register any doubt about the matter. The mathematical mind is not preoccupied with the matter to any greater degree either.

The mystery grows if one notes that, the more elevated the internal senses are, the more difficult it is to explain the production of the representation that is found in them. For example, by what representation does the sheep flee from the wolf before having experienced its ferocity? It is not, as St. Thomas notes, due to the form or color of the wolf, which are often little different from that of the sheepdog. It is that the sheep perceives in the wolf the natural enemy that it ought to flee.[18]

In this, we find something that does not have anything astonishing in its appearance, at least for common consciousness, but that causes the admiration of the philosopher who looks into the profound cause of this matter.

Here, we see a chiaroscuro that is most captivating. It is clear that the external bodies act upon the senses—but how? What is the intimate mode by which sensation is produced in the living eye while it is not produced in the very same eye immediately after death?

To deny the clear point on account of what is obscure would be to replace a mystery with an absurdity. Such a denial makes possible the materialism that imperiously reduces the superior to the inferior, spirit to matter, intellectual life to sense life, sense life to vegetative

---

[18] See *ST* I, q. 78, a. 4: "The sheep, seeing the approaching wolf, flees not on account of an unbecoming color, or figure, but on account of a kind of natural enmity." See also *De veritate*, q. 25, a. 2: "The sheep flees the wolf whose enmity it never senses."

John of St. Thomas has seen this difficulty very well, as one will realize in reading his *Philosophia naturalis de Anima*, q. 8, a. 4. Even Billuart, in his *Cursus theologicus*, in speaking of the mysteries of nature in order to distinguish them from those of grace, discusses the mystery of sensation, which has stopped all of the idealist philosophers. It seems that many try to avoid the problem rather than to resolve it.

[Tr. note: For recent work related to the power of estimation implied in the remarks about sheep and wolves, see Daniel De Haan, "Perception and the *Vis cogitativa*: A Thomistic Analysis of Aspectual, Actional, and Affectional Percepts," *American Catholic Philosophical Society* 88, no. 3 (2014): 397–437.]

life, and vegetative life to physico-chemical phenomena. In an inverse sense, the reduction of mystery to absurdity *also* lies at the root of that idealistic immaterialism that, with a spirit no less imperious, reduces matter to mind [*esprit*] or to the representation that mind has of the external world, a representation that has its laws and that would be "a well-connected dream," distinct from the other that is incoherent like a hallucination.

The philosopher who is at one and the same time spiritualist and realist knows that one can avoid the contradiction and give a solution to the stated difficulty, but he knows also that this solution remains and will always remain imperfect. In the chiaroscuro of which we speak, every obscurity is not suppressed. The true philosopher has a sense of mystery. Indeed, he has it more and more.

He says here, with St. Thomas, that the impression of external objects is received in an animated organ (e.g., the living eye) according to the nature of that animated organ—*quidquid recipitur ad modum recipientis recipitur* [whatever is received is so received according to the mode of the receiver].[19]

This is true. However, again, it is necessary to reconcile this principle with another—namely, that the *cause is superior to its effect* (or at least equal to it), that the agent is nobler than what it acts upon, that the more cannot come from the less.

To this, traditional realism responds that the *colored* material object, insofar as it currently has this or that determined quality, is *superior* to the animated organ that has not yet received the likeness of this form.[20] It recognizes, moreover, that the senses are *superior* to the material object inasmuch as the living, knowing faculty already exceeds, in a way, the conditions of matter, even though it remains intrinsically dependent upon the organism. Also, it is necessary to say that the rep-

---

19 See St. Thomas, *In II De anima* 12, lec. 24.

20 See *ST* I, q. 79, a. 3, ad 1: "Sensible things are found in act outside of the soul and therefore it is not necessary for there to be an agent sense." See also his commentary cited in previous footnote [*In II De anima* 12, lec. 24]: "Sense is receptive of the *species* without matter, as the wax is receptive [and] receives the sign of the ring without the gold or the iron. However, it receives the gold or iron sign—but not inasmuch as it is golden or iron." [Tr. note: To understand these words aright, be sure to see Simon's work on the metaphysics of knowledge, noted above on multiple occasions.]

resentation of the material object is *vital and psychological in dependence upon the sense faculty*, which is passive, however, before reacting by the very act of sensation—*sentire est quoddam pati (causaliter)*, antequam sit action sentientis [To sense is a certain kind of undergoing, causally speaking, before it is the action of the sensing being].

It is in this passivity of the sensing subject with regard to inferior things that we find something very difficult to explain. It is not surprising that it be so *each time that a participation in an absolute perfection (simpliciter simplex) appears*, whether it is concerned with being, life, knowledge, or intelligence. Certainly, sensation is not an absolute perfection, but rather, *the knowledge* in which it participates is an absolute perfection. And, when it begins with sense life or when it ceases upon death, we are faced with something profound of which the inner mode is not fully known to us.[21]

We do not know anything fully. All of the world says it. The sage loves to speak of the *docta ignorantia*, the learned ignorance.

There remains something mysterious each time that one passes from an inferior order to one that is more elevated. From one point of view, *sense is assimilated* (or, rendered similar) *to the colored object* by means of the likeness that it receives from it. Yet, from another point of view, *the sense*, even before reacting in virtue of this likeness, *mysteriously assimilates the latter*, which becomes in it something vital and psychological—in a certain manner, something spiritual.[22]

This mutual dependence is explained by the principle "Causae ad invicem sunt causae, sed in diverso genere [Causes are causes of each other, though in different genera of causation]."[23] The representative likeness (the *species impressa*) *is the ultimate disposition to the act of sensation*, which would not be vision of a given color rather than another, of such an object rather than some other, if this act did not proceed from a faculty *determined to know* this object rather than that other

---

[21] [Tr. note: This is why Aristotle opens the *Metaphysics* by using sight as an analogy for contemplative, speculative knowledge.]

[22] *Aliqualiter spiritalis*, as St. Thomas often says: like the animal's soul—which is not a body, which is simple, which dominates certain material conditions, above which the plant's life is not elevated—but which nonetheless is intrinsically dependent upon the animal organism and disappears with it.

[23] See Aristotle, *Metaphysics* 5.2, and St. Thomas's commentary on the passage.

one. Therefore, in one manner, this disposition (or, vital/psychological impression) that is the representation in some sense precedes the activity of the faculty; however, in another manner this impression is vital or psychological only in dependence upon this faculty. It is an application, one that remains mysterious, of the principle of the mutual dependence of causes, which intervenes everywhere the four causes (i.e., efficient and final, formal and material) come into play.[24] We have treated of these matters elsewhere at greater length. Here, we are speaking only by way of example.[25]

The Mystery of Causality

An example of what we are saying, one that is no less striking, can be found in the most insignificant case of transitive action—that is, in the production of the most insignificant of local motions.

For the common outlook (and even that of the experimental sciences), nothing is simpler than the case of one ball meeting another and putting it into motion after such a collision.

Looking upon the same situation, the philosopher ponders how the first ball can have an action upon the second. This is the great problem of *transitive action*, studied by Aristotle and the Scholastics: is it in the agent or in that upon which the agent acts? This same problem, as is well known, was taken up by Descartes and Leibniz, and everybody knows their divergence upon this point as upon numerous others.

When the first ball moves the second, does the movement *pass* (as is sometimes said) from the first into the second? No. Movement is

---

[24] St. Thomas says in *In IV Sent.*, d. 17, q. 1, a. 5, qla 3: "The ultimate disposition is the effect of the form from the perspective of formal causality; however, the ultimate disposition precedes the form from the perspective of material causality."

 [Tr. note: This exact text cannot be found in the cited text. See *In IV Sent.*, d. 17, q. 1, a. 4, qla 2. As a possible source, see John of St. Thomas, *Cursus philosophicus thomisticus*, ed. Beatus Reiser, vol. 2 (*Naturalis philosophiae*, vol. 1) (Turin, IT: Marietti, 1930), part III of *Naturalis philosophiae*, q. 2, a. 2: "Utrum corruptio et generatio sint eadem actio, ratione cuius generatio unius sit corruptio alterius" (603B15–608B36).]

[25] See Garrigou-Lagrange, *Le réalisme du principe de finalité*, 176–209 and 336–66. Also, Simon has recently treated these matters in *An Introduction to the Metaphysics of Knowledge*.

only an accident of the body in movement, and one and the same accident cannot pass from one subject to another. It is only *this* movement, for it is the movement of *this* subject and not *that* other. Therefore, it is necessary to say that the influx of the first ball *produces* a movement in the second; however, it is not the movement of the first that *passes* into the second.

Very well, but what is this influx from the first ball? This question brought Leibniz to a halt, leading him to deny the very reality of transitive action: "Monads have no windows by which anything can enter or leave them."[26] According to him, the apparent action of one upon the others is explained only by a pre-established harmony—that is, by a Divine action quite similar to that of which the occasionalists speak.

What, then, is this influx of the first ball into the second? Leibniz denied transitive causality only because he did not grasp profoundly the sense and scope of the Aristotelian distinction between *potency and act*. In his doctrine, Leibniz replaced the notion of potency with that of *force* (or, *nisus*), like the force of a taut spring. It is a notion that is totally different from that of potency, for the force of a taut (though not yet deployed) spring is more than potency. It is an act, an action, to which is opposed a contrary action.

It is necessary that we maintain the Aristotelian distinction between potency and act, a notion so in conformity with the first certitudes of natural reason (and necessary if we are to resolve the arguments of Parmenides). That is, this distinction is necessary in order to reconcile the principle of identity (or, the principle of contradiction) with the becoming and multiplicity found in things. Certainly, potency is a *mysterious middle* posed between being in act (*no matter how imperfectly in act it might be*) and nonbeing.[27] We hold that, if one maintains

---

[26] See Leibniz, *Monadology*, ch. 7.

[27] According to Parmenides, *being is, nonbeing is not*. Now, from being nothing can arise (*ex ente non fit ens*), for being already is and that which becomes is not yet. From being nothing can arise; just as one does not make a statue from a statue (because it already is). On the other hand, *ex non-ente non fit ens*, from nonbeing, it is no more possible that something might come about, for nonbeing is not, it is pure nothingness; and from nothingness, without any cause, nothing can come about. *Ex nihilo nihil fit*—a negative formula of the principle of causality, reduced thus to the principle of identity or contradiction: "Being is not nonbeing."

this distinction, one thus explains the causality of the first ball upon the second by saying that the action of the *active potency* of the first is exercised upon the *passive potency* of the second and that *their union gives birth to the movement produced.* This movement, the Thomists say, is educed from the potency of the mobile thing by the influence of the active power of the mover. They add that the transitive action, formally speaking—all while proceeding from the mover of which it is the accident (and, indeed, its second act)—has its terminus in the moved thing: *originative est ab agente et terminative est in passo* [as regards its origin, it is *from* the agent; as regards its terminus, it is *in* what is acted upon].[28] This remains somewhat mysterious, but it is necessary to say it in order to reconcile the principles with the facts.

The problem then rests upon the subject of the very production of this transitive action on which the movement perceived in the mobile thing depends. Is there *something new* in the *movement* thus produced, and is there something new in the *action* that produces it?

If there is nothing new, there is no causality, no *coming to be,* contrary to what Heraclitus has said (and after him, all of the evolutionists, in particular the author of *Creative Evolution*).[29]

Becoming, not able to have its origin either in being or in nonbeing, therefore is impossible—according to Parmenides.

But then Aristotle responds: Yes. . . . Unless it is the case that there is *a middle* between determined being (i.e., being in act) and pure nonbeing! This middle is *potency,* which is not imperfect act (even if ever so weak) as some suppose it to be. Instead, it is the *real capacity* for receiving act (i.e., passive potency) or of producing an act (i.e., active potency). Motion is born from the actual union of these two potencies. Potency remains, still, rather mysterious, for nothing is intelligible except insofar as it is in act or in relation to act. *Nihil est intelligibile nisi in quantum est in actu.* The Aristotelian notion of potency leads, as we know, to the admission that prime matter is *pure potency* and not imperfect act (even so minimal), as some suppose—*nec quid, nec quale, nec quantum.* The notion of potency likewise leads us to see in created essences a potency or real capacity, really distinct from the existence that it receives. These are two points of doctrine that have not been well understood by a number of well-known scholastics.

[28] See John of St. Thomas, *Cursus philosophicus thomisticus,* vol. 2, pt. I of *Naturalis philosophiae,* q. 14, a. 3 ("Utrum action transiens sit subjective in agente [Whether transitive action is in the agent as in a subject of inherence]").

[29] [Tr. note: He is referring to Henri Bergson, whose influence in French thought at the time was not insignificant, including in French Catholic thought. See Henri Bergson, *Creative Evolution,* trans. Arthur Mitchell (Mineola, NY: Dover, 1998).]

If there is something new, on the contrary, then it seems that there is *more* in the union of the effect and the cause than in the cause alone. And then, whence comes this *more being*, this greater perfection? As Parmenides has said, *this is a violation of the principle of identity* (or, of contradiction). It is not possible that, at one moment of time, there would be more being or perfection than at another. And this would be not only a violation of the principle of identity but even a *violation of the principle of causality*, which we wish to explain here, for according to this principle: *the greater does not come from the lesser*, the effect cannot be more perfect than the cause, and even the effect and the cause taken together cannot be something *more* (i.e., more perfect than the cause alone). It seems that this goes so far as to say that causality is not only something mysterious but, instead, that its concept destroys itself in being posited at all.[30]

---

[30] A difficulty of the same kind is posed on the subject of the *principle of inertia*, a difficulty that escapes a good number of physicists. They consider this principle of inertia either from the point of view of experimental physics or from the point of view of mathematical physics and do not seek in any way to reconcile it with the metaphysical principles of efficient causality and finality.

The philosopher, in contrast, considers the matter as follows. Supposing that there is no obstacle, not even the resistance of air, how can a *finite impulse* produce in a projectile a movement that would remain *forever*, in which there would remain always *something that is new*? How does a limited, *finite* impulse produce an effect that is neither finite nor limited? Even in admitting that there is an *impetus* in the projectile, an effect of the first impulsion, this impetus is itself finite. How could it produce a movement in which there would always be *something new, to infinity*? The gravity of the ancients explained for them the falling of bodies, but it produced only a limited movement up to the natural place of bodies. How, can *the impetus*, even conserved by God, always produce something that is new? Why does it itself endure if it is not a natural property of the bodies and if it is ordered to maintain a rectilinear movement that in itself is something accidental?

Moreover, how can it be, if *every agent acts for an end* (as the principle of finality states), that a finite impulsion produces a movement that is not toward a determined *end*, but a movement that (if there is no obstacle) *would endure forever, in aeternum*— and not only a circular motion whose end is the perpetual return to the point of departure, but a movement that is rectilinear and uniform.

In *De potentia*, q. 5, a. 5, St. Thomas writes, "*Since nature always tends in a determinate manner to one thing*, it is impossible that nature incline to motion itself. . . . Motion by its very nature is contrary to and cannot be understood as being an end, for motion is a *tendency toward something* else. [As St. Thomas continues: "It is a means, not an end, so to speak."] . . . *He who posits an infinite number of final causes destroys the end and the nature of the good.*"

Traditional realism does not ignore this difficulty in any way. It knows what kind of mystery is hidden in the least fact of causality. It says that, in movement or becoming, *there is something new* and that, on the other hand, it is necessary to maintain the principle of identity (or, of contradiction): "Being is being, nonbeing is nonbeing."

In order to explain the *newness* that is found in the effect produced by the causes that fall within the grasp of our experience, traditional realism says that it is often manifest that the *novitas effectus* [newness of the effect] presupposes a *new action* in the cause that we see act. For example, the movement of the ball presupposes the impact that is also new. However, St. Thomas adds, this cause (in which the action appears as something new) needs itself to be *premoved*—and premoved not only in the past, but *currently* by a superior cause. The fisherman who carries his net is himself carried by the boat, and the boat by the waves of the sea, the waves by the earth, the earth by the sun, and the sun by its innermost source of activity, but one cannot proceed forever to infinity in the current subordination of causes.[31] It must of necessity

---

According to St. Thomas, the First Mover produces movement in the world in view of a determined end up until the number of the elect is complete. The principle of inertia, as Henri Poincaré discusses in his book *Science and Hypothesis*, is proven neither *a priori* nor *a posteriori*. It is a postulate. How can this postulate of modern physics be reconciled with the metaphysical principles of efficient causality and of finality? Here is a question that does not torment the physicist, but it is posed by the philosopher. See Henri Poincaré, *Science and Hypothesis*, trans. J. Larmor (Mineola, NY: Dover, 2011).

[Tr. note: There are some infelicitous aspects to this way of posing the question. However, Maritain himself held views akin to this, although, with time, he came to understand "motion" as spoken of here as describing a *state* of active potency. Thus, *motion* (in the sense employed when speaking of inertia) is not the same as the "motion" that the natural philosopher knows to be the act of what is in potency inasmuch as it is in potency (or the imperfect act arising from the causal interaction of agent and patient). On this topic, much wisdom can be gained by reading Yves Simon, "The Science and Philosophy of Inertia," In *The Great Dialogue of Nature and Space*, ed. Gerard J. Dalcourt (Albany, NY: Magi Books, 1970), 37–58.]

[31] Already, *attraction* remains very mysterious, though one mathematically expresses its law: "The bodies of the universe are mutually attracted in direct proportion to their mass and in inverse proportion to the square of their distance." This law discovered by Newton does not tell us what is *the intimate nature of this force* called attraction or gravitation and of which weight [*pesanteur*] is only a particular case. Is it necessary to have recourse to a magnetic fluid similar to that by which one explains the properties of magnets? Here, we have only hypotheses. What is certain is the fact of movement, which requires a mover and a supreme mover.

come to a stop, so as to arrive at a Supreme Cause, which does not need to be premoved by a superior cause and which, therefore, *is Its own Action* instead of *having received it* (i.e., in place of having produced it *under* a superior influx). *Causa suprema debet esse suum agere, et proinde suum esse, quia operari sequitur esse, et modus operandi modum essendi* (The Supreme Cause must be Act Itself and, therefore, Being Itself, for action presupposes being, and the ultimate mode of action presupposes the ultimate mode of being). God alone is He Who Is—*ego sum qui sum*—in Him alone are essence and existence identical.

Thus is safeguarded the existence of becoming, the existence of something NEW that is found in it, and also the truth of the principle of IDENTITY (or, of contradiction).

Yes, but there remains here this marvelous mystery, which philosophical clairvoyance has divined in the least case of movement: there is something *new* in the effect, but there is *nothing new* in the Supreme Cause. St. Thomas forcefully and well said, "Novitas divini effectus non demonstrat novitatem actionis in Deo, cum actio sua sit sua essentia [The newness of a given Divine effect does not demonstrate that there is a newness of action in God, for His Action is His Essence]."[32]

Thus, we have arrived at the mystery of the coexistence of eternity and time, the coexistence of the Infinite and the finite: *Est novitas effectus in mundo sine novitate actionis in primo motore.* How can this be the case without there being some sort of internal contradiction? It is so because the Divine Action is at one and the same time eternal and free. *A free cause superior to movement and to time* (which is the measure of movement) *can produce, when it wishes, the movement that, from all Eternity,* It has decided to produce. In the unique instant of immobile eternity, this Cause has decided that *movement would begin* at a given fleeting instant that would be the origin of time (i.e., the measure of movement). Furthermore, in order to produce it in this instant of time rather than one before it, it is in no way necessary that there be *some-*

Attraction remains as mysterious for us as this property of weighty bodies that, they called gravity [*gravité*], was for the ancients.

[32] See *SCG* IV, ch. 35.

thing new in that Cause. Similarly, as St. Thomas notes,[33] the doctor who, in the morning, prescribes a medicine to be taken at night could, without the intermediary of anyone and without any new action, give it at night if his free will were capable *by itself* and itself alone, without the intermediary of any body, of producing this effect.

There is no contradiction in this, but the mystery remains—that of the coexistence of eternity and time: *Est novitas effectus in mundo sine novitate actionis in primo motore*.

Likewise, one may respond to the difficulty at hand, "Is there *more being* in the effect and the cause united together than there is in the cause alone?"

Yes—if it pertains to a finite or secondary cause; no—if it pertains to the Supreme Cause, which is infinite.

As the theologians say in common, "Post creationem sunt plura entia, sed non est plus entis quam antea [After creation, there are more beings, but there is not more being than before]." After creation, there are more beings, more living things, more intelligent beings, but there is not more being, nor more life, nor more wisdom, nor more goodness, nor more love. There is no more perfection than there was before creation, for before creation, there already was, from all eternity, Infinite Being, Infinite Life, Infinite Wisdom, Infinite Love.

If, when a disciple of St. Thomas understands his doctrine without improving it, there are more sages without there being more wisdom, then, for even greater reason is this the case when our limited knowledge is added to the Divine Omniscience.

The contradiction is avoided, indeed, but the mystery of the very order of nature remains here: that of the coexistence of the finite and the Infinite.

Mystery: it is what the philosophical spirit squeezes out of the perception of the smallest of facts, for example, from the least movement, which cannot be produced without the intervention of God the First Mover (i.e., cannot be produced without Divine promotion). And if the philosopher thus sees all of a sudden something very profound in the production of the least of local motions, such as that of a ball being

---

[33] See ibid.

pushed by another, all the more is there reason that he sees it in the production of the least of vital movements in the plant, or in the least case of an animal's sensation, or in the most insignificant of intellections or volitions in man.[34]

St. Thomas's Sense of Mystery

A restricted view of the doctrine of great, traditional masters such as Aristotle and St. Thomas can make us forget that they had *the sense of mystery*. They had it to a profound degree, for they had truly philosophical minds—the *habitus* of wisdom, wholly differing from that of the positive sciences and the geometric mind [*espirit*].

However, their elevation often passes by us unperceived, a bit like that of the Gospel, because it is united to a great simplicity that never breaks with common sense (or, natural reason). These great traditional thinkers carefully elevated themselves from the *vague concepts of common sense*, expressed by the nominal definition or by words that are used by everyone, to *the distinct concept* of philosophical reason. This concept is not different from the first one. It is the very same concept, but now in a more perfect state, as the infant becomes a man or as the man who is more or less asleep awakes.

Thus, it is not surprising that St. Thomas's doctrine, in many of its parts (not only in its least elevated ones, let us note), remains *accessible*

---

[34] Aristotle shows well the necessity of the agent intellect for knowledge of the universal, but the intimate mode by which the influence of the agent intellect exercises its influence remains quite mysterious. It is an *intellect that does not know but makes the knower to know*, a bit like the sun, which does not see but makes sight possible. A poet has said, "The sun is blind." No, it does not have a *privation* of sight; but it does not see. Likewise, the agent intellect is not blind, but it makes one to know without itself knowing. Negation is not a privation.

Likewise, one shows the necessity of a last practical judgment before free choice (or election). However, their mutual relationship remains mysterious enough, though wholly in conformity with the principle that "Causae ad invicem sunt causae in diverso genere [Causes are causes for each other, though in diverse genera of causality]." We have studied this question at length elsewhere in our *God: His Existence and His Nature: A Thomistic Solution of Certain Agnostic Antinomies*, vol. 2, trans. Bede Rose, vol. 2 (St. Louis, MO: B. Herder, 1949), 268–350.

to ordinary people who have elevated souls without these same people suspecting the superior intellectual power expressed in this doctrine.

It is sometimes said, "This speaker surpasses his listeners." Does this always arise from his superiority? Rather, is it not the case that he does not know how to adapt his thought to the intelligence of his listeners? If he wholly possessed it, he would find this adaptation and, by his artful skill, would come to discover the very nature of human intelligence present in each of his listeners. The superiority of Christ appears in the fact that he could render the highest of truths accessible to all. There is—granted, to a much inferior degree—something similar in the case of St. Thomas. Indeed, so well does he express his doctrine with simplicity and conformity to the common sense of man that the elevation of his philosophical spirit is sometimes veiled to the eyes of some who read his works.

Certain expositions of St. Thomas's doctrine, undertaken in a far too material manner, can make one believe that he had no sense of mystery. However, he eminently had a sense for the real and for the mystery hidden therein, as when he said, "*Before the consideration of our mind* [*espirit*], matter IS NOT form, and therefore it is *really distinct* from it; likewise, before our mind's consideration, created essence and personality ARE NOT their existence and therefore are *really distinct*—no angel, no man (with the exception of Christ) can say, 'I am the Truth and the Life'; God alone can affirm, '*Ego sum qui sum*'; *In solo Deo essentia et esse sunt idem.*"[35]

He eminently had the sense of the real and the mystery hidden in it—this Doctor who proclaimed the necessity of choosing between the existence of God (Who is essentially distinct from the world) and absurdity placed at the root of all things. The more perfect does not come from the less perfect in a kind of ascending evolution that would not have a cause superior to it. Becoming cannot have in itself its own *raison d'être*. St. Thomas says to us: The only one having in Himself His *raison d'être* is He Who is *Eternally Self-Subsistent Being*, Pure Act, He Who is not determinable in any further way, and Who cannot be

---

[35] See *ST* I, q. 3, a. 4. No created person (nor any created personality) is its own existence, but it has received such existence.

perfected in any way—*ipsum esse per se subsistens, cui nulla potest fieri additio.*[36] He alone, *without any new action,* can freely produce all that is *new* in the world and all that truly represents progress in it.

And if St. Thomas had this sense of mystery in the natural order, how much more did he have it in the order of grace—he who has affirmed more clearly than any of his predecessors the *distinction between these two orders* while not ignoring, however, *their harmony.* And in each supernatural mystery, St. Thomas has profoundly noted the most inti-mate unity in the greatest diversity—in the diversity of things that God alone can bring together and reunite. It suffices to recall here what the Holy Doctor has said concerning Eucharistic Communion:

> *O res mirabilis*
> *Manducat Dominum,*
> *Pauper, servus, et humilis.*
> (O, what a marvelous thing!
> The poor, the servant, the humble—
> They feed upon their Lord).

Contemplation is the sense of mystery. St. Thomas had this—above all at the end of his life when intellectuality, united in him to a superior spirituality, was more and more simplified, brought to its perfection in a contemplation that was so lofty that it no longer permitted him to dictate his *Summa theologiae.* In such a state, he could not descend into the detail of each article, into the three difficulties of the *status quaestionis,* into the *sed contra,* into the body or the responses to the objections. Having arrived at this age of the spirit's life, the intellect in St. Thomas could no longer be subjected to this complexity; it had become more and more contemplative and discovered more and more the supreme mystery on which the others depend and that cannot be expressed in human words.

This poses another question: *How does it happen that the human intellect,* though naturally united to the body, senses, and sense memory, *does not better adapt after sixty or seventy years* (as one sees in many

---

[36] See *ST* I, q. 2, a. 3; q. 3, aa. 5 and 8.

thinkers) *to the complexity of reasoned intellectual work*, which presupposes ever-renewed material information? *How does it happen that this
human intellect* (above all in those who have the philosophical spirit or
also among the ordinary who have lofty souls) after sixty or seventy
years *is ripe* (even from the natural point of view) *for an intellectual life
superior* to that supplied by libraries and all the means of information,
as long as the soul is united to the body?[37]

*　*　*

Consider yet another mystery that is singularly profound. The human
intellect is, by its very nature, united to the senses, for it is the *least among
intellects* [*la dernière des intelligences*], having for its proper object *the
least among that which is intelligible* [*le dernier des intelligibles*]—namely
the intelligible being of sensible things.[38] However, before a century
here below, it is ripe for a superior life that will endure for thousands
upon thousands of years—without end. In this state, it will preserve a
desire to be reunited to the body, a desire that will be given to it at the
resurrection. However, what a mystery: that of an intellect that nor-
mally needs the senses and that, nonetheless, lives separated from them
for centuries upon centuries before recovering them.

As in the case of the other mysteries we have considered, St.
Thomas shows, in the eight articles of *Summa theologiae* I, q. 89, his
profound sense for the mystery of the separated soul. Insisting on this
point does not lessen his doctrine; instead, it shows its true loftiness. It
is necessary to distinguish *the inferior sort of obscurity*, which arises from
incoherence and absurdity, from *the superior sort of obscurity*, which
comes from a light that is too powerful for the weak eyes of our mind.

Positivists, hearing this language, say that metaphysicians are
poets who missed their vocation. We can respond to them that, as St.
Thomas says, if poetry often uses *analogy* in order to enlarge *small*

---

[37] Even if the body would not be tired and would not be worn out, would not the human
intellect (from the simple point of view of the natural order) fatigue after three centuries of this inferior intellectual travail? Would it not aspire to a more elevated
contemplation?

[38] See *ST* I, q. 76, a. 5.

things, Wisdom uses it in order to stammer as well as it can concerning *things that are too lofty* to be expressed perfectly by us.[39]

In this attitude, we see the sense of mystery that, as in the case of St. Thomas, has *a sense for analogy* and that says, in accord with the formula of the Fourth Lateran Council, "Inter Deum et creaturam non est tanta similitudo, quin sit semper maior dissimilitudo notanda [Between God and creature, there cannot be any similarity expressed except insofar as there is always a greater dissimilarity noted in such expression]."[40]

Moreover, far from excluding certitude, this superior sort of obscurity is united to it; it does not truly begin unless it begins with certitude, and the two increase together.

Indeed, if someone still doubts that Infinite Mercy and Justice exist in God, he will not even pose to himself the problem of their intimate reconciliation with each other; however, the more one is certain of these two Divine Perfections, the more one glimpses the grandeur of each of them, and also the more does the mystery of their intimate

---

[39] See *ST* I, q. 1, a. 9, ad 1; I-II, q. 101, a. 2, ad 2.

[Tr. note: Analogy and metaphor have very close proportional structures, even though metaphor remains improper while properly proportional analogy attributes something properly and formally present in that of which the analogue is predicated. The philosopher often begins by stammering in metaphor before fully grasping things according to the strict laws of proper proportionality. See the profound words of Yves Simon in *Work, Society, and Culture*, ed. Vukan Kuic (New York: Fordham University Press, 1971), 168: "The use of metaphors in philosophy proper must either be rejected or at least strictly controlled; but in the phase of discovery, in the introduction to a subject, nothing is more natural than to use metaphors. In fact, a rich metaphorical imagination is an indispensable privilege of all creative philosophers. Philosophy will begin when metaphor is transcended, but in the introduction to philosophy we have to use metaphorical analogies."]

[40] St. Thomas's doctrine concerning analogy can be summarized in these terms: "Those things are called analogous for which the name is common, though the notion signified through the name is common only in a qualified sense to each (namely, common to them through proportionality), but simply speaking the notion is diverse in them." Thus, in God, existence is identified with essence, but in us, it is really distinct from essence; likewise, the knowledge of God is the cause of things, but for us [knowledge] is caused by them.

According to Suarez, in contrast, the analogous notion is *simplicter eadem, secundum quid diversa* [simply speaking the same, different in a qualified sense]. Indeed, in his doctrine, existence in us, just as in God, is not really distinct from essence and Divine knowledge (according to his theory of middle knowledge, i.e., of the *scientia media*) *depends* upon things, at least on future conditionals.

reconciliation in the eminence of the Deity (i.e., of the intimate life of God) appear to such a person. The more one is certain of the existence of God, the more does it appear that He lives in the inaccessible light, which the mystics call the *great darkness*, for this light is far too strong for the vision of a created intellect. These incredibly beautiful chiaroscuros are abundant in St. Thomas's works, for he feared neither logic nor mystery—and the first leads unto the second.[41] We see this in particular in what he has written concerning Divine causality and the free will of man or angel, and in what he has written concerning the efficacious grace given to one person (e.g., the good thief) and on the Divine permission of sin given to another who is less loved and less aided, though the obligation always remains *truly possible*. God never commands the impossible, but one person would not be better than

---

[41] St. Thomas never would have admitted like Suarez that the principle of contradiction is not applied in the case of the Trinity. It is applied there according to an eminent mode that remains hidden to us, and nothing can show that this mystery implies a contradiction. Recently, as regards a well-known text from the *De unitate intellectus*, ch.7 (*Valde autem ruditer argumentatur*, etc. [However, they argue crudely . . .]), one has written that St. Thomas lived in so great an intimacy with the mysteries of the faith so as to hasten to declare contradictory every *exception to metaphysical laws* that are the most certain among those rationally established. Without a doubt, one wished to say, "to natural laws," which are hypothetically necessary and outside of which miracles are possible. However, as regards "metaphysical laws," these are absolutely necessary and without possible exception, even by a miracle. If they suffer an exception, they would no longer be worth anything. For example, if this metaphysical law is true, "Act, not limited of itself, can be limited and multiplied only by potency—form can be multiplied only by the matter that receives it (or by an essential relation to such matter [in the case of the separated soul])"—if this metaphysical law is true, it is without any exception, as is the principle of contradiction, as well as that of causality.

As regards the text "Valde ruditer argumentatur," this matter is well explained by John of St. Thomas and by Jean Baptiste Gonet in their treatises on the angels, where they treat of the question "utrum sint plures angeli solo numero distincti intra eamdem speciem [whether there are multiple angels differing only in number within the same species]."

[Tr. note: It appears that Fr. Garrigou-Lagrange is referring to a discussion at which he was present in 1934 with Fr. Charles Boyer, S.J. Given the imprimatur date on the text, the remarks in this footnote were added relatively close to the completion of this book. The example seems to match Fr. Boyer's talk/article. See Charles Boyer, 'Valde ruditer argumentantur': S. Thomas concedit actum per miraculum multiplicari posse sine potentia receptiva," *Acta Pontificiae Academiae Romanae S. Thomae* 1 (1934), 129–34, completed in 2 (1934): 202–5.]

another person if it were not also the case that God loved one more than the other. Such is the mystery of efficacious grace and sufficient grace that is already posed with regard to the efficaciousness of Divine aid given in the natural order for accomplishing the moral law.[42]

This does not diminish St. Thomas's doctrine but, instead, draws attention to this superior obscurity. It better presents its high intellectuality and makes us note that reasoned study of this teaching ought to be brought to completion in contemplation. It is in this sense that we can understand in a vital and positive sense what is called the *docta ignorantia*, the learned ignorance.

Above Eclecticism

In the midst of these difficulties, the philosophical spirit, in order to find the truth (or at least the direction one may take toward the truth) senses that philosophical systems are generally true in what they affirm and generally false in what they deny, for reality is richer than any of them. Consequently, the philosophical spirit realizes that there are doctrines that are obviously erroneous and are opposed to one another, doctrines that are like the extremities of the base of a triangle or of a pyramid. Thus, the philosophical spirit is led to seek for the truth in the middle (and above) these extremes that represent the wandering paths of error. In elevating itself, the philosophical spirit finds in the middle of his journey *the opportunism of eclectics* who take something

---

[42] See *ST* I, q. 19, a. 8: "When a cause is efficacious to act, the effect follows upon the cause not only *according to what is done* but also according to its *manner of being done* or of being. . . . Therefore, since the Divine Will is *most efficacious*, it does not only follow that those things that God wishes to be done are done but also that they are done *in the mode* by which God wishes them to be done, . . . namely, either necessarily or contingently and freely."

See also *ST* I, q. 20, a. 3: "Since God's love is the cause of the goodness of things, one person would not be better than another if it were not the case that God willed to one person a greater good than He wills to another."

This principle virtually contains [i.e., within its illuminative power] the treatise on predestination, and it is not irreconcilable with this other: *God never commands what is impossible*, and He renders *truly possible* every accomplishment of His precepts. The intimate reconciliation of these two principles is the very mystery of predestination.

from the adverse systems but without any directing principle. Finally, the philosophical spirit seeks the truth in a summit that, at one and the same time, dominates the erroneous extreme positions as well as the eclecticism that remains midway.

Often, it does not succeed at defining this summit well, but it often senses it without seeing it, like the meeting of two sides of a triangle. One could give various examples of this.

And when the speculative difficulty is more or less vanquished, there remain all of the difficulties pertaining to action—for example, the current problems of economics or of the social order. Beyond individualism and communism, one senses the true doctrine of the common good in which the philosophical spirit harmonizes true charity and the four species of justice (i.e., commutative, distributive, legal, and that of equity). However, even when one has little by little balanced these things in thought and in discourse, much still remains to be done—indeed, sometimes everything remains to be done—in the order of sentiment, of will, and of action. It is necessary even to be attentive to avoid a certain unconscious Pharisaism and "phraseology of love" that would make one believe that one truly and profoundly *has* the sentiments and virtues about which one *speaks*—whereas, in order to have these at the desired degree, holiness is truly necessary.

The Spirit of Christian Philosophy

Christian philosophy possesses, more than any other philosophy, this sense of mystery of which we have spoken because, more than any other philosophy (without becoming identified with infused faith or with theology), it has a sense for God. Concerning this subject, we wish to note here one thing above all else. If the spirit of Christian philosophy does not come sufficiently from on high, and if it does not give enough place to mystery, it is replaced by another spirit that is no longer Christian, except only in name.

Without a doubt, Christian philosophy is distinct from the apologetics of Christian faith. On this point, M. Maurice Blondel tends to confuse the two.[43] Indeed, Christian philosophy does not need to receive from Divine Revelation notions like those of infused faith and of the supernatural mystery. It proceeds according to its proper principles and its proper method, already distinctly enough formulated by Aristotle.

However, Christian philosophy ought to depend upon a conformity with Christian faith, which is a true guiding star for it—in the words of Pope Leo XIII, *velut stella retrix*. Not only should it not say (even implicitly) something against the revealed doctrine proposed by the Church, but beyond this, it ought to have a positive conformity with it, orienting itself (according to its proper principles and methods) within the sense of revealed truths—for example, with regard to creation *ex nihilo* and *non ab aeterno*, also with regard to the nonrepugnance of the elevation of man to the life of grace. This conformity, as Jacques Maritain has explained well in his *Essay on Christian Philosophy*, ought to be objective in the sense that Christian philosophy cannot ignore revealed truth.[44] This conformity ought also to be subjective in the sense that it results from a comforting of the acquired *habitus* of wisdom by means of the virtue of infused faith—for example, as when a philosopher becomes a believer, thus adhering with a new force to the rational proofs for the existence of God (as the Author of nature) that he already knew before being a believer.[45] Thus, Christian philosophy does not differ *specifically* from that of an Aristotle (taken in what is true in it). That is, it does not have a new formal object. It is the same science, but in a *state* that is superior, just as the infant becomes man or like discursive theology in the intellect of a theologian who has received the light of glory.

Conceived in this manner, Christian philosophy has more of a sense of mystery than does any other philosophy. In particular, it is

---

[43] [Tr. note: On the thought of Maurice Blondel in the context of the controversies regarding Christian philosophy, see the works cited in note 1 above.]

[44] See Maritain, *An Essay on Christian Philosophy*. We fully accept Maritain's conclusions; they appear to us to be very excellently formulated.

[45] According to St. Thomas and the Thomists, although one cannot at the same time *believe and see* the same truth from the same point of view, one can, at one and the same time *believe* in the existence of God as the author of grace and *see* the demonstrative value of the proofs of the existence of God as the author of nature. In this case, the virtue of infused faith confirms from on high the value of the demonstration.

aware that it cannot demonstrate rigorously either the existence or even the intrinsic possibility of any of the supernatural mysteries. It can no more demonstrate rigorously the intrinsic possibility of the Beatific Vision than it can demonstrate the intrinsic possibility of the Trinity. In order to do that, it would have to demonstrate the intrinsic possibility of *eternal life*, of the light of glory, and of sanctifying grace. These objects are supernatural by their very essence; now, that which is SUPERNATURAL QUOAD ESSENTIAM is also supernatural *quoad cognoscibilitatem, quia verum et ens convertuntur*—it is supernatural as regards knowability, for truth and being are convertible.[46] Here, it is no longer a matter only of the mystery of the production of the least of local motions, nor of that of sensation, nor only of a miracle; it is a matter concerning the mysteries of the intimate life of God and its participation in us.

The just equilibrium of Christian philosophy is difficult to maintain from on high from a kind of fideism, on one hand, and from a kind of semi-rationalism, on the other. It is necessary for Christian philosophy to be faithful to the inspiration that comes from Divine Revelation. If the philosophical activity of a Christian, without advocating anything that is contrary to the faith, excludes more or less the superior inspiration that would fortify it from on high, what happens to it? This inspiration is inevitably replaced by an inferior spirit that is no longer Christian enough or that is not Christian at all. *The seriousness of the intellectual life is thus displaced*: one more or less depreciates superior values by giving more importance to others that are subordinate to them. One tends *to prefer the proper method* of research *to the truth*. The philosopher will thus arrive at an *anticontemplative* mentality and will lose the sense of mystery. He will even arrive at having an antiphilosophical mentality, for to prefer method to truth is *to prefer being of reason* [i.e., *ens rationis*] *to real being*. The latter is much richer than our thought, which is always lacking in some way, and it is precisely this

---

[46] We have developed this point at length already and we will return to it below in the second chapter of the second part of this book, "Can the Possibility of the Beatific Vision be Demonstrated?" See also our work *De revelatione per Ecclesiam catholicam proposita*, 3rd ed. (Rome: Ferrari, 1931), 1:397ff. [Tr. note: A translation of this work is anticipated in a future volume by Emmaus Academic.]

richness of the real in its various degrees that requires in the philoso-pher—above all in the Christian philosopher—the sense of mystery, a sense that here below grows with certitude instead of destroying it.

Chapter 4

The Intellectual Chiaroscuro

O NE OF THE MOST STRIKING ASPECTS in the study of the great problems of philosophy and theology is the union of light (indeed, sometimes a dazzling light) and a profound obscurity. However, we do not generally reflect enough on the nature of this obscurity—either on its causes (which are sometimes quite varied) or on the usefulness it can exercise as a kind of contrast, helping us understand the nature of truth.

The sense of mystery could not be lacking in the great Doctors of the Church, for it is the proper characteristic of superior intellects. Above all, it is found in those who are accustomed to immersing their attention in the profundities of the Passion of Jesus Christ, in the adoration-inducing secret of the Redemption in itself (as well as in relation to each one of us). From this, such superior intellects progressively elevate themselves to the heights of God's intimate life, which, in heaven, is the immediate object of the Beatific Vision. Thus, they ever aspire to see, to love, and to speak of that which no human language can express. *Oculus non vidit, nec auris audivit, nec in cor hominis ascendit, quae praeparavit Deus iis, qui diligunt illum* [Eye has not seen, nor ear heard, nor has it arisen into the heart of man, that which God has prepared for those who love Him] (1 Cor 2:9). It is this that produces the great enthusiasm of the saints.

In contrast, as Ernest Hello has written:

The mediocre man feels neither grandeur nor misery. In his judgments, as in his works, he substitutes convention for reality, approves that which finds a place in his private way of seeing things, condemns that which escapes the denominations and categories that he knows, has a dread for that which astonishes, never approaching the terrible mystery of life—the mediocre man avoids the mountains and chasms through which life leads her friends.[1]

In this chapter, we wish to note the sense of mystery that St. Thomas had, as much in the order of nature as in that of grace, about the problems that can be most captivating for the human intellect.

The Two Obscurities and the Two Clarities

It is important from the beginning to recall that the kinds of obscurity proper to the great problems of philosophy and theology are of very different natures. This difference is due to the causes from which they arise.

On the one hand, there is the kind of "obscurity from below," which itself is varied in nature. It comes from blind *matter*, for matter, in a sense, is repugnant to intelligibility, which is obtained by abstraction from matter.[2] "Obscurity from below" also arises from voluntary or involuntary *error* (often from errors opposed to each other while having the appearance of truth). Finally, such obscurity also comes from *moral disorder* or sin.

On the other hand, there is an "obscurity from on high," which

---

[1] Ernest Hello, *L'homme: la vie—la science—l'art*, 7th ed. (Paris: Perrin, 1903), 1.8 (pp. 66–67).

[2] The human intellect *abstracts the intelligible* from matter, which remains thus like a kind of residue, intelligible only with great difficulty. First matter (i.e., prime matter), which is only a *real capacity* for receiving substantial (i.e., specific) form of sensible beings—of air, water, dirt, roses, lilies, lions—is intelligible only by its essential relation to the determinations or perfections that it can receive. However, of itself, matter is nothing determined—*nec quid, nec quale, nec quantum*, etc. See Aristotle, *Metaphysics* 7.3.

comes from the transcendence of *the intimate life of God*, as well as from that which is a participation in it (i.e., the life of grace). As the matter from which we abstract the intelligible is (in a way) below the limits of intelligibility, the intimate life of God is above the limits of the intelligibility that is naturally accessible to us.

Moreover, between the two, the natural life *of the spirit* remains obscure for *the being that is least in the order of intellectual beings* (i.e., man), who needs the senses in order to know the *least among that which is intelligible* (found in the shadow of sensible things)[3] and who can therefore know *the spiritual* only in a negative manner as being immaterial. Man knows spiritual realities only in a relative manner in the mirror of sensible things, *in speculo sensibilium*.[4] Thus, the human intellect speaks, by using analogies based on the dimensions of space, of a "profound" spirit "elevated" to "vast horizons." However, it does not know here below the life of the spirit as an angel knows it, nor as the separated soul will know it immediately after death.

It is immensely important to distinguish well here at the beginning of our study of these matters between the obscurity that comes from below and the obscurity that comes from on high. God is invisible, incomprehensible, and ineffable thanks to His infinite elevation, but in Himself, He is light itself. The human individual is ineffable because of the matter that is in him as something inferior, the principle of individuation, which, because of its inferiority and its fundamental obscurity, in a way, is repugnant to intelligibility. Let us not confuse the obscurity that dominates the frontiers of intelligibility from on high with that which is beneath them.

* * *

Between these two, very different obscurities, there is an intellectual light, sometimes a very beautiful one, put in relief by a Plato, an Aristotle, and in a superior order, by the Gospel, by St. Paul, by the genius of an Augustine or a Thomas Aquinas. On some days, one is captivated

---

[3] See *Summa theologiae* [hereafter, *ST*] I, q. 76, a. 5.

[4] See *ST* I, q. 87, aa. 1–4.

by the opposition of this light and the profound shadows that are above and below it.

However, as there are two obscurities that are very different (that from on high and that from below), there are also *two clarities* of a contrary nature—true clarity and the false clarity. The latter, by its false brilliance, resembles the other just as a glass bead resembles a diamond.

Indeed, there is the *clarity* of spiritualism, *which explains the inferior by the superior*, according to the subordination of causes that lead us to the First Cause and to the Last End of the universe, to God the First Being, the First Intellect, and the Sovereign Good, to Him who alone can say, "I am He who Is"—"I am the Truth and the Life." Man can say, "I *have* truth and life." God alone can say, "*I am the truth and the life*" (John 14:6). One cannot repeat the point enough: there is an infinite distance between the verbs "to be" and "to have." And that which God alone can say of Himself, Jesus Christ has said of His own proper person. It is the true clarity in the midst of the shadows.

However, there is *the false clarity* of every doctrine that attempts (like, for example, materialism) *to explain the superior by means of the inferior*, according to a supposed *subordination*, not of causes but *of experimental laws*, in such a way that psychological laws are reduced to biological laws, which are said to be more general. Then, these biological laws are reduced to physico-chemical laws, and finally to the laws of conservation of matter and energy, which are given as the most universal and supreme principle of explanation—all in place of God, of Pure Act and the First Mover of spirits and bodies.

As one sees in the history of materialism (and also that of rationalism), generally, those who *pride themselves the most on their objectivity* are precisely those who most lack the superior sort of objectivity, which, in their materialism, they call "mere romantic subjectivism." All of this leads them to prefer to the superior sort of clarity the inferior sort of clarity, which becomes false thanks to the importance that they unduly give to it. From this arise the great errors that fill many books and so-called scientific reviews—that is, the denial of almost all of the superior truths, those that are the substance of the religion taught in the Catechism. The contrast between such so-called science and the

Catechism for children can be reduced to these words of the Savior: "I thank thee, Father, Lord of heaven and earth, that thou hast hidden these things from the wise and understanding and revealed them to babes; yea, Father, for such was thy gracious will" (Matt 11:25). Woe unto those who prefer to the clarity that comes from on high that which comes from below, a "clarity" that quickly becomes false.

Here, in materialism under its various forms, we have the most striking and the greatest example of this false sort of clarity. Obviously, there are many other and very subtle types of it as well. It is immensely important to distinguish the clarity of what is purely and simply true (*simpliciter verum*) and that of what is true only in a secondary and partial aspect, all while being essentially false (*verum secundum quid, et falsum simpliciter*). We have said that, even in the falsest of doctrines, there is a soul [âme] of truth. It would be better to say "a grain of truth," for the truth found in such doctrines (indeed, the truth rendering the error seductive and permitting it to be presented) is not the principle animator of the doctrine but, on the contrary, is placed in the service of the false principle that diverts that truth from its end. In such a false doctrine, truth is the slave of error, which is all the more dangerous in that it presents itself under the appearance of a great truth, just as perversity presents itself under the appearance of virtue.

Obviously, it is no less important to distinguish the true sort of clarity from the false kind than it is to distinguish the obscurity that comes from on high, arising from too great a light for our weak eyes, from that coming from below that is born from confusion, incoherence, and that often veils over a contradiction. St. Thomas often opposes the one to the other—in his articles, it is the opposition found between the difficulties posed at the beginning and the response that he makes to these opposed arguments.

Also, it is necessary to note that the apparent clarity of certain objections against the great mysteries of faith come from our imperfect mode of knowing. Here, it happens that we grasp more rapidly the strength of the objection [e.g., made against St. Thomas's position in the *Summa*] than that of the response. Why is this so? It is so precisely because the objection comes from our imperfect mode of knowing, always a bit material and mechanical, while the response given by a St.

Augustine or a St. Thomas is taken from what is most elevated in the ineffable mystery with which we are not familiar enough. Contemplation penetrates it only a little bit at a time, gradually and only to the degree that maturity of spirit is acquired.

Also, let us note, as regards true clarity, that there is a superficial, nearly sensible, sort and another that is elevated, which comes from the highest principles. Voltaire was speaking of the first when he said, "I am like the streams: I am clear because I am not profound."[5] The other, superior sort of clarity comes from the deepening of certain, elementary truths (e.g., the principle of causality, which leads all the way to the Supreme Cause). Ignorance of these high truths leads to a complexity that can appear to be learned but is "science" in name only.

Two Forms of the Probable

Finally, it is important to mention here that, between that which is evidently true and that which is evidently false, there are *two forms of the probable* that are very different from each other and that probabilism tends to confuse with one another—*the probably true* and the *probably false*. Obviously, it is a matter of great importance that we distinguish these two, as much in the speculative order as in the practical order. We could imagine them as follows:

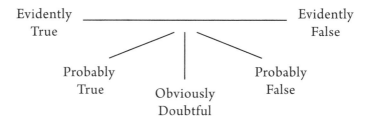

---

[5] [Tr. note: Lit. "Je suis comme les ruisseaux: je suis clair parce que je ne suis pas profond."]

In the eyes of theologians who reject probabilism, when something is *certainly more probable*, the contrary *is not probable*, and it is neither reasonable nor licit to act in this way. In other words: when a proposition is more probably true, the contrary or contradictory proposition is probably false, and it would be unreasonable to hold it, for in this adherence, the fear of error (*formido errandi*) would prevail over the reasonable inclination to adhere. Now, in every reasonable opinion, the inclination to hold something ought to prevail over the fear of error.[6]

Above that which is probably true and that which is evidently true, we find the superior kind of obscurity. Below them, there is the contrary kind of obscurity.

The superior kind of obscurity is called the "great darkness" by the mystics. The inferior kind of obscurity is that which is often spoken of in Scripture, in particular as when it is said in Matthew 4:16: "The people who sat in darkness have seen a great light, and for those who sat in the region and shadow of death light has dawned."[7]

The Art of Contrasts

The philosopher and the theologian both, in contemplating the intellectual panorama of the orders of nature and grace, seek to reduce the aforementioned double obscurity as much as possible by throwing

---

[6] Probabilists respond: "When something is certainly more probable, the contrary is not probable in the *strict and philosophical sense*, that is to say, worthy of adherence—we concede this. That it is not probable *in the broad and moral sense of the word* 'probable'—that is to say, founded upon serious reasons—this we deny, unless the less probable opinion concerns the same principle as the other opinion or the less probable opinion has very little probability." For a presentation of this manner of seeing things, see Benedictus Merkelbach, *Summa theologiae moralis*, vol. 2 (Paris: Desclée, 1931), 97.

This response, rejected by all the theologians who are opposed to probabilism, remains very weak from the fact that it concedes that the *moral sense* of a probable expression is no longer conformed to its *philosophical sense*. Moral thought ought to be founded upon a sound speculative philosophy.

[7] This is a citation of the Hebrew form of Isa 8:23 and 9:1. The Psalms also often speak of those who are in darkness and the shadow of death. See Ps 87:7 and 106:10, 14.

light on all possible matters. But perhaps they do not habitually make enough use of the marvelous opposition that exists here (as in the sensible order) between light and shadow.

Often, philosophers and theologians do not explain enough why certain summits of truth can appear to many people as being very close to grave errors—for instance, Thomism to Calvinism, or the true doctrine of abandonment to God that appears to be so close to quietism. A little deviation on the principles leads to monstrous errors!

When one has lived for many years, studying these problems, one is often struck by these magnificent chiaroscuros where obscurity takes on a value, for it powerfully places in relief the Divine Light and the rational light that illuminate us in our voyage toward eternity. John the Evangelist speaks of this lively opposition: "I am the light of the world; he who follows me will not walk in darkness, but will have the light of life" (John 8:12). Also, according to the report of Luke concerning Zechariah, the father of the forerunner gave thanks to God in his canticle (i.e., the *Benedictus*) for His promise "to give light to those who sit in darkness and in the shadow of death, to guide our feet into the way of peace" (Luke 1:79). Indeed, it was already said by the Psalmist, "Even though I walk through the valley of the shadow of death, I fear no evil for thou art with me" (Ps 23:4). We walk among the rays and the shadows.

The Sensible Chiaroscuro

This lively opposition of light and obscurity in the intellectual order can be better understood if one reflects for a moment on what great painters have said concerning chiaroscuro in the sensible order.

The term "chiaroscuro" is used to describe a way of painting. It refers to a manner of handling or distributing the light and darkness found in a painting in a way that helps to detach the figures in the painting. The chiaroscuro provided certain artists with a great resource for obtaining this relief. Painters enamored with light, such as the Véronèse and numerous other artists of the Venetian school, use it very little. They seek to indicate the plans of objects in the midst of nuances, tones, half-tones, and pristine colors. For them, the background of the painting is more often as luminous as the foreground. There is something similar, in the case of the intellectual viewpoint, in most of the philosophical and theological works that use very little (or virtually no) intellectual chiaroscuro. With great brevity, they provide an exposition of the errors and difficulties of great problems and exclude the shadows as much as is possible. However, it is also often the case that truth is very little placed in relief by this method. Thus, in many of the manuals of philosophy and theology, one does not see the difficulty that drives the very problems being discussed.

In opposition [e.g., to the Venetians], there are those painters whose style can be said to make things dark, accumulating shadows in certain parts, and bringing forth light in their paintings by means of restrained points of exit, as happens in the architecture of certain churches. They thus obtain effects of a great vigor but in detriment to the colors, the lightness, and the fluidity of certain shadows. This method has the added disadvantage of suppressing reflections. Many of the Flemish painters, as well as the Italian painters, of the sixteenth century fell into this excess. The grand master of the chiaroscuro is Rembrandt, who allowed only an eighth of his canvas for light. Great painters were preoccupied with regulating the proportions of the chiaroscuro by mathematical laws. Titian gave a quarter of his canvas to light, a quarter to half-tones, and a quarter to shade. Correggio followed rather closely to this given way of doing things. Today, drawings and etchings again make great use of the chiaroscuro.

There is something similar in music. Lyrical drama has had a great effect on it. Here, it merely suffices to recall certain leitmotivs of Wagner such as that of hatred or that of the lance, or again, the opposition of the two leitmotivs of the opening of the *Tannhaüser* (i.e., that of perdition and that of salvation).

One could speak also of Beethoven's symphonies: "They delighted in imitating storms, reproducing, in such a transposition, these striking contrasts of darkness and light that sometimes tear apart the visible horizon."

The Suprasensible Chiaroscuro in the Various Orders of Intellectual Knowledge

Mystics are the people who have been captivated by the suprasensible chiaroscuro—especially St. John of the Cross, in his *Dark Night of the Soul* and *Living Flame of Love*, and Blessed Angela de Foligno, in particular in her *Book of Visions and Instructions*, chapters 26 (The Great Darkness), 27 (The Ineffable), 28 (Certitude), 33 (True Love and Deceitful Love), 34 (The Cross and Blessing), 35 (Splendor), 46 (The Burning), 48 (The Light), 57 (Knowledge of God and of Self), and 65 (The Ways of Love).

Certainly, one can abuse the antithesis. The romantics very often fell into this abuse. However, one can also draw a true advantage from it, as the Church has done in giving precision to dogmatic formulas in opposition to contrary heresies, between which the truth is like a summit between two chasms. Thus, the Church's doctrine on grace and predestination rises like a culminating point between Pelagianism and Semi-Pelagianism, on one side, and Predestinationism, Protestantism, and Jansenism on the other.

All theologians know these vigorous oppositions. It is sovereignly important to treat them thoroughly, recalling that Providence, which permits an evil only for the sake of a greater good, likewise permits error and its various contrary wanderings only so that the truth can appear in a much greater relief. Therefore, just as the painter, in the chiaroscuro, uses darkness so as to make the light appear in greater relief, so too the philosopher can (and should) use errors opposed to one another, defining them very exactly, so as to place the truth into relief and to show what distinguishes the superior sort of obscurity to which the truth leads from the obscurity that is found in the incoherence and contradictions of the various forms of falsity.

*   *   *

Let us note here some cases of intellectual chiaroscuros that we have exposited elsewhere.

The Aristotelian doctrine of *act and potency* is elevated above the immutable monism of Parmenides and the absolute evolutionism of Heraclitus. Indeed, as nothing is intelligible except insofar as it is in act (i.e., is determined), this doctrine, which was given further development by St. Thomas, *is clear by the place that it gives to act and obscure by that given to potency*, which is a real capacity for perfection, a real capacity that is a *mysterious middle* between act (no matter how minimal that act may be) and pure nonbeing. *Real potency* (whether it be passive potency or active potency) is not nonbeing; nor is it negation, nor a privation, nor even the simple possibility that is a prerequisite for creation *ex nihilo*. However, for all that, it also is not act (no matter how imperfect one might suppose that act to be). Furthermore, it is *intelligible* only in relation to the act to which it is ordered: *nihil est intelligibile nisi in quantum est in actu*. Who could, before having ever seen an oak, know that the oak is found in potency in the seed found in the acorn?

Likewise, the doctrine of *matter and form*, which is elevated above mechanistic atomism and dynamism, while keeping whatever is true in each position, is intellectually *clear* by form and *obscure* by matter, pure potency.[8] Matter, as we have said, is repugnant to any sort of intelligibility, which is obtained by abstraction *a materia, saltem a materia singulari* [from matter, at least from singularizing matter]. There, we find the inferior sort of obscurity, below the frontiers of intelligibility.

On the contrary, when we raise our view from brute matter to plant life, we find that there is a superior sort of obscurity in defining *life*, for life as such is an *absolute perfection* (*simpliciter simplex*) attributable, analogically and in its proper sense, to God, angel, man, animal, and plant. Life is not a genus but, instead, is above every genus. It is an analogue, something difficult to define, for this definition must be able to be applied *in its proper sense* proportionally to God, who is Life Itself,

---

8   Prime matter can become air, water, earth, incandescent carbon; it can become plant or animal. However, in itself, it has none of these forms in act: *nec quid, nec quale, nec quantum*, as Aristotle has said. For this reason, it is *intelligible* only by its relation to the act (or, determined perfection) that it can receive. To say that it is a *real passive potency* is to say that it is a *real capacity for perfection*—not to produce but *to receive*. Likewise, the essence of every creature is a real capacity for perfection in relation to existence, for God alone *is* existence; we *have* existence; no creature can say, "I am existence [*l'existence*], truth, and life."

and to a blade of grass, which properly speaking is something living.[9]

The same difficulty arises when we elevate ourselves from plant life to the most elementary *tactile sensation*; with sensation, no matter how small, a new order appears—that of knowledge. Now, *knowledge*, like life, is an *absolute perfection* (*simpliciter simplex*), attributable, analogically and in its proper sense, to God. Therefore, it is necessary to define knowledge in general (which is not a genus but is an analogue) in such a manner that it can be attributed proportionally and in a proper sense to God and to the least tactile sensation of the most inferior animal. Therefore, it should be no surprise that we find here a superior sort of obscurity, one very different from that which is found in a materialistic or an idealistic theory of sensation. According to the Aristotelian and Thomistic conception, *cognoscens differt a non cognoscente prout potest QUODDAMMODO FIERI ALIUD A SE;*[10] the knowing being differs from the nonknowing being inasmuch as the former can, in a certain way, become *something other than itself*—that is to say, become (in a certain manner) the reality that is known. This conception is raised above the materialist theory, which fails to recognize the uniqueness of sensation, reducing it to something that is inferior to it. It is also superior to the idealist theory, which removes the real value and scope from sensation. To the eyes of a Thomist, these theories deny that which is clear in the fact of sensation on account of what is obscure in it, thus replacing that which is obscure in it with absurdity.

*   *   *

From a greater height, the Aristotelian theory of *intellectual abstraction*, thanks to the light of the agent intellect, dominates, at one and the same time, empiricist idealism and subjective idealism. However, it has its own mysterious side: the activity of the agent intellect, this

---

[9] See *ST* I, q. 18, a. 1 ("Quorum sit vivere [To what things does life belong]"); a. 2 ("Quid sit vita [What is life]"); a. 3 ("Utrum vita Deo conveniat [Whether life pertains to God]"); a. 4 ("Utrum omnia in Deo sint vita [Whether all things in God are life]").

[10] *ST* I, q. 14, a. 1. [Tr. note: See Réginald Garrigou-Lagrange, "Cognoscens quodammodo fit vel est aliud a se," *Revue néo-scolastique de philosophie* 25 (1923): 420–30. A translation of this article is anticipated in a future volume by Emmaus Academic.]

intellectual faculty that does not know but makes known, all by means of an activity intimately deep within us.

Likewise, the true notion of *free choice*, directed by the judgment of the intellect, differs from the intellectualist determinism of Leibniz, as well as the libertinism that makes an exception for freedom, placing it outside the direction of the intellect. However, free choice retains a mystery in the intimate relation of the last practical judgment and the voluntary choice, which, from *diverse points of view*, have a *mutual priority* to each other, according to the principle *causae ad invicem sunt causae, sed in diverso genere* [causes are causes for each other, though in diverse genera of causality]. In this fact, there is no contradiction, for it is from various points of view that, at the end of deliberation, the last free and practical judgment has a priority over the election and the latter over the former. However, there remains here something mysterious—without speaking of the actualization of the created choice by Divine causality, nor to speak of the possible deviation, which is sin.[11]

*   *   *

On numerous occasions, St. Thomas also noted that, for our intellect, *all that is related to love* remains rather obscure and often *unnamed*.[12] There are two reasons for this. First, our intellect knows better that which is in it than that which is in another faculty (e.g., the will). Thus is it that the just man is more certain of having Christian faith than of

---

[11] We have studied this double problem at length elsewhere. See Réginald Garrigou-Lagrange, *God: His Existence and His Nature: A Thomistic Solution of Certain Agnostic Antinomies*, vol. 2, trans. Bede Rose (St. Louis, MO: B. Herder, 1949), 268–350. [Tr. note: Maritain provides something of a précis of Garrigou-Lagrange's thought on this matter in the sixth chapter of the first part of Jacques Maritain, *Bergsonian Philosophy and Thomism*, ed. Ralph McInerny, trans. Mabelle L. Andison and J. Gordon Andison (Notre Dame, IN: University of Notre Dame Press, 2007), pt. 1, ch. 6. Fr. Garrigou-Lagrange himself refers to Maritain's text in Garrigou-Lagrange, *Le réalisme du principe de finalité* (Paris: Desclée de Brouwer, 1932), 93n1. The reader would also benefit to read Jacques Maritain, *Existence and the Existent*, trans. Gerald B. Phelan and Lewis Galantiere (New York: Pantheon, 1948), 47–61.]

[12] See *ST* I, q. 27, a. 4, ad 3; q. 28, a. 4; q. 36, a. 1; q. 37, a. 1 ("Processio amoris est minus nota et non habet nomen proprium [The procession of love is less known and does not have a proper name]").

having charity and being in the state of grace. Second, the good, which is the object of love, is not formally in the intellect as is the true that is the rectitude of our judgment. Instead, the good is in the things, and love *tends* toward it, like a *mysterious impulse* that is difficult to define, for all that which *tends* toward another thing remains, in a sense, *potential*, undetermined; only that which is in act and determined is, of itself, intelligible. Thus, the things of love are known by experience, though we are not able to render them perfectly intelligible. This interior experience, which St. Augustine expresses in saying, "Amor meus, pondus meum [My love is my weight]," contains a most captivating chiaroscuro, especially when it pertains to the living flame of love spoken of by St. John of the Cross.

*   *   *

Finally, the Catholic doctrines of Providence and Predestination also rise like a summit above two errors that are radically opposed—Pelagianism and semi-Pelagianism, on the one hand, and Protestantism and Jansenism on the other.

Against semi-Pelagianism, it is certain that nothing *would be better than* something else *if* it *were not more loved by God*, whose love is the cause of all good. This is what is said with exactitude by St. Thomas in *Summa theologiae* I, q. 20, a. 3: "Since God is the Cause of the goodness of things, one thing would not be better than another if God did not wish a greater good to one than to another." This principle of predilection, which virtually contains[13] all of the treatise on predestination, as well as that of grace, had been expressed by St. Paul when he wrote in 1 Corinthians 4:7: "For who sees anything different in you? What have you that you did not receive?" This is the foundation of Christian humility. St. Augustine insisted greatly upon this point against the semi-Pelagians.

However, on the other hand, speaking in contrast to Protestantism and Jansenism, it is no less certain that *God never commands the impossible.* He would be neither just nor merciful if He did not render

---

[13] [Tr. note: That is, as a cause contains its various effects within its power (*virtus*).]

the accomplishment of His precepts *really and practically possible, here and now*. As the Council of Trent[14] recalled against the Protestants that which was said by St. Augustine: "God never orders impossible things; however, in His ordering He does admonish you both to do what you can and to seek [from Him the Grace to do] what you cannot do."

Therefore, it is absolutely certain, for example, that, on Calvary, it was *really possible* that the bad thief could have accomplished his duty *and* that the good thief who *in fact accomplished* his duty was more loved and more aided by God.

However, as much as each of these two principles appear in their certainty when taken apart, so much too does their intimate reconciliation remain obscure.

To see how these two absolutely incontestable principles are intimately reconciled, it would be necessary to see how, in the eminence of the *Deity* (i.e., the interior life of God), His Infinite Mercy, Infinite Justice, and Sovereign Freedom are intimately reconciled. Now, no human intellect (nor, indeed, any angelic intellect) can see this before having received the Beatific Vision of the Divine Essence.

We have here a very manifest chiaroscuro: just as each of these aforementioned principles is clear in itself, so much too does their intimate reconciliation remain obscure—with this superior obscurity, which is nothing other than the "inaccessible light where God lives" (1 Tim 6:16).

We will return later to this subject,[15] as though to the leitmotiv of this work, for here we come to the greatest of mysteries in the order of things that are at once Divine and human, and it contains at one and the same time a mystery of grace, which in itself is luminous, and a mystery of sin, which in itself is shadow. What we have said thus far suffices to distinguish the obscurity that comes from on high and that which comes from below so as also to better distinguish true clarity from the "clarity" that is nothing but a false reflection of the former. As we have shown elsewhere,[16] there is in God (from our perspective) something that is *very*

---

[14] See Denzinger, no. 1536.

[15] In the sixth chapter of the next part of the book.

[16] See Réginald Garrigou-Lagrange, *Providence*, trans. Bede Rose (St. Louis, MO: Herder, 1937), 119–29.

clear for us to know: He is Omniscient Wisdom, the Sovereign Good, and He cannot will the evil of sin (neither directly nor indirectly); in these, there is a dazzling light. However, there is also in God something very obscure: the holy permission of evil and the intimate reconciliation of His Infinite Justice, Infinite Mercy, and Sovereign Freedom. They can be reconciled only in the eminence of the Deity, which by Its very elevation is invisible and incomprehensible to us.

How is it that this Invisible God contains, *at one and the same time*, for us, *such clarity* and *such obscurity*? How is it that there is this chiaroscuro, at once so alluring and so mysterious?

It comes from the fact that we know the Divine Perfections only in their reflection in creatures, and thus, when we are able to enumerate them well enough, we do so like a child who spells out or distinguishes the syllables of a word. However, we cannot see how these Infinite Divine Perfections are united in the intimate life of God. This manner of union is too luminous for us; it is too lofty to be reflected in the mirror of created reality. Vis-à-vis God, we are a little like people who have never seen white light but, instead, have seen only the seven colors of the rainbow, thus knowing only the name of whiteness. Our limited concepts, by which we represent to ourselves the spiritual physiognomy of God, harden it a little like the small squares of a mosaic; and this is why we yearn for a knowledge that is superior to the multiplicity found in discourse, why we yearn for a simple contemplation of the mystery of the intimate life of God.

*   *   *

Among the contemplatives, those who most have the sense of mystery are those who love God most ardently and love souls in Him. As one of their great admirers has written:

> Love hears what one does not say; it reads what one does not write; it divines what must be divined in order to grow. It increases its discoveries; it is enriched by its treasures; and then it complains of being poor—so that it can extract new secrets. . . .

The language (of the great contemplatives) is a hand-to-hand combat with things that cannot be spoken. . . . Their eloquence consists in complaining of not being able to put into words what they have felt. . . . Colliding in its flight with ineffable secrets, with unrevealed mysteries, it has the appearance of an eagle who, having taken off from the heights of a mountain where the snow is eternal, arrives in regions where, even for it, there is no longer air suitable for breathing. Thoughts are lacking for it. Their intellect descends again, struggling against words, which fail, each in their own turn; it engages in a battle against them, . . . where it is at one and the same time conquered and victorious. . . . There, abysses are glimpsed; there are magnificent attempts at speaking the Ineffable. . . . Human intelligence appears short and brief, and the soul rests assured in its own thirst. For God is declared infinite—and the treasures of eternity are not exhausted.

In this ascent, the final light eclipses all the others; all lights are shadows in comparison with the last light. The treasuries into which the great contemplative's gaze searches are forever inexhaustible; and eternity promises to their ever-renewed joy fresh springs that will never be exhausted.[17]

---

[17] See Ernest Hello's introduction in Angela of Foligno, *Le livre des visions et instructions de la bienheureuse Angèle de Foligno*, trans. Ernest Hello (Paris: A. Tralin, 1914), 17–20.

Part II

THE MYSTERY OF THE RELATIONSHIP BETWEEN NATURE AND GRACE

Having spoken of the sense of mystery in general (above all in the philosophical order) it is appropriate to consider it in the theological domain by pausing to consider the relations of the natural and the supernatural.

From this point of view, we will here treat of the following subjects:

1. The existence of the supernatural order (or, of the intimate life of God)
2. Whether the possibility of the Beatific Vision can be demonstrated
3. The eminence of the Deity, Its attributes, and the Divine Persons
4. Two very different forms of the Supernatural: miracles and grace
5. The supernaturality of faith
6. The Divine Predilection and the possible salvation of all
7. Created, purely spiritual beings and their limits[1]
8. The spiritual chiaroscuro in certain trials of the life of the soul

---

[1] [Tr. note: This is omitted from the text, though clearly he is paralleling the structure of the chapters to follow, and so I have added it here.]

Chapter 1

The Existence of the Supernatural Order: The Intimate Life of God

I N ORDER TO SHOW what ought to be the sense of mystery (above all for the theologian), we will now pause to consider in particular the chiaroscuro found in two great problems pertaining to the relation of nature and grace: (1) Is the existence of the order of supernatural truth demonstrable? (2) Can the possibility of the Beatific Vision also be rigorously demonstrated?

The first of these two questions, which we have treated at length in the past,[1] has recently been taken up with regard to an important text of the *Summa contra gentiles* [hereafter, *SCG*].[2] Let us examine the difficulties that are proposed to us.

A Capital Text of St. Thomas

St. Thomas has written in *SCG* I, chapter 3: "*It is most evidently apparent that there are certain truths about Divine Matters that totally exceed the ability of human reason.*"

As has been recently noted:

---

[1] See Garrigou-Lagrange, *De revelatione per Ecclesiam catholicam proposita*, 3rd ed. (Rome: Ferrari, 1931), vol. 1: 337–70. [Tr. note: A translation of this work is anticipated in a future volume by Emmaus Academic.]

[2] See Adam Corvez, "Est-il possible de démontrer l'existence, en Dieu, d'un ordre de mystères strictement surnaturels?" *Revue thomiste* 37 (1932): 660–67.

Our Doctor asks himself (here) if there are in God mysteries that are strictly supernatural. This is our own question. Without any doubt, he responds, *'evidentissime apparet.'* And why? Because we do not attain the Divine Substance in itself 'quidditatively'; it is only known to us in a very imperfect manner in the mirror of creatures in which the virtuality of their cause is not exhausted. If there are already so many secrets remaining veiled to us in the sensible beings that surround us, how much more should the Divine Essence contain ineffable mysteries.[3]

Then, the same commentator adds:

In this place are reasons of mere suitability, and this is well shown by the practical conclusion stated by St. Thomas: "*Non* igitur omne quod de Deo dicitur, quamvis ratione investigari non possit, *statim quasi falsum est abiiciendum* [Therefore, not everything that is said concerning God, even though it may not be able to be investigated by reason, *should be rejected immediately as something seemingly false*]." It is not necessary to reject immediately, under the pretext that one cannot demonstrate them, incomprehensible mysteries like that of the Trinity. There is nothing impossible *a priori* regarding the fact that there might be in God absolutely transcendent truths that are strictly supernatural; however, we are far from proving rigorously and demonstratively concerning their existence.

Is this truly the sense of the words of St. Thomas, *evidentissime apparet*, and the argument that follows this? Did he wish to give here only "reasons of mere suitability" and not a demonstrative reason?

*   *   *

First, let us remark that, if he proved only that the order of supernatural truths is *really possible* in God (i.e., that it is not intrinsically repugnant

---

3   Ibid., 665.

a parte rei), the existence of this order would follow immediately, for "*in necessariis*, existentia sequitur immediate possibilitatem; in hoc necessaria different *a contingentibus* [*in necessary things*, existence follows immediately upon possibility; in this, necessary things differ *from contingent ones*]." If we could demonstrate by reason alone that the Trinity is really possible in God (i.e., that it is not intrinsically repugnant *a parte rei*), it would follow that the Trinity exists.[4] However, the only thing that theologians can show is that *nobody can prove* that there is a contradiction in the enunciated dogma of the Trinity.[5]

However, if we are no longer speaking about the intrinsic possibility and existence of *a given* supernatural mystery in particular but, instead, are speaking only *in a general and global way* of the possibility and *the existence of the order of these mysteries in God*, is our reason also powerless?

---

[4]   Thus, Rosmini was condemned for wishing to prove by means of a *reduction ad absurdum* the *intrinsic possibility* of the Trinity and its existence, since the Trinity is necessary and not contingent like the Incarnation. See Decree of the Holy Office, *Post obitum*: "When the mystery of the Most Blessed Trinity has been revealed, its existence can be demonstrated by merely speculative arguments, negative indeed, and indirect; yet such that through them the truth is brought to philosophic studies and the proposition becomes scientific like the rest" (Denzinger, no. 3225). From this position, one arrives at semirationalism—that is, the confusion of the natural and supernatural orders. And, if several semirationalists recognized that one cannot prove the existence of the Incarnation, it is not because, to their eyes, it is *essentially supernatural* but, instead, because it was *contingent*, like the instant of the beginning of the physical world or the hour of its end.

[Tr. note: Concerning Rosmini, more will be said in note 9 of the next chapter.]

[5]   This is why St. Thomas said, *In Boetium de Trinitate*, q. 2, a. 3: "In sacred doctrine, philosophy can be used in three manners: first, to demonstrate those things that are preambles of faith; second, in order to make more known, by way of certain likenesses, things pertaining to faith; and (third), to resist those things *which are said against faith*—whether by showing that they are *false* or *that they are not necessary*."

Also, as the Thomists commonly say, as for example Billuart in *Cursus Theologicus*, *De Trinitate*, diss. proem., a. 4: "Nor also can the *possibility* of this mystery (of the Trinity) be proven by means of natural reason alone. I deny that it can be proven that this mystery does not involve a contradiction *positively* and *evidently*; however, I concede that it can be proven that this mystery does not involve a contradiction *negatively* and *by ways of probable arguments*. Indeed, this suffices so that this mystery not be judged to be impossible, not however that it be known to be *evidently possible*."

Does St. Thomas mean nothing more than this in saying that the existence of the supernatural order *evidentissime apparet* (*Summa contra gentiles* [hereafter, *SCG*], I, ch. 3)?

When St. Thomas, in the passage cited from *SCG* I, ch. 3, writes, "*It is most evidently apparent* that there are *certain truths* (without determining any in particular) *about Divine matters* that *totally exceed* the ability of human reason," does he wish to be content with giving a "reason of mere suitability," as he does much later when it is a question of each of the supernatural mysteries in particular—the mysteries of the Trinity, the Incarnation, and the Beatific Vision?

What is the sense of this *evidentissime apparet*, this "most evidently apparent"?

First of all, never does St. Thomas present "reasons of mere suitability" in this manner. For example, as regards the mystery of the Trinity taken in particular, he says, "Positing that the Trinity exists, reasons of this kind *confirm* (or, agree with) it; *however, this should not be taken as saying* that by means of these reasons *the Trinity of Persons is sufficiently proven*."[6] Here, we are far from *evidentissime apparet*.

Besides, the sense of these very strong words are determined by what follows, by the very nature of the argument proposed by St. Thomas. Let us reread it, weighing out each word and observing that he wishes to show that there are truths in God that surpass not only the natural[7] powers of the human intellect but also those of the angelic intellect—whether created or creatable.

By means of an attentive study of this text, we will see that St. Thomas's proof is taken from something neglected in objections that have been addressed to our position elsewhere. The central matter is that the *formal object of the Divine Intellect* infinitely surpasses *the proper object of every created (or creatable) intellect*. Furthermore, it also follows that what pertains *per se primo* (i.e., essentially and immediately) to this proper formal object of the Divine Intellect is that it cannot be known *naturally* by any created (or creatable) intellect.[8]

---

6 *Summa theologiae* [hereafter, *ST*] I, q. 32, a. 1, ad 2.

7 [Tr. note: The French text reads "surnaturelles," but that does not make sense in context.]

8 In formulating these objections, our interlocutor has not paid attention to the fact that the argument being critiqued is considering *the Deity, not materially ut res est* [i.e., insofar as it is a thing] but, instead, *formally ut obiectum est* [i.e., insofar as it is an object]. This is a distinction that is familiar to every theologian (see Cajetan, *In*

Indeed, if there is a formal object that can constitute a new and wholly transcendent order, it is manifestly that of the Divine Intellect. Just as, above the inorganic kingdom and that of plant life, there appears the animal kingdom with sensation and the formal object of sensation (*non ut res, sed ut obiectum est*), and above these appears the kingdom of man with *the proper object of the human intellect* and, above that, the angelic realm with *the proper object of angelic intellection*; thus, too, the kingdom of God or the supernatural order of truth and life (supernatural for man and angel) appears with *the formal object of the Divine Intellect,* inaccessible to the natural powers of every intellect

---

ST I, q. 1, a. 3, no. 5), and that should not escape the apologist if he wishes to treat with some small profundity the questions that he poses to himself. It goes without saying that we maintain what we have written elsewhere (see *De revelatione*, ch. 2) that apologetics cannot adequately accomplish everything that it ought to do unless it is indeed a reasoning office of theology that, as a form of wisdom, defends its proper principles instead of leaving their defense to some other science. See *ST* I, q. 1, a. 8.

Thus, it is commonly taught in theology that the very God (the very Divine Reality *ut res est*) can be known in a very different manner, *ut obiectum est*. Thus it is that God is known *sub ratione entis* [from the notional perspective of being] by metaphysics, whose formal object is being insofar as it is being. Likewise, God is known *sub ratione Deitatis clare visae* [from the very perspective of the Godhead, clearly seen] by Himself and by the blessed. Likewise, He is known *sub ratione Deitatis obscure revelatae* [from the perspective of the Deity itself obscurely grasped by revelation] by infused faith. The formal motive of infused faith is *revelation formalis* [formal revelation, or "revelation, formally speaking"], and that of sacred theology is *revelation virtualis* [virtual revelation, or revelation considered in the breath of what is contained within the illuminative power of its data and light, illatively drawing conclusions from revealed principles or explicatively defending and meditating upon the revealed principles of theology].

Thus, as is fairly commonly taught, "The formal object *that* is known in sacred theology [obiectum formale *quod* sacrae theologiae] *is God from the perspective of His Deity*; the formal object *by which* [theological knowledge is attained] is divine virtual revelation." For example, see Billuart, *Cursus theologicus*, diss. proem., a. 5. The same point can be found in numerous other Thomists.

By this fact, sacred theology is very superior to natural theology, which is only a part of metaphysics.

Supposing this terminology, which is well known, we have thus formulated the argument that has been critiqued in the following manner: "From created realities, one cannot know in a positive manner *God from the intimate perspective of the Deity*. Now, the natural objective medium of any created intellect cannot be anything other than a created reality. Therefore, from its natural objective medium, no created intellect can, *in a positive manner*, know those things that pertain *immediately* to God *from the perspective of the Deity*: hence, this constitutes a supernatural order of truth."

that has been created or could ever be created. And when we say, "*The proper formal object* of the Divine Intellect," we certainly do not mean the *Divine Essence* as it is known in the mirror of creatures (that is to say, *in an inferior formal object*) as *the hidden root of the Divine Attributes that are naturally knowable,* something spoken of in philosophy. We mean *the Divine Essence* taken in itself, *the Deity as such,* not inasmuch as it is *being, one,* and so on, but inasmuch as it is the *Deity, the intimate life of God.*[9] St. Thomas expresses his point in *Summae theologiae* [hereafter, *ST*] I, q. 1, a. 6:

> Sacred doctrine (above and beyond metaphysics) *most properly determines matters concerning God,* from the perspective of the Highest Cause—not only according to that which is knowable [about Him] by means of created realities, which the philosophers knew, as is said in Romans 1:19: "That which is known about God is manifest in them," but also according to WHAT IS KNOWN BY HIMSELF ALONE ABOUT HIMSELF and by others by means of communicated revelation.

It is clear for the sole reason that the Divine Intellect ought to have a *proper formal object,* and if there is a formal object that can constitute a new and absolutely transcendent order, it is this one. We can naturally know God *sub ratione entis,* as the First Being, the First Truth, the First Goodness, the First Intellect, and so on—for being, truth, and goodness can be *naturally participated* in the created order and, therefore, are naturally known. However, can we *naturally* know God *sub ratione Deitatis,* as God, in His intimate life in what is eminently proper to Him? For this, it would be necessary that the Deity as such could be *naturally participable* in the created order; it would be necessary that one could say of human nature or of angelic nature (whether created or creatable at some higher degree than any other created) that it is a

---

9   As the sense of taste grasps, for example, milk as sweet and not from the perspective of being (*gustus attingit dulce ut dulce non ut ens est*), the philosopher grasps God as being and not as God: *Philosopus attingit Deum, ut ens est et primum ens, non vero ut Deus est, sub intima et propria ratione Deitatis.* Such is the common terminology in theology, and apologetics cannot ignore this distinction.

formal participation in Divine Nature. That is true only by *grace*, which is a participation in the intimate life of God. To say that of a created nature would be to admit, as we will see, to a pantheistic confusion of this created nature (which could not be elevated to a superior order) and God.

Do we not have here the sense of the *evidentissime apparet* of St. Thomas in *SCG* I, ch. 3? Let us read all of this text, emphasizing that which is most formal in it:

> Now, in things pertaining to God, we hold that there is a *twofold manner of truth.* Pertaining to God, *there are some things that exceed all of the ability of human reason*, such as the fact that God is three and one (i.e., strictly supernatural mysteries).[10] *However, there are other things to which even natural reason can reach*, such as that God is, that God is one, and other things of this sort (i.e., natural truths which remain however mysterious due to the *mode* according to which being, unity, goodness, etc., are found in God). Even the philosophers have proven demonstratively these things concerning God, led as they were by the natural light of reason.
>
> Now, *it is most evidently apparent* that there are *certain truths about Divine Matters that totally exceed the ability of human reason.* (This is indeed concerned with the existence in God of the order of supernatural mysteries, taken *in general*, without aiming at any one of them in particular.)
>
> Now, *since the principle of all science*, which reason perceives about anything, is *the understanding of the very essence of that being* (for, according to the doctrine of Aristotle [*Posterior analytics* 2.3] *the principle of demonstration is "that which is,"* i.e., *the essence of the thing*), it is necessary that, according to the manner by which the essence is understood, so too will be the manner of those things that are known concerning that thing. Whence, if the human intellect comprehends the essence of

---

[10] [Tr. note: Throughout, all remarks in parenthesis are those of Fr. Garrigou-Lagrange in the midst of the passage.]

something, e.g., a stone or triangle, *no understanding of that thing* will exceed the ability of human reason.

However, this does not happen for us in the case of God. (This is not only a probable form of reasoning but is a matter certain even by reason alone.) For *the human intellect by its natural power is not able to reach a full grasp of His Very Essence* (i.e., of God) since our intellect, in this present life, knows by beginning with the senses. Therefore, those things that do not fall under the senses cannot be grasped by the human intellect except inasmuch as knowledge of them can be gathered from the senses. However, sensible realities cannot lead our intellect so that *in these the Divine Essence would be seen* ESSENTIALLY (i.e., quidditative knowledge of God *sub ratione Deitatis*) *since sensible things are effects that do not equal the power of their cause.* However, our intellect is led from sensible things to knowledge of God so that it knows *concerning God that He is* and *other such things that ought to be attributed to the First Principle.* (From that, St. Thomas is not content to conclude, "Therefore, the Divine Essence, as the hidden roots of the Divine Attributes that are naturally knowable, remains mysterious." He goes further.) *Therefore, there are some intelligible truths about Divine realities that can be penetrated by human reason*, BUT THERE ARE SOME THAT ENTIRELY EXCEED THE POWER OF HUMAN REASON.

Among these latter sorts of truths, he placed, at the beginning of this selection, "That God is three and one," and he says, "Quod autem *sint aliqua* (without precisely stating any supernatural mystery in particular) intelligibilium divinorum, quae humane rationis *penitus excedant ingenium, evidentissime apparet.*" It is most evidently apparent that there are *certain truths about Divine Matters* that *totally exceed* the ability of human reason.

Is this an argument "from mere suitability," as are those invoked to manifest the truth of the dogma of the Trinity in particular? One sees, on the contrary, by the necessity of the invoked premises,[11] that St. Thomas wishes to provide a demonstrative argument, and this is why he has written, "evidentissime apparet."[12]

The following argument, formulated by St. Thomas in the same location, is even stronger, for it holds (one sees it by the very letter of the argument) not only for the natural power of the human intellect but also for that of the angelic intellect (whether as created or for any creatable angelic nature). Indeed, precisely speaking (and merely to reiterate what we have already stated), this argument is founded upon this fact: the *proper formal object of the Divine Intellect* infinitely surpasses *the proper object* of every human or angelic intellect, and therefore, what pertains *per se primo* (essentially and immediately) to this formal object of the Divine Intellect—that is, *to the Deity as such* (and not to God as the First Being, the First Intellect, naturally knowable)—cannot be naturally known (even obscurely) by any created intelligence. It is the order of the intimate life of God as such.

In fact, St. Thomas continues in the same passage from the *SCG*:

> Now, this same point is easily understood *based on the various grades of intellectual beings*. (It is even an easy thing to understand, at least for those who are wise, est enim *quid per se notum pro sapientibus* quod ea quae pertinent per se et immediate ad obiectum formale et proprium intellectus divini superant omnino vires naturales cuiuslibet intellectus creati; "for it is *something known of itself by the wise* that those things that pertain *per se* and immediately to the formal and proper object of the Divine Intellect entirely exceed the natural powers of any created intellect." St. Thomas shows it easily by what follows.)
>
> Now, consider two people, one of whom understands

---

[11] In order to know all that is intelligible in a thing (*omnia intelligibilia alicuius rei*), it is necessary to attain unto its very essence. Now, the human intellect does not naturally attain unto the Divine Essence as such. Therefore, [the human intellect does not naturally not know all that is intelligible in the Divine Essence]. [Tr. note: The French drops off, as frequently is found in scholastic disputations, indicating something like "Q.E.D." at the end of a mathematical proof.]

[12] See also the commentary of Sylvester of Ferrara that accompanies this text in the Leonine edition.

something with greater intellectual subtlety than does the other person. That person whose intellect is more elevated can understand many things that the other in no way can grasp, just as is obvious in the case of a simple person who in no way is able to grasp the subtle considerations undertaken in philosophy. *However, the intellect of an angel exceeds much more power of the human intellect than does the intellect of the greatest philosopher in comparison with the simplest idiot. . . .* Indeed, the angel knows God *from a more noble effect* than man knows Him (namely, from the angel's own proper essence, which is purely spiritual). *. . . Even more greatly does the power of the Divine Intellect exceed the angelic intellect than does the angelic intellect exceed the power of the human intellect.* For this very Divine Intellect is equal in its capacity to its own substance, and therefore *perfectly knows of it* WHAT IT IS and knows all things that are understandable about it; in contrast, *the angel (at least by means of its natural powers of cognition) does not know about God WHAT HE IS,* because the very substance of the angel, through which it is led into knowledge of God, *is an effect that is unequal to the power of its cause.* Whence, the angel, *by means of its natural knowledge, cannot grasp everything* that God in Himself knows; nor, does human reason suffice for grasping everything that the angel knows by his own natural power.

This argument, like the preceding, rests on premises that are certain and not only probable, and one cannot see in it only a "reason of suitability." It is why St. Thomas wrote at the beginning: "*It is most evidently apparent* that there are *certain truths about Divine Matters* that *totally exceed* the ability of human reason."

Now, the argument that we proposed in *De revelatione*[13] is only a summary of these arguments of St. Thomas. There, we wrote:

From created realities, one cannot, *in a positive manner,* know God *from the intimate perspective of the Deity.*

---

[13]   Garrigou-Lagrange, *De revelatione*, 1:348 (in ch. 11).

Now, the natural objective medium of any created intellect cannot be anything other than *a created reality*.

Therefore, from its natural objective medium, no created intellect can, *in a positive manner*, know those things that pertain *immediately* to God *from the intimate perspective of the Deity*: hence this constitutes a supernatural order of truth.

So that one does not misunderstand the sense of the expression "*immediate* ad Deum sub intima ratione Deitatis," we added in a note, "*Immediate* is the same as *per se primo*, just as man is *per se primo* rational while *per se non primo* he is living (i.e., animal) and *per accidens* is white or has musical abilities."

All of this comes down to the following: That which pertains essentially and immediately to THE PROPER FORMAL OBJECT OF THE DIVINE INTELLECT IS INACCESSIBLE TO THE NATURAL POWERS OF EVERY INTELLECT THAT HAS BEEN CREATED (OR EVER COULD BE CREATED) and, therefore, constitutes the order of supernatural truth. This is said to avoid the risk of a pantheistic confusion of the created intellect and the Uncreated Intellect: *they cannot have the same specifying formal object*. By its natural powers, our intellect cannot attain the formal object of the Divine Intellect (even if it were only in a very vague manner). To do that, it would already be of the same order and it would be necessary to say of our natural intellect what is said of sanctifying grace; namely, that it is a participation in the Divine Nature. From that moment on, the elevation of our intellect to a supernatural order would be impossible. It would already belong to this order by its own nature.

*   *   *

Deus sub ratione Deitatis, this is what St. Paul called "the depths of God" in the famous text in 1 Corinthians (2:9–11):

What no eye has seen, nor ear heard, nor the heart of man conceived, what God has prepared for those who love him, God has revealed to us through the Spirit. For the Spirit searches everything, even the depths of God. For what person knows a man's thoughts except the spirit of the man which is in him? So also no one comprehends the thoughts of God except the Spirit of God.

Just a moment ago, St. Thomas said to us, on the subject of the *existence of the supernatural order* of truth and life in God, "Evidentissime apparet" and "Facile est videre." St. Paul has already said himself at the end of the text that we have cited (1 Cor 2:10–11):

> For the Spirit searches everything, even the depths of God. *For what person knows a man's thoughts* (that is, in his intimate life, in the intimate conversation that each man has with himself) *except the spirit of the man which is in him? So also no one comprehends the thoughts of God* (in his intimate life, in His Deity as such) *except the Spirit of God.*

This is what St. Thomas called, as we have already seen, in *ST* I, q. 1, a. 6, "That which is known concerning God only by Himself and by others by means of revelation."[14]

In his commentary on 1 Corinthians 2:10–12, St. Thomas writes, "However, the *depths of God* are those things that remain hidden and not those which can be known about God by means of creatures, which seem to be only, so to speak, on the surface of God."

If the intimate life of each man is known only to himself and to God, if it is not revealed to others, for all the stronger reason is the intimate life of God known only by Him alone and to those to whom he wishes to reveal Himself. This is not something that is simply probable; it is a certain fact, even to the eyes of reason left to its power alone, at least from the time that the problem is posed.

---

[14]   See also: *SCG* I, ch. 9; II, ch. 4; IV, ch. 1; *ST* I, q. 62, a. 2, etc.

Response to Difficulties

We see, therefore, the answer to the objections formulated against our position.[15] They consider *the Deity* only materially, *ut res est*, not formally, *ut est obiectum* notum "soli Deo et aliis per revelationem."

First objection: "*The mode* according to which a given natural attribute (i.e., a naturally knowable Divine Attribute) exists—Goodness, for example—is also absolutely proper and incommunicable as such: the Divine Goodness, which we know by our reason, is it for all of that of the strictly supernatural order?"

Response: Certainly not, for we know without revelation that it exists in God "formally and eminently," and we know it analogically *by means of participated goodness* without, however, knowing *the mode* according to which it is found eminently in God, founded without any real distinction from the other absolute perfections—wisdom, justice, and so on. On the contrary, in order to know what the *Deity as such* is, we cannot, without revelation, know it analogically by a *participation in it*, for it is not able to be participated in by created natures. It itself is *this inaccessible eminence* in which the *simply simple* perfections that are capable of being participated in naturally are identified without being destroyed. By means of our natural powers, we cannot know *what the Deity is*, nor can we know that which pertains to it *per se primo*, essentially and immediately, as we know that being rational pertains to man. In comparison to the Deity, we are a little like men who have never seen white light but have seen only the seven colors of the rainbow and who know that these seven colors are derived from an eminent source without being able to say what it is.[16]

---

[15] See Corvez, "Est-il possible de démontrer l'existence, en Dieu, d'un ordre de mystères strictement surnaturels?"

[16] There is, however, this difference: the seven colors are in the white light only *virtualiter eminenter*, while the Divine perfections, naturally able to be participated in and naturally knowable, are in the Deity *formaliter eminenter*. Sic Deitas simul est ens et formaliter *super ens* [Thus, the Deity is at once being and formally *above being*]. See Cajetan, *In ST* I, q. 39, a. 1, no. 7: "The divine reality is prior to being and to all of its differentiations: for it is *above being*, and *above one*, etc."

[Tr. note: This will be discussed again below. In words that recall Cajetan's own remarks as recounted by Fr. Garrigou-Lagrange, much light is shed on this point in

In order to understand this better, it is necessary to recall that the *Deity as It is in Itself* (*Deitas sicuti est et clare visa*) contains *actu EXPLICITE* (in act explicitly) the Divine Attributes, while God known as *Subsistent Being Itself* contains them only *actu IMPLICITE* (in act implicitly); indeed, one *deduces* them progressively from the fact that God is Being Itself, and there is, between the Divine Nature thus imperfectly conceived and the Attributes, a *minor distinction of reason*,[17] which, as a distinction, is in no way found in the Divine Reality. Such is the common opinion of the Thomists, and it suffices that one reflect upon it in order to see that such is the case.[18] God is not a *heap of naturally knowable perfections*; He is much more than that.[19]

---

the brief but profound text found in Emmanuel Doronzo, *Introduction to Theology* (Middleburg, VA: Notre Dame Institute Press, 1973), 48: "*Deity* means God considered in his most intimate essence, or according to what makes God to be God and distinguishes him from all creatures. Hence, Deity is something different from and beyond all those divine attributes which are in some way common to creatures, such as being, one, true, good, intelligent, willing, potent, acting, etc. All such attributes are really found in creatures, although in God they are in an infinite manner proper to God, and, in this sense of infinity, they are proper to God. But infinity itself is a negative concept, that is, absence of limit in a positive perfection; hence it cannot be the intimate and proper essence of God. All the other positive attributes of God, as those we just mentioned, are only analogical concepts taken from creatures, and therefore they do not express the proper and inner essence of God. This essence, rather than being, unity, truth, goodness, intelligence, will, power, is *something above being, unity, truth, etc.*, which founds and explains all such attributes in an infinite and simple way. *That something is what we call Deity.*"]

[17]   [Tr. note: On this, the reader will benefit from a careful reading of John of St. Thomas, *The Material Logic of John of St. Thomas: Basic Treatises*, trans. Yves R. Simon, John J. Glanville, and G. Donald Hollenhorst (Chicago: University of Chicago Press, 1955), q. 2, a. 3 (pp. 76–88).]

[18]   See in the Commentators on St. Thomas, at the beginning of the Treatise on God, the classic thesis: "The Divine Attributes are distinguished from one another and from the Divine Essence by means of a *virtual distinction* (or, a *distinctio rationis ratiocinatae minori*) by the mode of implicit and explicit." It is clear that this *distinction of reason* no longer exists in the Beatific Vision, which attains unto God immediately as such and in Himself.

[19]   If that which is formally constitutive of God *as He is in Himself* were not the *Deity*, but instead *Subsistent Existence Itself*, God would be a *heap of ordered perfections*, a sum of ordered perfections. Indeed, as we have just said, God known as Self-Subsistent Being contains the attributes that are deduced from it [i.e., Self-Subsistent Being] only *actu IMPLICITE*; deduction *explains* something with regard to our intellect. On the contrary, the *Deity as It is in Itself*, such as It is seen by God and by the blessed,

While Goodness is *able to be participated in naturally*, the *Deity* as such cannot be. To say that it is would be to admit to the pantheistic confusion of God and a created nature that would be essentially a participation in the Divine Nature and that, if it were endowed with an intellect, would have the same specifying formal object as the Divine Intellect, the same specifying formal object at least obscurely known, as the intellect of the most ignorant man has the same specifying object as the intellect of the greatest philosopher.

Second Objection: The Divine Essence, the object of natural theology,[20] is not, however, a strictly supernatural mystery.

Response: The Divine Essence is known in natural theology not *sub ratione Deitatis*, but *sub ratione entis, in speculo sensibilium*, in an inferior formal object.

To attain in this way unto God from the outside, from the perspective of being (i.e., as the First Being and the First Ordering Intellect), is not also to attain Him in that which is most intimate to Him.

Instance: "And how do I know of *this most intimate* [life], which includes mysteries *of which nature* (i.e., created)—however beautiful that it would be, so beautiful that it could be—*would be incapable of manifesting anything* to any created or creatable intellect?"

Response: "This most intimate" is *the proper formal object of the Divine Intellect*, which infinitely surpasses the proper object of every created or creatable intellect. It is the Deity as such, which cannot be naturally participated in. If it were participated in by a greatly elevated angelic nature, this nature would be endowed with a natural intellect having the same formal object as the Uncreated Intellect. Thenceforth, this angel will not be able to be elevated to a supernatural order

---

contains the Divine Attributes *actu EXPLICITE*, without the least real distinction (i.e., anterior to our mind's consideration).

[20] [Tr. note: I have replaced "theodicy" with "natural theology." Fr. Garrigou-Lagrange maintained the vocabulary of the curriculum of his time, derived in many ways from the Leibnizian/Wolffian classification of the philosophical disciplines. However, against what some have asserted, he *was not* a partisan of this classification's actual ordering of philosophical disciplines. He maintains only the names, not the realities signified by them. See Réginald Garrigou-Lagrange, "Dans Quel Ordre Proposer Les Sciences Philosophiques," *Revue thomiste* 40 (1924): 18–34.]

[because it was already supposedly supernatural by the very object of its intellect].[21]

Without a doubt, this appears to us much more clearly after revelation, but even without revelation, philosophers can know that God, whom they attain as the *First Being*, has an *intimate life*, which we cannot naturally know. Therefore, this intimate life of God, *as such*, constitutes a highly elevated order of knowledge, an order of inaccessible mysteries. And, in this, there would be only one mystery: the formal constitution of the Deity such as It is in Itself, *sicuti est* (and not as known in an inferior formal object). This would suffice, and to be elevated to know it would require being elevated to an absolutely superior order of truth and life, inaccessible to the natural powers of every created or creatable intellect.

Last objection: "However one argues concerning the intimate life of God, this life does not necessarily entail supernatural mysteries. If it exists in God, what we know solely by faith is (as theology says to us) that '*such things do not pertain to the order of the Divine Essence*, but to *that of the Persons*, which is not engaged in creation since the creative power of God is common to the whole Trinity'" (*ST* I, q. 32, a. 1).

Response: The Deity as such (or, the intimate life of God) includes in Itself a *unity* that is absolutely eminent, inaccessible to reason, that precisely subsists in spite of the Trinity of Persons. It includes also an *infinite fecundity ad intra*. This fecundity is manifested to us without a doubt by the Trinity of Persons, but the Father begets not by free will but by His Nature: "Filius est genitus ex natura vel substantia Patris."

Let us not forget either that sanctifying grace is a participation in the Divine Nature and not of the Divine Persons.

Thus, it remains necessary to maintain, without attenuating the matter, what St. Thomas has written in *SCG* I, ch. 3: "Quod qutem sint *aliqua* intelligibilium divinorum, quae humanae rationis *penitus excedant* ingenium, *evidentissime apparet.*" In other words, there are in the Deity—the *formal object* of the Divine Intellect, infinitely supe-

---

[21] This angel could be elevated only to the order of the Hypostatic Union, about which we are not here concerned; and even it would not be *its person* that would be elevated to it.

rior to the proper object of every created intellect—*intelligible truths, inaccessible to every created intellect* (i.e., supernatural mysteries). We cannot, without revelation, know the least of them or name a single one of them, but they are there. Otherwise, there would be between the proper object of the Divine Intellect and that of the created intellect only the difference of the obscure in comparison to the clear (or, that of the vague [*confus*] in contrast to the distinct), like that which exists between the knowledge had by the least cultivated man and that had by the greatest philosopher. The distance between the greatest philosopher and that of the least of angels is even greater. And therefore, the difference is incomparably greater yet when it pertains to the formal object of the Divine Intellect, as well as what pertains to it *per se primo* (i.e., essentially and immediately): "Multo amplius intellectus divinus excedit angelicum, quam angelicus humanum" (*SCG* I, ch. 3).

There is an abyss between, on the one hand, knowing the existence of the Deity *in speculo sensibilium* [in the mirror of sensible things] (in an inferior formal object) as the hidden roots of the Divine Perfections that can be participated in naturally and can be known naturally and, on the other hand, knowing the Deity as God alone knows It naturally and as He alone can make It known to other intellects by means of a supernatural revelation.

In that latter case, one knows God "not only according to that which is knowable about Him by means of created realities but *also according to that which is known by Himself alone about Himself, and by others by means of communicated revelation.*"[22] There is already a great distance between knowing the Sovereign Pontiff externally, by what all the world can know, and knowing the secrets of his intimate life. All the more does this hold if the matter pertains to the intimate life of God— not only of his free acts but also of His Divine Nature inasmuch as it is Divine (i.e., of the Deity as such), of that which St. Paul calls τα βάθη του Θεού, "The depths of God."

---

[22] *ST* I, q. 1, a. 6.

Chapter 2

Can the Possibility of the Beatific Vision Be Demonstrated?

W E HAVE SEEN THAT THE EXISTENCE of the order of supernatural truth is rigorously demonstrable. Is it necessary to say the same about the possibility of the Beatific Vision?

After having identified, on this particular subject, a number of studies, of which we have taken account, a question has been posed to us in an article in the *Bulletin thomiste*:[1] why, after having admitted the *demonstrability of the existence of a supernatural order of truth and life in God*, do we not admit also *the demonstrability of the possibility of the Beatific Vision*.[2]

We have explained our perspective on this point at length in a work soon to be released in a new edition, and in it, we have explained and defended the position generally adopted by Thomists.[3]

As we said in the preceding chapter, the proof of the existence in God of *a supernatural order of truth and life* comes down to saying that the *formal object* of the Divine Intellect (i.e., the Deity) infinitely sur-

---

[1] See A. R. Motte, O.P., "Désire naturel et béatitude surnaturelle," *Bulletin thomiste* 3 (1932): 651–75.

[2] "How," one says to us, "has Fr. Garrigou-Lagrange not seen the connection of the two theses? The argument that he gives against the second, if it held, would also hold against the first" (ibid.). See Réginald Garrigou-Lagrange, *Le réalisme du principe de finalité* (Paris: Desclée de Brouwer, 1932), 275n2.

[3] See *De revelatione per Ecclesiam catholicam proposita*, 3rd ed. (Rome: Ferrari, 1931), 1:ch. 12. [Tr. note: A translation of this work is anticipated in a future volume by Emmaus Academic.]

passes the *proper object* of every created or creatable intellect, which cannot naturally know God except in the mirror of created things and which, therefore, cannot know the *intimate life of God* (i.e., *the Deity*), which cannot be participated in by a created nature, no matter how perfect it might be. In this created nature, there is a participation in being, truth, good, intellect, and will; however, there is not a *participation in the Divine Nature* (i.e., in the *Deity*). Otherwise, its definition would be identified with that of sanctifying grace, and one would thus be led to the pantheistic confusion of created nature with the nature of God.

This point has been very clearly acknowledged in the review in the *Bulletin thomiste* of which we have spoken. The reviewer, Fr. A. R. Motte, O.P., has perfectly understood what, in our eyes, is the very teaching of St. Thomas. He expresses the matter well in saying:

> Here, it concerns *an order* of mysteries or, if one prefers, the singular mystery of the Divine Being in its Deity. Now, this mystery escapes (in its essence)[4] every manifestation by way of creation, the world necessarily being incapable of expressing its *quid est*, its essence. Therefore, it is indeed a supernatural mystery in the strictest sense, as naturally impenetrable as the particular mysteries that it envelops. It is differentiated from these latter mysteries with regard to our capacities for knowledge insofar as its *existence* can be recognized, while theirs cannot. (Indeed, one conceives, we say, that there *exists* in God an intimate life, and a formal object of His intellect, which are *naturally unknowable* for every created intellect, having as it does an inferior proper object.) . . .
>
> *The matter is entirely different with regard to the particular mysteries*; without being more supernatural in their essence, in order for their existence to be known, they presuppose certain particular determinations that no longer have a necessary relation with our idea of the First Cause as does the idea of the Deity *ut sic* [as such]. The mysteries are totally hidden

---

4   [Tr. note: The remarks in parentheses are Fr. Garrigou-Lagrange's.]

in the mystery of God, whereas this latter (all while necessarily concealing its content from us) at least allows itself to be recognized from the outside [i.e., "externally," as it were] as a reality.[5]

Such is, well expressed, the position that we have always defended as being the very doctrine of St. Thomas, in particular in *Summa contra gentiles* [hereafter, *SCG*] I, ch. 3. However, what follows from it?

The Nature of the Problem

From this doctrine, is it now necessary to deduce that *the possibility of the Beatific Vision* can be rigorously *demonstrated*? It is astonishing that we have not seen the connection between these two theses!

We respond (and it is the teaching generally received among Thomists): The Beatific Vision (i.e., eternal life) *is a particular mystery of the Creed*, like that of the Holy Trinity and the Redemptive Incarnation. Therefore, the recognized thesis that has just been explained and that precisely distinguishes the mystery of God and the particular mysteries, far from leading us to admit the demonstrability of the possibility of the Beatific Vision, wholly removes this conclusion.

In the preceding thesis, one was concerned only with the existence of the *order* of supernatural mysteries *in general*, without determining any in particular. Having proven the existence of AN ORDER OF NATURALLY UNKNOWABLE MYSTERIES, it does not follow in any way that the possibility of any one of them (e.g., eternal life) would be NATURALLY DEMONSTRABLE. Moreover, the contrary must be concluded.

Now, with regard to a particular mystery, that of the Beatific Vision, which is nothing other than the mystery of eternal life, St. Thomas says the following in *Summa theologiae* [hereafter, *ST*] I-II, q. 114, a. 2:

---

5   Motte, "Désire," 650.

Eternal life is a particular good exceeding the measure of created nature, for it even exceeds its *knowledge* and its *desire*, as is said in 1 Cor 2:9: "Neither has eye seen, nor ear heard, nor has it arisen in the heart of man. . ."

The same can be seen in *In* 1 *Cor* 2, lec. 2; *In* 2 *Cor* 5, lec. 2; *In* III *Sent.* d. 23, q. 1, a. 4, sol. 3, and d. 33, q. 1, a. 2, sol. 3; and *De veritate*, q. 22, a. 7, and q. 14, a. 2. Indeed, in the last, we read:

The other [final good] is the good exceeding the measure of human nature, for natural powers do not suffice for its attainment, neither in *knowledge* nor in *desire*.

One sees that this formula is frequent in the works of St. Thomas, in his last ones as much as in his earliest works. And he applies it not only to man but also to the angels, for he says in his exposition of his definitive opinion on the necessity of grace for the angels in *ST* I, q. 62, a. 2:

As was shown above (cf. *ST* I, q. 12, aa. 4 and 5) when God's cognition was discussed, *to see God through His essence* (in which consists the ultimate beatitude of a rational creature) is above the nature of any created intellect. Whence, *no rational creature can have a movement of will ordered to that beatitude unless it is moved by a supernatural agent*; and this movement we call the help of grace. Therefore, it must be said that the angel can only be converted by his will to that beatitude through the help of grace.

And in the response to the first objection to the same article:

To the first objection, it must be said that an angel naturally loves God inasmuch as God is the principle of his natural being. However, here we are speaking about turning to God *inasmuch as God is beatifying* by vision of His Essence.

In his commentary on *SCG* III, ch. 51, Sylvester of Ferrara insists on this same distinction.

Here, it is no longer a matter of knowing whether there is in God an order of naturally unknowable mysteries. We are wondering whether the Deity, which in Its Essence is naturally unknowable, CAN BE SUPERNATURALLY KNOWN—not if It in fact will be known, but if It *can be*.

We are wondering if, while exceeding the proper object of every created intellect, the Deity (or, God seen face to face) exceeds the adequate object of the created intellect. We are wondering if this adequate object is not only *being* insofar as it is being (the object of metaphysics) known *in speculo creato* but also being according to all of its extent, *ens secundum totam latitudenem entis*, of such a sort that nothing escapes it, not even the intimate life of God, immediately visible. We are asking if a created intellect (whether angelic or human) *can be elevated* to the immediate vision of the Divine Essence, whether it can be elevated to see God as He sees Himself, without the intermediary of any creature, with no created mirror (whether sensible or spiritual).

This mystery is *supernatural* not only like the miracle, which is supernatural only *quoad modum productionis suae* [with regard to the mode of its production] but, instead, is ESSENTIALLY supernatural, *quoad substantiam vel essentiam*. While the resurrection of Lazarus supernaturally gave him *natural life*, eternal life (or, the Beatific Vision) is *essentially* supernatural. It is a formal participation in the intimate life of God. There is an abyss between these two forms of the supernatural.

What follows from this? Everyone grants that, if it concerns the *existence* of this particular mystery, one cannot know it without revelation since it is a contingent matter depending uniquely upon the free will of God, who could or could not elevate us to the supernatural life of grace and of glory.

However, on account of this *contingency*, according to St. Thomas (see *ST* I, q. 46, a. 2), revelation is also necessary to let us know that the physical world began (as well as when it began and when it will come to an end).

When it is a matter concerning eternal life, it is not only a question of a contingent fact depending upon the good pleasure of God; it is a matter concerning *a mystery that is essentially supernatural,* like the Trinity and the Incarnation.

Now, is its possibility rigorously demonstrable?

Certainly, one can give (along with St. Thomas) excellent and strong reasons why it is fitting. Indeed, since we naturally know that there exists a First Cause, we have an inefficacious and conditional *natural desire to see this First Cause.* On the other hand, since we know not only the nature of sensible things but also *universal being,* there is, in this fact, *a sign* that the *adequate object* of our intellect exceeds its proper object (see *ST* I, q. 12, a. 1, and a. 4, ad 3).[6]

---

6   [Tr. note: On these points, a summary statement from Fr. Garrigou-Lagrange's student Fr. Austin Woodbury is likely helpful. See Austin Woodbury, *Natural Philosophy: Treatise 3, Psychology,* The John N. Deely and Anthony F. Russell Collection, Latimer Family Library, St. Vincent College, Latrobe, PA, no. 920 : "The proper object of the human intellect, in state of union with the body, is the quiddity or 'nature existing in corporeal matter' of a thing represented by an image of the imagination, but as it is universal"; ibid., no. 904:

> The adequate object of [the] human intellect is at least material being and whatsoever other being according as it has analogical community therewith. For a power that apprehends essences is a power that knows things under the reason or character of being, as said above (no. 895C); for essence and being are convertible; for being is nothing else than essence having being [i.e., existence] (actually or potentially). But [the] human intellect, as said above (nos. 646–48; nos. 650–51; no. 889; no. 895), apprehends the essences of things.
>
> But the reason why [the] human intellect apprehends the essences of things is: that the human intellect receives forms immaterially: not as they are the forms of this individual matter, but as they are forms; and therefore receives forms immaterially: not merely as that whereby something manifests itself exteriorly—as sense receives forms—but as they are determinative of the quiddity of a thing, as said above (no. 648; no. 889Ad2b).
>
> But from this, that our intellect knows things under the reason or character of being, it follows that our intellect is cognoscitive of whatsoever has the character or reason of being at least according as it is manifestable whether immediately or mediately by the formal reason whereunder our intellect understands. But the formal reason whereunder our intellect naturally understands is that degree of immateriality that is immateriality through abstraction from individual matter, as said above (nos. 653–56).
>
> But: what is immediately manifested by this degree of immateriality is the entity of material things (see nos. 653–56), as will be shown more copiously in the following chapter; *while mediately manifested by this degree of immateriality are other beings according as they have (at least analogical community with material beings).* Therefore, our intellect is cognoscitive of material being

However, can one thus *rigorously* demonstrate the possibility of the Beatific Vision or *the possibility of our elevation* to this Vision?

First and foremost, that which is supernatural with regard to its very essence is also supernatural with regard to its very knowability. As is commonly said by the Thomists, "Quod est supernaturale quoad essentiam est supernaturale quoad cognoscibilitatem quia verum et ens convertuntur."

When it was a matter of the *order* of supernatural mysteries *taken in general*, we were able to prove its existence, for it was only a matter of proving the existence of an order that is INACCESSIBLE in itself, in its essence, *to our natural knowledge*. Thus, we reached it only NEGA- TIVELY in proving that it exists.

Here, it is a matter of saying POSITIVELY whether the Beatific Vision is possible. It is a matter of knowing whether its intrinsic pos- sibility is demonstrable solely by reason, supposing at least that the question has been posed as a result of Divine Revelation.

*   *   *

Reason already sees that this vision is possible only by means of a *supernatural elevation*—and by "supernatural," I mean not merely *quoad modum* (as would be a miracle) but QUOAD ESSENTIAM.[7]

Is this supernatural elevation that we attribute to grace and glory possible? There certainly exists in us an *obediential potency* or *apti-*

---

and of whatsoever else has the reason or character of being at least according as it has analogical community with material being. (Emphasis added.)

Strictly speaking, the adequate object includes the proper and common objects of the intellect, the latter including in itself the mediate and extensive objects. The mediate object is whatever is manifested mediately by the proper object. The exten- sive object is "that towards which the power is only not repugnant by virtue of its order towards its proper object (i.e., by virtue of its nature)." See ibid., no. 902 for a schematic summary. Woodbury's complete treatment deserves consultation by the interested reader.]

[7]   [Tr. note: That is, formally supernatural and not merely supernatural as regards the mode of production or the mode of ordination to a supernatural end. This will be discussed at greater length below in ch. 4: "Miracles and Grace—Two Very Different Forms of the Supernatural."]

tude to receive everything that it pleases God to accord to us, and the Divine Power is limited only by contradiction or repugnance to existence. *Is the essentially supernatural gift* (of whatever name one might give it: grace or the light of glory), which is necessary for our elevation to immediate vision of the Divine Essence, possible? Is it not intrinsically repugnant? In other terms, is a formal participation in the Divine Nature (i.e., the intimate life of God) possible? In order to respond concerning the possibility of the Beatific Vision, we absolutely must resolve this question, for *one cannot demonstrate the possibility of the end* (i.e., the Beatific Vision) if one cannot know *the possibility of the indispensable means*. It is not a matter of knowing whether God *wishes* to give us such means. Instead, it is a matter of knowing whether or not such means are possible.

Certainly, as we have already said, there are arguments of suitability for responding affirmatively. Moreover, theology establishes that no *intellect can prove the impossibility of grace* or of the light of glory, and by that fact, one can demonstrate *negatively* the possibility of such things. That is to say, one can show that nobody can definitively establish that there is a contradiction in this mystery.

However, can theology prove its possibility *positively*? In no way can it do so, for it concerns the intrinsic possibility of something *supernatural by its very essence* (and, therefore, by its very knowability): *quod est supernaturale quoad essentiam est supernaturale quoad cognoscibilitatem, quia verum et ens convertuntur.*[8]

---

[8]   Such is the common teaching of theologians concerning the supernatural mysteries taken each one in particular. They agree in saying, for example, on the subject of the Trinity: "I deny that it can be proven that this mystery does not involve a contradiction *positively* and *evidently*; however, I concede that it can be proven that this mystery does not involve a contradiction *negatively* and *by ways of probable arguments*. Indeed, it suffices that this mystery not be judged to be impossible, not however that it be known to be *evidently possible*."

See (for example) Billuart, *de Trinit.*, diss. proem., a. 4. Also, St. Thomas says in *Boetium de Trinitate*, q. 2, a. 3: "In sacred doctrine, we can use philosophy . . . in order . . . to resist those things *which are said against faith*, either by showing them to be *false* or by showing them *not to be necessary*."

*   *   *

However, can one rigorously prove, at least in an *indirect manner*, the possibility of the Beatific Vision by consideration, not of the grace to receive it, but of our conditional, inefficacious desire to see the First Cause in Himself?

Even in an *indirect* manner, we cannot rigorously demonstrate the possibility of supernatural mysteries, each taken in particular. Rosmini was condemned[9] for having claimed to have demonstrated *indirectly* the possibility of the Trinity.[10] It would follow furthermore, concerning the Trinity, that, if one could demonstrate its possibility even in an indirect manner, one could demonstrate additionally its existence, for its existence is *not contingent* but necessary—*in necessariis autem existentia sequitur immediate possibilitatem; in hoc necessaria different a contingentibus.*

As regards other supernatural mysteries, like the Incarnation and eternal life, they are naturally unknowable for us—not only because of their *contingence* (like the day of the end of the physical world or the day upon which it began) but also due to their *essential supernaturality*. And, from this point of view, no more than for the Trinity, one cannot rigorously demonstrate the possibility of such mysteries, even by means of an indirect argument or by a *reductio ad absurdum*.[11] The proofs that one can give in these matters are excellent proofs of suitability, very profound proofs even, but they are not rigorously demonstrative.

---

9   [Tr. note: Bl. Antonio Rosmini-Serbati (1797–1855) had his work *Delle Cinque Piaghe della Santa Chiesa* placed on the index during his lifetime. After his death, forty propositions taken from his works were condemned. He was later rehabilitated and beatified for his heroic virtue in 2007. Details on his rehabilitation should be interpreted in light of the 2001 decree by then-Cardinal Ratzinger, "Note on the Force of the Doctrinal Decrees concerning the Thought and Work of Fr. Antonio Rosmini Serbati," promulgated July 1, 2001. *Rosmini* was rehabilitated, not the conclusions that might be drawn from his works by those who are not careful.]

10   See Denzinger, no. 3225.

11   On the contrary, whatever many contemporary philosophers may say about it, one can demonstrate that the denial of the principle of causality implies contradiction.

The Common Solution of Thomists

To reject this position does not mean only that one must distance oneself from what Cajetan has said on *ST* I, q. 12, a. 1 (an interpretation that was defended just a few years ago by Fr. Del Prado).[12] To reject this position means that one must distance oneself from the greater part of Thomists, who more generally follow the interpretation of Sylvester of Ferrara, who appears to us, as we have said elsewhere, to be best [concerning this matter].[13]

Sylvester of Ferrara writes:

> By our natural powers, we desire the vision of God inasmuch as it is a *vision of the First Cause*, not inasmuch as it is a vision of the object of supernatural beatitude. For, by our natural powers, it can be known that God is the cause of other things; however, we do not naturally know that He is the object of supernatural beatitude.[14]

One does not see Sylvester of Ferrara claiming to demonstrate rigorously, by the existence of this desire to *see the First Cause*, the possibility of the absolutely immediate vision of the Divine Essence. Here we find a very important argument from suitability but not a demonstration.

Bañez, who gives precision to the nature of this desire by saying that it is conditional and inefficacious, writes on *ST* I, q. 12, a. 1:

> To the fourth conclusion, §3: With regard to the testimony of St. Thomas from this article where he says, "Now, there is in man, etc. [i.e., a natural desire for knowing a cause when he knows an effect],". . . we respond that he is not speaking here of an absolute desire but of a conditioned one. Whence, *this reasoning does not demonstrate it to be possible*, for it is an article of faith.

---

[12] See Norbert del Prado, *De veritate fundamentali philosophiae christianae* (Fribourg, CH: Ex Typis Consociationis Sancti Pauli, 1911), 581–639.

[13] Garrigou-Lagrange, *De revelatione*, 1:395 (ch. 11, no. 4).

[14] Sylvester of Ferrara, *In contra gentes* III, ch. 51. [Tr. note: *Contra gentes* is the common variant of the time for *SCG*.]

John of St. Thomas, writing on *ST* I, q. 12, a. 1, also insists on the conditional character of this inefficacious desire. He says, on this article, in disp. 12, a. 3, no. 12:

> A simple or *inefficacious* desire only regards the absolute *goodness* of an object *without an order toward the pursuit of it* (and *a fortiori* toward knowledge of it); for, we desire and will many goods that we judge to be impossible, like wishing never to die and other such things.

It is clear that God cannot be seen without supernatural assistance. It is also naturally certain *that it would be good to see God*. From this arises the conditional and inefficacious natural desire. Inasmuch as this desire is *natural*, instead of something solely fanciful, we have here a serious argument from suitability, one that even is very profound. However, inasmuch as this desire is *conditional* and *inefficacious*, the possibility of the Beatific Vision is not rigorously demonstrated. It would certainly be very good for us to see God, if He can and wants to elevate us to this Vision. *Is grace*, something essentially necessary to this elevation, *possible?* We cannot demonstrate it. It is only very probable, as it is very probable that our intellect, being wholly spiritual (i.e., immaterial), can be informed even by the highest intelligible, which is God seen face to face. And nobody can prove the contrary.

It is very probable that the *Divine Essence, known immediately and supernaturally*, does not surpass the adequate object of our intellect[15] and that this formal object therefore tremendously surpasses *being insofar as it is being*, known *in speculo sensibilium* and the object of metaphysics. However, this cannot be demonstrated, for the Divine Essence, immediately known (i.e., the intimate life of God), is of an essentially supernatural order.

We can naturally know that the Divine Essence exists as an object

---

[15] [Tr. note: See the text (Woodbury, *Natural Philosophy: Treatise 3, Psychology*) and comments above in note 6. In particular, pay heed to the discussion of *nonrepugnance* at the end of the note. The importance of this point will be increasingly evident as Fr. Garrigou-Lagrange discusses the Thomist position on obediential potency in contradistinction from the Suarezian position.]

that is *naturally unknowable* in its essence; however, we cannot demonstrate that it *can be supernaturally known* by us as it is in Itself. One sometimes has given, following St. Thomas, demonstrations presupposing one premise from faith, but such is not our concern here.

*   *   *

This teaching is exposited with clarity by the Salmanticenses, Gonet, Gotti, Billuart, and many others who see in this teaching the teaching of St. Thomas himself and the teaching of the best Thomists.

The Salmanticenses, in their discussion concerning *ST* I, q. 12, a. 1, tract. 2, disp. 1, dub. 3, expressly pose the question "whether the possibility of the vision of God through His essence can be known evidently by a created intellect by the light of nature." They respond, in contrast to Gonzales and Vasquez, in no. 39:

> The natural light of reason, considered essentially and precisely according to its own nature, cannot know or demonstrate in a clearly evident manner that the vision of God through His Essence is possible for a created intellect. This assertion is plainly clear from what St. Thomas says in *ST* I-II, q. 109 a. 1; Cajetan, Francisco Zumel, and Machin follow, as well as others among Thomists in the present such as Sylvester Mazzolini in his *Conflatus* I, q. 12, a. 1, Medina and Martinez on *ST* I-II, q. 5, a. 1, Alvarez in his twenty-eigth disputation, and Suarez in the second section of his thirtieth metaphysical disputation. Others could be listed as well.
>
> Now, the reason for this position is as follows. *Vision of God* as He is in Himself *is something that is supernatural in an essential manner* [*secundum suam substantiam supernaturalis*]. . . . However, a created thing that is supernatural in an essential manner has neither a cause nor an effect in the natural order.
>
> (In addition,) the possibility of an end cannot be demonstrated if the possibility of the means cannot be known in an evident manner, for *an end is not sought, except through the means*. . . . However, the means needed for knowing the afore-

mentioned Vision (namely, grace, faith, hope, charity, etc.) are supernatural things that to the same degree also exceed the capacity of the natural light of reason.

(Ibid., no. 47):

By the natural light of reason, it is not evident that the adequate object of the intellect is *being inasmuch as it abstracts*[16] *from the natural or the supernatural*. Whence, he who asserts that the object of the intellect is only natural being cannot be convinced of the falsity of this position in a manner wholly evident by means of the power of the natural light of reason.

*   *   *

Likewise, Jean Baptiste Gonet in his *Clypeus theologiae thomisticae*, on *ST* I, q. 12, disp. 1, a. 4, §1:

It is certain and doubtless in everyone's view that the *existence* (or futurition) of the Beatific Vision cannot be demonstrated by the natural light of reason, for since it is something that is not owed to the intellectual creature [i.e., to its own created nature] and is something immediately *depending only on the will of God*, it is therefore able to be known certainly by revelation. Also, it is certain that one cannot exhibit the *impossibility* of the Beatific Vision. . . .

Now, what is constantly tossed about in controversy is *whether this possibility* can be demonstrated in an evident manner by the natural light of reason. For, Scotus (in treating IV *Sent.*, d. 49, q. 8) and Gabriel Vasquez (in his treatment of *ST* I-II, disp. 20, ch. 2, *partem affirmativam*) hold that it can be. However, others deny it. We are in their company.

I say: *The possibility of the vision of God, as He is in Himself,*

---

16 [Tr. note: It is implied that this would be a kind of imperfect abstraction like that involved in the analogy of proper proportionality.]

cannot be demonstrated by the natural light of reason alone; nor can it be known in an evident manner. . . . This conclusion is proven based upon *ST* I-II, q. 109, a. 1. . . .

Supernatural things, are called supernatural inasmuch as they exceed the entire order of nature. However, they would not so transcend the entire order of nature if they had a necessary connection with the effects of nature (a point that is obvious of itself.) Therefore, [if something has a necessary connection with the effects of nature, such a thing is natural, not supernatural.][17]

Now, this is confirmed [in the following manner]. . . . The possibility of the end cannot be demonstrated unless the possibility of the means can be known in an evident manner because the end is not sought except insofar as it is sought through the means. However, the possibility of the means leading to the clear vision of God (which without a doubt are grace, faith, hope, and charity) cannot be known in an evident manner solely by the natural light of reason; for since these things are supernatural things, they exceed the capacity of the natural light of reason. Therefore, nor can the possibility of Beatific Vision be shown by the natural light of reason.[18]

*   *   *

In the eighteenth century, Vincenzo Ludovico Gotti, in his *Theologia scholastico-dogmatica, De Deo*, q. 1, *De Possibilitate visionis Dei* [Concerning the possibility of vision of God], dub. 3, §1 (on *ST* I, q. 12, a. 1), examines the same question: "Whether by means of natural reason it can be known that the vision of God is possible?" He responds like the preceding Thomists:

---

[17] [Tr. note: In a style that becomes rather regular from the fourteenth century onward, the text just drops off, stating "therefore," which implies, "You draw the conclusion."]

[18] See also Gonet's solution to the objections taken from Scotus and Vasquez. [Tr. note: For this location in Gonet's text, the Paris edition of 1875, published by Vivès, the sections are marked with §, but Fr. Garrigou-Lagrange's text abbreviates them as "chapters" within the given article.]

First of all, I say: One cannot demonstrate solely by the natural light of reason that the clear vision of God is possible. Now, this is proven as follows. Because the natural light of reason can show us only that which is natural, as well as that which has a connection with natural effects. However, the vision of God inasmuch as it is utterly supernatural has no connection with natural effects because something is called supernatural when it is above the whole of nature, as well as above all the demands of nature. Therefore, [one cannot demonstrate, by the natural light of reason alone, the possibility of the Beatific Vision]. Again, St. Thomas bears witness to this in his remarks in *ST* I-II, q. 109, a. 1. . . .

Now, it is naturally evident that an abstractive[19] knowledge of God is contained within the scope of the created intellect's object; however, *God as clearly seen* is not so contained. This is so because, as such, inasmuch as it is a supernatural object, it exceeds the powers of the natural light of reason. And although by the light of nature it is certain that being, abstracting from God and creatures, is the (adequate) object of the intellect, it is not evidently certain, however, that a created intellect can attain God clearly and intuitively, and not only abstractively.

Nor can an angel, even though it wholly comprehends the scope of the human intellect, naturally *know that it can be elevated to the Beatific Vision* and, hence, that this is even possible. For the angel does indeed comprehend the natural power of the human intellect and it knows all the acts that it can naturally elicit; however, it does not comprehend its *obediential potency* or the acts to which it can be elevated. Therefore, it cannot know *certainly* such a possible vision of God. *Obediential potency is ontologically* [*entitative*] *natural,* nay, rather, it is the intellect's very nature; *however, it is terminatively* [i.e., *as regards the terminus of its potency*] *supernatural* and therefore its terminus cannot be known by the powers of nature. (This

---

[19] [Tr. note: Concerning the important distinction between abstractive and intuitive cognition, see note 31 below.]

pertains to the obediential potency that is presupposed for elevation to the order of grace and of glory and not the obediential potency presupposed for a miracle, for it is certain that reason alone can demonstrate the possibility of a miracle.)[20]

(Gotti continues:) *Secondly, I say: It can be shown, in a way, by the powers of nature that the vision of God is not impossible*—either by offering reasons that show its suitability or probability (even though they are not demonstrative), or by responding to the arguments that can be made against its possibility. . . . (Thus,) the reasons that St. Thomas expresses in *Summa contra gentiles* III, ch. 50, are indeed *very probable* and are *effective ad hominem* (as they say) against the Gentile philosophers, against whom he is arguing in this book, because they are taken from principles admitted by them; . . . however, they are not demonstrative arguments.

For, we can doubt whether, just as, on account of His very excess of intelligibility, God cannot be adequately and comprehensively known by any creature, so too, He cannot be known *quidditatively* unless, from another source, faith shows the manner by which His infinite quiddity is united in a *finite manner* to a created intellect.

Also, the second reason offered (i.e., taken from the desire of seeing the cause, having already seen and known the effect, which is vain and frustrated if knowledge [lit., *visio*] of the cause is not possible) is not demonstrative, for, since such a natural desire, as we say, is neither efficacious nor absolute but, instead, inefficacious and conditioned, the aforementioned reason does not prove in an evident manner that knowledge of the cause is possible absolutely but, instead, only that it is suitably and probably the case. For, since this desire is very suitable to nature, and as it is found in many, it is very suitable that it not be frustrated, and therefore *with great suitability, one proves the possibility of the thing desired.*

---

[20] [Tr. note: The parenthesis is Fr. Garrigou-Lagrange.]

*   *   *

Therefore, Billuart is the faithful echo of the Thomists who preceded him when, in expressly posing the very same question in *De Deo*, diss. 4, a. 3, appendix,[21] he writes, twenty years after Gotti:

> *Intuitive vision of God is utterly supernatural, not only ontologically speaking but also as regards truth and knowability;* . . . it has no connection with a natural cause or effect.
>
> When we say that there is in man a natural desire of seeing God after we have seen His effects, . . . we are speaking about an appetite elicited from previous knowledge[22]—not, indeed, absolutely and efficaciously, . . . but only conditioned and inefficaciously (*"if only it could come about, inasmuch as it is possible"*). From such a desire for the Beatific Vision, since it can (absolutely speaking) be frustrated, one cannot demonstratively prove the possibility of the Beatific Vision but can only do so with probability and can persuade morally regarding it.

The Value of the Thomists' Common Solution

A preliminary remark will illuminate this matter.

It can seem very simple to say, *"Man naturally desires to see God, whom he knows to be the First Cause of the universe."* However, this affirmation, so simple in appearance, poses very great problems.

It has not been noted enough that, in the thought of St. Thomas, the question of the natural desire to see God has much resemblance

---

[21] [Tr. note: Article 3 addresses the question "whether the intellect that is supernaturally aided can see God as He is in Himself?" This appendix to article 3 then addresses this subsidiary question of "whether the possibility of the Beatific Vision can be demonstrated or known by the natural light of reason alone?"]

[22] [Tr. note: A thorough understanding concerning the distinction between natural and elicited appetites is one major component for understanding these matters aright. See Robert Sullivan, *Man's Thirst for Good* (Westminster, MD: Newman Press, 1952). Also, we will discuss below in a footnote the excellent work by Lawrence Feingold on closely related matters.]

to that of the universal salvific will of God, about which St. Thomas speaks in *ST* I, q. 19, a. 6, ad 1. In the two cases, it pertains to an act of *will* called *antecedent* and not *consequent and efficacious*. God wills, in a certain way, that all men may be saved. However, in fact, all men have not been saved (though He wishes with an efficacious and consequent will the salvation of the elect, who are infallibly saved without their freedom being violated at all). Likewise, man naturally desires to see God, but it does not follow at all that he will in fact arrive at seeing Him.

The two problems, which are illuminated in light of the same principles, can appear at first to be very simple if one only considers them superficially. However, a more attentive view permits one to glimpse their depths and what in them is difficult to express, whence comes the necessity of the multiple distinctions that rightly have been made by Thomistic theologians in order to avoid every error here. These distinctions can appear too complicated. However, it is very difficult for discursive reason to dispense with them, and they are well within the normal scope of that which St. Thomas says about the *antecedent will* in *ST* I, q. 19, a. 6, ad 1:

> To understand this matter, it must be considered that everything insofar as it is *good* is thus *willed* by God. However, something can be *in the first consideration of that thing*, according to which it is absolutely considered to be *good* or bad; or however, *it can be considered with something added to it* (which is a consequent consideration of it) and, then, it may be changed to the contrary. . . .
>
> Thus, God antecedently wills that all men be saved; however, He consequently wills that some are damned on account of the demand of His justice. However, we do not, without qualification, *will that which we will antecedently,* but instead will it *in a qualified sense,* for the will is compared to things according to what is in the things themselves; however, in themselves, there are particularities. Whence, *we simply will* something inasmuch as we will that thing considered in all of its particularized circumstances—and this is to *will consequently.* Whence, it can be said that the just judge *in an unqualified*

sense wills the hanging of a murderer, though he *wills in a qualified sense* for the man to live, namely inasmuch as he is a man. Whence, such a thing can be better called a willingness [lit., *velleitas*] than an absolute will. And thus it is obvious that whatever God wills without qualification, He does; however, that which He antecedently wills, He does not do.

Since all men are not, in fact, saved, it is necessary to say that *God* wills *to save all* not in an absolute and efficacious way, but in a conditional and inefficacious way. However, this Will is the principle of sufficient graces, which render the accomplishment of the precepts truly possible for all adults.

Likewise, man naturally *desires to see God*, whom he knows to be the First Cause of the universe. However, man also sees that he cannot, by his natural powers, attain to this vision. Therefore, his natural desire is not absolute and efficacious, but only conditional and inefficacious: *If God wishes gratuitously to elevate to this vision, to the order of grace* that is immensely superior to that of human nature or even to that of angelic nature.

Furthermore, the desired thing (one cannot think enough upon this point) *is of a supernaturality far superior to that of a miracle.*

We are familiarized with the expression "to see God immediately," and we forget the essentially supernatural elevation of that Vision. A good number of those who have written recently on this question forget that it pertains to a Vision whose supernaturality is *very superior* to that, for example, of the resurrection of the dead. If it pertained only to the desire for corporeal resurrection, one could demonstrate the possibility of the thing, for miracles are supernatural only in their cause and in their manner of production. However, they are naturally knowable as regards their existence and possibility.

The immediate vision of the Divine Essence, like *the grace and the light of glory* that alone render such Vision possible, is *essentially and intrinsically* supernatural in its very being, and therefore, neither its existence nor its possibility are naturally demonstrable.

The arguments invoked in favor of this possibility are those about which St. Thomas wrote in *SCG* I, ch. 8:

Human reason is related *to knowledge of a truth of faith* (e.g., eternal life), which can be known only by those who see the Divine Essence, such that it can collect together certain true likenesses of such a truth; however, these *do not suffice so that the aforementioned truth may be comprehended by being known in a quasi-demonstrative* or per se manner. However, it is useful for the human mind to exercise itself in making these sorts of reasons, even though they be weak, *so long as there is no pre-sumption of demonstrating* or comprehending them; for, to be able to have some insight concerning the highest things, even by a small and weak consideration of them, is a cause of the greatest joy.[23]

Again, in *ST* I–II, q. 109, a. 1, he writes:

The human intellect cannot know higher intelligibles (to knowledge of which we cannot arrive by way of sensible real-ities), unless it is perfected by a more powerful light, such as the light of faith or of prophecy, which is called *the light of grace* inasmuch as it is added to nature—"Eye has not seen, nor has ear heard, nor has it arisen in the heart of man, what God has prepared for those who love him" (1 Cor 2:9).

---

[23] [Tr. note: The remark is taken from a famed passage in Aristotle's *Parts of Animals* 1.5.644b22–645a4: "Of substances constituted by nature some are ungenerated, imperishable, and eternal, while others are subject to generation and decay. The former are excellent and divine, but less accessible to knowledge. The evidence that might throw light on them, and on the problems which we long to solve respecting them, is furnished but scantily by sensation; whereas respecting perishable plants and animals we have abundant information, living as we do in their midst, and ample data may be collected concerning all their various kinds, if only we are willing to take sufficient pains. Both departments, however, have their special charm. The scanty con-ceptions to which we can attain of celestial things give us, from their excellence, more pleasure than all our knowledge of the world in which we live; just as a half glimpse of persons that we love is more delightful than an accurate view of other things, whatever their number and dimensions. On the other hand in certitude and in completeness our knowledge of terrestrial things has the advantage. Moreover, their greater nearness and affinity to us balances somewhat the loftier interest of the heavenly things that are the objects of the higher philosophy"; trans. W. Ogle in *The Complete Works of Aristotle*, vol. 1, ed. W. D. Ross (Princeton, NJ: Princeton University Press, 1995)].

In order to summarize in a few words the Thomists' common position, let us say:

[Major:] That which is substantially supernatural is also supernatural with regard to its knowability, for truth and being are converted.[24]

[Minor:] Now, the Beatific Vision is substantially supernatural.

[Conclusion:] Therefore, the Beatific Vision is supernatural with regard to its knowability; hence, its possibility cannot be demonstrated by the sole light of reason.

Recent works on this subject have not destroyed this argument; many of them have even failed to examine it.

If one were to demonstrate positively the possibility of a supernatural mystery: in the case in which its existence is *necessary* (e.g., the Trinity), one would demonstrate it as well; or, in the case in which its existence is *contingent*, it would be indemonstrable by reason of its contingence (like future contingents in the natural order) but not by reason of its essential supernaturality.

This position, very exactly taken by the Thomists whom we have cited, is founded upon the elementary truths of theology, truths that appear more profound as one meditates upon them for a long time. We first studied this position thirty-five years ago, and after [we have] often returned to it many times, it always appears to us to be better founded.

Before beginning to revise this thesis, it would be necessary that one be very certain not to misconceive its foundations, and it would be necessary that one grasp the doctrine of St. Thomas better than the Thomists of whom we have spoken. To flatter oneself that one

---

[24] This major premise does not contradict in any way the preceding thesis that proves the existence in God of a supernatural order, for that thesis proves it precisely as the existence of *an order of truths inaccessible to our natural knowledge*. And among these truths there is that which concerns eternal life (i.e., the Beatific Vision).

has penetrated it better may perhaps not be lacking in presumption.[25]

To our eyes, it would not be a form of progress were one to revise

---

[25] The revision of the Thomist positions relative to the distinction of nature and grace could lead us much further than we think and could begin a period of decline in a moment above all when, from diverse quarters, there is reported a decline in speculative studies, despite the abundance of publications. The most opposed of these are sustained with equal assurance, and often the questions become more confused the more that they progress. It is not without concern, for example, that one sees a certain number of professors of philosophy and theology sustain today that the denial of the principle of causality does not imply a contradiction. They do not even realize that, in supporting this position, they deny the ontological necessity and the demonstrative value of the traditional proofs for the existence of God. It is a position obviously very far from that which supports the possibility of rigorously demonstrating by reason alone the possibility of the Beatific Vision; however, it could nonetheless very well be that certain minds, under the influence of the philosophy of action, admit at one and the same time these positions, which are so different from one another.

To deny that the natural desire to see God is *conditional* would lead one to say with Baius that it is *absolute* and *efficacious*.

[Tr. note: He refers here to Michael Baius (1513–1589), the Leuven theologian whose work on Augustine met with condemnation. The aforementioned philosophy of action above all hints at the works of Maurice Blondel (1861–1949), who was very influential in certain Catholic philosophical and apologetic circles. He was not of small influence on Cardinal Henri de Lubac (1896–1991), whose positions on the natural desire to see God were posed as an explicit challenge to the position espoused by Garrigou-Lagrange. When reading his annotation of letters he exchanged with Étienne Gilson, one can sense De Lubac's continued anger at what he perceived to be aggressions by Garrigou-Lagrange. See *Letters of Étienne Gilson to Henri de Lubac*, ed. Henri de Lubac, trans. Mary Emily Hamilton (San Francisco: Ignatius Press, 1988), 91–126.

There are remarks made by Cardinal De Lubac that require careful contrast to other sources concerning Fr. Garrigou-Lagrange's character. It is far from clear that the history that is commonly presented regarding him is fair. It has been common to speak ill of him. However, one can merely cite the words of Maritain, who himself had his own falling out with Garrigou-Lagrange. See Jacques Maritain, *Notebooks*, trans. Joseph W. Evans (Albany, NY: Magi Books, 1984), 168–69: "I transcribe my notes of 1937 without attenuating anything in them; I insist only on remarking that our differences in political matters never diminished the affection and the gratitude which Raissa and I had for him. (And he for his part, even when he found fault with me, did what he could to defend me.) This great theologian, who was little versed in the things of the world, had an admirably candid heart, which God finally purified by a long and very painful physical trial, a cross of complete annihilation, which, according to the testimony of the faithful friend who assisted him in his last days, he had expected and which he accepted in advance. I pray to him now with the saints in Heaven." On Garrigou-Lagrange's character, see also, Richard Peddicord, *The Sacred Monster of Thomism: An Introduction to the Life and Legacy of Reginald Garrigou-Lagrange*, O.P. (South Bend, IN: St. Augustine's Press, 2005), 24–53.]

this position. It would be a regression, a regrettable confusion that would bring about confusion concerning the very notion of *supernatural mysteries*, whose essential supernaturality is very superior to that of a naturally knowable miracle.[26] Now, this distinction, which is at once elementary and fundamental in theology, is in part misunderstood today by those who hold that, *without the grace of faith*, a miracle is not discernable with certitude. At the same time, there is something quite paradoxical—namely, that many of them hold at the same time that the possibility of the Beatific Vision is naturally demonstrable.

For our part, we defend the inverse of this. Miracles are naturally discernable. The [First] Vatican Council is clear on the matter:

> If anyone says, . . . *that miracles can never be recognized with certainty* and that the divine origin of the Christian religion cannot be *legitimately proven* by them, let him be anathema.[27]

> However, in order that the obedience of our faith be nevertheless in harmony with reason [cf. Rom 12:1], God willed that exterior proofs of his revelation, viz., divine facts especially *miracles* and prophecies, should be joined to the interior helps of the Holy Spirit; as they *manifestly display* the omnipotence and infinite knowledge of God, they are the most certain signs of the Divine Revelation, adapted to the intelligence of all men.[28]

On the contrary, concerning the possibility of each essentially supernatural mystery, even that of the Beatific Vision, it is necessary to say with the same Council:

> For divine mysteries by their very nature so *exceed the created intellect* that, even when they have been communicated in rev-

---

[26] We have shown the consequences elsewhere. See Garrigou-Lagrange, *De Revelatione*, 1: chs. 5, 6, 11, and 12. See also Garrigou-Lagrange, *Réalisme du principe de finalité*, pt. 2, ch. 7.

[27] First Vatican Council, *Dei Filius*, can. 3.4 (Denzinger, no. 3034).

[28] Ibid., ch. 3 (Denzinger, no. 3009).

elation and received by faith, they remain covered by the veil of faith itself and shrouded, as it were, in darkness as long as in this mortal life "we are away from the Lord; for we walk by faith, not by sight" [2 Cor 5:6–7].[29]

If anyone says that in Divine Revelation no true and properly so called mysteries are contained but that all dogmas of faith can be understood and demonstrated from natural principles by reason, if it is properly trained, let him be anathema.[30]

The mystery of eternal life (i.e., the Beatific Vision) is not only indemonstrable as regards its existence (like the case of a simple future contingent of the natural order); it surpasses our intellect not only by its contingency but also by ITS ESSENTIAL SUPERNATURALITY. And therefore, its intrinsic possibility cannot be rigorously demonstrated.

If there is not in this position the presumption of demonstrating [*praesumptio demonstrandi*] that St. Thomas points out, there is also no "fearful minimalism." On the contrary, what we speak of is a very certain affirmation of the transcendence of every essentially supernatural mystery. It is the opposite position that leads one to minimize the supernatural and that seems to fear it; such a position has lost the sense of mystery.

Thus, we firmly maintain, with all the Thomists whom we have cited, that the possibility of the mystery of the Beatific Vision (or, of eternal life) is not rigorously demonstrable.

*   *   *

One understands very well that St. Thomas, in *ST* I, q. 12, a. 1, says that *to deny* the possibility of the Beatific Vision would be *praeter rationem*, contrary to reason. Indeed, nobody can prove that it is impossible.

However, the argument given in the same text to show that it is possible would be absolutely rigorous only if *intuitive knowledge* (and

---

[29] Ibid, ch. 4 (Denzinger, no. 3016).
[30] Ibid, can. 4 (Denzinger, no. 3041).

not abstractive knowledge)[31] *of the essence* of the First Cause were *necessary* for explaining the natural effects of this Supreme Cause.

Now, this is not the case, for these effects of the natural order are not a participation in the Divine Nature, in the Deity (as is the case for sanctifying grace). Instead, God produces them by His Intellect and Will according to the Divine Ideas.[32] Therefore, in order to know things in the natural order by their Supreme Cause, it is *indeed* necessary, without a doubt, to *know* that God, the First Being, is also the First Intellect and the First Will. However, it is not necessary to *see* the Divine Essence.

However, our abstractive knowledge of God allows many obscurities to remain, particularly those concerning the intimate reconciliation of certain Divine Attributes or the reconciliation of their acts. How is it that the free creative act is not something contingent in God, which [it] could not be, and is reconciled with the absolute necessity of God, to whom one can add no accident, *cui nulla potest fieri additio*? How is it that the Divine permission of physical and moral evil (sometimes ever so great) is reconciled with His Supreme Goodness and with His All-Powerfulness? Also, how is Infinite Mercy reconciled with Infinite Justice?

---

[31] [Tr. note: The distinction between intuitive and abstractive cognition was at best inchoate in the works of St. Thomas. By the time of Bl. Duns Scotus, it begins to play a pivotal role, one that would have significant outcomes in all of the *scholae* of the later Middle Ages and beyond, especially in nominalism. According to the position accepted by Fr. Garrigou-Lagrange, the distinction between abstractive and intuitive cognition can be simply understood as pertaining to the distinction between knowing something without or with the physical presence of that which is known. It is one thing to know intellectually a tree's essence; it is another for a tree to be present *here and now*. Intuitive cognition adds no quidditative note to what is known, only attention to the existential presence of what is known. In our current state, such presence is known only through our senses. Indeed, this is what makes the external sense powers unique—namely, that they form no expressed concepts, something that *is* required for the imagination, memory, estimative/cogitative power, and intellect. Thus, short of the Beatific Vision (which is possible only with the light of glory elevating our intellects), we have no *strictly intuitive knowledge of God*. For the Thomist position on these matters, see John of St. Thomas, *The Material Logic of John of St. Thomas: Basic Treatises*, trans. Yves R. Simon, John J. Glanville, and G. Donald Hollenhorst (Chicago: University of Chicago Press, 1955), q. 23, a. 1 (pp. 405–21).]

[32] See *ST* I, q. 14, a. 8; q. 15; q. 19, aa. 3 and 4.

Because of the obscurities that abstractive knowledge of God allows to remain, for the angel as for man,[33] there is born the conditional desire: "Nevertheless, if I could see God, immediately as He sees Himself! If I could see the intimate reconciliation of the divine perfections in the Deity, what happiness that would be for me! What beatitude, if God elevated me to such a Vision!"

From the fact that this natural desire exists, it is *very likely* that this Vision is possible. However, given that this desire is conditional, it does not follow that God wishes to elevate us to this Vision, and it is not even *rigorously* demonstrated that *He can do it*. Indeed, a question remains: Is the *essential supernatural* assistance, absolutely and manifestly necessary for this Vision, possible? Such assistance would need to be *a formal participation in the intimate life of God*, of the Deity. Is this formal participation possible? We cannot demonstrate this by reason alone, for reason is incapable of knowing positively *this intimate life of God*. Reason knows only that it surpasses the proper object of every created intellect and that it constitutes the proper object of the Divine Intellect.

Therefore, although it seems to many people evident and certain that there is not an impossibility from our side of things, it is not certain that this impossibility does not exist as regards the indispensable means for this Vision and from the perspective of God Himself. Even if it were evident that an essentially supernatural grace is possible, would it be rationally certain that God can be seen without the intermediary of any created idea? Can He, without imperfection, play the role of the *species impressa* and the *species expressa*?[34] Can reason, by its

---

[33] [Tr. note: Hence, we can see here that "abstractive" cognition does not primarily deal with the human need to "abstract" from sensual and perceptive knowledge. Instead, it is about physical presence and absence in the act of knowledge. Even the *natural* angelic knowledge of God lacks this direct physical presence. There is an infinite gulf between this knowledge and the angel's experience of the Beatific Vision.]

[34] [Tr. note: Note well his qualifying words "plays the role." See Garrigou-Lagrange, *The One God*, trans. Bede Rose (St. Louis, MO: B. Herder, 1946), 340–41: "St. Thomas's conclusion is: God's essence cannot be seen by any created likeness representing the divine essence in itself as it really is. All the disciples of St. Thomas unhesitatingly accept this conclusion, saying that there can be no question either of an impressed or expressed species in the clear vision of God. Or else they say that, according to the imperfect way we conceive it and speak of it, the divine essence takes the place of both the impressed and the expressed species. This terminology is interpreted in a

power alone, respond to this question? Does there not remain a doubt on this point: perhaps a *created idea* is needed? And if so, would God be seen truly *as He is in Himself*? Can a created idea, no matter how perfect one may suppose it to be, express that He is in Himself Him who is Pure Act, Being Itself, Intellection Itself, an Eternally Subsistent, Pure Intellectual Flash of Light? Finally, can the *Infinite* be seen *modo finito* [in a finite matter] by a vision that is immediate without being comprehensive?

There are many other very difficult problems, almost as many as those relative to the possibility of the Incarnation: Can God, without imperfection, *immediately terminate* our vision in the order of knowledge, and can the Word of God, without imperfection, *immediately terminate* an individuated human nature?[35]

Now, one commonly admits that the possibility of the Incarnation is indemonstrable. Nobody can, with certainty, demonstrate that the Incarnation is impossible, but the reasons that we give for its possibility are only reasons of suitability. Let us recognize that, in this order, they are very strong, above all this one that St. Thomas himself gives in *ST* III, q. 1, a. 1:

> It pertains to the nature of the good that it communicate itself to others. . . . Whence, it pertains to the nature of the Highest Good that it communicate Itself in the highest manner to the creature, which indeed was maximally done by this, namely that He thus conjoined to Himself the created nature so that one person is made up of these three (the Word, soul, and body), as St. Augustine says in *De Trinitate* 13.17. Whence it is obvious that it was fitting for God to be incarnate.

---

benign sense by the Thomists, but it is faulty; for the impressed and expressed species take, so to speak, the place of the object, as representing it. And therefore to say that the divine essence takes the place of the species, is to say that it acts as substitute for the same. However, this terminology is permissible according to our imperfect mode of conceiving it, just as we say that God enters into logical relations with creatures."]

[35] The philosopher and the apologist scarcely ask themselves these questions, but they are familiar to the theologian. Now, those who hold that one can rigorously demonstrate the possibility of the Beatific Vision are more often among the philosophers than among the theologians—and this problem is properly in the domain of theology.

Although suitability is more than simple possibility, the possibility of the Incarnation is not rigorously demonstrated by this profound reasoning, no more than the possibility of the Trinity is rigorously demonstrated by this very excellent principle enunciated by St. Thomas in *ST* I, q. 27, a. 1, ad 2 (see *SCG* IV, ch. 11):

> That which proceeds internally (*ad intra*) by way of intelligible procession, does not need to be different from that from which it proceeds; nay, rather, the more perfectly it proceeds, the more it is one with that from which it proceeds. . . . Whence, since the Divine Understanding is utterly perfect, it is necessary that the Divine Word be perfectly one with Him from Whom He proceeds without any difference in Nature.

Here, we are faced with sublime reasons of suitability, extremely profound ones, more than can be put into words, but they are not demonstrations. They are, I do not say demonstrations, but an evidence of another order—that which the inscribed polygon (of which one forever multiplies the sides) is to the circumference [of the circle in which it is inscribed]. At the limit, the polygon is identified with the circle, but the limit is to infinity.

One will never succeed at multiplying the sides of the polygon as much as is possible. Likewise, *reason can never succeed at deepening these reasons of suitability as much as is possible*, but the more it does deepen them, the more it sees that it cannot transform them into a demonstration. (It is thus even for the angels, even for the loftiest of angels.)

Why is this so? It is so because that which is *at the limit* is not a rational demonstration; it is something far superior: It is the supernatural Vision—either of the Trinity, of the Incarnation, or of that which formally constitutes eternal life.

And therefore, as paradoxical as it may at first appear, those who hold that these reasons of suitability are demonstrative reasoning grasp neither their elevation well enough nor at what height is found the mystery of which they speak. To say that they are demonstrative is to diminish them in this sense; it is to say that they are of our domain and our scope, when, in fact, *they pass far higher* but according to the mode of probability, the only one that is possible in these superior regions.[36] This is why St. Thomas says to us, "To be able to have *some insight concerning the highest things, even by a small and weak consideration of them,* is a cause of the greatest joy."[37] This is what the semi-rationalism that seeks to demonstrate the mysteries has not understood.

These reasons of suitability are less than rational demonstrations from the point of view of their *mode of knowledge* (i.e., that of their certitude and rigor), but they are superior to demonstrations if one considers the *elevation of their object*. Indeed, they tend to make us conceive a truth that escapes demonstration, not because it is below what is demonstrable but because it is *above what is demonstrable*—infinitely above it. These reasons of suitability are, in the act of faith, the object of the *cogitation* about which is spoken in the classic definition: to believe is to think with assent. As St. Thomas explains the matter in *De veritate*, q. 14, a. 1:

> In scientific thought, cogitation leads to assent, and the assent brings reasoning to a rest. However, in faith assent and cogitation are quasi-equals. For *assent is not caused by the cogitation but by the will.* However, because the intellect is not in this way terminated at one thing so that it is led to its own proper term (which is vision of something intelligible), it therefore happens that *its movement is not yet quieted* but has cogitation and inquiry about the given thing that it believes, although it does most firmly assent to it. For inasmuch as the intellect *is considered in itself*, it is not satisfied, nor is it terminated at one thing but is only terminated in an extrinsic manner.[38] And thence it is that the intellect of the believer is said to be *captive, for it is bound by alien terms and not by its own.*

---

[36] And if one forces them to descend from this essentially supernatural domain, where they penetrate only by way of probability, *what will remain* in this superior domain for manifesting in a certain way the suitability of essentially supernatural mysteries? Here, we touch upon an extremely interesting question concerning the frontiers of the highest metaphysics and theology.

[37] *SCG* I, ch. 8.

[38] [Tr. note: I.e., by the will's role in the assent of faith.]

Thus, the possibility of eternal life is a truth that is *above all demonstration*, superior to the demonstrative power of a created intellect, whether it be angelic or human. When we consider this proposition, "Eternal life is possible," our mind remains in *cogitatio*; it finds the most elevated of reasons of suitability, which, thanks to the mode of probability, *exceed* the sphere of the demonstrable. The *cogitatio* does not succeed at *seeing* with certitude that the predicate of this proposition agrees with its subject, for the latter expresses a reality that is supernatural in its essence and, therefore, also in its knowability—*verum et ens convertuntur*. And therefore, as we believe in the existence of eternal life, we also believe in its possibility. We do not know it. We are in a domain superior to that of demonstration. In this sense, to wish to make reasons of suitability into demonstrative reasoning would be to diminish them and to lose sight of the grandeur to which their very serious probability manages to elevate itself.[39]

---

[39] Let us remark on this subject that one notices rather often among many contemporary theologians a double form of inadvertence. Many say that we prove the noncontradiction of supernatural mysteries. However, we show only by the solution to difficulties that one cannot demonstrate that there is a contradiction in supernatural mysteries. However, their nonrepugnance (or their intrinsic possibility) *nec probatur, nec improbatur, sed suadetur* [is neither proven nor disproven; it is suggested persuasively]. Secondly, many also by inadvertence speak as though the mysteries of eternal life or that of the Incarnation escape demonstration only on account of their contingence and not by their essential supernaturality.

Chapter 3

The Eminence of the Deity, Its Attributes, and the Divine Persons

O NE OF THE CULMINATING POINTS of St. Thomas's doctrine about which Cajetan's commentary very well shows the elevation and radiance is that which concerns the Deity and its relations with the proper object of theology: the Divine Attributes, the Divine Persons, sanctifying grace, and even the profound problem of predestination. To recall Cajetan's teaching concerning these diverse matters permits us to glimpse the synthesis that was formed little by little in this great mind, which was able to express an original work, though he wished only to be a commentator on St. Thomas so as to defend the *Summa theologiae* against the multiple and repeated attacks made against it.

The Deity and the Proper Object of Theology

The Thomists generally teach that the formal, specifying object of theology is God from the perspective [*sous la raison*] of the Deity (*sub ratione Deitatis*) inasmuch as He can be known by *virtual revelation*. In this way, theology differs from the part of metaphysics that is called "natural theology,"[1] which is concerned with God from the perspective of being (*sub ratione non Deitatis sed entis*), known by the light of

---

[1] [Tr. note: See note 20 in the first chapter of section II, which cites Réginald Garrigou-Lagrange, "Dans Quel Ordre Proposer Les Sciences Philosophiques," *Revue thomiste* 40 (1924): 18–34.]

reason. Theology also differs from the theological virtue of faith, which is concerned with God in His Deity (or, in His intimate life) known not only by the light of virtual revelation but also by formal revelation.[2]

This teaching, commonly received by the Thomists, comes in large part from the precisions brought about by Cajetan for the sake of explaining and defending the first question of St. Thomas's *Summa theologiae* [hereafter, *ST*]. What he has written on this subject shows forth all of the elevation of this teaching.

The holy Doctor had said in *ST* I, q. 1, a. 6, "Sacred doctrine *most properly* determines matters concerning God, . . . not only according to that which is knowable [about Him] by means of creatures, which the philosophers knew, . . . but also *as regards what is known by Himself alone about Himself* and by others by means of communicated revelation." Also, he states in *ST* I, q. 1, a. 7: "God is the subject of this science." Likewise, see his response to the first objection to this same article.

In nos. 4–10 of his commentary on *ST* I, q. 1, a. 3, Cajetan uses this fact to show well the unity of theology. He notes that the unity and diversity of sciences depends upon the unity and diversity of the *formal reason of their object, as an object.* Thus, natural philosophy treats *mobile being* (i.e., according to the first degree of abstraction), mathematics treats being from the perspective of *quantity* (i.e., according to the second degree of abstraction), and metaphysics of *being inasmuch as it is being* (i.e., according to the third degree of abstraction, *ab omni materia*, under the natural light of the intellect). Theology treats of God from the perspective of the *Deity*, known in the light of Divine Revelation.

However, Cajetan adds, the revealing Divine light, which alone

---

[2]   For example, see Jean Baptiste Gonet, *Clypeus theologiae thomisticae*, vol. 1, disp. procem. (*De natura et qualitatibus theologiae*), a. 3, no. 22: "I say that the formal and specifying object of Theology is God, from the perspective of the Deity, as He falls under virtual revelation. Thus, the very Deity is the *ratio formalis quae*; however Divine Revelation that is virtual and mediate is the *ratio formalis sub qua*. However, the extensive and terminative material object is whatever might be revealed by God. Nearly everyone now agrees about this claim."

Likewise, see Charles René Billuart, *Cursus theolog.*, diss. proem., a. 5. We have exposited this doctrine at length elsewhere. See Garrigou-Lagrange, *De revelatione per Ecclesiam catholicam proposita*, 3rd ed. (Rome: Ferrari, 1931), 1:6–28 [Tr. note: A translation of this work is anticipated in a future volume by Emmaus Academic].

can make the Deity (i.e., the intimate life of God) known positively, is multiple. It can give *evidence of the Deity*; thus, it specifies the Beatific Vision. Likewise, it could *reveal God only obscurely*, as it specifies infused faith. Likewise, it could *abstract from evidence and lack thereof*; thus, it specifies our theology, which exists in an imperfect state and without evidence here below and in a perfect state in the blessed who have evident knowledge [*ont l'évidence*] of supernatural truths.[3]

One better grasps the sense and scope of this teaching by considering the explication given by Cajetan on *ST* I, q. 1, a. 7, concerning this proposition of St. Thomas: "God is the subject of this science (namely, sacred theology)":

> Notice each term in the title to his question. The term "subject" stands for the formal subject, and the term "God" is to be taken in a formal sense, i.e., *inasmuch as He is God*. . . . And to maintain the integrity of this doctrine, you must penetrate what this *"inasmuch as he is God"* conveys, using the declaration made by Scotus on this question (cf. Prol. *Sent.*, q. 3), namely how man can be understood in four ways: (1) quidditatively, inasmuch as he is man; (2) as a substance, and so he is conceived of *in communi*; (3) as naturally tame, and so he is conceived *per accidens*; . . . (4) as the noblest of animals, and thus he is conceived *in relation to something else*.
>
> So, in the aforementioned proposition, proceeding in reverse order, God can be considered as: (4) the Highest Cause . . . and thus is considered *in relation to something extrinsic*; (3) He can also be considered as wise, good, just, and universally according to notions that can be attributed of Him, and thus He is considered *quasi per accidens*; (2) He can also be considered *as being, act*, etc., and thus He is considered *in communi*. And to these three modes that are quasi-simple are reduced composite considerations such as *pure act, first being*, etc. For, in such things, God is considered as He stands under a *common concept*, as well as *relative* or *negative* ones, as is obvious.

---

[3]   See Cajetan, *In ST* I, q. 1, a. 2, nos. 10–12.

However, before all of these modes, God can be considered *according to His own quiddity*, for, according to the order of nature, this is the first notion of all and is the foundation of the others: and we circumlocute [*circumloquimur*] around this quiddity by means of the name DEITY.

In this very place, Cajetan shows well that, when St. Thomas teaches that the formal subject of theology is God, he means to say: God inasmuch as He is God, *not only from the perspective of first being, or pure act, or supreme goodness, but from the perspective of the Deity in its most proper depths*, God in that which constitutes His intimate life.

If someone objects that the theologian cannot, however, say here below what God is (*quid sit Deus*), we must respond with St. Thomas[4] that the theologian does not see what God is, but he knows imperfectly what God is by means of what God has obscurely revealed concerning His intimate life in the mystery of the Trinity, as well as in regard to the fact that He is not only the Author of nature but also the *Author of grace*, which is a participation in the *Deity*. Here, we enter into a superior order, one that is properly Divine, that of the Kingdom of God—of God conceived as not only the Author of created natures (e.g., human or angelic) but also as *Father*, as the Author of grace.

In light of this fact, we can see the elevation of theology, though it remains inferior to the faith from which it proceeds here below, as well as to the Spirit's gifts of understanding and wisdom that enable us to penetrate and to savor the principles of faith, which theology analyzes conceptually and from which it deduces its conclusions.

Theology considerably surpasses even the loftiest metaphysics. The latter considers first and foremost creatures and knows God only by way of the reflection of His perfections found in this created mirror. That is, metaphysics knows God by the perfections that are *analogically and evidently*[5] common to the Creator and His works: being, unity, truth, goodness, intelligence, love, and so on. On the contrary, *theology*

---

[4]   See *ST* I, q. 1, a. 7, ad 1.

[5]   There are other analogies that are not naturally obvious [or, evident], such as those of paternity, filiation, and spiration, which God could use to reveal the secret of His intimate life—the mystery of the Trinity. Metaphysics does not know these things.

considers God first and foremost; and it does so according to what is most intimate in Him—namely, *according to the Deity*, in the eminence of Which *are identified* all the perfections that are analogically common to Him and to creatures. However, theology considers these attributes as expressions of His intimate life,[6] which is above all manifested by the revelation of the mystery of the Trinity, on which depend the mysteries of the Incarnation of the Word and the Mission of the sanctifying Holy Spirit. Thus, there is an immense difference between knowing God only in an external manner [as one does in metaphysics] and, to use an expression of St. Paul, knowing obscurely "the depths of God" (1 Cor 2:10)—just as there is a great difference between knowing a man externally and knowing the secrets of his heart.

It follows from this that *the Deity* (or, the intimate life of God), which is the proper object of the Divine Intellect, is inaccessible to every intellect that has been created or ever could be created. It manifestly constitutes *an essentially supernatural order* of knowledge, and *none* of the mysteries of this order can be naturally known, nor can they be demonstrated, even after revelation has been made.

Cajetan even insists on this point so much when commenting on *ST* I, q. 12, a. 1, that he appears to deny even the conditional and inefficacious *natural desire* of seeing God immediately.[7] In any case, he certainly does not admit that one can demonstrate positively by reason alone the possibility of eternal life, nor that of sanctifying grace or of the light of glory that would be necessary for the Beatific Vision. All of those matters are of a sphere that surpasses rational demonstration; it is of an incomparably more elevated order—that of the formal object of the Divine Intellect, superior to the proper object of every intellect that has been created or ever could be created.[8]

---

6 Thus, it treats of Providence not merely in the natural order but in that of grace. Thus, theology speaks *expressly* of Predestination.

7 [Tr. note: This text in Cajetan has recently received attention in the excellent work of Lawrence Feingold on this question: *The Natural Desire to See God According to St. Thomas and His Interpreters*, 2nd ed. (Naples, FL: Sapientia Press, 2010), esp. 167–82.]

8 See Cajetan, *In ST* I, q. 12, a. 4.

The Deity and the Divine Attributes

Theologians have often debated concerning the nature of the distinction existing between the Divine Nature and the Divine Attributes. Nominalists have wished to see here only a verbal distinction, like that between Tully and Cicero. It would follow, then, that the Divine Justice and the Divine Mercy would be synonyms and that one could indifferently employ one or the other of these expressions, saying, for example, that God punishes by His Mercy and pardons by His Justice—something that cannot be upheld. On the other hand, Duns Scotus holds that there is between the Divine Nature and Divine Attributes (as well as among these latter) a *distinction* that is not only virtual but *formal and actual*. To that, the great majority of theologians, in admitting the virtual distinction, respond: A formal and actual distinction would be *anterior to our intellect's consideration*; it would be a *real distinction* contrary to the Divine Simplicity, for there is in God a real distinction only in the case of the Divine Persons on account of their opposition of relation, in virtue of the principle that was very clearly expressed by the Council of Florence: "These three Persons are one God, not three gods, because there is one substance of the three, one essence, one nature, one Godhead, one immensity, one eternity, and everything [in them] *is* one where there is no opposition of relationship."[9]

On this point, like the preceding one, Cajetan expresses his habitual precision, showing very justly how one must understand St. Thomas. The Common Doctor had written, in *ST* I q. 13, a. 5:

> When the term "wise" is said of man, we signify a certain perfection that is *distinct* from man's essence, as well as his power, his existence, and other such things. However, when we say this name of God, we do not intend to signify *something distinct* from His essence, power, or existence. And thus, when the word "wise" is said of man, in a certain sense it circum-

---

9   Council of Florence, *Cantate Domino* (Denzinger, no. 1330). [Tr. note: This is the text from Denzinger. Fr. Garrigou-Lagrange has a slightly shortened form of the Latin: "In Deo omnia sunt unum et idem, ubi non obviat relationis oppositio [(In God, everything is one and the same where there is no opposition of relationship).")]

scribes and comprehends the thing signified. However, this is not the case when it is said of God. In that case, it *leaves behind* [lit., *relinquit*] *the thing signified as being non-comprehended and exceeding the signification of the name.*[10] Whence, it is obvious that it is not according to the same notion [lit., *rationem*] that the term "wise" is *said* of God and of man. And the same point applies to other terms as well. Whence, no term is univocally said of God and of creatures.

Duns Scotus was not satisfied by this way of seeing things. Thus, he wished to establish between the Divine Attributes a formal-actual distinction: an *actual* distinction of *formalities*, rather than of realities. Otherwise, according to him, one could say, "God punishes by His Mercy and pardons by His Justice." This would introduce universal confusion.

Cajetan, in nos. 7–16 of his commentary on *ST* I, q. 13, a. 5, responds by saying that the attributes for which the formal concept does not imply an imperfection *are formally in God* (more than virtually), but they are *not formally distinct*; they are identified (without being destroyed) in the eminence of the formal notion of the *Deity*. They formally *are* there, but their *distinction* is only virtual.

Let us see his exact words in no. 7:

> *Formaliter* can be understood in two ways. *In one way,* if we imagine that the particular formal notion of *wisdom* and that of *justice* are one formal notion, *so that this one notion is not some third notion,* but is only the particular notion of wisdom and justice. Now an identity of such things is simply speaking impossible, implying two contradictories. . . . (Whence) if they are one notion, therefore they are one *third notion*: and that

---

[10] [Tr. note: Although there are many controversies here regarding analogy and knowledge of God, on this matter, the reader would benefit greatly from reading Jacques Maritain, *The Degrees of Knowledge*, trans. Gerald B. Phelan (Notre Dame, IN: University of Notre Dame Press, 1995), 215–59. Though his remarks pertain primarily to the natural order (i.e., metaphysics and the *various manners of deploying analogy therein*), they shed great light on these issues.]

which is essentially one [lit., *secundum se*] is not other.

In another way can this be understood, if we imagine the notion *of wisdom* and the notion of *justice* to be enclosed eminently *in one formal notion of a superior order* and to be identified formally. And this identity is not only possible but in fact is the case for all of the perfections in God. For it must not be thought that the *proper* formal notion of wisdom is in God but, instead (as is said in St. Thomas's own words), the notion of Wisdom is in God, not as is *proper* to wisdom itself, but, instead, as is *proper to something superior*, namely the *Deity*; and common in this eminent and formal way are found also Justice, Goodness, Power, etc. For just as the *thing* that is wisdom [i.e., the reality pertaining to wisdom] and the *thing* that is justice [i.e., the reality pertaining to justice] in creatures is elevated *into one superior thing* of a superior order, namely the Deity, and therefore are one thing in God; so too *the formal notion* of wisdom and the *formal notion* of justice are elevated *into one formal notion* of a superior order, namely the proper notion of the Deity, and they are united in the formal notion that *eminently* contains both of them, *not only virtually*, as light contains the notion of heat, *but formally*, as the notion of light contains the notion of being a power of heating.[11] Whence, in his divine genius, St. Thomas most subtly stated the matter: Therefore the notion of wisdom is one thing in God and another in creatures; and because of this, the term is *not* commonly said of them *according to one notion*.

Cajetan explained in the sixth chapter of his *Analogy of Names* that the analogical notion that pertains to God and to creatures expresses a perfection that is not *simpliciter eadem* [without qualification the same] in God and in us but, instead, is *proportionaliter eadem* [proportionally

---

[11] Whence, the expression *formaliter eminenter* [formally eminently], when one says that the Deity contains *formaliter eminenter* absolute perfections such as intelligence and *virtually eminenter* mixed perfections such as rationality. We might say by way of example: White light *formally* contains the power of producing the seven colors in the rainbow; although it only *virtually* contains the colors themselves.

the same].[12] Thus, the wisdom of God is the cause of things, but ours is measured by things. And if, in us, practical wisdom is formally ordering (*ordinativa*), in God it is something that eminently contains this active ordination—*aliquid eminenter praehabens in se esse ordinativum.*[13]

Numerous corollaries derive from this doctrine, and they are often indicated by Cajetan.[14] We will recall here only one that is particularly important. It is relative to the infallibility of the Providential decrees (whether positive or permissive) and to predestination.

However, contrary to his normal practice, Cajetan unfortunately did not formulate this corollary well. Because of this, it has attracted criticism by Sylvester of Ferrara and many other Thomists.

In no. 8 of his commentary on *ST* I, q. 22, a. 4, after having recog-

---

[12] [Tr. note: See Tommaso de Vio Cajetan, *The Analogy of Names, and the Concept of Being*, trans. Edward A. Bushinski and Henry J. Koren (Eugene, OR: Wipf and Stock, 2009), 46–51. As the reader may know, there are great controversies regarding Cajetan's work on analogy. Although we could cite a number of positions, on the negative register, a forceful account is that found in Bernard Montagnes, *The Doctrine of the Analogy of Being According to Thomas Aquinas*, trans. E. M. Macierowski and Pol Vandevelde, ed. Andrew Tallon (Milwaukee, WI: Marquette University Press, 2008).

For a general defense of Cajetan's position, one should consider together the work of Long and Hochschild, who respectively plumb the metaphysical and logical/semantic issues at play here: see Joshua P. Hochschild, *The Semantics of Analogy: Rereading Cajetan's De Nominum Analogia* (Notre Dame, IN: University of Notre Dame Press, 2010), and Steven A. Long, *Analogia Entis: On the Analogy of Being, Metaphysics, and the Act of Faith* (Notre Dame, IN: University of Notre Dame Press, 2011). Likewise, see James Anderson, *The Bond of Being: An Essay on Analogy and Existence* (St. Louis, MO: B. Herder, 1954). Above all, however, see the lucidly clear work of Yves Simon, "On Order in Analogical Sets," in *Philosopher at Work: Essays by Yves R. Simon*, ed. Anthony O. Simon (Lanham, MD: Rowman & Littlefield, 1999). Simon very carefully exposits the issue of analogy without becoming enmeshed in the polemics that often obscure these matters.

One should also consult Réginald Garrigou-Lagrange, *God: His Existence and His Nature: A Thomistic Solution of Certain Agnostic Antinomies*, vol. 2, trans. Bede Rose (St. Louis, MO: B. Herder, 1949), 144–207.]

[13] See Cajetan, *In ST* I, q. 13, a. 3, no. 7.

[14] We can infer from this that the *Deity*, considered in Itself, contains the Divine Attributes *actu explicite* [explicitly in act] in the following sense: namely, if one *sees* the Deity, one would have no need to deduce them but would instead see them actually and explicitly contained in it. In contrast, the *Divine Nature*, humanly conceived as *Subsistent Being*, contains the attributes only *actu implicite*. It is necessary to deduce them progressively.

nized that, generally speaking, the doctors say that what is foreseen and willed by God is inevitable, Cajetan writes:

> However, I—not that I may oppose myself against the torrent, *nor for the sake of asserting*, but standing always in captivity of intellect in obedience to Christ—*suspect* that in a certain fashion *to be foreseen* places in the foreseen event neither contingency nor necessity, as is said in the words of the article, because God is a super-exceeding cause, *eminently pre-holding* [lit., *praehabens*] *necessary and contingent things*; . . . Thus, elevating on high the eyes of our mind, God himself, of His excellence, which is higher than we are able to understand, thus foresees things and events such that *to be foreseen by Him* follows *something higher* than avoidability [*evitabilitas*] or inevitability [*inevitabilitas*]. And if it is so, the intellect rests not upon the evidence of truth that has been grasped [*inspectae*], but by the inaccessible height of hidden truth [*veritatis occultae*].

Here, Cajetan, like certain virtuosos, appears to have forced the note a bit and to have misplaced the accent a little. Also, his manner of expressing himself here is not generally admitted by other Thomists.[15]

---

[15] See Sylvester of Ferrara, commenting on *SCG* III, ch. 94, near the end: "I do not approve of that response. . . . For that which is avoidable [*evitabile*] and inevitable [*non evitabile*] are opposed as contradictories. . . . It is necessary that something else be said *about the foreseen thing*, namely, whether it is something that is avoidable or inevitable and, thus, the same difficulty remains because there seems to follow from this an incertitude in Divine Providence if one holds that it is *avoidable*; however, it seems that the necessity of all things follows if one holds that it is *inevitable*. Therefore, the response that is taken from St. Thomas in this place is more fitting and better satisfying. . . . Because Divine Providence is most efficacious, it cannot be the case that at one and the same time something is foreseen and [it does] not *occur in the manner that it is foreseen*."

Sylvester maintains here the common manner of expressing this: contingent facts happen *infallibly* according to conditional necessity and in a manner nevertheless *contingent* because they proceed from a proximate cause that is not determined *ad unum*; and the infallible motion of God, like His decrees, safeguards the mode of contingence (and even *actualizes* it *strongly and sweetly, fortiter et suaviter*).

Here, in fact, Cajetan does not appear to have expressed himself very well. On the contrary, he could have said, very justly and as we will see him do in his remarks on

It is necessary for us to maintain that contingent facts foreseen by God happen *infallibly* even though they remain *contingent* due to their relation to their proximate cause, which is not determined *ad unum* [to one thing], and also due to their relation with the Divine motion that does not destroy contingency (nor freedom) but, on the contrary, activates freedom within us by producing in us (and with us) all the way up to the *free mode* of our acts—that is, their *dominating indifference* with regard to any particular good desired.[16] Cajetan never put that in doubt; he says it many times, even in the commentary about which we are speaking. However, the formulation of certain parts of the text that we have just considered is unfortunate. He expresses himself better in his commentary on the ninth chapter of St. Paul's letter to the Romans.

What *does* most certainly derive from the doctrine that he invokes concerning the eminence of the Deity (and that he does express elsewhere,[17] in accord with all the Thomists) is as follows. There are two principles here. Each of them, taken in separately, is absolutely certain. However, their *intimate reconciliation in the eminence of the Deity* is inaccessible to every created intellect (whether human or angelic) so long as it has not received the Beatific Vision. What are these two principles?

On the one hand: "Given that God's love is the cause of all that is good, nothing would be better than something else if it were not loved

---

ST I, q. 39, a. 1 (no. 7): "There is in God one formal notion, not purely absolute nor purely respective, *not purely communicable, nor purely incommunicable*, but *most eminently and formally containing* both whatever absolute perfection there is and whatever the relational nature of the Trinity [lit., *Trinitas respectiva*] requires." Indeed, although the contingent event is either avoidable or inevitable, God the Father can communicate His Nature but not His relation of Paternity. The eminence of the Deity contains formally-eminently that which is communicable and that which is not.

[16] [Tr. note: The clearest explanation of the traditional doctrine on freedom of the will can be found in Yves R. Simon, *Freedom of Choice*, ed. Peter Wolff (New York: Fordham University Press, 1999). See also Réginald Garrigou-Lagrange, *God: His Existence and His Nature*, vol. 2, trans. Bede Rose (St. Louis, MO: B. Herder, 1949), 268–350; Garrigou-Lagrange, *Le réalisme du principe de finalité* (Paris: Desclée de Brouwer, 1932), 93n1; Jacques Maritain, *Bergsonian Philosophy and Thomism*, ed. Ralph McInerny, trans. Mabelle L Andison and J. Gordon Andison (Notre Dame, IN: University of Notre Dame Press, 2007), pt. 1, ch. 6; Maritain, *Existence and the Existent*, trans. Gerald B. Phelan and Lewis Galantiere (New York: Pantheon, 1948), 47–61.]

[17] See Cajetan *In ST* I, q. 20, aa. 3 and 4; q. 23, a. 5, nos. 7ff and 13–18.

more by God."[18] This is the very formula of the principle of predilection such as is found in St. Thomas.[19] In this sense, Jesus said, "Without me, you can do nothing" (John 15:5) in the order of salvation; and, in speaking of the elect, he added, "Nobody can snatch them from my Father's hand" (John 10:29). Likewise, St. Paul said, "Who is it that distinguishes you? What do you have that you did not receive?" (1 Cor 4:7). What could give a more profound lesson in humility?

On the other hand: God never commands the impossible and, by love, renders *truly possible for all* (above all to those who are dying) *the accomplishment of His precepts*; and they are not deprived of final grace unless they refuse it by resistance to the final call, as happened to the bad thief.

As was said by St. Prosper, in the words repeated by a Council in the ninth century:[20] "If certain people are saved, it is by the gift of the Savior; if others end in perdition, it is by their fault." Here we have a formula that reunites the two aspects of the mystery and the two principles that we have recalled here.

Each of these, taken apart, is true, that of predilection as much as that concerning the possible salvation of all. However, how are these two, so incontestable principles able to be intimately reconciled? No created intellect can see their intimate reconciliation before the Beatific Vision. To see this reconciliation would be to see, in fact, how Infinite Mercy, Infinite Justice, and Sovereign Freedom *are reconciled in the eminence of the Deity.*[21]

---

[18] [Tr. note: This principle will generally be rendered as saying "no one," given the context of free human agents. However, as will be seen below, in its strictest form from St. Thomas, it universally applies to all beings.]

[19] See *ST* I, q. 20, a. 3: "Cum amor Dei sit causa bonitatis rerum, non esset aliquid alio *melius*, si Deus non vellet uni *maius bonum* quam alteri." See also a. 4: "Ex hoc sunt aliqua meliora, quod Deus eis maius bonum vult."

[20] See Council of Quiercy: "That some, however, are saved is the gift of the one [who saves]; that some, however, perish is the fault of those who perish" (Denzinger, no. 623).

[21] And even the blessed, who see the Deity and how these three perfections are reconciled in It, cannot see the reason for the sovereignly free good pleasure, which makes it the case that God ever relieve certain sinners at the very end but not do so for others. In this matter, St. Thomas says (in *ST* I, q. 23, a. 5, ad 3) that there is a *simplex velle* (simple will), which Cajetan explains just as all the Thomists (*In ST* I, q. 23, a. 5, no. 13ff).

We believe this is what Cajetan wished to say above all else concerning this great problem: To see the intimate reconciliation of the principles of which we have spoken, it would be necessary to see the Divine Essence. The more these principles to be reconciled become certain for us, the more (by contrast) does the eminence of the Deity appear *obscure*, with a transluminous obscurity—that is, the intimate life of the Deity, in which they are united, where Cajetan loved to repose himself.

The Deity thus conceived corresponds to what the mystics have called the great darkness, or the "inaccessible light, where God lives" (1 Tim 6:16), the brilliant light that appears to us as darkness because of the weakness of the eyes of our spirit, just as the sun appears dark to the night owl.[22]

We will return to this point in chapter six below, concerning the problem of evil.

Here, theology arrives in a certain sense at mysticism. And there is in this place something very important for providing a just idea of the mystery of the Holy Trinity. Cajetan has seen this point very well.

The Deity and the Divine Persons

There was on this point a controversy among the theologians similar to that relative to the distinction of the Divine Attributes and the Divine Nature. The great majority of theologians admit, in these two cases, a *minor virtual distinction* of such a kind that the Divine Nature, such as we conceive it, contains *actu-implicite* the attributes and subsistent relations constitutive of the Divine Persons (the relations of paternity, filiation, and passive spiration).

As is known, Duns Scotus held here that there is an actual-formal distinction between the Divine Essence and the three persons. To this, the Thomists generally respond: This distinction, which is more than virtual, but actual-formal, must exist *before our intellect's consideration* and, therefore, is *real*. From this, how can one avoid the condemna-

---

[22] [Tr. note: A classic line from the beginning of Aristotle's *Metaphysics*.]

tion declared against Gilbert of Poitiers by the Council of Reims[23] and renewed by the Fourth Lateran Council?[24]

Cajetan, in the very profound response that he makes to Scotus concerning this, sheds a great light on the matter. It is certainly one of the most beautiful pages of all of his works. It is found in his remarks concerning *ST* I, q. 39, a. 1, and is concerned with maintaining the true meaning of these revealed propositions: The Father *is* God, the Son *is* God, the Holy Spirit *is God*, but the Father *is not* the Son, *nor are* either of These the Holy Spirit.

The verb "to be" here, like in every affirmative proposition, expresses the real identity of the subject and the predicate; and the negation "is not" expresses the real distinction of the Divine Persons among themselves.

Cajetan admirably shows that if the Divine Nature, such as we imperfectly conceive it, contains *actu-implicite* the attributes and the Divine Relations, the *Deity such as it is in Itself* and seen by the blessed contains them *actu-explicite* in a unique formal notion that is absolutely eminent.

Let us look now at this text of incomparable grandeur and strength—namely, his remarks in no. 7 of his commentary on *ST* I, q. 39, a. 1:

> The Relation, or Person, does not differ in reality, but only in reason, from the Divine Essence. . . .
>
> In evidence of this, know that *just as in God*, according to reality [*secundum rem*]—or in the real order—*there is one thing* [*res*] not purely absolute nor purely respective, nor a mixture composed or resulting from both; but most eminently and formally having that which is respective (nay, rather, of many respective things) and that which is absolute; *so too in the formal order*—or, the *order of formal notions*—in itself, i.e., not as is said by us, *there is in God one formal notion, not purely absolute, nor purely respective*, not purely communicable, nor purely incommunicable; but *most eminently and formally containing whatever*

---

is of absolute perfection and whatever the relational nature of the Trinity [Trinitas respectiva] requires. Now, it is necessary that it be so, for it is necessary that to any most simple thing that is of itself maximally one that there correspond one adequate formal notion—otherwise it would not be *per se primo* one intelligible by some intellect. And this is confirmed, for the Word of God is only one. However, it is fitting that a word, if it is perfect, be adequate to that of which it is [the word].

However, we err if we proceed from the absolute things and respective things to God because we imagine that the distinction between the absolute and the respective is somehow *prior to the Divine Nature [quasi priorem re divina]* and therefore end up believing that the Divine Nature must be placed under one of those two members [i.e., that which is absolute or that which is respective]. However, the complete opposite is the case, for the Divine Nature is prior to being and all of its differences: it is *super ens, super unum*, etc. . . . And therefore . . . the absolute and the relative are elevated to one "thing" and one Divine Formal Notion. (That is: They are formally and eminently in God.)

Whence, we can respond to the first objection made by Scotus (namely, if it were a thing of one notion [*res unius rationis*] it would be either only communicable or only incommunicable) . . . by denying the conditional assumption. For from this (namely, that it is of one notion in itself [*unius rationis in se*]), it does not follow that *therefore it will be either only communicable or only incommunicable*. Instead, it is the case that it is both communicable and incommunicable—and this is so on account of that Formal Notion.

All of this can be reduced to a deep understanding of the following simple statement of truth. The Father *is* God; equally the Son *is God* and the Holy Spirit *is* God. In these affirmative propositions, the verb "is" expresses the real identity of the subject and the predicate; whereas, when we say that the Father *is not* the Son, we affirm their real distinction.

That which we have read in Cajetan under a form that brings to mind the flamboyant, [late] Gothic [style] of the fifteenth century had been said in a much simpler form by St. Thomas, notably in two places in his *Summa theologiae*.

First, consider the end of *ST* I, q. 28, a. 2, ad 3:

> Because *the perfection of the Divine Essence is greater than what can be comprehended by the signification of any name*, it does not follow, if a relative name . . . does not signify something perfect, that the Divine Essence must be imperfect, for the Divine Essence comprehends in Itself every kind of perfection, as was already shown above in *ST* I, q. 4, a. 2.

Likewise, consider the end of *ST* I, q. 27, a. 2, ad 3:

> *In the very perfection of the Divine Being [esse]* is contained both the Word intelligibly proceeding and the Principle of the Word, and also whatever pertains to His Perfection.

This teaching of St. Thomas, admirably placed in relief by Cajetan (under the pressure of Scotus's objections) has been maintained by all the Thomists. They are in accord in saying against Scotus's *formal-actual* distinction what one reads, for example, in Billuart (see *Cursus. Theol. de Trinitate*, diss. 2, a. 3: "Concerning the Identity and Distinction of the Relations from the Essence"):

> *Thus there would not be saved in God the notion of Act that is Most Pure, Most Simple, and Infinite.* . . . For, in this hypothesis (i.e., that of the formal-actual distinction) the Divine Essence would be conceived with a foundation in reality that is *in potency* to the relations and actualizable by them as by something extraneous, . . . just as animality is conceived as being in potency to rationality, actualizable by it as by something extraneous.[25]

---

[25] [Tr. note: If the reader feels a bit overwhelmed by some of this, it is helpful to read Réginald Garrigou-Lagrange, *The Trinity and God the Creator*, trans. Frederic C. Eckhoff (St. Louis, MO: B. Herder, 1952), 109–45.]

The conception that Cajetan proposes to us concerning the *eminence of the Deity*, containing *formally and eminently* the Divine Attributes and the Divine Relations, safeguards completely the Simplicity and the Infinity of God as Pure Act, Who cannot be conceived as being subsequently determinable or actualizable.[26]

In the great text of Cajetan that we have cited, some are astonished, perhaps, by this proposition that calls to mind [Pseudo-]Dionysius [*Denys*]: "The Divine Reality is prior to being and all of its differences; it is therefore *super ens et super unum*, etc."

This means, as Cajetan explained in the same place, that the *formal notion of the Deity* is superior to all of the formal notions that It contains *formally eminently*. Agnosticism would follow from this if the Deity contained them only *virtually eminently*, as It contains mixed perfections (as when one speaks metaphorically, "God is angry"). However, It contains the aforementioned things *formally* in its emi-

---

[26] Moreover, one knows how Cajetan conceives of *personality*. He remarks with St. Thomas in *ST* III, q. 4, a. 2 (no. 8) that *person is a first subject of attribution (suppositum)* endowed with an intellect, to which one attributes an intellectual nature, existence, and operations. He concludes on this matter that *personality is that by which* precisely the person is constituted as a *first subject of attribution* of all that follows upon it: "*Id quo* aliquid *est quod* per se separatim existit et operatur."

Now, that cannot be any of the parts that are attributed to it, neither the nature nor the existence, but it is (at their junction, like a point is the junction of two lines) *that by which* the intellectual nature becomes immediately *capable of existing* in Peter or in Paul, in me or in you. Here we have the metaphysical sense of these personal pronouns that everybody employs. *That which exists* is not the nature; *it is the subject* to which this nature is attributed as the essential part.

We have shown elsewhere the excellent foundation of this conception of the matter. See Garrigou-Lagrange, *Our Savior and His Love for Us*, trans. A. Bouchard (St. Louis, MO: B. Herder, 1958), 92–100. As subtle as it appears to some, it is a simple explication of what is contained in the common sense notion of person. Moreover, one cannot identify (as Fr. Billot wished) created personality with created existence. That would ultimately lead one to deny the real distinction between created essence and existence. In fact, as the human essence *is not* its existence, likewise the *person of Peter* (and even the personality of Peter) *is not* its own existence, which is in it a contingent predicate. It is in this that Peter differs from God: *Only God is His own Existence*. The person of Peter (which formally contains his personality) is only *quid capax existendi* [that which is capable of existing].

[Tr. note: As an aid to understanding this issue, see R. P. Phillips, *Modern Thomistic Philosophy: An Explanation for Students*, vol. 2, *Metaphysics* (Westminster, MD: Newman Press, 1962).]

nence. The Deity is thus superior to being, unity, goodness, wisdom, love, mercy, and justice. However, these latter are *formally* in it (more than the seven colors are in white light). While whiteness is not blue, the Deity is True, One, Good, Intelligent, and so on. Moreover, these perfections can *exist in a pure state* only in the Deity. Pure Being in the state of Pure Act cannot be found except in the Deity—and there it is identified with all the other absolute perfections: Unity, Goodness, Wisdom, Love, Mercy, and Justice. Pure Being ought to be not only intelligible but actually known and identical to Subsistent Intellection. And if, in this identification, these absolute perfections *are not destroyed*, it is because they demand this identification, and this identification is accomplished in a *superior* formal notion. Indeed, if mercy is identified with justice, not only in the superior perfection of the *Deity* but also in the very perfection that is *justice*, it would be destroyed. In order that these absolute perfections be safeguarded in this identification, in order that they be there *formally* (and not only virtually like the seven colors found in white light), it is necessary that this identification occurs in something that is *eminent*—in the eminence of the *Deity*. This is the profound meaning of the classic expression: "Simply simple perfections are *formally and eminently* in God and *not only virtually* in Him as are the mixed perfections."

All of this supposes that being is not univocal, as Scotus would have it, but instead, analogical.

The exact sense of the expression "the Deity is above being" appears again in what remains for us to say concerning the very essence of sanctifying grace.

The Deity and the Essence of Grace

The Deity of which we have spoken is not able to be participated in in the natural order, no matter how perfect we may presume that natural order to be. The nature of the most elevated angel could not be a participation in the Deity. This participation can be found only in sanctifying grace, "By which we are made to be sharers in the Divine Nature" (2 Pet 1:4), for only grace is a radical principle of *strictly Divine operations*. It disposes us for seeing God immediately as He sees Himself and to love Him as He loves Himself.

It was this fact that made St. Thomas say, "Bonum gratiae unius maius est quam bonum naturae totius universi."[27] The least degree of sanctifying grace is worth more than all of the natures of the universe taken together, including all of the angelic natures in it. This is the profound meaning of "all things on account of the elect" and "Blessed are the poor in spirit, for theirs is the kingdom of heaven" (Matt 5:3). The Deity can be participated in only by grace.

On the contrary, all of the Absolute Perfections that are found in the eminence of the Deity can be *naturally* participated in by creatures. The stone participates in *being*, the plant in *life*, the animal in *knowledge*; man and angel participate naturally in *intelligence, wisdom, love, mercy, justice,* and so on. However, no nature that is created or ever could be created can *naturally* participate in the *Deity* (i.e., the intimate life of God); no created nature can be the radical principle of operations that are, strictly speaking, Divine.

Only sanctifying grace is a real, physical,[28] and formal participation in the Divine Nature as such (i.e., in the Deity, the intimate life of God), for it disposes us to see Him as He sees Himself, to love Him as He loves Himself. Sanctifying grace disposes us positively and radically for essentially supernatural operations, ones that are, strictly speaking, divine, that have the very same formal object as God's Uncreated Intellection and Uncreated Love.

Sanctifying grace is not only a participation in the Divine Nature inasmuch as It is *Being* or inasmuch as It is *Intellectual*; it is a participation in It inasmuch as It is *Divine*, a participation in the Deity, a participation in the intimate life of the Most High.

It was necessary for Cajetan to be led to highlight this fact by all that we have seen from him concerning the Deity. Indeed, he has not failed in defending, against Scotus, the *essential supernaturality* of sanctifying and habitual grace.

---

[27] *ST* I-II, q. 113, a. 9, ad 2.

[28] [Tr. note: One might also say "ontological." The sense is the same as that of the classic term "physical premotion."]

On this subject, one of the principal texts of Cajetan is found in *ST* I, q. 12, a. 5, nos. 9, 11, and 12.

It is known that Duns Scotus[29] has held that, if God so wished, the Beatific Vision of the Divine Essence could have been in us (and in the angels) not a fruit of supernatural grace but a natural perfection. From such a perspective, one no longer sees *grace* and the light of glory as being *essentially supernatural gifts*, since both of them could be a *natural gift*. Does this not destroy the very notion of grace, the essence of this gratuitous gift? Grace would no longer be essentially gratuitous. It could be the very nature or a natural property of man or angel!

From this point of view, Scotus held that man and angel do not necessarily need an essentially supernatural gift in order to see God immediately. According to him, it could be that it would suffice that one be supernaturally accorded a natural gift, like natural sight was supernaturally given by a miracle to the man born blind.

Cajetan, in his commentary on *ST* I, q. 12, aa. 4 and 5, shows on the contrary, following St. Thomas, that *no created intellect (nor any that could be created)* can, by its own natural powers, *attain, even in a vague manner* [*confusément*], *the proper and formal object of the Divine Intellect*, which is the Divine Essence, immediately known. If the matter were otherwise, a created intellect would be of the same nature as God; it would be a formal participation in the Deity. Since every intellect is specified by its formal object, this would be the pantheistic confusion of the Divine Nature with a created one. *The univocity of being*, held by Scotus,[30] also leads to the same consequence, for univocal being should be diversified, like a genus, *by differences* that would be *extrinsic* to it, differences that would be outside of being like rationality is extrinsic to animality. Now, nothing is outside of being; its different modalities are in it *actu-implicite*, and it is contained in them, for these modalities are still of being.[31]

---

[29] See Duns Scotus, *In III Sent.*, d. 14, q. 1, and *In IV Sent.*, d. 44, q. 11. [Tr. note: Likely following the Leonine Edition's dated annotation, Fr. Garrigou-Lagrange does not distinguish between the editions of Scotus, i.e., the *Lectura*, the *Ordinatio*, and the *Reportationes* that we have of his works from the last days of his lecturing in Paris.]

[30] See Scotus *In I Sent.*, d. 3, qq. 1 and 3; d. 8, q. 3.

[31] Although rationality is not animality, it is the case that substantiality, vitality, animality, etc., are still of being. Being is therefore not univocal, but rather, analogical

Also, Cajetan, on the subject of the essential supernaturality of sanctifying grace and of the light of glory, concludes in his commentary on *ST* I, q. 12, a. 5, nos. 11 and 12:

> The proportion between the light of glory and the Divine Essence, not in *esse naturae* but in *esse intelligibili* [i.e., intentionally], *is a proportion of a property connatural to the nature from which it flows.* That this is so was proven from what has been said. The light of glory is nothing other than the *power*, as a proper disposition, *that unites to the Divine Essence* as intelligible form and as making of Divine Vision; it is obvious from what has been said that the light of glory pertains to these two matters. However, *to have the Divine Essence as intelligible form*, and, *similarly, to see God, are connatural only to God.* Therefore, the light of glory is connatural only to the Divine Nature. And from this it follows that *the Divine Essence and the light of glory are of the same order*, as in the same way an ultimate disposition and form are of the same order, namely according to connaturality. . . . And therefore, in the very words [of the article] it is said that the *light of glory cannot be connatural to anyone unless that thing is carried over into the Divine Nature* (that which would be a pantheistic confusion of the Divine Nature with a created nature).

---

according to a similitude of proportions. See Cajetan on *ST* I, q. 13, a. 5. Likewise, see his commentary on the *De ente et essentia*, q. 3, and his treatise *On the Analogy of Names*, ch. 6. In those places, he critiques at length Scotus's arguments against analogy in favor of univocity of being. One sees by these arguments that he [Scotus] is concerned with a univocity that is not only logical but also metaphysical, which merits the critiques that generally are made by Thomists such as Capreolus, Cajetan, John of St. Thomas, et al. We have examined this point elsewhere. See Réginald Garrigou-Lagrange, *God: His Existence and His Nature*, 2:203–67.

Moreover, the Church has never spoken of univocity, but of analogy between God and the creature. She has even said, at the Fourth Lateran Council: "Between Creator and creature no similitude can be expressed without implying a greater dissimilitude" (Denzinger, no. 806).

Likewise, the [First] Vatican Council, in *Dei Filius*, ch. 4, said: "Nevertheless, if reason illuminated by faith inquires in an earnest, pious, and sober manner, it attains by God's grace a certain understanding of the mysteries, which is most fruitful, both from the analogy with the objects of its natural knowledge and from the connection of these mysteries with one another and with man's ultimate end" (Denzinger, no. 3016).

[Tr. note: See note 12 above.]

Moreover, from these points, the *falsity of Scotus's opinion* is obvious in I quaest. Prol. on I Sent., where he wishes that *the natural and supernatural do not distinguish things but relations to active causes*. Accordingly, if the light of glory, charity, and the gifts of the Holy Spirit, as well as other things of this sort, are all *supernatural beings*, it is not only because they can be caused *only by a supernatural agent* but because NO CREATURE THAT HAS EVER BEEN MADE OR EVER COULD BE MADE CAN BE CONNATURAL TO THEM; on account of this, they are called SUPERNATURAL entities, NAY RATHER, entities OF THE DIVINE ORDER.

This pertains to the very definition of the supernatural and of the distinction between the *essential supernaturality* of sanctifying grace and the supernaturality *of miracles*. Grace is supernatural by its very essence and cannot naturally be known (*because truth and being are convertible*); whereas, miracles are only supernatural by the mode of their production and are, by that fact, naturally knowable. The resurrection of a dead person supernaturally renders natural life unto that person.

As Cajetan adds, in the same place (no. 9), in order to respond to the objections of Scotus, who tends to confound these two forms of the supernatural:

Whence, it is obvious that the case is not the same as regards *the illuminated blind person* and *the illuminated intellect* (i.e., illuminated by the light of glory): for in the former, the power given is *natural*, though *supernaturally given*; however, in the latter case, the power given is *supernaturally given* and *is supernatural*.

There is an immense difference between, on the one hand, the essential supernaturality of grace and the light of glory and, on the other hand, the supernaturality of a miracle, for instance the healing of a man who is born blind. This miraculous healing *supernaturally* renders unto such a person the *natural* power of sight, while, grace and the light of glory are an *essentially supernatural life, vita nova*. It is concerned with nothing less than the very essence of eternal life: "Gratia Dei vita aeterna" (Rom 6:23).

Cajetan speaks here very firmly, for he is convinced that many of the capital theses of Duns Scotus (in particular that of the univocity of being and that of the distinction that is only contingent, and not necessary, between nature and grace), if they were true, would destroy the principles formulated by St. Thomas. As Cajetan has written in the preface to his commentary on *ST* I:[32]

> Nor have theologians failed to attack, thinking thus to acquire a name for genius or doctrine if (in the manner of generals who attack the most fortified point) they concentrate their fire on this part [i.e., the *Prima pars*]. *But John Duns Scotus (eminently in comparison with others) has labored in this matter with subtlety and in abundance, as you see, strove to undermine nearly every word of this part.*[33]

Moreover, Cajetan is persuaded that Scotus's thesis concerning the absolute nonnecessity of the light of glory for the Beatific Vision cannot be sustained after the Council of Vienne. He writes in no. 9 of his commentary on *ST* I, q. 12, a. 5:

> And heed well that Scotus, with those who follow him, can no longer have their position sustained concerning this matter, for in Clement the Fifth's *Ad nostrum, de Haereticis* they are expressly condemned of error who say *the soul does not need the elevating light of glory in order to see God.* Thus you can discern that the Church, embracing the doctrine of St. Thomas, has determined *not only the need for the light but also its cause,*

---

[32] See *Sancti Thomae de Aquino opera omnia,* Leonine edition, vol. 4 (Rome: 1888), p. xx.

[33] [Tr. note: For an account of this passage defending Cajetan's anti-Scotistic flourish (which is clearly rhetorical) against the dismissal of Etienne Gilson, see Ralph McInerny, *Praeambula fidei: Thomism and the God of the Philosophers* (Washington, DC: Catholic University of America Press, 2006), 39–68 (esp. 40–44). I am generally following McInerny's translation of the first sentence, as he renders Cajetan's forcefulness with clarity.]

namely so that the soul may be elevated to such a vision, as is said in the words [of St Thomas].[34]

Cajetan's teaching, thus defending St. Thomas, is followed by all Thomists.[35]

One sees that Cajetan passes a severe judgment on Scotus's voluntarism, which makes the distinction of nature and grace depend upon the Divine Freedom, thus leading the distinction to become not necessary but contingent.

---

[34] At the Council of Vienne, in the Constitution *Ad nostrum qui,* this error of the Beghards was condemned: "Any intellectual nature in its own self is naturally blessed, and the soul does not need the light of glory raising it to see God and to enjoy him beatifically" (Denzinger, no. 895).

 Also, the [First] Vatican Council said in *Dei Filius,* ch. 4: "The perpetual common belief of the Catholic Church has held and holds also this: *there is a twofold order of knowledge, distinct not only in its principle but also in its object;* in its principle, because in the one we know by *natural reason,* in the other by *divine faith;* in its *object,* because *apart from what natural reason can attain,* there are proposed to our belief *mysteries that are hidden in God* that can never be known unless they are revealed by God. . . . *For divine mysteries BY THEIR VERY NATURE so exceed the created intellect that,* even when they have been communicated in revelation and received by faith, they remain covered by the veil of faith itself and shrouded, as it were, in darkness as long as in this mortal life 'we are away from the Lord; for we walk by faith, not by sight (II Cor. 5:6f)" (Denzinger, nos. 3015–16).

 These terms show that the Council is concerned with a distinction of orders, a distinction that is *not contingent* (or, founded upon the good pleasure of God), *but necessary* (or, founded upon the transcendence of the Divine Essence, the proper object of the Divine Intellect, and thus inaccessible to the natural forces of every intellect that has been created or ever could be created).

[35] For example, see Gonet, *Clypeus theologiae thomisticae,* vol. 4, *De gratia,* disp. 2, a. 3 ("Whether habitual grace is entitatively [i.e., ontologically] supernatural"): "The opinion of Scotus is generally rejected, for it does not distinguish between the *intrinsically supernatural,* or *quoad entitatem,* and the *extrinsically supernatural,* or *quoad modum;* it is opposed to the common consensus of the theologians, who admit that we have gifts that are supernatural intrinsically and entitatively; nay, rather, it is against the faith providing for such gifts."

 [Tr. note: To make Gonet's passage slightly more readable, I follow Fr. Garrigou-Lagrange's own French translation of the text, provided in the next chapter, though I have chosen to retain certain aspects of Gonet's original that Fr. Garrigou-Lagrange changed (albeit only slightly).]

* * *

He is no less severe against this same voluntarism that leads Scotus to hold these propositions:

> No act is bad from its genus, or only by its object, except that of hating God.[36]

> It does not seem that concerning a creature there is some sin that is mortal from its genus but only from the Divine precept, such as committing adultery or killing a man, for were God to revoke the precept, that would not of itself be bad.[37]

Otherwise, according to Scotus, the Divine Will would be determined by something other than itself.

Cajetan responds in no. 3 of his commentary on *ST* I-II, q. 100, a. 8 ("Whether the precepts of the Decalogue can be dispensed"):

> Indeed, the Divine Will is not determined to will something outside of Itself *to be or not to be.* . . . However, it is necessary for Scotus himself and everyone to admit, saying there are some *precepts that are per se good* and *prohibitions that are per se bad,* such as the precepts of the natural law and the first precepts of the Decalogue. Obviously, as concerns these precepts, it is not a matter of them existing or not existing; *instead, the matter pertains to their rectitude or lack thereof. In this way is the Divine Will determined, namely that It cannot be in dissonance*

---

[36] *In IV Sent.*, d. 26, a. unica. [Tr. note: Here, Fr. Garrigou-Lagrange cites the Wadding edition of Scotus, published by Vivès in 1894. This dated edition is in the process of being superseded.]

[37] *In IV Sent.*, d. 50, q. 2, Scotus also says in *In IV Sent.* of the *Reportatio parisiensia*, d. 28, q. unica: "No act is good in genus from the object alone except to love God, . . . and the only act that is bad from its genus, which is opposed to that aforementioned act, with respect to the same object, is to hate God, who in no way can be 'circumstanced' [lit., *circumstantionari*] as He is good. Therefore, every other act, which is with respect to another object, is indifferent and can be subjected to circumstances for good or bad."

with those things which are right, nor can it be in agreement with those that lack rectitude . . . (or better) just as the Divine Intellect is naturally determined only to knowing God Himself and all that naturally shines forth in Him; so too the Divine Will (is determined) to the willing of God Himself and all that is naturally right; things of this sort exist only in God before they are communicated by Him.

This is extremely important, above all if one thinks of men who do not have faith, who do not know Divine Revelation. If Scotus's position were true, it would follow that no precept of the natural law (except that of loving God) would be necessary, as the positivists hold. Homicide would not be intrinsically evil.

*   *   *

In order to return to the essence of sanctifying grace, it is clear that Cajetan, in defending its *essential supernaturality* (which is far superior to the supernaturality of miracles), only comes to repeat what St. Thomas often affirmed, in particular, in texts such as:

ST I-II, q. 112, a. 1:[38] The gift of grace exceeds every faculty of a created nature, since it is nothing other than a kind of participation in the Divine *Nature,* which exceeds every other nature. . . . For thus it is necessary that only God *deifies* [*deificet*], by communicating *fellowship in the Divine Nature* through a certain participation of likeness, just as it is impossible that something can enflame, except fire itself.

ST I, q. 62, a. 2: *To see God through His Essence* is *above the nature of any created intellect* (as shown in *ST* I, q. 12, aa. 4 and 5). . . . And therefore, it must be said that an angel, could not have been turned to that beatitude by his will except by the aid of grace.

---

[38] [Tr. note: Fr. Garrigou-Lagrange incorrectly has *ST* I-II, q. 112, a. 2.]

It is clear that, for Cajetan, all these points of doctrine derive from the conception that one must have of the *eminence of the Deity*, which *cannot be participated in naturally*, whereas the simple perfections (such as being, life, intelligence, wisdom, and love) can be participated in naturally and, thus, are naturally known.

From this, one sees why he holds that the proper object of sacred theology is God *sub ratione Deitatis*, while that of natural theology is God *sub ratione entis*. One sees also why the *formal notion of the Deity* contains *formally eminently* all of the Divine Attributes and the subsistent, real relations that constitute the Divine Persons. In this, we see manifestly one of the culminating points of St. Thomas's doctrine about which it was difficult to show better the elevation and radiance. This represents one of the great merits of Cajetan in the theological synthesis that he presents, a synthesis that, in its master principles [*lignes maîtresses*], dominates opinions and appears indeed to belong to theological science itself. One sees that this great theologian, who was a virtuoso in logic, was also someone with a great degree of the sense of mystery, and by that fact, he finds himself among the contemplatives.

Chapter 4

Miracles and Grace—Two Very Different Forms of the Supernatural

I N ORDER TO DETERMINE BETTER what ought to be the sense of mystery for the theologian, we will study here the profound distinction that separates the supernaturality of the miracle from the supernaturality that is much more elevated in the case of infused faith and grace. We will summarize here what we have said at greater length in our work *De revelatione*.[1]

Whence Comes the Confusion in Many Controversies Relative to the Supernatural?

One of the principal sources of confusion in debates related to the fact of revelation, to the discernability of miracles and the supernaturality of faith, seems to be the imprecision of definitions often given for the supernatural *quoad substantiam vel essentiam* and for the supernatural *quoad modum*.

When we maintain that natural reason can know with certitude if a fact is truly miraculous and thus demonstrate by this sign the fact of revelation, it is often objected to us, "If the miracle and the fact of rev-

---

[1] See Garrigou-Lagrange, *De revelatione per Ecclesiam catholicam proposita*, 3rd ed. (Rome: Ferrari, 1931), 1:191–97, 458–515. [Tr. note: A translation of this work is anticipated in a future volume by Emmaus Academic.]

elation are supernatural, how is it that they can be known naturally?" We respond, "The miracle is supernatural only *as regards the manner* of its production and *not as regards the very essence* of the effect produced. For example, corporeal resuscitation *supernaturally* renders life to a corpse but it does not thereby give it a *supernatural* life. The natural life miraculously rendered is naturally knowable in itself and also as an effect properly attributable to the First Cause. Only the Author of life can render life to that which is dead.[2] He alone has *immediate* power over the being (inasmuch as it is being)[3] of created things (over matter,[4] over substance) and therefore, only He can, without prior accidental dispositions,[5] substantially reunite the soul to the body—i.e., to resuscitate it."[6]

Moreover, even if the resuscitated corpse receives, like that of our Lord, the properties of a glorious body,[7] these properties (e.g., its brightness) are naturally knowable because they are supernatural only

---

[2] *ST* III supplement, q. 75, a. 3.

[3] *ST* I, q. 45, a. 5; *ST* III, q. 75, a. 4.

[4] See *ST* I, q. 105, a. 1; q. 110, aa. 2 and 4.

[5] [Tr. note: E.g., as when an animal's body slowly deteriorates due to illness, ultimately leading to substantial corruption, i.e., death.]

[6] See *De potentia*, q. 6, a. 7 ("Whether angels or demons can assume a body"), ad 4: "*Nothing has a power surpassing its being* [*esse*]; for the power of every being [*omnis res*] flows from its essence or presupposes its essence. Now since *the soul by its being* [*esse*] *is united to the body as form*, it is not in its power to release itself from its union with the body; similarly too, it is not in the power of the angel that it be united to a body according to *existence* [*esse*] as form; however, it can assume a body in aforementioned mode, to which it is united as the mover and as figure to its shape."
   With the help of these principles, it would be easy to demonstrate that God alone can revive a dead person: God alone has over being itself and the substance of things a power that is not only mediate (by the intermediary of accidents) but also *immediate*. Now, the substantial reuniting of the soul to the body without preliminary accidental dispositions presupposes this immediate power. Therefore, God alone can achieve it. Natural agents can only produce a living substance by way of generation as a result of indispensable accidental dispositions. To show the rigor of this argument, it would suffice to recall the principal theses of St. Thomas's metaphysics concerning the *proper* effects of the First Agent—effects that by definition surpass *all natural powers, whether known or unknown, created or able to be created.*

[7] The glorious Resurrection is a miracle of the first order (or, *quoad substantiam*), according to St. Thomas. The case of Resurrection that is not that of the glory of heaven is a miracle of the second order (or, *quoad subiectum in quo est*). See *ST* I, q. 105, a. 8.

by the *mode* of their production and in no way *essentially* supernatural, as is sanctifying grace. The glorification of the body constitutes, without a doubt, a miracle *quoad substantiam*[8] because it is an effect that surpasses all *created powers*, but it does not by that surpass all *created natures*. The glorification of the body is thus a *miracle quoad substantiam* without being *supernatural quoad substantiam* as is, for example, grace, which is a participation in the Nature of God. As St. Thomas says in *ST* III supplement, q. 85, a. 2, ad 1:

> The (bodily) brightness [*claritas*] of glory will be of another genus than the brightness of nature, *as regards the cause* but not *as regards the appearance* [*speciem*]. Whence, just as the brightness of nature by reason of its appearance [*speciem*] is proportioned to sight, so too is the brightness of glory.

Thus, the apostles were able to know naturally and to see with their eyes the glorious body of the Resurrected Christ and be assured of His identity.[9]

---

[8] See ibid.

[9] See *ST* III, q. 55, a. 6:

> Christ manifested His resurrection in two ways, namely *by testimony* and *by argument* (or by sign). And *each kind of manifestation was sufficient in its own kind*. For in order to give *testimony* He made use of two things, . . . the angels . . . and the Scriptures that He Himself proposed. . . . Also, *the arguments* were sufficient for showing the Resurrection was true and glorious. However, He showed that it was a true resurrection, in two ways.
>
> *In one way, he did so from the perspective of the body.* Concerning this, He showed three things. First, He showed that it was a *true and solid* body, not a body that was a mere phantasm (or rarified like air): "Feel and see, for spirit does not have flesh and bones as you see me to have" (Luke 24:39). Second, He showed them that it was a *human body* by showing unto them a true figure, which they saw with their eyes. Third, He showed them that it was *one and the same body* that He had before by showing to them the scars of His wounds: "See my hands and my feet, for I am myself" (Luke 24:39).
>
> Now, *in a second way*, He showed them the truth of His resurrection *from the perspective of the soul* now reunited to its body. Concerning this, He showed the matter by means of the activities of the threefold kinds of life. First, He did so as regards *the activities of nutritive life* in that he ate and drank with his disciples. Second, He did so *as regards the activities of sensitive life* by responding to the questions raised by His disciples as well as by greeting

This response is often poorly understood because some do not always realize well enough what distinguishes the modally supernatural from the essentially supernatural. And some, at times, seem to confuse this latter with the miracle *quoad substantiam*. However, they differ from one another as much as invisible and Divine grace[10] differs from the visible brightness of the glorious body.

Concerning grace, which is incomparably more valuable than miracles, it is said, "The good of one person's grace is greater than the natural goodness of the entire universe."[11]

---

them when they were present. By doing this, He showed that He both saw and heard. Third, He did so *as regards the activities of intellective life* by speaking to them and discussing the Scriptures. . . .

Also, He showed the *glory* of his resurrection to His disciples by the fact that He came among them by passing through doors that were closed. . . . Likewise, it pertained to a property of his glory when suddenly "He vanished from their eyes" (Luke 24:31), for by this it was shown that it was in His power to be seen and not to be seen.

Now, to the first objection, we say that *although each argument taken singularly would not suffice for PERFECTLY manifesting the resurrection of Christ, nonetheless when they are all together they PERFECTLY manifest the resurrection of Christ*, maximally on account of the testimony of Scripture and of the words of the angels and also on the assertion of Christ himself, confirmed by miracles."

And in a. 5 it is said, "Christ through the evidence of signs showed Himself to be resurrected."

In the response to the objection cited above, "maximally" is related to the "perfectly" that precedes it. It does not mean that the signs (*argumenta*) independent of the testimony of Scripture, angels, and Christ are insufficient. On the contrary, he said at the beginning of the article, "Each kind of manifestation was sufficient in its own kind." What is there to say? The arguments or sensible signs are sufficient in their order, that is for giving a particular proportionate certitude—namely, that which is called physical certitude: "Feel and see." The testimonies of Scripture, the angels, and Christ, are sufficient for giving certitude of a superior order—namely, supernatural certitude. The manifestation of the Resurrection is therefore as perfect as is possible: the conjunction of a miracle of the first order and of the prophecies, in addition to the affirmation made by the angels and Christ confirmed by the new miracle of the Ascension. And, by *faith* in the Resurrection, the apostles had been led to *see* the Resurrected Christ. "Just as man comes from the hearing of faith unto the Beatific Vision, so too did men come *to the vision of the Resurrected Christ* through those things that they first heard from the angels" (*ST* III, q. 55, a. 2, ad 1).

10 See *ST* I-II, q. 113, a. 5: "Without revelation, nobody can know whether or not he or she has grace but can only know it conjecturally through certain signs."

11 *ST* I-II, q. 113, a. 9, ad 2.

The same difficulty in making a response reappears when, as regards the fact of revelation, we respond, "This fact is naturally knowable and certain by miracles inasmuch as it is supernatural at least *as regards the manner of its production*, by means of the miraculous intervention of God in the world, like the physical miracle that confirms it. However, this same fact of revelation is altogether the motive and object of faith (*quo et quod creditur simul*)[12] inasmuch as it is *essentially* supernatural. For example, consider the Salmanticenses's *de Gratia* (tract. 14, disp. 3, no. 40):

> While, by way of his natural powers, man can rely upon the testimony of God as the Author and End of the natural order, nonetheless he cannot by these natural powers believe by relying upon the aforementioned sort of powers inasmuch as [in this case] it is a testimony of God the supernatural Author and End and inasmuch as it founds supernatural certitude.

This response, which truly conforms to the principles of St. Thomas, allows us to demonstrate that faith is at one and the same time *reasonable* (by the evident credibility that precedes it) and *essentially supernatural* (by its formal motive and its object). However, it is often poorly understood and always, for the same reason, because of a lack of the precise notions of what is essentially supernatural as opposed to what is modally supernatural.

Now, there are two opposed reproaches that are registered against this response. On the one hand, some believe that it misunderstands the completely supernatural character of faith.[13] On the other hand,

---

[12] See Cajetan, *In ST* II-II, q. 1, a. 1, no. 11. Likewise, see Capréolus, John of St. Thomas, Bañez, Gonet, Billuart, and Zigliara.

[13] Thus, Fr. Rousselot writes: "How does it come about that a theologian (i.e., Fr. Gardeil) who is so independent of modern prejudices and entirely possessed, if one dares to say it, by St. Thomas's great theses, how is it that this ever clear-sighted adversary of the supernatural *quoad modum*, the merely veneered supernatural, is able still to preserve in his synthesis this *little morsel of Scotism*? Here again, the philosophical prejudice is revealed. He appears to forget that, in the intellective act, the causality of the *light* (which is of the subject) does not number alongside the causality of the notes perceived in the object and cannot, by consequence, be opposed to it. He

others do not see the necessity of an essentially supernatural formal motive for theological faith (and as supernatural, inaccessible to reason).[14] However, St. Thomas has said that the infused moral virtues differ by their formal object from the acquired moral virtues.[15] All the more should infused faith have a formal motive superior to that of acquired faith such as the demons have. The Salmanticenses[16] explain very well why, on this point, St. Thomas, the Thomists, St. Bonaventure, and Suarez (all partisans of supernatural faith *quoad substantiam*) are opposed to Scotus, the nominalists, and Molina (all partisans of supernatural faith *quoad modum*).

These latter generally allege against the Thomists a text of St. Thomas taken from *ST* II-II, q. 171, a. 2, where the holy Doctor wishes to show that prophecy is not a *habitus* and where he responds, to the

---

appears to believe that to affirm the subjective necessity of the light of grace would be to deny the full objective sufficiency of the motives of credibility" (Pierre Rousselot, "Remarques sur l'histoire de la notion de foi naturelle," *Recherches de sciences religieuse* 4 [1913]: 33).

In reality, Fr. Gardeil conserved exactly the parallelism of the subjective light and the object of knowledge when he held that [one the one hand] the fact of revelation, inasmuch as it is the simple miraculous intervention of God in the world (supernatural *quoad modum* confirmed by miracles), is knowable by the light of reason and that [on the other hand] the same fact, inasmuch as it is *supernatural quoad substantiam*, can be attained only by the light of faith. It is the same as what was said by the Salmanticenses in the selection above.

[Tr. note: A full version of Rousselot's essay can be found in Pierre Rousselot, *Essays on Love & Knowledge*, trans. Andrew Tallon, Pol Vandevelde, and Alan Vincelette, ed. Andrew Tallon and Pol Vandevelde (Milwaukee, WI: Marquette Unviersity Press, 2008), 183–224.]

[14] For example, J. V. Bainvel, *La Foi et l'acte de foi* (Paris: Lethielleux, 1908), 168: "It is beyond doubt that, in general, human acts are specified by their formal object (or what comes to say the same, by their formal motive). However, that the act, *inasmuch as it is supernatural* would always have a supernatural motive and that the absolute necessity of grace for supernatural acts holds precisely to the disproportion of the faculty with this formal motive (or object)—this is what more than one person contests, in emphatically noting the confusion that their adversaries seem often to make between the specification of the act as moral and its specification as a supernatural act.

"We do not care in the end.... What is necessary to hold is that the act of supernatural faith does not differ *as psychological act, as an act of faith*, from the act of natural faith."

Fr. Bainvel seems to represent here the extreme opposed to the theory of Fr. Rousselot.

[15] See *ST* I-II, q. 63, a. 4, ad 1.

[16] See Salmanticenses, *Cursus theologicus, De gratia*, tract. 14, disp. 3, dub. 3.

third objection, [that] it is necessary for us to have a supernatural *habitus* in view of acts that are supernatural *quoad modum*, like the acts of faith and charity; there is no need for *habitus* in view of acts that are supernatural *quoad substantiam* such as prophesying or doing miracles.[17]

The Thomists,[18] have often explained that, in this response (like that concerning the division of miracles found in *ST* I, q. 105, a. 8), the supernatural *quoad substantiam* is taken in relation to the efficient cause and not in relation to the formal cause, and that it is therefore synonymous with the extraordinary supernatural, whereas the supernatural *quoad modum* is here synonymous with the ordinary or habitual supernatural that requires a *habitus*. Despite this explanation, which is manifestly founded upon the context,[19] the partisans of supernatural faith *quoad modum* always renew this objection.

The obscurity of these various controversies appears to arise from the same cause: namely, the imprecision of definitions generally given for the supernatural *quoad modum* and the supernatural *quoad substantiam*, which is sometimes confused with the *miracle quoad modum* and the *miracle quoad substantiam*, or, again, with the ordinary supernatural and the extraordinary supernatural.

This imprecision itself arises from the fact that, in many treatises on dogmatic theology, the divisions of the supernatural are only

---

[17] See *ST* II-II, q. 171, a. 2, ad 3: "To the third objection, it must be said that every gift of grace elevates man to something that is above human nature. Now, that can be in a twofold manner. In one way, it can be in regard to the substance of the act, such as to miracles and to know hidden and uncertain things of Divine Wisdom; and to these acts there is not given a habitual gift of grace. In another way, it can be something above human nature as regards the mode of the act, not, however, according to its very substance—for example to love God and to know Him in the mirror of created things; for these there is given a habitual gift of grace."

[18] E.g., John of St. Thomas, *Cursus theologicus*, De gratia, disp. 20, a. 1, solv. obj.

[19] It is obvious elsewhere that, for St. Thomas, as for all the theologians, the supernaturality of sanctifying grace is superior to that of the graces freely given [*gratis datae*]. See *ST* I-II, q. 111, a. 5: "Sanctifying grace [*gratia gratum faciens*] is much more excellent than graces freely given." See Gonet, *Clypeus theologiae thomisticae*, De gratia, disp. 2, a. 1, §2: "Sanctifying grace [*gratia gratum faciens*] is of a higher order and perfection than are graces freely given, as St. Thomas teaches here in a. 5. . . . The first is a participation in the Divine Nature, as it is nature; the second, however, only participates in some attribute of God, e.g., his knowledge or power." Gonet is particularly clear regarding the notion of supernaturality and is scrupulously Thomistic.

juxtaposed. Sometimes, there are a dozen acceptations for the word enumerated, but then the author neglects to order them philosophically. [Matthias] Scheeben himself, who in his dogmatic theology exposited at length the theory of the absolute supernatural, was then content with juxtaposing too simply the fundamental notions of his treatise.

On the contrary, the Thomists have philosophically classified the various acceptations of the word "supernatural" according to the four causes—as one sees in John of St. Thomas,[20] the Salmanticenses,[21] and even in Suarez, who expresses himself the same on this matter.[22]

It is this division that we wish simply to recall.

The Division of the Supernatural

Above all else, "supernatural" signifies that which is above nature.

Now, what should we understand by "nature"? St. Thomas, following Aristotle, gave precision to the common notion of nature.[23] In each being, nature is the very essence of this being inasmuch as it is the fundamental principle of its activity. Thus, we say, "Man naturally desires to know."

From this perspective, what then does "natural" signify? Something is "natural" for each being if it is fitting for it according to its nature[24] and, above all, according to its very *nature* along with its *faculties* and the *activity* of which the nature is the principle. However, it also pertains to the *end* to which a thing is essentially ordained—thus, we speak of the natural end of man—and the Divine *concurrence* that is necessary for the exercise of its natural activity—thus, we speak of the natural concurrence of God without which second causes cannot act.[25]

---

[20] See John of St. Thomas, *Cursus theologicus, De gratia*, disp. 20, a. 1, solv. arg. no. 4.

[21] See Salmanticenses, *Cursus theologicus, De gratia*, tract.14, disp. 3, dub. 3, no. 24.

[22] See Suarez, *De gratia*, bk. 2, ch. 4.

[23] See Aquinas, *In II phys.*, ch. 1, lecs. 1 and 2. Also, *In V meta.*, lec. 5; *ST* I, q. 29, a. 1, ad 4; III, q. 2, a. 1.

[24] See *ST* I-II, q. 10, a. 1.

[25] [Tr. note: The reader should be aware that Fr. Garrigou-Lagrange is using "concurrence" loosely. He is no Molinist.]

Now, in contrast to "natural" taken in this sense, we oppose: (1) that which is violent (i.e., *against nature*); (2) that which, without being against nature, is *preternatural* (e.g., the state of the human soul in separation from its body);[26] and (3) that which is neither against nature nor only preternatural but is *supernatural* (or, that which exceeds the proportion of nature).

From other points of view, "natural" is opposed to that which is free, artificial, or fortuitous. The free action, like the work of an artisan or the artist, is not determined by nature. It demands a new determination resulting from deliberation. As regards the fortuitous, such things are produced in nature but only accidentally and as though it had been intended and willed.

Now, how must we understand the "supernatural"? For a given being, it is that which surpasses the proportions established by the nature of this being without, however, being contrary to it; as St. Thomas often says, "Quod excedit proportionem naturae." More explicitly, the supernatural is that which surpasses the natural powers and the demands of this or that being but would be fitting to it if it were gratuitously given to it. The error of naturalism is precisely the confusion of the supernatural with that which is against nature.

The supernatural is called relative when it only surpasses a given determined nature (e.g., human nature but in no way an angelic nature).

The supernatural is called absolute or Divine when it surpasses every nature that has been created or ever could be created.

It is this absolute or Divine supernatural that is important to divide in a necessary and adequate manner. The division of the Thomists is as follows:[27]

---

[26] Also, one sometimes designates by the word "preternatural" the relative supernatural (whether angelic or demonic) or even that which is supernatural *quoad modum* (i.e., miracles), but neither of these senses are the strict meaning of the word "preternatural."

[27] See John of St. Thomas, *Cursus theologicus, De gratia*, disp. 20, a. 1, solv. arg.:

> It must be noted that *supernaturality* can pertain to a thing from the perspective of three principles, namely *from an efficient cause, a final cause, or a formal cause*. It cannot pertain to the perspective of material cause, as the material cause is the very subject in which such supernatural forms are received, and this is the soul itself or one of its powers, which are natural beings [*entia nat-*

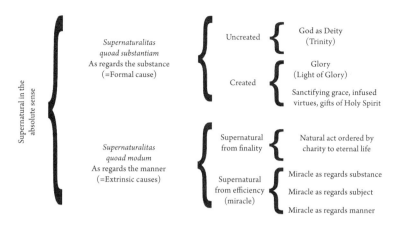

[To help give some initial clarity to the division, Fr. Garrigou-Lagrange places footnotes in the diagram, attached to "Miracle as regards substance" and "Miracle as regards manner."[28]]

---

uralia], although they receive [them] on account of an obediential potency.

From the perspective of efficient cause, something is called supernatural when it is *done in a supernatural manner,* whether the thing thus done is supernatural or natural, just as the resurrection of a dead person or the illumination of a blind person are supernatural *quoad modum,* though the thing made is natural, namely the life of a man or the power of sight.

From the perspective of final cause, that is called supernatural which *is ordered to a supernatural end from without* [*ab extrinsico*], just as the act of temperance, or some other acquired virtue, if it is ordered by charity toward merit of eternal life, receives in itself a *supernatural mode of ordination* toward such an end. And in this manner, the *humanity of Christ* has a supernatural mode of union to the Word to which it is ordered as toward an end and a term of union.

From the perspective of formal causality, something is called supernatural *when from its formal, specificative notion* [*ratione*] *it regards* [*respicit*] *a supernatural object.* And that is called *supernaturality quoad substantiam,* which is so with regard to the species and nature of the act, which is taken from the formal object.

[Tr. note: Although Fr. Garrigou-Lagrange does not cite the edition of the *Cursus theologicus,* it is almost certainly Joannis a S. Thoma, *Cursus theologicus,* new edition, vol. 6 (Paris: Vivès, 1885).]

28 [Tr. note: The footnote for "Miracles as regards substance" reads: "In the class of miracles as regards substance, we include prophetic knowledge of a future contingent of the natural order. However, revelation of a truth that is essentially supernatural (e.g., the Trinity) is itself supernatural *quoad substantiam,* as is the infused faith regarding this truth." The note on "Miracles as regards manner" reads: "In the class of mir-

This division is necessary, immediate, and adequate. Logic teaches, in fact, that a division that is not accidental but, instead, necessary (*per se*) ought to be made according to the formal reason of all that it divides, and it is adequate when it is exhaustive.[29] Now, we have defined the absolute supernatural as "that which *exceeds* every nature that has been created or could be created." Therefore, the division ought to be taken according to the very foundation of this *excess*, and this foundation can be only intrinsic or extrinsic. Thus, the supernatural will be essentially different according to how it surpasses every nature that has been created or ever could be created, surpassing them *either by intrinsic causes or only by way of extrinsic causes.*

The *intrinsic* causes of a thing are the essential principles that constitute what it is. Aristotle and the scholastics call them the formal and material causes. Now, it is clear that a thing cannot be superior to all natures that have been created (as well as all natures that ever could be created) by means of its material cause. However, if this superiority pertains to it by its *formal cause* (i.e., by the intrinsic principle that constitutes it and specifies it), one will say that it is *supernatural quoad substantiam vel essentiam.* Indeed, it exceeds, by its very essence, not only all created *powers* but, instead, all created or creatable *natures.* Such is the very essence of God, as well as sanctifying grace, which is a participation in the nature of God,[30] as well as the infused virtues and

---

acles as regards the manner of production, we include, for example, *instantaneous* knowledge of a human science or a foreign language, forms of knowledge that can be acquired only over time. Similarly, we could include the inspiration for infallibly judging (*modo infallibili*) that which reason already knows naturally and can already judge with chances of error. Indeed, St. Thomas says in ST I-II, q. 174, a. 2, ad 3: 'If the intellectual light is divinely infused into someone, not for the sake of knowing something supernatural but, instead, for judging with the certainty of divine truth those things that human reason can know, such intellectual prophecy is below the kind of prophecy joined to imaginary visions leading to supernatural truth.'"]

[29] [Tr. note: For a brief, accessible explanation of logical division as a preparation for definition, see Vincent E. Smith, *The Elements of Logic* (Milwaukee, WI: Bruce, 1957), 66–74. The interested researcher would benefit from consulting the treatment of division in Austin Woodbury, *Logic*, The John N. Deely and Anthony F. Russell Collection, Latimer Family Library, St. Vincent College, Latrobe, PA, nos. 183–94.]

[30] See *ST* I-II, q. 112, a. 1.

the gifts that derive from habitual grace like a property derives from something's essence.[31]

On the other hand, the *extrinsic* causes of a thing are the efficient cause and the final cause. That which is supernatural, not at all by its formal or specifying cause, but only by its extrinsic causes, is called *supernatural quoad modum*. And this supernatural is subdivided, like the extrinsic causes that provide its foundation, into the supernatural *quoad modum* of *efficiency* and the supernatural *quoad modum* of *finality*.

The modal supernatural pertaining to efficiency pertains to *miracles*. The miraculous effect (e.g., life rendered unto a corpse) is natural as regards the formal principle that specifies it and, for that reason, it is naturally knowable. It is supernatural only by the *mode of its production*, for God alone can produce something outside the ordinary course of nature. In no way does it surpass *all created natures*. It surpasses only all *created or creatable powers*.

This modal supernatural is itself subdivided according to the various ways that it surpasses all created *powers*:[32]

1. It can surpass them *by its very essence*. Thus, no created cause can produce the glorification of the body; such a glorification is a corporeal overflow from the soul's own glory. However, this glorious brightness does not in any way surpass all created *natures*. It is a sensible brightness that is naturally knowable,[33] and by its formal cause it is of an order infinitely inferior to the grace and glory of which it is only a corporeal manifestation.

2. The miraculous effect surpasses all created powers *as regards the subject* in which it is produced (and not as regards its essence) when these powers can produce the effect in another subject. Thus, nature can produce life, but not at all in a corpse.

3. The miraculous effect surpasses all created powers only by the *mode* according to which it is produced—for example, instantaneous healing of a sickness that would have naturally healed only with time.

---

[31]   See *ST* I-II, q. 110, aa. 3 and 4.

[32]   See *ST* I, q. 105, a. 8.

[33]   See *ST* III supplement, q. 85, a. 2, ad 1.

However, outside of the modal supernatural of efficiency, there is a modal supernatural of *finality*. This sort of finality is that which, while being natural because of its formal and specifying principle, is *extrinsically ordained to a supernatural end*—for example, an act of acquired natural virtue, like temperance, ordered by charity to eternal life. This act, of itself natural, receives from charity an accidental mode that makes it a meritorious act.[34]

We must note that this division is not opposition by opposed *things*, but rather by opposed *notions* [*rationes*]. Thus it is that one and the same thing (e.g., grace) will be at one and the same time supernatural *quoad substantiam* and supernatural *quoad modum*; the same holds for the fact of revelation that makes us know strictly supernatural mysteries. However, we will call specifically supernatural *quoad modum* that which has only this sense (i.e., is not also supernatural *quoad substantiam*). St. Thomas makes the same remark with regard to the division of the good into the fitting [*honestum*], useful, and pleasurable.[35]

The overall framework of this division of the supernatural is imposed, it seems, upon all theologians. What they dispute is only to what categories a given supernatural gift pertains.

Nominalists, who do not take into account the irreducibility of essences, judging all things by concrete facts and not by the formal reasons of things, have generally seen in the life of grace (and, hence also, in the infused virtues) only a modal supernatural *ex fine*, which their adversaries have called *veneered* [*plaqué*] supernatural. William of Ockham, Gabriel Biel, and Peter of Ailly have held that sanctifying grace is not supernatural by its very essence and that it has a saving value only because of a contingent institution made by God, as metal has value as money only because of a law expressed by the civil authority.[36]

Durandus of St. Pourçain, John Duns Scotus, and Luis de Molina have peculiar affinities with the nominalists on this point (as upon

---

[34] See *ST* I-II, q. 109, a. 4.

[35] See *ST* I, q. 5, a. 6, ad 2. [Tr. note: Thus the fitting good is desirable. However, desirability strictly *of itself* is indifferent to virtue or vice. Fr. Garrigou-Lagrange is drawing a parallel between this case and those of the *supernatural quoad substantiam* and the *supernatural quoad modum*.]

[36] See Salmanticenses, *Cursus theologicus, De gratia*, tract. 14, disp. 4, dub. 2, no. 34.

many others).[37] Cajetan, whom some contemporary theologians wrongly place among the partisans of supernatural faith *quoad modum tantum*, says in his commentary on *ST* I, q. 12, a. 6 (no. 12):

> Based on what St. Thomas says in this article, we see the obvious falsity of Scotus's opinion expressed in the prologue to the beginning of his commentary on the first book of the *Sentences*, namely where he wishes to hold that the natural and supernatural do not distinguish *things* but only *relations to active causes*.

Likewise, Gonet states:[38]

> The opinion of Scotus is generally rejected, for it does not distinguish between the *intrinsically supernatural*, or *quoad entitatem*, and the *extrinsically supernatural*, or *quoad modum*; it is opposed to the common consensus of the theologians who admit that we have gifts that are supernatural intrinsically and entitatively; nay, rather, it is against the faith providing for such gifts.[39]

---

[37] See Scotus, *In* I *Sent.*, d. 17, q. 3, no. 33, and elsewhere. See Molina, *Concordia*, q. 14, a. 13.

[38] See Gonet, *Clypeus theologiae thomisticae, De gratia*, disp. 2, a. 3 ("Whether habitual grace is a form that is entitatively supernatural").

[39] After the division of the supernatural exposited above, one can easily explain the passage of St. Thomas in *ST* II-II, q. 171, a. 2 ad 3, that is given to us in opposition by the partisans of the supernatural *quoad modum tantum*. In that passage, St. Thomas, having as his end to show that prophecy is not a *habitus*, wishes to say that it is an extraordinary supernatural gift and not one that is habitual. And, if he says that it is supernatural *quoad substantiam* and that charity and faith are supernatural *quoad modum*, he intends it in relation to the *efficient cause* and not in relation to the *formal cause*. Thus, this terminology corresponds to that which is used in the division of miracles in *ST* I, q. 105, a. 8. And it goes without saying that he cannot hold that the supernaturality of *graces freely given* (the gift of prophecy and the gift of miracles) is *formally* (*entitatively*) superior to the supernaturality of sanctifying grace, charity, and faith; with the ensemble of theologians, he constantly teaches the contrary. See *ST* I-II, q. 111, a. 5; q. 114, a. 10, ad 1; q. 113, a. 9.

[Tr. note: I am following the original text, as discussed above in note 35 of the previous chapter.]

In opposition to the nominalists, to Durandus, and to Scotus, the Thomists (and also Suarez[40]) hold that habitual grace, the infused theological and moral virtues, and the gifts of the Holy Spirit are supernatural *quoad substantiam* (or, by their *formal object*). This is the teaching of the great theologians and it is difficult for us to understand how many contemporary theologians overlook an essential element of this doctrine and deny an essentially supernatural formal object for the theological virtues, one that is inaccessible to natural faith, all the while striving to hold that these virtues are supernatural *quoad substantiam*. From this perspective, one can no longer see what separates, as a psychological act (*in esse physico*), the acquired faith of the demon and infused theological faith. They no longer differ except from the moral point of view.[41] One finds in many contemporary theologians the nominalist or empiricist tendency that judges everything by way of concrete facts and not by the formal reasons of things, which alone can render the facts intelligible. The Salmanticenses raise the point with an indignation that recalls the same sort of indignation raised by St. Anselm against the nominalists of his day:

> Nothing in true philosophy would remain unwavering concerning the *species* and the distinction of powers and *habitus*; likewise, we would be compelled to establish a new foundation that was not taught by Aristotle, St. Thomas,[42] and the other leaders of the other Schools. And while younger theologians may admit this with ease, we would have no leader from among the ancients. This would fall immediately into the greatest loss

---

[40] However, Suarez does differ from the Thomists in that he admits there to be an *active* obediential potency.

[41] In a recent opusculum, Emmerich David strives to show that, according to St. Thomas, supernatural acts do not have a proper formal object. The author recognizes that St. Thomas is interpreted in a different way by his principle commentators. If this essentially nominalist and Molinist thesis were true, it would be necessary to conclude that Ockham and Molina understood St. Thomas better than the entire Thomistic school! See Emmerich David, *De objecto formali actus salutaris* (Bonn: Hanstein, 1913).

[42] See Aquinas, *In II De anima*, lec. 6. Also, *ST* I, q. 77, a. 3; I-II, q. 63, a. 3, ad 1.

of true wisdom; whence, with regard to this matter, it is necessary to hinder them with all our strength.[43]

In fact, an abyss separates truly great theology from nominalism, which, as a doctrine, is not only mediocrity, but misery itself. Metaphysically, it naturalizes everything in our supernatural life, just as it reduces reason merely to experience. It is well known that Luther was formed in the school of the nominalists, and their theory of the supernatural prepared the way for his theory, as well as that of Baius.[44]

If one does not forget the Thomist principles and the division of the supernatural that was explained above, it is easy to understand that the fact of revelation can be rationally certain inasmuch as it is at least supernatural *quoad modum*, as a straightforward intervention of God, like the miracles that confirm it; whereas it is altogether the formal motive and the object of faith (*quod et quo creditur*) inasmuch as it is supernatural *quoad substantiam*. This is what the Salmanticenses say in the text that we cited in the beginning,[45] and this is what St. Thomas himself has said, most particularly in *In V John* lec. 6, [Marietti] no. 9,[46] when he distinguished (with regard to the fact of revelation) *the*

---

[43] Salmanticenses, *Cursus theologicus, De gratia*, tract. 14, disp. 3, dub. 3, no. 60.

[44] See the forty-second proposition of Baius (condemned in Pius V's bull *Ex Omnibus Afflictionibus*): "The justice by which the sinner is justified through faith consists formally in the *observance* [*oboedientia*] of the commandments; it is the justice of works. It does not consist in any sort of (habitual) grace infused in the soul by which man becomes God's adopted son, is internally renewed, and *is made a sharer in the divine nature* so that, renewed in this way through the Holy Spirit, he may henceforward lead a good life and obey the commandments of God" (Denzinger, no. 1942). *This represents the reduction of the supernatural order to the moral order.* Supernatural life, to take the metaphysical point of view, is thus destroyed.

From this, one sees the naturalist danger of the doctrine according to which the act of infused faith does not necessarily need a formal motive that is *essentially supernatural* (and that is sufficiently distinguished *by its moral motive* from the *natural/acquired* faith that is found, for instance, among the demons).

[45] See Salmanticenses, *Cursus theologicus, De gratia*, tract. 14, disp. 3, no. 40.

[46] St. Thomas, *In Ioan.* 5, lec. 6, Marietti no. 9: "God testifies to something in a twofold manner, namely, sensibly and intelligibly. He does so *sensibly* just as through a sensible voice (and miracles, as was said a little earlier); and in this way was testimony made to Moses on Mount Sinai. . . . However, He testifies *intelligibly* by inspiring in the hearts of those who believe what they ought to believe and hold. . . . Therefore, you (i.e., the unbelieving Jews to whom Jesus was speaking) were able to receive the

sensible testimony, which is Divine and supernatural only as regards efficiency [*effective*] and could be known naturally by the Pharisees and demons, and the *intelligible testimony*, which is the *voice of the Father* understood by supernatural faith and is understood neither by the Pharisees nor by the demons—*neque vocem eius unquam audistis*. The demon, just like the heretic, attains only unto the supernatural mysteries *materially*; he cannot attain unto them *formally* inasmuch as they are supernatural by their essence. However, nominalism cannot perceive this distinction.

By that, one explains that faith is at one and the same time *reasonable* (i.e., based upon the evident credibility that it presupposes) and *essentially supernatural* (i.e., by its formal motive and its first object). Therefore, faith is *in itself*, despite its obscurity, more certain than the eyes of flesh by which we know the miracle, indeed more certain than our adherence to the principle of contradiction.[47] Certain with a supernatural certitude *quoad substantiam*, it is supported by the *very voice of the Father* who makes Himself heard to us when the Church, His instrument [*son organe*], proposes revealed truth to us.

Christ could say on the one hand:

---

first kind of testimony, for it was from God only *effectively* (i.e., according to supernaturality pertaining to efficient causality), as was said—those words and sights [*species*]. However, you did not understand these words—*neque vocem eius umquam audistis*, etc.—that is, you were not among those partaking in them. . . . That is, you did not have that intelligible testimony and, therefore, did He add, '*Et verbum eius non habetis in vobis manens.*' . . . However, every word inspired by God is *a kind of participated likeness of Him* (i.e., according to supernaturality *quoad substantiam*)."

The Salmanticenses (and other Thomists) merely express the same doctrine when they say, "While, by way of his natural powers, man can rely upon the testimony of God as the Author and End of the natural order, nonetheless he cannot by these natural powers believe by relying upon the aforementioned sort of powers inasmuch as [in this case] it is a testimony of God the supernatural Author and End and inasmuch as it founds supernatural certitude" (*De gratia*, trans. 14, disp. 3, dub. 3, no. 40).

One can say that miracles reveal God as the *Author and Master of nature* (as opposed to the *Author of the order of glory and grace*). Indeed, inasmuch as He is the Author of the natural order, God can do miracles because He is the *free* Author of this order. And this is why the philosophy that considers God only as the Author of the natural order treats of the possibility and the discernability of miracles.

47 See *ST* II-II, q. 4, a. 8.

For the works which the Father has granted me to accomplish, *these very works which I am doing, bear me witness* that the Father has sent me. (John 5:36)

And immediately after that, He adds:

And the Father who sent me has himself borne witness to me. His voice you have never heard, his form you have never seen; and you do not have his word abiding in you, for you do not believe him whom he has sent. (John 5:37–38)

On the contrary, insisting again upon the absolutely and essentially supernatural character of faith, our Savior said to Peter: "Blessed are you, Simon Bar-Jona! For flesh and blood has not revealed this to you, but my Father who is in heaven" (Matt 16:17).

Three things, says St. Thomas,[48] lead us to faith: (1) natural reason; (2) the testimony of the Law and the prophets; and (3) the preaching of the apostles and their successors. However, when man thus led has arrived at faith, then he can say, "The formal motive by which I believe is none of the three preceding things; the formal motive for my belief is the First Truth Himself" ("Quando per hoc homo manducatus credit, tunc potest dicere, quod propter nullum istorum credit; nec propter rationem naturalem, nec propter testimonia legis, nec propter praedicationem aliorum, sed propter *ipsam primam Veritatem tantum*").

---

[48] See *In IV John*, lec. 5, no. 2.

Chapter 5

The Supernaturality of Faith

I N T H E P R E C E D I N G C H A P T E R, we discussed the divisions of the absolute supernatural. As we said there, something can be supernatural in two manners, either *intrinsically, by its very essence* (by that which specifies it formally, as in the case of grace and the infused virtues), or else *extrinsically* (whether by the *manner* [*mode*] of production, as in the case of miracles, or by the *manner* [*mode*] according to which it is extrinsically ordered to a supernatural end, as is the case of an intrinsically natural act ordered by charity to eternal life). That which is intrinsically supernatural is called supernatural *quoad substantiam* (or, as regards its substance/essence);[1] that which is only extrinsically

---

[1] Only the Uncreated Supernatural is substantial in the sense that It alone exists as *substance*; the created supernatural *quoad substantiam* can be only an *accident*. However, the *essence* of this accident is *supernatural* (the essence of grace, the theological virtues, the seven gifts of the Holy Spirit). Thus, the expression *supernaturale quoad substantiam* signifies *supernaturale quoad essentiam*. The actual grace necessary for the exercise of the infused virtues and the gifts of the Holy Spirit is also essentially supernatural. Some thinkers sometimes confuse the miracle *quoad substantiam* with the supernatural *quoad substantiam*. This obviously is an error, given what we have said. On this, see the table laid out in the previous chapter.

[Tr. note: Fr. Garrigou-Lagrange is being a little loose with the language here. God does not exist in the *category* of substance. Although unable to be defined through proximate genus and specific difference, we can give a quasi-definition of substance as "a thing to whose nature it belongs to exist not in something else." As Aquinas notes in *ST* I, q. 3, a. 5, ad 1, "substance" includes the notion of the given *essence* that *exists* in this particular way (i.e., such as not to be in another). This implies a distinction between essence and existence that is not acceptable for the Divine simplicity. Thus, while substance provides the closest analogate in our experience for articulating the Divine Aseity, we should be careful with our words on this matter. Regarding this quasi-defi-

supernatural is called supernatural as regards the mode of efficiency or finality. This division is adequate, like the division of the four causes, for it is obvious that a thing cannot be called supernatural by its material cause (i.e., by the subject into which it is received), for this subject is the very nature of created beings considered with regard to its obediential potency. (See again the table laid out in the previous chapter.)

We add that a virtue can be *intrinsically* supernatural (i.e., *quoad substantiam*) only if the formal object (or formal motive) that *specifies* it is itself essentially supernatural and inaccessible to reason and acquired faith. We say this in virtue of the fundamental principle that states: every virtue is specified by its object and its formal motive, without which, the species of the habit cannot remain—*species cuiuslibet habitus dependet ex formali ratione obiecti: qua sublata, species habitus remanere non potest.*[2]

From this, it follows, according to St. Thomas (in the same article), that the heretic who rejects the formal motive of Divine faith on a point no longer adheres supernaturally to the dogmas that he pretends to maintain. From which it follows as well that the natural faith of demons forced to believe by the evidence of miracles[3] can differ *specifically* from theological faith only if it has a different formal motive. The faithful, *sub illuminatione et inspiratione Spiritus Sancti,*[4] listen to the *voice of the Heavenly Father* by the instrument [*organe*] of the Church. The demon, deprived of all interior supernatural light, does not hear the voice of the Heavenly Father. He finds only the miracles that stop him from denying the *intervention of the Author of nature* in the prophet and in the Church. Such is the teaching of St. Thomas and the Thomists. Suarez sees this to be not only the doctrine of a school, but, instead, the classical teaching of the theologians.[5]

---

nition of substance, see John F. Wippel, *The Metaphysical Thought of Thomas Aquinas* (Washington, DC: Catholic University of America Press, 2000), 228–37.]

[2] *ST* II-II, q. 5, a. 3. [Tr. note: See also Réginald Garrigou-Lagrange, "Actus specificantur ab obiecto formali: De universalitate huiusce principii," *Acta Pont. Acad. Rom. S. Thom. Aq. Et Rel. Cath,* n.s., 1 (1934): 139–53. A translation of this article is anticipated in a future volume by Emmaus Academic.]

[3] See *ST* II-II, q. 5, a. 2, ad 2.

[4] See declarations from the [First] Vatican Council and the Council of Orange in Denzinger, nos. 3010 and 375–77, respectively.

[5] Suarez, *De gratia,* bk. 2, ch. 11, no. 8.

The Nominalist Theory of the Supernatural

However, it was misunderstood by the *nominalists*, who judge everything by the facts of experience and not by the formal reasons of things, which alone can render the facts to be intelligible. Ockham, Gabriel Biel, and Peter of Ailly held that sanctifying grace is not supernatural by its very essence and that it has a supernatural value only in virtue of a contingent institution by God, like metal having value as money only because of a law promulgated by the civil authority.[6] Likewise, for them, the infused virtues (notably theological faith) were supernatural only by their *mode* inasmuch as they were ordered to an extrinsic supernatural end. According to Ockham, the certitude of theological faith is founded immediately and formally on the natural, acquired faith that is born from the examination of the miraculous signs of revelation.[7] From this point of view, it is very difficult to show in what way supernatural faith is more certain than acquired natural faith, as well as how supernatural faith is specifically distinct from it.

Given these general facts, one ought not be surprised that the nominalists were accused by the Thomists[8] (and also by Suarez[9]) of logically tending to Semi-Pelagianism and Pelagianism. Indeed, according to the nominalists' principles, one rightly can ask how the act of *theological faith* differs from the *natural faith* such as is found even among the demons. One will answer, first of all, that theological faith differs from such natural faith because of the *good will* involved with the former and that there is no need for the foundational good will that is that of charity, since unformed theological faith can exist in the soul in a state of mortal sin.

Without a doubt, but why does not a *natural good will* suffice for theological faith, according to the nominalists' principles? Thus, there would be a *natural faith of authority* that differs from the *scientific faith* of the demon but, at the same time, is infinitely distant from the *supernatural faith of authority* that is conceived of in a sound theology. And if

---

6   See Salmanticenses, *Cursus theologicus, De gratia*, tract. 14, disp. 4, dub. 2, no. 34.

7   See Suarez, *De gratia*, bk. 2, ch. 11 no. 32.

8   See Billuart, *De gratia*, diss. 3, a. 2, §11.

9   See Suarez, *De gratia*, bk. 2, ch. 11.

natural faith can attain unto the formal motive of theological faith, why could it not be the case that natural love of God could attain unto the formal motive of supernatural charity? Is it not obvious that, from this perspective, we find ourselves in an open form of Pelagianism?

Indeed, the Pelagians said (as recalled by St. Thomas in *ST* II-II, q. 6, a. 2) that man, in order to have faith, needs only to receive the external revelation of God, confirmed by signs, and by his natural powers alone believes in this externally proposed revelation. The Semi-Pelagians said that at least the beginning of faith can come from us without grace. Now, the nominalists avoid heresy inasmuch as they recognize the necessity of grace in order to believe as is fitting for salvation—*ut oportet ad salutem*. However, they hold that the act of faith thus produced is not *essentially supernatural* and that, considered in its essence and in its formal motive, it does not exceed natural powers. The necessity of grace was only a *necessity of fact*, not *a necessity of right*. God had thus willed it. From this perspective, the distinction between the natural and the supernatural depends upon the free will of God.[10] This parallels very well the contingentism of nominalist theology, which does not consider the necessity of essences, reducing essences to collections of individuals.

This nominalist theory of the supernatural, which is not without affinity with Semi-Pelagianism, paved the way for Lutheran theology, which is a pessimistic form of naturalism, while Pelagianism is an optimistic form of this error. As is well known, Luther was formed in the nominalist school of thought and held that grace is not a participation of the Divine Nature in us but, instead, the external pardoning of our faults accorded to us by God—a mere extrinsic denomination. Baius claimed, "The justice that justifies the impious by faith consists formally in *obedience* to the commandments which is the justice of works, and *not in infused grace*, by which man is adopted as God's child, revived and thus made a participant in the Divine Nature."[11] This represents the

---

[10] Ockham even went as far as to say that the distinction of moral goodness and badness depends upon the free will of God, as though the absolute power of God could command us to hate Him.

[11] See the forty-second proposition of Baius (condemned in Pius V's bull *Ex Omnibus Afflictionibus*): "The justice by which the sinner is justified through faith consists for-

reduction of the supernatural order to the moral order and the renewal of the Pelagian confusion of the natural and the supernatural (though by presenting the opposite sense). The Pelagians, in denying original sin, exaggerated the powers of nature and rendered grace to be useless. Luther, Baius, and the Jansenists, in emphasizing the consequences of original sin, exaggerated the needs and demands of nature and made grace a thing due to nature for accomplishing one's moral obligation.

Later on, under the influence of Cartesianism, as Fr. Bainvel remarks:

> In the 17th century and for a good part of the 18th century, theology thus emancipated from scholasticism nearly came to the point of forgetting sanctifying grace and supernatural gifts. Sin and grace were only considered as being moral denominations answering to the idea of philosophical and natural integrity. [Ultimately,] this was to suppress . . . the reality of the supernatural except in name only. These ideas were current for a long time, notably in France and in Germany; the faithful still retain something of it today.[12]

Before the Council of Trent's condemnation of the Lutheran theses regarding grace, and before the condemnation of Baius, certain theologians like Duns Scotus[13] and Durandus of St. Pourçain,[14] followed by

---

mally in the *observance* [*oboedientia*] of the commandments; it is the justice of works. It does not consist in any sort of (habitual) grace infused in the soul by which man becomes God's adopted son, is internally renewed, and *is made a sharer in the divine nature* so that, renewed in this way through the Holy Spirit, he may henceforward lead a good life and obey the commandments of God" (Denzinger, no. 1942).

[12] J. V. Bainvel, *Nature et Surnaturel*, 3rd ed. (Paris: Beauchesne, 1905), 73.

[13] See *In I Sent.*, q. prolog. See also *In I Sent.*, d. 17, q. 3, no. 33. [Tr. note: Again, recall that Fr. Garrigou-Lagrange does not explicitly differentiate between the various versions of Scotus's work in the *Lectura*, the *Ordinatio*, and the Parisian *Reportationes*.]

[14] Durandus saw the same with regard to the priestly character, holding it to be merely a relation of reason (i.e., an extrinsic denomination). See Billuart, *De sacram.*, d. 2, a. 2. [Tr. note: Durandus (ca. 1275–1334), who has been mentioned on several occasions, has been the subject of several recent studies. He was a Dominican who also was a kind of proto-nominalist, forcefully opposed by his Dominican confrere, Hervaeus Natalis, who was the French provincial of the Dominican order from 1309 to

Molina,[15] held that theological faith is supernatural only *quoad modum*. This position was ever combatted by the Thomists. Cajetan said, in no. 12 of his commentary on *ST* I, q. 12, a. 5, against the Scotist theory of the supernatural, "From these points (in St. Thomas's article), the *falsity of Scotus's opinion* is obvious in I quaest. Prol. on I Sent., where he opines that *the natural and supernatural do not distinguish things but relations to active causes*"—as though there were in us only a modal supernatural pertaining to efficient causality or to final causality and not something that was essentially supernatural.

In What Sense is Infused Faith Essentially Supernatural? Is It Due to Its Formal Object?

After the Council of Trent, the Thomists rejected again more categorically Scotus's opinion. Gonet, answering whether habitual grace is supernatural by its very essence (i.e., entitatively), wrote:

> The opinion of Scotus is generally rejected, for it does not distinguish between the *intrinsically supernatural*, or *quoad entitatem*, and the *extrinsically supernatural*, or *quoad modum*; it is opposed to the common consensus of the theologians, who admit that we have gifts that are supernatural intrinsically and entitatively; nay, rather, it is against the faith providing for such gifts.[16]

1318, as well as the master general of the order from 1318 until his death in 1323. See Elizabeth Lowe, *The Contested Theological Authority of Thomas Aquinas: The Controversies between Hervaeus Natalis and Durandus of St. Pourçain*, Medieval History and Culture 17 (New York: Routledge, 2003); Isabel Iribarren, *Durandus of St. Pourçain: A Dominican Theologian in the Shadow of Aquinas* (Oxford: Oxford University Press, 2005).]

[15] Molina, *Concordia*, q. 14, a. 13.

[16] Jean Baptiste Gonet, *Clypeus theologiae thomisticae, De gratia*, disp. 2, a. 3. [Tr. note: As noted above, this follows the original Latin with an eye to Fr. Garrigou-Lagrange's translation.]

All the Thomists speak like Gonet.[17] Moreover, the most faithful commentators of Scotus, like Francesco Lychetus (ca.1465–1520), recognized that, after the Council of Trent, it is necessary to acknowledge that grace and infused virtues like faith are supernatural *quoad substantiam*. Lychetus writes on this:

> From the time of the Council of Vienne up to the time of the Council of Trent, it was only more probable that there be *habitus* that are essentially [*per se*] infused. And after the Council of Trent that greater certitude was upheld, and more truly seems to me that it is a matter of faith itself, [namely,] that certain ontological aids [*aliqua auxilia physica*] are given as essentially infused aids for the sake of those sorts of acts.[18]

Likewise, the Salmanticenses could write:

> It must be presupposed that the habit of theological faith is essentially [*per se*] infused and, thus, infused according to a supernatural nature [*quoad speciem supernaturalem*]. Indeed, all theologians now agree on this point—and, rightly so. On the one hand, because it appears as being defined by the Council of Trent in Session 6, chapter 7, canons 11 and 12. Therefore, those important Doctors [*graves Doctors*], who teach that it is certain as a matter of faith [*secundum fidem*], are not lacking. On the other hand, it is so because theological faith is of the same order as sanctifying grace, which certainly is ontologically [*entitative*] supernatural.[19]

Suarez speaks in the same manner as well.[20]

However, if all the scholastic theologians since the Council of Trent recognize that habitual grace and theological faith are supernatural

---

[17] For example, see the works of John of St. Thomas, Tomás de Lemos, the Salmanticenses, and Billuart.

[18] Lychetus, *In Scot.*, III *Sent.*, disp. 25, q. 2, n. 72 (Vivès edition, 15:200).

[19] Salmanticenses, *Cursus theologicus, De gratia*, tract. 14, disp. 3, dub. 3, no. 25.

[20] See Suarez, *De gratia*, bk. 2, ch. 11.

quoad substantiam, a number of them[21] (among whom one finds a nominalist tendency) claim that theological faith does not need an essentially supernatural formal object or formal motive (i.e., one that is inaccessible to natural or acquired faith) for the Council's position to hold.[22]

Fr. Bainvel, without wishing to take part in the debate, very justly exposited this theory when he wrote:

> It is beyond a doubt that, in general, human acts are specified by their formal object (or what comes to say the same, by their formal motive). However, that the act, *inasmuch as it is supernatural would always have a supernatural motive* and that the absolute necessity of grace for supernatural acts holds precisely to the disproportion of the faculty with this formal motive (or object)—*this is what more than one person contests,* in emphatically noting the confusion that their adversaries seem often to make between the *specification of the act as moral and its specification as supernatural act.*[23]

We have responded (as discussed in the previous chapter):[24] however, then, supernatural faith and natural faith (founded on the

---

[21] E.g., Giles de Coninck, Jacques Granados, Juan Martínez de Ripalda, Juan de Lugo, et al.

[22] This thesis was recently displayed in Emmerich David's small work, *De objecto formali actus salutaris.* There, the author holds that the saving act does not have a proper formal object. Fr. P. M. Martin, O.P., a reviewer in the *Revue des sciences philosophiques et théologiques,* Oct. 1913, has seen (like we have) the nominalist thesis latent in this position. He adds, on p. 802: "M. David has believed it possible—but with what pains!—to reclaim the lofty patronage of St. Thomas. What a vain effort! The reader, thus warned, will note . . . that the sense of the terms employed by St. Thomas is different from the sense given them by the author."

[23] J. V. Bainvel, *La Foi et l'acte de foi,* (Paris: Lethielleux, 1908), 168.

[24] See Salmanticenses, *Cursus theologicus, De gratia,* tract. 14, disp. 3, dub. 3, no. 31, where they respond in the same manner to Molina: "From the doctrine of this author, it follows that the *habitus* of theological faith is not necessary; for, *that joining together [coaptatio] and proportioning to a supernatural end above and beyond natural acts can very well be communicated to them without a supernatural habitus* that proximately elicits the act, as comes about in that acts of natural virtues, which are meritorious in the just man. . . . Additionally, from this position, it would happen that the assent of theological faith, considered in itself, would have nothing more than, or would no more lead to the supernatural end, than do the acts of the natural virtues."

purely rational knowledge of the miraculous signs of revelation) would no longer differ except from a *moral* point of view. Is this not to return to the nominalism of Ockham and Biel and, likewise, to favor the position of Baianism?

In recent days, numerous theologians have attempted to show that theological faith can remain *ontologically supernatural without having an object or motive that is essentially supernatural* (and, by that very fact, inaccessible to natural faith). It seems that we are no longer aware of the principle that ought to be fundamental in these matters: *species cuiuslibet habitus dependet ex formali ratione obiecti*.[25] We can understand, then, why they have striven to maintain a position like:

> An act can be considered in its *logical species*: in such a case *its substance is its essential tendency toward its proper object*; its mode is constituted by the accessory differentiations that do not alter this principal element. However, in contrast, it can be envisioned in its *ontological species*—i.e., *its substance is then the physical energy that produces it*. Its mode is made up of the secondary determinations that it can receive from the fact of its production—slow or fast, easy or difficult—or from its acceptation for a given end. . . . One sees that the expression "supernatural *quoad substantiam*" carries with it an equivocation. In the *ontological* sense of the term, the Jesuit theologians have spoken on behalf of the strict (entitative) supernaturality of the act of faith. As regards the *logical* sense of the word, the Jesuits (except the Suarezians) generally hold for the substantial identity, certainly not of scientific faith and the faith of authority, but of a faith of natural authority and a faith of supernatural authority. The notional elements in them would be the same.[26]

---

[25] See *ST* II-II, q. 5, a. 3.

[26] [Tr. note: Fr. Garrigou-Lagrange does not note the source of this interlocutor. I have not been able to track down the article or text either.]

This is indeed what we have said: "Many modern theologians reject an essentially supernatural formal motive or object[27] to the theological virtues, an object or motive that would be inaccessible to natural faith, all while endeavoring to maintain that these virtues are supernatural *quoad substantiam*."[28] One is astonished to see such a doctrine suspected of naturalism: "Therefore," one asks, "is it nothing other than an *ontological* specification, which transports the act into the divine order?"

But the whole question is a matter of knowing precisely if that which is called by the grand expression "ontological specification" can remain without that which they call, in a disdainful enough tone, the "logical specification." In other words, can the act of theological faith be *essentially* supernatural (because of the physical energy that produces it) if it is not supernatural by its essential tendency to its proper object? Furthermore, if it does not have an object or motive that is inaccessible to natural faith, why would it necessarily require an essentially supernatural energy to produce it? Can intellection be *essentially* different from sensation by the physical energy that produces it if it is not essentially different by its essential tendency to its proper object? And, if its proper object is not inaccessible to sensation, why does it necessarily need a purely spiritual energy in order to produce it? Here, we see a metaphysical impossibility. According to the principle *species cuius libet habitus dependet ex formali rationi obiecti*, every faculty and every virtue, being *essentially relative*[29] to an object, is specified by this object and does not have an intrinsic specification independently from the object; failing this, it would no longer be *essentially* relative and would become an absolute. If sensation were not specified by its proper object, why would it be incapable of attaining to the proper object of intellection? What then would happen to the proofs of the spirituality of the human soul? Does not such a misconceiving of the formal object

---

[27] Logical specification, according to the new terminology.

[28] Ontological specification. [Tr. note: These two notes are reversed in what appears to be an editing error in the original. Based on the context, this appears to be the correct form Fr. Garrigou-Lagrange wanted.]

[29] [Tr. note: Transcendentally relative (*relatio secundum dici*). This is not relation in the strict sense (*relatio secundum esse*). "Object" here pertains to the formal object, not the brute thing as thing (or, material object).]

(or proper motive) of supernatural faith (thus rendering it accessible to natural faith) metaphysically destroy the objective foundation of the supernaturality of faith? The entire matter is found in that question.[30]

We do not believe that we will surprise anyone in posing this question, for we have only repeated what has always been said by the principal Thomists against the nominalists, Scotus, and Molina (and that has also been said in a very clear manner by Suarez). We have exposited elsewhere[31] at length the Thomist doctrine on this fundamental point that is at the very heart of all theology. It is so important because it pertains to nothing less than the essential distinction between the natural and the supernatural in us. In order to show that we have advanced nothing new on these points, it will suffice here for us to reproduce the principal assertions of the theologians who defend our thesis.

From among these theologians, we will select the man who is least suspected of being excessively rigorous against the nominalists and against Scotus and Molina—namely Suarez. Then, we will see how the Thomists and St. Thomas himself express themselves. Likewise, we will see that which springs from the very language of Scripture and the Church.

* * *

Suarez, who often searched for a midpoint between St. Thomas and Scotus never was very exacting with regard to the essential distinction between the natural and the supernatural. He even held that there is an *active obediential potency* that, to Thomists' eyes, virtually contained the confusion of the two orders. It seemed this way because this potency would be *essentially natural* with regard to its principle (i.e., as being a

---

[30] To say that the *act* of faith is ontologically not specified by its formal motive or its object but, instead, *by the principle* that produces it, *by the infused virtue,* is to reverse the order of things. The virtue is specified by the act (*potentia dicitur ad actum; potency is said with regard to act*) and the act by its object. And, anyway, this would only push back the question one level, for the virtue itself would indeed need to be specified by the object to which it is essentially ordained.

[31] See Garrigou-Lagrange, *De revelatione per Ecclesiam catholicam proposita,* 3rd ed. (Rome: Ferrari, 1931), 1:458–515. [Tr. note: A translation of this work is anticipated in a future volume by Emmaus Academic.]

property of nature) while also being *essentially supernatural* with regard to the object that would specify it. To the Thomists this is a contradiction in terms.[32]

Now, while Suarez was not very exacting regarding the distinction between the natural and supernatural orders, he is clear enough in the question with which we are now occupied and follows the Thomists, at least roughly. In *De gratia*, bk. 2, ch. 11, he asks, "Solely by natural powers, without the aid of grace, can one have an acquired faith that would have *the same* formal motive as infused faith?" He then enumerates the reasons alleged by certain theologians in favor of an affirmative answer to this question, indeed the same ones produced today by many. Then, he notes that Scotus, the nominalists, Molina, and [supposedly] Cajetan[33] proceed to answer, "Yes." Suarez himself responds in the negative with Thomists like Bartolomé de Medina, Domingo Bañez, Domingo de Soto, and John Capreolus,[34] showing that it is also the position of Bonaventure (*In III Sent.*, d. 23, a. 2, q. 2), Richard (*In III Sent.*, a. 7, q. 2), Alexander of Hales (*In III Sent.* q. 64, a. 2), St. Thomas (*ST* II-II, q. 1, a. 1; q. 5, aa. 2 and 3, corp. and ad 1; *In III Sent.*, d. 24, a. 1, q. 1, and innumerable other locations). He even adds: "Commonly, Doctors writing concerning faith." In fact, all the great theologians write in this manner.

---

[32] See John of St. Thomas's treatment in *ST* I, q. 12, disp. 14, a. 2, no. 11 (in vol. 2 of the *Cursus theologicus*) and Billuart in his treatment in *ST* I, q. 12, diss. 4, a. 5, §3: "*This active obediential potency* implies a contradiction, for it is natural and supernatural at one and the same time. It is natural because it would be congenital to all natural agents and follows upon their nature as a property. It is supernatural because it is immediately ordered to a supernatural effect. Secondly, *this active obediential potency would destroy the entire order of grace*; for having posited this potency, grace would be superfluous, given that all the supernatural effects that are attributed to grace and the other supernatural *habitus* could possibly be done through this active obediential potency."

John of St. Thomas (in the aforementioned passage) justly sees in this Suarezian conception of obediential potency the departure point for the divergences between Suarez and the Thomists in matters treated in the treatise on grace, notably concerning the interpretation of the maxim "Facienti quod in se est deus non denegat gratiam [God does not deny the grace to him who does what lies within his power]." [Tr. note: See *ST* I-II, q. 109, a. 6.]

[33] However, Cajetan teaches the contrary against Scotus. See his remarks on *ST* I-II, q. 1, a. 1.

[34] For Capreolus, see *Defensiones theologiae, In III Sent.*, d. 24, q. 1, a. 3, ad *argumenta Scoti*.

Then, Suarez defends his thesis in two ways—theologically and philosophically. Theologically, in nos. 11–13, 17, and 21, he notes the danger of Pelagianism. If the formal motive of Divine faith indeed is not supernatural and inaccessible to natural faith, then interior grace is no longer necessary for producing the act of faith according to this motive. From this perspective, it seems sufficient to have external revelation confirmed by miracles that are naturally knowable. In no. 17, Suarez adds:

> However, to say that a larger grace or aid is only required so that the assent may be more perfect in its being [*in genere entis*],[35] although *from the power of the object* [*ex vi obiecti*][36] it would not be necessary, greatly approaches what Pelagius said, namely that grace is required only for making our actions to be done more easily. Likewise, it seems to be a flight invented solely for the sake of escaping the testimony of the Councils and the Fathers.

Philosophically, Suarez, like the Thomists, holds the fundamental principle: habits are specified by acts, and acts are specified by objects (nos. 22 and 23). He presents an objection to himself akin to what is held by many today:

> Some respond that those acts *are formally and essentially distinguished through their entities, though it is not necessary to seek something formally distinct from the perspective of the object.*

And to this, Suarez responds that that is nothing less than the destruction of all philosophy:

> However, this means nothing other than overturning the principle of the distinction of acts by their objects. [Indeed,] it means nothing other than overturning the whole of philos-

---

[35] According to the new terminology, discussed earlier, "ontological specification."
[36] According to the new terminology, "logical specification."

ophy, which teaches that motion and everything essentially including a relation to something other than itself [*habitudinem ad aliud*] (whether predicamental or transcendental)[37] have their *species* (and, consequently, their distinction) *from the termini or objects to which they are oriented* [*a terminis vel obiectis quae respiciunt*].

In sum, Suarez presents his adversaries with the choice: either choose the denial [*négation*] of the necessity of grace or that of philosophy. He refutes various objections, particularly that which is often reproduced today: if Divine faith has a formal motive that is inaccessible to naturally acquired faith, psychological experience ought to testify it; now, it does this in no way. "What convert, at the moment of his first act of faith, or what Catholic after a fault against faith, has ever observed in himself this passage from the natural vision to the supernatural vision of the motive or object of faith?"[38]

Have we ever claimed that there is a supernatural vision—a kind of small Beatific Vision—in the obscurity of Divine faith? Certainly, there is an *illumination by the Holy Spirit* (affirmed by the council of Orange[39] and the [First] Vatican Council[40]). *And can it be that this illumination remains without a formal effect* in the intellect of the faithful person? However, psychological experience does not suffice for making us discern with evidence this supernatural effect of the Holy Spirit's illumination from the effects of the natural light of our intellect. As Suarez notes:

---

[37] [Tr. note: To express it another way, whether it be a *relatio secundum esse* or a *relatio secundum dici*, although the distinction between *relatio secundum esse* and predicamental relations (i.e., "real" *relationes secundum esse*) is not clearly articulated here.]

[38] [Tr. note: The quote is not readily discovered, though Fr. Garrigou-Lagrange directly quotes it here.]

[39] Denzinger, no. 377.

[40] First Vatican Council, *Dei Filius*, ch. 3: "Still, no man can 'assent to the Gospel message,' as is necessary to obtain salvation, 'without the illumination and inspiration of the Holy Spirit, who gives to all delight in assenting to the truth and believing it'" (Denzinger, no. 3010).

Since in these acts both natural and supernatural motives are always concurrently in operation in some manner, as I have said, man never discerns with sufficient evidence, whether or not he is moved and acts from a purely supernatural reason, and this is enough that never can he altogether be certain concerning faith or its action [*vel sua operatione*], although he can strongly conjecture regarding it.

St. Thomas even notes that, in the case of the prophetic instinct, which is something imperfect as revelation, the prophet supernaturally judges without always fully discerning that he judges supernaturally:

Concerning those things which the prophet knows by way of an instinct, it sometimes happens that he cannot fully discern whether he has thought this by way of a Divine instinct or by way of his own spirit.[41]

St. Augustine said the same thing concerning this *instinctus*, "which human minds underwent, without knowing it."[42]

Therefore, no less than the Thomists, Suarez saw the danger in the doctrine that he combats. However, the Salmanticenses reproach him for a concession that he makes to his adversaries. After they noted themselves that nothing would remain in philosophy concerning the specification of powers and of *habitus* [by their formal objects], the Salmanticenses add:

We cannot praise Suarez, who, after having defended the common sentiment on this matter in many ways, then deviates from the first principle in this matter. He does so by admitting that *by [God's] Absolute Power*, it can be the case that in one and the same faculty there can be two specifically distinct acts which have the same formal object.[43] By this, Suarez enfeebles and

---

[41] *ST* II-II, q. 171, a. 5.

[42] Augustine, *On the Literal Meaning of Genesis* 17.

[43] However, Suarez does not make this concession for two acts, one of which is natural and the other supernatural; he makes it only for two natural acts.

enervates all that he previously had said, for the specification
that concerns the essence of things abstracts from dispositions
relative to the ordinary or extraordinary power of God.[44]

Moreover, his theory of *active* obediential potency no less compromises
the essential distinction between the natural and the supernatural
orders.[45]

Did not St. Thomas himself respond in advance to the nominalists
by determining against the Pelagians the cause for which interior grace
and the supernatural *habitus* of faith are necessary for one to adhere
formally to the revealed mysteries?

> Since, in assenting to the things that are matters of faith,
> man is elevated above his nature, it is necessary that he have
> this from a supernatural principle that moves him interiorly,
> namely God.[46]

The absolute necessity of grace is due to the disproportion
between our natural intellectual powers and the supernatural object to
be believed, as well as the supernatural motive for which it is necessary
for one to believe. It is necessary to adhere not only to the sensible
testimony of miracles that are naturally knowable but also to the essentially supernatural testimony of the Heavenly Father (i.e., the testimony
of God as the principle of the supernatural order). As St. Thomas says
in a text already cited above,[47] only the faithful illuminated interiorly by
the Holy Spirit can hear this testimony:

> God testifies to something in a twofold manner, namely sensi-
> bly and intelligibly. He does so *sensibly* just as through a sensible
> voice (and miracles, as was said a little earlier); and in this way
> was testimony made to Moses on Mount Sinai. . . . However,
> He testifies *intelligibly* by inspiring in the hearts of those who

---

[44] Salmanticenses, *Cursus theologicus, De gratia*, tract. 14, disp. 3, dub. 3, no. 60.

[45] See John of St. Thomas, *Cursus Theologicus, In ST* I, q. 12, q. 12, disp. 14, a. 2, no. 11.

[46] *ST* II-II, q. 6, a. 2.

[47] Aquinas, *In Ioan.* 5, lec. 6, Marietti no. 9.

believe what they ought to believe and hold. . . . Therefore, you (i.e., the unbelieving Jews to whom Jesus was speaking) were able to receive the first kind of testimony, for it was from God only *effectively* (i.e., according to supernaturality pertaining to efficient causality), as was said—those words and sights [*species*]. However, you did not understand these words—*neque vocem eius umquam audistis, etc.*—that is, you were not among those partaking in them. . . . That is, you did not have that intelligible testimony and, therefore, did He add, '*Et verbum eius non habetis in vobis manens.*' . . . However, every word inspired by God is *a kind of participated likeness of Him* (i.e., according to supernaturality *quoad substantiam*).

The Salmanticenses summarize this doctrine of St. Thomas by going to the foundation of the question that Suarez only saw half of, apparently:

Man can indeed, by his natural powers, rely upon the testimony of *God, the Author of nature* (and cause of the naturally knowable miracle), but he cannot, without supernatural grace, rely upon the testimony of God, the *Author of the supernatural order*, upon the voice of the Heavenly Father, who is the principle of a supernatural certitude.[48]

This distinction is imposed in order to avoid confusing supernatural faith with natural faith, no less than to provide for the distinction between charity and the natural love of God, and this would be to adopt Baius's error rather than to deny it. Indeed, one knows Baius's thirty-fourth proposition: "The distinction of a twofold love of God, namely, a natural love whose object is God as the Author of nature and a gratuitous love whose object is God as beatifying, is meaningless and imaginary; it has been devised as a mockery of the Sacred Scriptures and of the numerous testimonies of ancient authors."[49]

---

[48] Salmanticenses, *Cursus theologicus, De gratia*, tract. 14, disp. 3, dub. 3, no. 40.

[49] Pius V, *Ex Omnibus Afflictionibus* (Denzinger, no. 1934). Likewise, the Rosminian proposition is condemned: "God is the object of the beatific vision insofar as he is the

Without grace, we cannot hear the essentially supernatural testimony of the Spirit who, as St. Paul says, "reveals the depths of God" and the riches of His intimate life: "God has revealed to us through the Spirit. For the Spirit searches everything, even the depths of God" (1 Cor 2:10). The order of agents ought to correspond to the order of ends, and action ought to be specified by its object. Therefore, in order to reveal strictly supernatural mysteries, it is necessary that there be a revealing action of the same order (supernatural *quoad substantiam* and not only *quoad modum*). It is the formal motive of our infused faith. It remains from this point of view inaccessible to natural (or, acquired) faith.[50]

Indeed, this is why Scripture and the Church both attribute revelation to God precisely inasmuch as He is the Heavenly Father and not, precisely speaking, inasmuch as He is the Author of nature. The Free Author of nature can indeed perform miracles. For this reason, one discusses the possibility of miracles in philosophy, which considers

---

author of works *ad extra*" (Decree of the Holy Office, *Post obitum*, in Denzinger, no. 3238). [Tr. note: Regarding Rosmini, see the remarks in note 9 above in the second chapter of this section.]

[50] If God had only supernaturally revealed to us *natural truths of religion* (e.g., the universal extent of His Providence, the immortality of the soul, etc.) and had confirmed His word by miracles, revelation would have been supernatural *quoad modum tantum*. That is, it would have been supernatural only with regard to its manner of production and not *essentially supernatural* (i.e., on account of its object).

In contrast, the Revelation of the Old Testament and the New Testament is *doubly supernatural—quoad modum* and *quoad substantiam*—on account of its formal object: the essentially supernatural mysteries of God's intimate life.

From that moment of revelation onward, it can be *naturally known* under one or the other of its aspects (inasmuch as it is confirmed by miracles and other signs). Likewise, it can be *supernaturally known* under its most elevated aspect. Such is the very simple application of the classical distinction (rejected by Baius) between *God the Author and Master of nature* and *God the Author of grace.*

Recently, it has been written that this doctrine is not conformed to that of St. Thomas and that it was constituted by the Thomists of the sixteenth century. From this point of view (which is one representing a quite material *literalism*), that which is only *implicitly* in the very terms of St. Thomas would not be conformed to his doctrine.

Moreover, the distinction proposed here by the Thomists is even *explicitly* used by St. Thomas. For example, see *ST* I, q. 62, a. 2, ad 1: "The angel naturally loves *God* inasmuch as He is the *Principle of natural being* [lit., *esse*]. However, here we are discussing conversion toward *God* inasmuch as *He is Beatifying* through vision of His Essence." This distinction, here expressed by St. Thomas concerning the love of God, obviously holds for our knowledge of God as well.

God *sub ratione entis, non sub ratione propriissima Deitatis* [from the perspective of being and not from His most proper perspective as the Deity Itself]. In order to reveal the supernatural mysteries, God acts *sub ratione Deitatis*,[51] according to His intimate life, which He wishes to communicate to us, not only so that He may make us to be His creatures but also so that He may make us to be His children. Thus is it that Scripture and the Church ever attribute revelation to the Heavenly Father or to the Holy Spirit. See the scriptural texts cited by the [First] Vatican Council in the chapter on revelation:[52]

> But we impart a secret and hidden wisdom of God. . . . None of the rulers of this age understood this. . . . But, as it is written, "What no eye has seen, nor ear heard, nor the heart of man conceived, what God has prepared for those who love him," God has revealed to us *through the Spirit*. For the Spirit searches everything, even the *depths of God*. For what person knows a man's thoughts except the spirit of the man which is in him? So also no one comprehends the thoughts of God except the Spirit of God.[53]

The Creed speaks of the "Holy Spirit . . . who has spoken through the prophets." Likewise, yet another text cited by the Council:

> At that time Jesus declared, "I thank thee, *Father*, Lord of heaven and earth, that thou hast hidden these things from the wise and understanding and revealed them to babes; yea, *Father*, for such was thy gracious will. All things have been delivered to me by my *Father*; and no one knows the Son except the *Father*, and no one knows the Father except the Son and any one to whom the *Son* chooses to reveal him."[54]

---

[51] To repeat again the point from St. Thomas, *ST* I, q. 1, a. 6: "That which is known concerning God only by Himself and by others by means of revelation that has been communicated."

[52] First Vatican Council, *Dei Filius*, chs. 2 and 4 (Denzinger, nos. 3004 and 3015).

[53] 1 Cor 2:7–11.

[54] Matt 11:25–27.

The God Who reveals is not only the First Cause, the Author of the universe known by Plato and Aristotle. The God Who reveals is the Heavenly Father; He is God in His intimate life, Triune and One. As Jesus says to Peter, "Blessed are you, Simon Bar-Jona! For flesh and blood has not revealed this to you, but *my Father* who is in heaven" (Matt 16:17). Likewise, our Lord said:

> [But the testimony which I have is greater than that of John; for] the works which the Father has granted me to accomplish, these very works which I am doing, bear me witness that the Father has sent me. And the Father who sent me *has himself borne witness to me.* His voice you have never heard, his form you have never seen; and you do not have his word abiding in you, for you do not believe him whom he has sent.[55]

This is the passage that we cited above in the context of St. Thomas's commentary. The Old Testament made the point equally: *Deus salutaris noster,* God our deliverer.

Likewise, the *prima credibilia* that one absolutely must believe in order to be saved—namely, *quod Deus est et remunerator est* [i.e., that God exists and that He rewards according to one's deeds]—look directly upon God the *Heavenly Father,* the Author of the supernatural order, and not only God the Author of nature. It is only from this point of view that they imply the mystery of the Holy Trinity and can be known only by means of revelation.[56] Thus was it that Innocent XI

---

[55] John 5:36–38.

[56] On this subject, St. Thomas says (in *ST* II-II, q. 1, a. 7):

> The articles of faith stand in relation to the teaching [*doctrina*] of faith just as do *per se nota* principles in the teaching [*doctrina*] that is had by way of natural reason. A particular order is found in these principles, as certain ones are contained in others in a simpler manner—just as all principles are reduced to this as to a first, namely, "It is impossible to affirm and to deny [i.e., one and the same thing at one and the same time in one and the same respect]," as is obvious from Aristotle's discussions in the fourth book of the *Metaphysics.* Similarly, all the articles of faith are implicitly contained in certain first things that are believed [*in aliquibus primis credibilibus*]; as it is believed that *God exists* and *that He has Providence concerning men*—as is said in Heb.

condemned the proposition: "Faith, in the broad sense, which is based on the testimony of creatures or on a similar reason, is sufficient for justification."[57] Also, the Thomists generally maintain that the Christian philosopher who has demonstrated the existence of God the Author of nature can (and ought) to believe in the existence of God the Author of the supernatural order.[58]

What difficulty is there in distinguishing in the fact of revelation an exterior aspect that is accessible to reason and another intimate aspect that is accessible only to the interior light of faith? For example, the fact that Jesus Christ died on the Cross out of love for us can be known by reason alone, which sees this fact (as do liberal Protestants) as being a heroic love and the greatest example of moral courage. However, this same fact can be known by faith that sees in it an act that is not only essentially supernatural but also theandric, having an infinite value. Thus too is the infallibility of the Church manifested exteriorly by the notes of the Church, and her intimate nature is a matter of faith.

Therefore, it is not astonishing that the Thomists (and also Suarez) have always seen there to be a kind of affinity with Semi-Pelagianism in the doctrine that would hold that infused theological faith does not have its own proper formal motive, one that is essentially supernatural and inaccessible to natural faith (whether that faith be scientific or from an authority). The teaching of the Thomists is well summarized

---

11:6, "*Accedentem ad Deum oportet credere est, et quod inquirentibus se remunerator sit.* For he that approaches God, it is necessary for such a one to know that God exists and that He rewards those who seek Him."

For, in the Divine Existence is included all that we believe to exist eternally in God, in whom our beatitude consists. However, contained within faith in Providence there are included all those things temporally dispensed of by God for the sake of man's salvation, such things being the way to salvation. . . . Therefore, it must be said thus, namely, that with regard to the essence [*substantiam*] of the articles of faith, there has not been an increase in them through the passing of time, for whatever was believed at a later time was contained in the faith of the Fathers who came before, although it was so contained in an implicit manner. However, as regards further explication [of what was already implicitly contained], the number of articles did increase.

[57] Denzinger, no. 2123.

[58] See Gonet, *Clypeus theologiae thomisticae, De fide,* a. 6, §2.

by Billuart:[59] In order to respect the Council of Orange, it does not suffice that one say that grace is required in order to believe *ut oportet ad salutem* [as is necessary for salvation], for he who believes based upon the true formal motive of Divine faith already believes *ut oportet* [as is necessary]; and, if this formal motive is accessible to natural faith, one no longer sees why grace is necessary. One returns to a simple necessity of fact (and not of right), recognized by the nominalists so as to avoid heresy. Thus, one loses the sense of mystery in the very order of grace.

Solution of Difficulties

First objection: It has been objected against the principle concerning the specification of acts by their formal object that the eagle's vision is specifically distinct from the dog's vision and, nevertheless, they have the same formal object—color.

To this objection, it is necessary that we respond in the same manner as does Cajetan.[60] Between these two, there is only a *material difference*: that of the eagle's eye, which differs from the dog's eye. There

---

[59] See Billuart, *De gratia*, diss. 3, a. 2, §2.

[60] See Cajetan, *In ST* I, q. 77, a. 3, no. 6: "Note that we can speak of the powers of the soul in two ways. In one way, *inasmuch as they are powers* (namely, formally); and this is the meaning of the words here present. In another manner, we can speak of them *inasmuch as they are properties* of a given nature; and this is not the manner in which we are speaking here. For, according to this manner of speaking, they are distinguished on account of the diversity of natures in which they exist, as Averroes states in his commentary on the first book of the *De Anima* (no. 53): 'The members of man are diverse in species from the members of the lion.'"

Thus, the eagle's eye differs from the dog's eye, but the vision of the eagle does not specifically differ as vision from that of the dog. The principle invoked ought to be understood formally and not materially. On the subject of the principle in question (i.e., "faculties, *habitus*, and acts are specified by their formal object"), someone has recently written: *non generatim valet* [this does not hold in general]. This would be a metaphysical principle that would have exceptions. However, a metaphysical principle having exceptions no longer is a metaphysical (i.e., absolutely necessary) principle. Of it, one would say what one does of insipid salt: *it is good for nothing more except being thrown outdoors and trodden upon by men*. Now, it is by means of this principle that one establishes the specific difference between imagination and the intellect, that which is the foundation of the proof of the spirituality and immortality of the soul.

is not a formal difference concerning *vision inasmuch as it is vision*. At best, between these two visions as such there is an accidental difference, like the difference between normal vision and the vision of someone suffering from myopia. The principle that we have invoked ought to be taken *formally*; the act, *as act*, is specified by the formal object toward which it tends.

Second objection: *The principal difficulty* that one raises against our thesis is that the psychological experience of a believer does not succeed at discerning the supernatural formal motive from any other naturally knowable motive: "What convert, at the moment of his first act of faith, or what Catholic after a sin against faith, has ever observed in himself this passage from the natural vision to the supernatural vision of the motive or object of faith? What believer . . . has ever been able to translate a single note of his vision of faith, which was exclusively reserved to him?"

We have never spoken of a *supernatural vision*. Instead, we have spoken of Divine faith under the "illumination of the Holy Spirit," as mentioned by the Council of Orange and the [First] Vatican Council. Can it be that this illumination would be received in our intellect without producing a formal effect in it? What would be the use of it? Nothing is vain, above all in the supernatural order; however, it is quite surprising that someone wishes to discern clearly this formal effect by means of psychological experience, that one holds that "experience suffices to determine[61] this debate." This debate is not of the experiential order but, instead, of the metaphysical order—indeed, much more, it is of the wholly supernatural and theological order. Only the gifts of supernatural revelation and the rational notions in which they are expressed can resolve the question. The light that illuminates theological science[62] is not experience but, instead, is virtual revelation—that

---

[61] [Tr. note: Reading *dirimer* in the sense of *déterminer*. The word *dirimer* is perhaps a French neologism being taken from the Latin *dirimere*, meaning, among other things, "divide" or "dissolve." The later sense is being assumed here in a broad sense. In various French works, Fr. Garrigou-Lagrange on occasion slips into Latin, so perhaps that happened here to a degree.]

[62] For there certainly exists, beneath the Church's definitions, a theological science and not only theological hypotheses.

is, revelation inasmuch as it virtually contains [i.e., in its illuminative power] the conclusions deduced by the aid of a rational premise.

The recourse to "experience sufficing to determine[63] the debate" reminds one of empiricists who admit only sensible phenomena and ask that one show them *substance,* as though it were only a deeper kind of phenomena again accessible to the senses. The mechanists ask the vitalists to show them the vital principle, as though it resembled a will-o'-the-wisp. In order to admit the essential superiority of intellection over sensation, as well as the essential distinction of their formal objects, nominalists require that someone make them see a purely spiritual reality, a pure spirit. The nominalist Durandus of St. Pourçain reduced the priestly character to being only an extrinsic denomination, a relation of reason, likely because he had never had experiential knowledge of it. The theologians of the seventeenth and the eighteenth centuries who, after Descartes, denied the distinction between substance and accidents no longer could admit that there are supernatural accidents, thus reducing the life of grace to that which psychological experience manifests to us regarding it. Likewise, supernatural life was reduced to moral life.

Here below, we know only the intelligible in the sensible, and the supernatural that is essentially distinct in us from our natural activity is not so separated from it that we could experientially distinguish it with evidence from that which is not it [i.e., from our natural activity]. As we said above, according to St. Thomas, even the prophet himself, when he receives only a prophetic instinct, cannot always discern whether the light thus illuminating his mind is that of God or the light of the principles of natural reason.

Without such a discernment being necessary, the faithful, under the illumination and the inspiration of the Holy Spirit (about which the Council of Orange and the [First] Vatican Council speak), hears *the voice of the Heavenly Father* by the instrumentality [*l'organe*] of his Church. Thus, the believer attains in the obscurity of faith a formal motive inaccessible to the demon, as well as to natural faith of authority. The most insightful natural intellect, inasmuch as it has not received

---

[63] [Tr. note: The same *dirimer.*]

the grace of faith, notices only externally the miracles or other signs that prevent him from denying the intervention of the *Author of nature* in the prophet or in the Church. Hence, he can only *materially* understand Divine Revelation and supernatural mysteries.

The matter is very simple. Only an example is needed to make it well understood. A symphony of Beethoven can be heard in two very different ways. On the one hand, there is the person who, without being deaf, has no musical sense and hears it only *materially*. Of such a person, we say that he does not have an ear for it. We may ask him, "Have you heard this symphony?" To this, he can respond, "Yes." Then, we may ask, "Is it truly a masterpiece?" To this, he cannot respond, "No"; it would be foolish to deny what is universally recognized by those who are good judges in this matter. Thus, too, for the demon, it would be an act of foolishness to deny the fact of revelation, which is greatly evident by way of its signs. The symphony of Beethoven is listened to in a wholly different manner by a true musician who grasps its *formal motive*. Not that he immediately perceives Beethoven's genius; he attains unto it only by the material execution of his work, but in this execution, he attains unto that which is the soul of the symphony. Nevertheless, can he indicate *a single note* that had not been heard materially by the other listener? No—the untrained musician truly heard, materially speaking, all the notes; however, the soul of the symphony escaped him. To put the matter aright, we can say that he heard their sounds and did not hear the symphony.

So too is the case of the reader of the Gospel. The most powerful of natural intellects, without the grace of faith, *materially* understands the supernatural meaning of the mysteries of God. Properly speaking, what he perceives is the human meaning of the words of which the Creed is composed. It is a bit like the way that an animal *materially* hears a human word without perceiving the intelligible meaning of the word. In contrast to this, the supernaturalized intellect of the humblest of believers understands [*entend*] the Gospel as the musician hears [*entend*] the symphony of Beethoven. From the supernatural point of view, one can say of the believer, "He has an ear for it." By means of faith, he supernaturally hears the voice of the Heavenly Father, not in an immediate manner as the prophet hears it, but, instead, by the instrument of the

Church. Thus he hears formally "the depths of God" that the Divine Voice reveals. He formally believes in it, while the demon can say only one thing—it is not possible to deny it. These mysterious words are confirmed by the very Author of nature; indeed, it is necessary to admit that, in a material manner, they cannot be false.

Now, one may object, "The notional elements are the very same for supernatural faith and for natural faith"—that is, it is the very same dogmatic formula.

But, the believer does not believe the dogmatic formula of the Trinity; the believer believes the very mystery hidden in God—the profound depths of God. The formula is only a means of knowledge. On this, see St. Thomas's words in *ST* II-II, q. 1, a. 2:

> The act of believing does not find its termination in the *uttered, complex expression* [*enunciabile*][64] but in the *thing*. For, we only form complex expressions so that we may have knowledge of things through them; as this is in scientific knowledge [*scientia*], so too in faith.

Therefore, we can summarize our thesis by reducing it to an argument: Faculties, *habitus*, and acts are specified by their formal object and motive. Now, the formal object of Divine faith is God considered in His intimate life (i.e., according to the proper notion of the Deity). In no way is it God considered according to the common notion of being accessible to reason alone; it is the supernatural mystery of God's intimate life. The formal motive of this Divine faith is the authority of God as Revealer, inasmuch as He is not only the Author of nature but [beyond this] is the Author of the order of grace and glory. Therefore, Divine faith is essentially supernatural and not only supernatural *quoad modum* (as the nominalists hold).

---

[64] [Tr. note: The intellect's second act creates complex intelligibilities upon which judgment is rendered. On this important Thomistic doctrine, see: Jacques Maritain, *An Introduction to Logic*, trans. Imelda Choquette (London: Sheed & Ward, 1946), 84–98; Yves Simon, *An Introduction to the Metaphysics of Knowledge*, trans. Vukan Kuic and Richard J. Thompson (New York: Fordham University Press, 1990), 136–58.]

Also, in order to use the concession made by adversaries since the Council of Trent, one can give the conclusion in place of the minor premise and propose the argument as: *Habitus*, virtues, and also acts are specified by their formal object and motive. Now, one concedes, since the Council of Trent, that the *habitus* of theological faith is supernatural *quoad substantiam*. Therefore, this *habitus* and its acts ought to have an essentially supernatural formal motive inaccessible to natural faith. How could an essentially supernatural certitude be founded formally upon a motive that is naturally knowable?

Finally, it is a matter of faith that, without grace, one cannot believe *ut oportet ad salutem*, as is necessary for salvation. Now, to believe in virtue of the true formal motive of Divine faith is to believe already as one ought, *ut oportet*. Therefore, this motive is inaccessible without faith.

One can see in the Salmanticenses the response to the objections that have been made against these arguments.[65]

The doctrine that we have explained here is not only an opinion of a particular school, as Suarez notes along with the Thomists. It is the *classical doctrine*. And the preachers who must explain what faith is in all of its profundity and elevation do not speak in any other way. They reflect the Gospel. It suffices for us to cite, for example, this passage from Monsignor Charles Louis Gay, who writes (as I imagine, at least) without thinking according to one school rather than some other:[66]

> By speaking exteriorly the living word of His intimate life, God addresses Himself to us; He necessarily speaks a language that we can understand. Merely considering, for now, His intellectual communications, He gives His infinite thoughts in finite words, in well-known, ordinary words whose meaning is perfectly determined in advance. As such, when God uses these words, each of us can perceive them and understand them in

---

[65] See Salmanticenses, *Cursus theologicus, De gratia*, tract. 14, disp. 3, dub.3.

[66] Charles Louis Gay, *De la vie et des vertus Chrétiennes considérées dans l'état religieux*, 3rd ed., vol. 1 (Paris: Oudin, 1983), 158–61. [Tr. note: Msgr. Gay was also Titular Bishop of Anthedon and Auxiliary Bishop Emeritus of Poitiers in the last quarter of the twentieth century.]

their human meaning. God does more, and He should do more: for, in this matter, it is not enough that we know that someone speaks. It is necessary above all that we know who speaks—and He who speaks is God. Therefore, He speaks in God; that is to say, He vests His words with inimitable characteristics.

He is not content with imparting to them this intrinsic beauty that cannot be lacking to them but that His very excellence holds above the reach of a great number. He shows them, confirms them, and accredits them to the eyes of all by means of all kinds of works of His mighty hand and principally by incontestable miracles, of such a kind that not only can one reasonably hold them to be divine but also one can hold them to be of such a sort that, without deceiving common sense and without betraying its proper reason, one cannot confuse them with those that are in no way Divine. Thus, He overwhelms them with radiances that are personal to Him, and in thus showing [*montrant*] Himself, He proves [*démontre*] them.

Does it follow that the senses and reason suffice for us to be able to penetrate into this ultimate sanctuary of things? Certainly not. It is true that they can give us a physical knowledge or an historical knowledge of supernatural Divine facts—and this is their most eminent form of employment. Indeed, their concurrence is here indispensable. Without them, the act of faith would be impossible in its roots. They are the soil where this seed acts and that serves to support it. However, for that which is the real, commanded, meritorious perception of the revealed supernatural, the most exquisite senses and the most applied reason remain wholly incapable. *Faith* alone can give it to us; and not only *is it necessary so that we can adhere to the intimate depths of revelation (i.e., to the Divine reality enunciated in human language)*, but also we cannot have it without grace, which inaugurates it in us, rendering us adequate to the evidence upon which it is based. . . . One can say like the Jews, "This marvel is obvious; it can be in no way denied," and at the same time add like them, "Therefore, let us threaten the men who did it and force them to be silent" (cf. Acts 4:16–17).

Without faith, the most intelligent and most learned man remains the purely natural man whom St. Paul calls *animal* and of whom he says that, "He does not perceive that which is of the Spirit of God." Granted, this man can very well perceive something of God: for this, it suffices that he be reasonable. However, that which is of the "Spirit of God," i.e., the revealed divine, the supernatural divine, . . . to him all of that is folly, nonsense; in the end he can comprehend nothing of it. *Animalis homo non percipit ea quae sunt Spiritus Dei: stultitia enim est illi et NON POTEST intelligere* [The animal man cannot perceive those things which are of the Spirit of God; for it is foolishness to him and he IS NOT ABLE to understand it].[67]

Besides, were the human mind capable of this complete adherence to the testimony that God renders, by way of miracle, to His own word, there would still remain the heart, which necessarily has its part here, truly its very large part. For it is a fact of experience that nobody believes unless he truly wants to believe.

Thus does the Christian sense express itself. According to it, faith is essentially supernatural, for it is necessary for it to adhere to an essentially supernatural reality for an essentially supernatural motive, confirmed moreover by signs that are naturally knowable. Such is it that, *in order to adhere to the intimate depths of revelation—that is, to the supernatural mystery of God's intimate life—the grace of faith is necessary* not only with a necessity of fact instituted by God, but *with an absolute necessity founded upon God's very Essence. It is founded upon a distinction* that is not contingent—namely, the *absolutely necessary distinction of the natural and the supernatural*, the distinction of a created intellectual nature and of the Divine Nature inasmuch as it is Divine. On this condition alone are the foundations of theological science absolutely necessary, and it merits the name of science—a science immediately subordinated to that of God and of the blessed.[68]

---

[67] See 1 Cor 2:14.

[68] See *ST* I, q. 1, aa. 2, 5, and 6.

It is on this point that the nominalists have misconceived the matter, stopping themselves at the facts of experience without looking into the formal reasons of things. Only such formal reasons can render the facts intelligible. There is no exaggeration in saying that an abyss separates nominalism from true theology. Theology is no longer found in it except in a state of corruption. However, the Christian sense takes its revenge; it aspires to the true supernatural, inaccessible to natural faith, and here below, it adheres to it with an absolute, supernatural certitude, superior in itself to the natural certitude by which our reason adheres to the truth of the principle of contradiction: "Much more certain is man concerning what he hears from God, Who cannot be deceived, than he is about those things which he sees by way of his own reason, which can be deceived."[69]

Faith thus conceived is truly "the substance of the things for which we hope."[70] Likewise, one can easily understand why it demands to blossom forth in supernatural contemplation, as St. John of the Cross writes:

> Faith, as the theologians say, is a supernatural *habitus* of the soul, altogether certain and obscure. The reason for its obscurity is that it inclines us to believe truths revealed by God Himself, truths that exceed the natural light [of our intellect] and that exceed the scope of the entirety of human understanding. . . . The brilliance of the sun sometimes dazzles us and blinds us. Thus is it with the *light of faith, which by its intensity infinitely surpasses the light of our own understanding.* . . . It is precisely because faith produces an obscure night in the soul that it illuminates, "*Et nox illuminatio me in deliciis meis* [And the night will be my illumination in my delights]" (Ps 139:11 [Vulgate 138:11]). The night of faith ought thus to be our guide in the delights of contemplation and of union with God. The object

---

[69] *ST* II-II, q. 4, a. 8.

[70] Heb 11:1. [Tr. note: On this point, the reader can benefit from reflecting on the words of Pope Benedict XVI in *Spe Salvi* (2007), §7.]

that it manifests to us here below is the Holy Trinity whom we will contemplate without veil in eternity.[71]

This doctrine manifestly presupposes that infused faith is essentially supernatural because of its specifying formal object. If this formal object were accessible without the infused virtue of faith, the latter would be useless. Likewise, infused hope and infused charity would be useless. It would suffice that one have the kind of natural good will of which the Pelagians speak.[72]

This teaching is of capital importance for him who wishes to maintain *the sense of mystery* in the order of grace, where it is needed more than anywhere else.

---

[71] St. John of the Cross, *Ascent of Mount Carmel* 2.3 and 2.9. [Tr. note: The reader would benefit greatly from reading Fr. Garrigou-Lagrange's other works on the spiritual life, especially, *Christian Perfection and Contemplation, The Three Ages of the Interior Life,* and the small text *The Three Conversions in the Spiritual Life.* All three of these works are available in reprint editions and fully exposit his thought on these matters. A profound philosophical study of these matters can be found in Jacques Maritain, *The Degrees of Knowledge,* trans. Gerald B. Phelan (Notre Dame, IN: University of Notre Dame Press, 1995), 263–408.]

[72] We have discussed this doctrine at much greater length in *De revelatione,* 1:458–515. Likewise, we discuss it with respect to spirituality in *Christian Perfection and Contemplation,* trans. M. Timothea Doyle (St. Louis, MO: B. Herder, 1958), 48–80.

Chapter 6

The Divine Predilection and the Possible Salvation of All

IN ORDER TO GRASP more profoundly what the sense of mystery ought to be (most especially in the case of the theologian), let us consider what was said by one such as St. Thomas in his writings concerning the great problem of the Divine Predilection and the possible salvation of all.

In the fourth chapter of this part, we noted that, when St. Thomas addresses this difficult question, following St. Augustine, he firmly holds two principles. On the one hand, against Pelagianism and Semi-Pelagianism, he firmly holds that *nothing would be better than something else if the former were not loved more by God, Who is the Cause of all that is good.*[1] On the other hand, he holds at least as firmly to a principle that would be misunderstood after St. Thomas's day by Protestantism and Jansenism—namely, that *God never commands the impossible* and that, in His love, He makes it *really and practically possible, here and now,* for every adult to accomplish His precepts at the very moment when He so obliges them. The Council of Trent affirms this, using the very words of St. Augustine.[2]

---

[1] See *ST* I, q. 20, a. 3.

[2] In the Decree on Justification, ch. 11, Trent recalls this doctrine against the Protestants, citing the words of Augustine (see *De natura et gratia*, ch. 43, no. 50): "For God does not command the impossible, but when he commands he admonishes you to do what you can and to pray for what you cannot do, and he helps you to be able to do it. 'His commandments are not burdensome' (1 John 5:3); his 'yoke is easy and [his] burden light' (Matt 11:30)"(Denzinger, no. 1536).

Thus, it is absolutely certain that, on Calvary, it was *really and practically POSSIBLE* (*here and now*) for the bad thief to do what was right and that the good thief, who IN FACT ACCOMPLISHED *his duty*, was loved more and aided more by God. "For who sees anything different in you? What have you that you did not receive?" (1 Cor 4:7).

However, as much as each of these two principles, taken apart, is certain, so too is their intimate reconciliation obscure. To see this reconciliation, it would be necessary to see how *Infinite Justice, Infinite Mercy*, and *Sovereign Freedom* are reconciled in the eminence of the Deity (i.e., the intimate life of God). Only thus would one understand the God Who wished to be merciful to one of the two thieves more than to the other without, however, rendering it impossible for the other to accomplish his duty, but on the contrary, rendering it really *possible* for him *here and now*.

Let us recall here the clearest texts of St. Thomas concerning the two opposed aspects of this mystery, as well as concerning what, in their reconciliation, remains hidden to every created intellect (whether human or angelic) before it receives the Beatific Vision.

God Never Commands the Impossible, but He Makes It Really Possible for Every Adult to Accomplish His Duty

This principle, utterly misunderstood by the first Protestants, as well as by the Jansenists, is often affirmed by St. Augustine, in particular in the famous text of *De natura et gratia* mentioned above [note 2] as being cited in the eleventh chapter of the sixth session of the Council of Trent.

It is a principle that is evident in the rational order, for God would be neither good, nor wise, nor just, nor merciful if He were to command even once something that were *impossible*. In this case, it would mean

---

Likewise, the contradictory proposition was condemned—namely, the first of Jansenius's five propositions (Constitution *Cum Occasione*; Denzinger, no. 2001). If God were to command the impossible, He would be neither just nor merciful.

that sin would be, strictly speaking, *inevitable*. From this, it would no longer be a sin and it could not be punished justly. Punishment would no longer be justice but, instead, cruelty.

This truth, evident in the rational order, is confirmed by revelation in a thousand ways, in particular in the two scriptural texts cited by the Council of Trent in the aforementioned text. The Lord says in Matthew 11:30, "My yoke is easy, and my burden is light," and one reads in 1 John 5:3: "For this is the love of God, that we keep his commandments. *And his commandments are not burdensome*." The man who in fact freely resists the Lord's commandments, *is able* to not resist them.

When commenting on Matthew 11:30, St. Thomas says that, if the Lord's yoke is rather difficult to carry at first, it becomes easy and sweet for him who loves, even in difficult circumstances.[3]

In *ST* I-II, q. 106, a. 2, ad 2, St. Thomas similarly writes:

> If one sins after having accepted the grace of the New Testament, he deserves a great punishment, inasmuch as he did not utilize the help given to him: *for the new law taken in itself gives aid sufficient to avoid sinning*.

Furthermore, it is certain that, although the just man can sin (and sometimes does sin), habitual grace and the infused virtues that derive from it give him the *real ability* for accomplishing saving and meritorious acts; this ability grows with actual sufficient grace, which arouses a good thought, then a good desire, which morally inclines to the saving choice, without however making us produce the act.[4]

To say that sufficient grace, which gives the *real ability* for accomplishing precepts, is not truly sufficient because *it does not make one accomplish them in fact*, would be to say that it is not sufficient because it is not, in fact, efficacious. From this point of view, it would be necessary to say that the architect who is not actually building a house does

---

[3] In his *Commentary on Matthew*, St. Thomas says, "Love makes every difficult and impossible thing to be easy. Whence, if one loves Christ well, nothing is difficult for that person, and therefore the new law is not burdensome." See also *ST* I-II, q. 107, a. 4.

[4] See *ST* I-II, q. 109, aa. 1 and 2, where habitual grace (and the infused virtues) are clearly distinguished from actual grace, "*by which* man is moved to acting well."

not have sufficient technical knowledge for building it. From such a perspective, we *could not* do anything unless we were actually doing it. There would be no *real potency* except when there would be *act* (at least imperfectly), as said the ancient Megarians, against whom Aristotle established the distinction between potency and act.[5] As he put it, the sitting person has the *real ability* to stand but not the act of standing; likewise, the standing person has the *real ability* of sitting, although he cannot be, at one and the same time, both sitting and standing.

To say that sufficient grace, which gives *the real ability* for accomplishing a saving act (without yet making it accomplished), is not sufficient (i.e., that it does not render this accomplishment really to be possible) is to say something akin to "the sleeping man is blind." In reality, he who sleeps, although he sees nothing, has the *real ability* to see.

*   *   *

St. Thomas shows well that, *if someone* with the aid of actual, prevenient grace, *does that which is in his power to do, God will not refuse him habitual or sanctifying grace.*[6] Even if he were born in the forests and never has heard the preaching of the Gospel, and if he nevertheless does (with the help of prevenient grace) what his conscience says, he will receive other assistance and will be led from grace to grace, up to the grace of faith and justification by means known to God, and finally to salvation.[7] God never commands the impossible, and He

---

[5] See Aristotle, *Metaphysics* 9.3. See also St. Thomas's commentary on this book, lec. 3.

[6] See *ST* I-II, q. 109, a. 6, ad 1: "The conversion of man to God indeed occurs through free choice of the will; and for this reason is he commanded to convert himself unto God. However, the free choice of the will cannot be converted unto God unless it is so converted by God Himself to Himself, as is said in Jeremiah 31:18: 'Convert me and I will be converted [*converte me et convertar*], for You are the Lord my God,' and in Lamentations 5:21: 'Convert us Lord to you, and we will be converted [Converte nos Domine ad te et convertemur].'"

[7] See *ST* I-II, q. 89, a. 6: "When he begins to have the first use of his reason . . . the first thing that then occurs in thinking to this man is that he should deliberate concerning himself. And if he then orders himself to a due [or, fitting, moral] end, the remission of original sin will follow through grace." Likewise, see *De veritate*, q. 14, a. 11, ad 1 (a text forgotten by the Jansenists): "It pertains to Divine Providence that He provide

makes it possible for all adults to accomplish His precepts.

The Divine refusal of the efficacious grace of conversion (*denegation divina gratae, vel subtractio gratiae*)[8] is a punishment that presupposes at least an initial fault (a resistance to prevenient sufficient grace). Therefore, this Divine refusal (or, this Divine subtraction) must be distinguished from the *Divine permission* of this

---

to each person those things that are necessary for salvation, so long as such a person does not, for his own part, provide an impediment. Now, if someone were brought up in this way (i.e., in the woods) and, being led by natural reason, were to seek the good and flee from what is evil, it must most certainly be held that unto such a person, God either *would reveal, by an internal inspiration,* that which it is necessary to believe, or that He would send some preacher of the faith to him, just as He sent Peter to Cornelius [see Acts 10]."

Pius IX speaks similarly in the encyclical *Quanto Conficiamur Moerore* (1863) (Denzinger, no. 2866).

[Tr. note: In common awareness, this topic has been popularized in terms of Rahner's notion of "anonymous Christianity." Fr. Garrigou-Lagrange's discussion of the matters shows that an entirely different tradition of Catholic theology can speak with this level of breadth and openness without taking the doctrinal risks that one finds in Fr. Rahner's work. To see a lengthier treatment of this topic from a perspective that was almost certainly inspired by Fr. Garrigou-Lagrange, see Jacques Maritain, "The Immanent Dialectic of the First Act of Freedom," in *The Range of Reason* (New York: Charles Scribner's Sons, 1952), 66–85. For a generous critique of Maritain's position, see Lawrence Dewan, "Natural Law and the First Act of Freedom: Maritain Revisited," in *Wisdom, Law and Virtue: Essays in Thomistic Ethics* (New York: Fordham University Press, 2008), 221–41. The reader should be aware that Fr. Dewan's approach to Thomism is not isomorphic with that of Maritain (and, also, Fr. Garrigou-Lagrange).]

[8] Concerning the *subtractio gratiae* (or, *denegatio gratiae*), which is wholly different from the *Divine permission* of sin (above all, of the first sin), see *ST* I-II, q. 79, a. 3 ("Whether God is the cause of spiritual blindness or hardness of heart?"): "God by His own judgment does not give the light of grace to those *in whom He finds there to be an obstacle.*" See again, ibid., ad 1: "Since spiritual blindness and hardness of heart from the perspective of *the subtraction of grace* are *a kind of penalty,* from this perspective they do not make man to be worse; instead, *having been made worse through his fault,* he incurs this, as he does other punishments."

However, the mystery reappears inasmuch as this fault would not have happened if God did not permit it, and permitted it in this man instead of in that one.

[Tr. note: On this thorny topic, much can be gained by surveying: Réginald Garrigou-Lagrange, *Predestination,* trans. Bede Rose (St. Louis, MO: B. Herder, 1939); Garrigou-Lagrange, *Providence,* trans. Bede Rose (St. Louis, MO: B. Herder, 1954); Jacques Maritain, *God and the Permission of Evil,* trans. Joseph Evans (Milwaukee, MI: Bruce, 1966); Michael D. Torre, *Do Not Resist the Spirit's Call: Francisco Marín-Sola on Sufficient Grace* (Washington, DC: Catholic University of America Press, 2013).]

fault. To confuse the one with the other would be to admit the principle undergirding Calvinism.[9]

*   *   *

It follows from these principles, as is commonly admitted by the Thomists, that the *efficacious grace* that is the cause of an imperfect act like
attrition [i.e., imperfect contrition] is *sufficient* in relation to a perfect
act like [perfect] contrition. It gives the proximate ability without,
however, in fact making one do this act of [perfect] contrition. In other
words: the grace that is termed "sufficient" in relation to a perfect act is
efficacious in relation to a less perfect one.

From this, it also follows that efficacious grace (e.g., of [perfect]
contrition) is offered in the sufficient grace (relative to the same act),
as the fruit is offered in the flower. However, sin can render sufficient
grace sterile, as hail falling on a flower-covered tree renders sterile a
tree that promised to bear much fruit.

Sin will not be produced without a Divine permission, and it will
be followed by a penalty (above all, the Divine subtraction of grace,
which one must not confuse with the Divine permission of sin, since
the latter precedes the fault instead of following upon it).

Here, we see a chiaroscuro. It is clear that there must be a sufficient grace that renders possible the accomplishment of the precepts
and that, if one does not resist this sufficient grace, one will receive
efficacious grace.[10] However, the mystery remains in this: *the fact of
resisting* the prevenient sufficient grace *is already an evil*, a deficiency,
which cannot come from God but, instead, uniquely comes from our
defectibility (i.e., from the deficient secondary cause). In contrast, *the
fact of not resisting* prevenient sufficient grace *is already something that
is good*, and therefore it does not come uniquely from us but, instead,

---

[9] On the Divine permission of sin, see *ST* I-II, q. 79, a. 1: "It happens that [God] does
not provide aid to some for avoiding sin, which aid were He to give, they would not
sin. But He does all this according to the order of His wisdom and justice." God *is
not bound* to prevent a naturally defectible creature from always failing, but He can
permit this failure for a greater good. See *ST* I, q. 22, a. 2, ad 2; q. 23, a. 5.

[10] See *ST* I-II, q. 112, a. 3.

comes also (and, indeed, above all) from God who is the Cause of all good.[11] Thus, a mystery remains: Why does God permit that a given person resists His preveniences while He gives to another such that he does not resist? This is the mystery that was expressed thus by St. Augustine: "Why he draws this person, and does not draw that other one—do not wish to judge this, if you do not wish to err."[12]

Nobody Would Be Better than Another if He Were Not Loved More by God

Thus, are we led to the other aspect of the mystery—whence it comes, in the final analysis, that a given person is *better* than another.

Philosophical reason, when it is not misled, already is sufficient for telling us that *God*, the Sovereign Good, *is the source of every finite good*—that is, that creatures are good because God wills good for them, produces it in them, and aids them in their own coming to perfection. From this, it follows that nobody would become *better* than another if he were not loved more by God—that is, if God had not willed from all eternity that there would be *more good* in such a one. Thus speaks right reason in the natural order.

Scripture speaks in the same way, in the order of grace.

The Savior, who says to us, *"Without me, you can do nothing"* (John 15:5), in the order of salvation, says also about the subject of the Divine predilection for the little ones to whom God gives humility because He wishes to make them good, "I thank thee, Father, Lord of heaven and earth, that thou hast hidden these things from the wise and under-standing and revealed them to babes; *yea, Father,* [I thank thee] *for such was thy gracious will*" (Matt 11:25–6). Also, He says in John 10:27–29: "My sheep hear my voice, and I know them, and they follow me; and I give them eternal life, and they shall never perish, and no one shall snatch them out of my hand. My Father, who has given them to me, is

---

[11] See St. Thomas's commentary on the twelfth chapter of Hebrews, lec. 3: "The very fact that someone does not place an obstacle to grace is itself something that proceeds from grace."

[12] Augustine, *In Ioan.*, tract. 26.

greater than all, and *no one is able to snatch them out of the Father's hand."* Likewise, in His priestly prayer before His Passion:

> [Father,] I have guarded them, and none of them is lost but the son of perdition, that the scripture might be fulfilled. . . . Father, I desire that they also, whom thou hast given me, may be with me where I am, to behold my glory which thou hast given me in thy love for me before the foundation of the world" (John 17:12, 24).

St. Thomas's commentary on all these texts of St. Matthew and St. John excellently places in relief the Divine predilection, as do texts from St. Paul that we will cite as well.

In 1 Corinthians 4:6–7, St. Paul writes:

> [I have applied all this to myself and Apollos for your benefit, brethren, that you may learn by us not to go beyond what is written,] that none of you may be puffed up in favor of one against another. *For who sees anything different in you? What have you that you did not receive? If then you received it, why do you boast as if it were not a gift?*

Likewise, in Philippians 2:13, St. Paul writes, "God is at work in you, both to will and to work for his good pleasure." Again, in Ephesians 4:7, "But grace was given to each of us *according to the measure of Christ's gift."* Again, in Romans 9:14–16:

> What shall we say then? Is there injustice on God's part? By no means! For he says to Moses, "I will have mercy on whom I have mercy, and I will have compassion on whom I have compassion" (cf. Exod 33:19). So it depends not upon man's will or exertion, but upon God's mercy.

Similarly, he writes in Romans 11:7, "What then? Israel failed to obtain what it sought. The elect [among the gentiles and in Israel] obtained it." Also, Romans 12:3:

For by the grace given to me I bid every one among you not to think of himself more highly than he ought to think, but to think with sober judgment, *each according to the measure of faith which God has assigned him.*"

*   *   *

All these inspired words are summed up in this principle: "Given that God's love for us is the cause of all good, nothing would be better than something else if it were not loved more by God." It is the principle of predilection, clearly formulated by St. Thomas in *ST* I, q. 20, a. 3 ("Whether God equally loves all"):

> *Since God is the cause of the goodness of things,* as was discussed in the preceding article, *one being would not be better than another if God did not love one more than another.*

And, again, *ST* I, q. 20, a. 4 ("Whether God always loves better things more greatly"):

> God's will is the cause of goodness in things, and so *something is better because God wills a greater good to it.* Whence it follows that He loves it more greatly.

And, again, *ST* I, q. 20, a. 4, ad 1:

> Not only does God love Christ more than all mankind; He also loves Christ more than the whole universe of creatures. This is so because He wishes a greater good to Christ, for He gave him the name, which is above every name, inasmuch as Christ was true God.

God loves Christ more than all mankind and more than all the universe, since He has predestined Him to be His unique Son—and that before the foresight of any of the Savior's merits, since these merits presuppose the Divine Filiation.

This principle of predilection, thus formulated, contains within its illuminating power[13] the treatise on predestination (*ST* I, q. 23, aa. 2–5) and that of grace, whether concerning habitual grace and its degrees or actual grace (whether it be sufficient or efficacious).[14]

Without difficulty, St. Thomas has been able to find this principle in Scripture, in the Second Council of Orange against the Semi-Pelagians, and in the works of St. Augustine. This latter wrote: "Why is it that of two adults, that one rather than another is called to conversion and, likewise, of two children that one receives the remission of sin in baptism while the other does not [receive baptism]? The judgments of God are inscrutable."[15]

---

[13] [Tr. note: Literally, "virtually," i.e., as an effect is in a cause. Fr. Garrigou-Lagrange was always sensitive to finding the ruling principles of a topic, for it is only in light of its principles (whether they be primary or secondary, though above all its first principles) that a science has its surety and unity. His method is akin to that which he describes in the method of Fr. Ambroise Gardeil, O.P.: "Father Gardeil was one of those who thought that the explication of the *Summa theologiae* of St. Thomas consisted especially in underlining the great principles which enlighten the whole thing, in calling attention to the most elevated summits of this mountain chain." Text cited in Richard Peddicord, *The Sacred Monster of Thomism: An Introduction to the Life and Legacy of Reginald Garrigou-Lagrange*, O.P. (South Bend, IN: St. Augustine's Press, 2005), 117.]

[14] Concerning the efficaciousness of Divine motion, see *ST* I, q. 19, a. 8; q. 23, a. 4; I-II, q. 10, a. 4; q. 112, a. 3. In the last article, he writes, "God's intention cannot fail, as Augustine says in his book on the Predestination of the Saints (*De dono perseverantiae* 15), 'By God's good gifts whoever is liberated, is most certainly liberated.' Whence, if from God's intention in moving someone, that man whose heart he moves were to attain (habitual) grace, he will infallibly attain it."

See also *ST* I-II, q. 112, a. 4 ("Whether grace is greater in one person than in another"): "The preparation for grace is not in a given man except inasmuch as his free will is prepared by God. Whence, *the first cause of this diversity* [among people] must be taken as being *on the part of God Himself, who in various manners dispenses the gifts of His grace* so that the beauty and perfection of the Church may arise in various grades. . . . Whence, the Apostle says in Eph. 4:7, 'To each grace is given according to the measure of Christ's gift.'" Likewise, see St. Thomas's commentary on Matt 25:15: "He who strives more, has more grace; however, *that he strives more, is due to a higher cause.*" Also, see his commentary on Eph 4:7.

[15] St. Augustine, *De dono perseverantia* 9: "Thus, in the case of two little ones who are equally bound by original sin, why is it that one is taken and the other is left? Likewise, in the case of two wicked men who are already mature in age, why is it that one is called so that he may follow the call, while the other is not called (or is not called in such a manner)? The judgments of God are inscrutable. Likewise, in the case of

Likewise, St. Prosper speaks in the formulas that were promulgated in the Council of Orange.[16]

In the *City of God*, in speaking not only of men but also of the angels, St. Augustine wrote, "Although all the angels (e.g., Lucifer as well as Michael) had been created equally good, some fell by their bad will, *while others who were* MORE GREATLY AIDED attained unto this perfect beatitude, from which they have certitude of never falling."[17] It

---

two pious men, why should one be given perseverance to the end of life and the other should not be given it? Here, the judgments of God are even more inscrutable. However, it must be most certain to the faithful that the former is among the predestined and the latter not. 'For if they had been of us,' said one of the predestined [i.e., St. John the Evangelist], who had drunk this secret from the Lord's Breast, 'Certainly would such a person have remained with us' (1 John 2:19)." Likewise, see Augustine, *De dono perseverantia* 12.

16   See the Second Synod of Orange, can. 9: "For as often as we do good, God operates in us and with us, that we may work" (Denzinger, no. 379). This is taken from sent. 22 of St. Prosper of Aquintaine's *Sententiae ex operibus S. Augustini delibatae*.

See also Second Synod of Orange, can. 12: "How God loves us. God loves us as we will be by his gift, not as we are by our merit" (Denzinger, no. 382). This is taken from sent. 56 of St. Prospser.

See also Second Synod of Orange, can. 20: "But man can do nothing good unless God enables him to do it" (Denzinger, no. 390). This is taken from sent. 315/317 of St. Prosper.

It is from a text of St. Prosper that the Synod of Quiercy draws: "The omnipotent God wishes 'all men' without exception 'to be saved' [1 Tim 2:4], even if not all are saved. That some, however, are saved is the gift of the one [who] saves; that some, however, perish is the fault of those who perish" (Denzinger, no. 623). This penultimate proposition of Quiercy represents an enunciation of the principle of predilection: "That some, however, are saved is the gift of the one who saves."

Likewise, the Council of Tusey in 860, where the controversies brought against Gottschalk of Orbais were brought to an end, states from the beginning the principle that clarifies this entire problem: "In heaven and on earth God does everything that He wills (see Ps 134/135:6); for nothing happens in heaven or on earth unless God favorably does it (if it is something good) or if he justly permits it to be done (if it is an evil)" (PL 126:123).

In other words, nothing good happens in fact unless God has efficaciously willed it, and nothing evil happens unless God has permitted it. St. Thomas says the same in *ST* I, q. 19, a. 6, ad 1: "Whatever God *without qualification* [*simpliciter*] wills, that He does."

17   On this text of St. Augustine, see what a great number of Thomists have written at the beginning of their treatises on grace, under the title "Utrum tam Adamo quam angelis fuerit necessaria gratia per se efficax ad perseverandum [Whether essentially (*per se*) efficacious grace was necessary as much for Adam as for the angels to persevere]." In particular, see John of St. Thomas, Gonet, the Salmanticenses, and Billuart.

is in this chapter that St. Augustine shows that no creature can *make itself better* than another without being more loved and assisted by God: "The will of the angel, however good it might be, would have remained helpless in its desire, unless He who, out of nothing, had made [the angel's] good nature capable of enjoying Him, first excited in him a desire [for Himself], and *made him to be better by filling him* [with Himself]." Nothing good occurs unless God has willed it, and no evil occurs unless He has permitted it.

Likewise, in *City of God* 14.17, St. Augustine writes, "Who would dare to say or believe that it was not in God's power to prevent the fall of man or that of an angel?" In fact, God permitted the fall of Lucifer, without provoking it. He did not permit a similar fall in the case of Michael; however, He helped him to arrive at the terminus of his way, and for this, St. Michael ought to render Him thanks eternally (as should all the elect). The elect have been loved more, whether they be angels or they be men—and this in virtue of the principle that could not escape the lofty contemplation of St. Augustine: "As the love of God is the cause of all created good, nothing would be better than something else if it were not more loved by God." When St. Thomas formulated this principle of predilection,[18] he did not enunciate some truth that had been overlooked by the author of the *City of God*. St. Augustine had grasped the profound sense of the words of the Psalms that say to us that *God is the Author of every good*, that *no good* occurs unless He has willed it, *no evil* unless He has permitted it.[19] Very often did he comment upon the words of the Savior, "Without me, you can do nothing," and those of St. Paul, "What do you have that you have not received?"

*   *   *

This principle of predilection is *absolutely universal* and without any possible exception, like every metaphysical principle. It is applied to all good acts, whether they be natural or supernatural, easy or difficult,

---

[18] See *ST* I, q. 20, aa. 3 and 4.

[19] See St. Augustine, *Retractions* 1.9: "Because *all good things*—the great, the middling, and the small—*are from God*, it follows that *the good use of free will* also be from God," as much for angels as for men.

done in the state of innocence or after original sin; and it holds for the angels as much as it holds for men. This is why St. Thomas formulated it in a most universal manner: "Since the love of God is the cause of the goodness of things, *a given being* would not be *better* than another if God did not will a *greater good* to one than to the other."[20] This holds without exception, even for inanimate creatures.

The absolute universality (or, metaphysical value) of this principle has eluded the Molinists; too often, however, do people miss the fact that it also has eluded their Jansenist adversaries. Jansen held that the principle of predilection (along with grace that is efficacious of itself, which is inseparable from it) holds only in the case of fallen man, *titulo infirmitatis* [due to his weakness] and not *titulo dependentiae a Deo* [due to his dependence upon God]. The principle of predilection would be true neither for the angels nor for unfallen man.

The Augustinians Noris and Berthi, writing in the era of Jansenism, also thought this, all while, against Jansen, admitting truly sufficient grace and the free will of fallen man. From this point of view, St. Michael, by his free choice, would have become *better* than Lucifer without having been *more loved* and more aided by God. The elect [élus] angels would not have been *more loved*. Now, by the very fact of being *electus a Deo* [chosen by God] one is more greatly loved, according to the very notion of Divine choice [*élection*], which presupposes His love [*dilection*].[21]

Molina more greatly infringes upon the principle of predilection when he writes in his *Concordia*, q. 14, a. 13, disp. 12:

> It can happen, that of two who *with equal help* are called interiorly by God, one is converted according to the freedom of his choice and the other remains in infidelity. . . . Nay, rather, it can happen that someone preceded [*praeventus*] and called *with far*

---

20   *ST* I, q. 20, a. 3.

21   See *ST* I, q. 23, a. 4: "*Dilection* is presupposed by *election* [or, choice] according to its very notion, and so too is election presupposed to the notion of predestination." This holds in virtue of the very principle enunciated in the same article, "The Will of God, by which He wills a good to a given thing *by way of His love* [*diligendo*], is *the cause* for that good being given to that given thing in preference to others."

more help, is not converted according to his will, and another person with far less is converted.[22]

Expressed more briefly: "With the help of *equal* grace, nay rather *of less* grace, can he who is aided rise up [*resurgere*], while another having more does not rise up and perseveres in being hardened."

This represents the negation of the intrinsic efficaciousness of the grace that we call efficacious, which is followed by its effect. This Molinist position is attenuated in the congruism of Suarez, where the principle of predilection still is stamped with relativity, given that "congruous grace" is not efficacious of itself.[23]

The congruism of the Sorbonne, proposed in the eighteenth century by Tournely and many others, also denied the universality of this principle, given that eighteenth-century congruism held that intrinsically efficacious grace, necessary for the accomplishment of *difficult* saving acts, is not needed for accomplishing *easy* saving acts. These theologians thus admitted that, of two men *equally loved* and *aided* by God, one sometimes by an easy act becomes *better* than the other.

Without realizing what is happening, this doctrine tries to suppress the mystery found in these matters, and it appears acceptable to many from the practical point of view. Nonetheless, from the speculative point of view it has all the difficulties of Molinism with regard to easy acts and all the obscurities of Thomism for difficult acts. It represents a kind of eclecticism that stops halfway, while it should lift itself higher.

As we have said: *the very fact of not resisting* grace is *a good* and therefore does not uniquely come from us but also from God; while *the*

---

[22] [Tr. note: Fr. Garrigou-Lagrange cites the Parisian edition of 1876, pp. 51 and 565.]

[23] [Tr. note: To understand what Fr. Garrigou-Lagrange means by "being stamped (or struck) with relativity," see Garrigou-Lagrange, *Predestination*, 160–61: "But in the opinion of the Thomists, this theory still limits the universal validity of the principle of predilection and stamps it with the seal of relativity, in that it retains the main structure of Molinism, which is the *scientia media* or the denial of the intrinsic efficacy of the Divine decrees and of grace. It remains true, then, according to this conception of the *scientia media*, that human effort makes grace efficacious instead of being the result of the efficacy of this grace; so that if two men or two angels are equally helped by God, it may happen that one of them becomes better than the other, though this one was not helped more, and did not receive more than the other." See all of 160–62 for his complete discussion of the matter.]

fact of resisting is *an evil* that can issue forth only from the defectibility of the deficient cause, following upon a Divine permission that allows this evil to arise without being its cause,[24] and which allows it to occur in a given man rather than in another.

The Mystery of the Intimate Reconciliation of Justice, Mercy, and Sovereign Freedom

How is a reconciliation brought about with regard to the two principles that we have examined, these two principles that are absolutely certain (in both the order of nature and that of grace) when taken apart? Let us state them directly again. On the one hand, "*God never commands the impossible* and [He does] render the accomplishment of His precepts really possible for all adults." On the other hand, "Given that the love of God is the cause of all that is good, *nothing would be better than something else if he were not more loved by God.*"

The intimate reconciliation of these two principles is nothing other than the intimate reconciliation of Infinite Justice, Infinite Mercy, and Sovereign Freedom. Indeed, St. Augustine says, "When the aid of grace is given to certain ones, *it is by mercy*; if it is refused to others, *it is by justice*, as a penalty for a preceding sin or at least for original sin."[25] This text is cited by St. Thomas and is known well by theologians.[26]

Now, before receiving the Beatific Vision of the Divine Essence, no created intellect, whether angelic or human, can see how Infinite Mercy, Infinite Justice, and Sovereign Freedom are intimately reconciled *in the eminence of the Deity* (i.e., the intimate life of God). Even those who see God face-to-face and who grasp that Justice and Mercy

---

[24] We have treated this subject elsewhere at greater length. See Réginald Garrigou-Lagrange, "La grâce infailliblement efficace par elle-même et les actes salutaires faciles," *Revue thomiste* 30 (1925): 558–66, completed in 31 (1926): 160–73. Also, see the article "Predestination" in the *Dictionnaire de Théologie catholique*. [Tr. note: For some context concerning the discussion in the aforementioned article, the reader will likely be aided by Torre, *Do Not Resist the Spirit's Call*.]

[25] St. Augustine, *De correptione et gratia* 5; St. Augustine, *Epist.* 190 (157), ch. 3; St. Augustine *De praedestinatione sanctorum* 8 (9).

[26] See *ST* II-II, q. 2, a. 5, ad 1.

are *really identified in the Deity (without being destroyed)* cannot see the reason why God's good pleasure rests on Peter rather than upon Judas. There, we are confronted with an act of Sovereign Freedom.[27] It is what makes the saints say that there is no sin committed by another man that we *may not* commit in our own weakness if we were in the same circumstances and under the same influences and that, if *we in fact have persevered*, it is because we have been upheld by God, it is because His mercy has preserved us.[28]

By His mercy, God *often* raises up sinners, and certain ones of them He *always* raises up. It is the terrible and mild [*doux*] mystery of predestination.

The man who was often relieved by the Divine Mercy and who then falls again can, trembling, say to himself, "After such ingratitudes, will the Lord accord unto me efficacious grace, which raises up?" The Master is free to raise up such a man a hundred times and to leave him, in the end, in his sin, while he can raise up another in giving unto him perseverance to the end.

In so acting, God takes from nobody what is due to him.

As St. Thomas notes in *ST* I, q. 23, a. 5, ad 3, in the parable of the workers at the last hour, the Master says to the one who has worked from the time of morning and is now murmuring, *"Friend, I am doing you no wrong;* did you not agree with me for a denarius? Take what belongs to you, and go; I choose to give to this last as I give to you. *Am I not allowed to do what I choose with what belongs to me?* Or do you begrudge my generosity?" (Matt 20:13–15).[29]

Such is the response made by Sovereign Freedom, which sows the Divine seed into souls more or less generously according to His good pleasure without doing injustice to anyone. In the order of gratuitous things, He can give more to one and less to another, as it pleases Him.[30]

St. Paul also writes in Romans 9:20–24:

---

[27] See *ST* I, q. 23, a. 5, ad 3.

[28] Thus speaks St. Augustine.

[29] [Tr. note: The French makes the same closing point in a way slightly different from the RSV. It reads: "And will your eye be bad because I am good?"]

[30] See *ST* I, q. 23, a. 5, ad 3.

But who are you, a man, to answer back to God? Will what is molded say to its molder, "Why have you made me thus?" Has the potter no right over the clay, to make out of the same lump one vessel for beauty and another for menial use? *What if God, desiring to show his wrath*[31] and to make known his power, has endured with much patience the vessels of wrath made for destruction, *in order to make known the riches of his glory for the vessels of mercy, which he has prepared beforehand for glory*, even us whom he has called, not from the Jews only but also from the Gentiles?[32]

And this is applicable not only to peoples but also to individuals, of whom it is said, in Ephesians 1:11–12, "In him, according to the purpose of him who accomplishes all things according to the counsel of his will, we who first hoped in Christ have been destined and appointed to live for the praise of his glory."[33]

Here, we are confronted with a mystery that is inaccessible to every created intellect—how Infinite Justice, Infinite Mercy (which is exercised even in regard to those who are lost), and Sovereign Freedom are intimately reconciled in the Deity (i.e., the intimate life of God). It is difficult to speak of these matters better than St. Thomas does in *ST* I, q. 23, a. 5, in his celebrated response to the third objection. This is one of the most sublime chiaroscuros of theology. However, in order to avoid deviating, theological speculation must be brought to completion here in silent contemplation.

---

[31] I.e., His avenging justice.

[32] It is as though one were to ask, "Where is the injustice in this?" [Tr. note: In the selection from Romans, Fr. Garrigou-Lagrange's French is even stronger than the RSV. Where the latter speaks of a vessel for "menial use," the French reads "a vase of ignominy."]

[33] See Eph 1:5 and Rom 8:29–30.

The Divine Permission of Sin Differs from the Subtraction of Grace

The mystery becomes particularly more obscure if one traces all the way back to the *permission of the first sin,* for permission of the second sin is already in some manner a penalty for the first one that has been committed. However, the permission of every first sin could not be a *penalty.* And if one confuses the permission of the first sin with the *Divine subtraction of grace,* which is a penalty, one will be led to say that there is a *penalty* that has preceded *every fault*—and this would lead one to the principle of Calvinism. We will bring ourselves to a halt for a moment concerning this particularly mysterious point. Here, the smallest fault concerning principles would lead us to enormous errors.

The difficulty comes above all from the fact that the Divine permission of sin implies the nonconservation in the good; for, if God were to conserve a created will in the good, as He conserves it in existence, sin would not occur. And, St. Thomas has written in *ST* I-II, q. 79, a. 1:

> It happens that God *does not provide* help for some to avoid sin, such help being of a character that if He were to provide it they would not sin; however, He does all this according to the order of His Wisdom and Justice, since He is Wisdom and Justice. Whence, it is not imputed to Him that someone sins as though He were the cause of the sin. For example, the pilot is not called the cause of a ship's being wrecked from the fact that he *did not steer it* except when *he ceases* [*subtrahit*] to steer *when he is able and bound* to steer.

God has *permitted* sin in Lucifer as much as He has permitted it in St. Michael the Archangel. He can permit it that a defectible creature fails. He was not bound to prevent this failure; nor was He bound to preserve the creature forever in the good. If He were bound to preserve it, sin would never happen. In fact, it comes not from God but from the defectibility of the creature.

The only thing that is important for us to see here is that the Divine permission of sin (and the nonconservation in the good that it implies) is not also an *evil*. It is a *non-good* (in view of a superior good); while the *Divine subtraction* of grace is an *evil*—namely, that of punishment, which presupposes the evil of a fault (at least an initial one).[34]

Not to Give Versus to Refuse

In order to shed light on this problem, it is necessary to see well the difference that exists between *not giving* and *refusing*—i.e., between not giving a gratuitous assistance and refusing it.

For example, in relations between men, there is a great difference between *not giving* one's hand to someone and *refusing* to give it to him. In many cases, I am *not required* to go to a given person myself and stretch out my hand to him. If I do so, it is out of amiability, goodness, or condescension without being in any way obliged to do it. If I do not do it and this person, seeing me give my hand to another person, is offended that I did not give it to him, I am not the cause of his offense. It is he who offends himself. Later, noticing this matter and seeing that this person is sensitive and quick to be offended, injured, and upset, that he is touchy, suspicious, and defiant, I then decide not only *not to go* to him but, positively, *to avoid him*, and even to *refuse* to have relations with him. Here, we see the difference between *non velle* [not to will] and *nolle* [to not will]. There is a great difference between, on the one hand, this latter sort of refusal, motivated by the sensitivity and the

---

[34] One must not confuse the simple *negation* with the *privation* of that which is due. Now, evil is defined not as the *negatio boni*, but as the *privatio boni debiti* [the privation of a due good]. There is a great difference between the *non-good* (or the *less-good*) and the *evil*.

For example, one can see this in considering the distance that exists between the least form of generosity and pusillanimity. In a good act, which is saving and meritorious but also remains imperfect, the imperfection is not an evil, it is a *non-good*, the absence of a perfection that is not *due* or obligatory, though it would be desirable.

If one confuses the *less good* with the *evil*, one will be led to confuse the two orders of good and evil and, by that, to confuse the *less-evil* with *a good*, as do those who believe that it suffices for one to slow one's fall toward immorality in order to rise up.

We have treated this problem elsewhere in Réginald Garrigou-Lagrange, *The Love of God and the Cross of Jesus*, trans. Sr. Jeanne Marie, vol. 1 (St. Louis, MO: B. Herder, 1948), 318–44.

bad character of the aforementioned person and, on the other hand, the initial fact of not having given him my hand upon my arrival.

This sheds light on the problem of the Divine permission of the first sin of the angel (and, as well, the first sin of man). St. Michael the Archangel would not be *better* than Lucifer if he had not been *more loved* and *more aided* by God, who is the Source of all good. This archangel during the time of his testing,[35] knew better than St. Paul the sense of the expression "what have you that you have not received?" It is God who has made the first step toward him and has, so to speak, extended His hand to him.

God was not required to have the same gratuitous goodness, the same condescension, for Lucifer. He was *not obliged* to have the same *efficacious prevenience*. If Lucifer is, so to speak, offended, God is *not the cause* of his offense. He only has *permitted* it (or, has allowed it to come about). And then the Divine Justice can *refuse* grace as a punishment for this fault.

For all that, it takes only a moment, just as it only takes a moment between two men who are approaching each other, for one to be offended and upset that the other man did not extend his hand to him. The instantaneous exchange of two glances suffices to separate forever a vulgar man from a saint who is in no way responsible for this separation.

Examples of this kind are not rare in the lives of the saints. They illuminate the problem that occupies us. God is in no way responsible for the fact that Lucifer separated himself from Him.

Take another, less lengthy example. You invite many people to an event. The first of them, believing that the first place is due to him, takes the first place before you even offer it to him, and then you set it aside for another. You can request that he give up this first place, as was said in the Gospel parable (Luke 14:15–24). Lucifer was invited; he wished to take the first place for himself. He fell by pride and presumption, of which God is in no way the cause.

---

[35] [Tr. note: I.e., at the very first instant of its creation in which he made his choice for the good or the bad. See *ST* I, q. 62, aa. 1–3, and Jacques Maritain, *The Sin of the Angel*, trans. William L. Rossner (Westminster, MD: Newman Press, 1959).]

Here, the smallest error, the smallest confusion between the Divine permission of the first sin and the Divine subtraction of efficacious grace—the smallest error in understanding the difference between the *non-good* and the *evil*—will lead to the enormous errors of Calvin. *Parvus error in pricipio, magnus est in fine* [A small error at the beginning is a large one by the end].

This principle—*parvus error in principio, magnus est in fine*—explains why certain summits of truth appear to many to be rather close to very grave errors. This arises from one not being attentive to the exact formulation of these lofty truths. The least deviation from this height leads to a disastrous fall, as does the smallest wrong step on the edge of a precipice at a mountain's summit.

This also explains why objections made against these lofty truths often seem clearer than the just response given to such objections. It is that the objection arises from our inferior, superficial, quasi-mechanical way of conceiving, with its dependence upon sensible things, while the response is taken from that which is most elevated in the ineffable mystery against which the objection is formulated. The objection is understood immediately, while it is necessary to reflect on the response for a long time in order to understand it well.[36]

---

[36] This is what we can observe with regard to the following objection: "If affirmation is the cause of affirmation, negation is the cause of negation; for example, the rising of the sun is the cause of day, and the setting of the sun is the cause of the night. Now, the collation of efficacious grace is the *cause* of the saving act. Therefore, the noncollation of efficacious grace is the *cause* of a sin of omission"; in other words, God is the cause of a sin of omission.

One first responds indirectly that this would be, on the part of God, a *Divine negligence*, which is a contradictory thing.

Moreover, one can respond more directly as follows. The major premise of the objection is true, if it pertains to a solely physical cause, such as the rising of the sun. However, it is not true if it pertains to *two causes*, one of which is *indefectible* and the other one, at the same time, *free, defectible,* and *deficient.* In this latter case, the sin of omission arises only from the defectible cause. The Divine permission is not the *cause*; it is only a *condition* without which sin would never be produced.

The Measure and Boldness of St. Thomas in These Questions

In the midst of all these difficulties, one can say that St. Thomas has proceeded with a measure and security that was equaled only by his boldness and the elevation of his contemplation.

When one rereads what the Angelic Doctor has written on pre-destination, which we have summarized here,[37] and when one notes, in particular, the rigor of the two principles that are placed in equilibrium with one another (i.e., that of the possible salvation of all and that of predilection) by noting the mysterious summit toward which they converge, one can say of the Angelic Doctor that which has been said concerning a great contemplative of the Low Countries:

> He is aerial like a chant and rigorous like a star (i.e., like the course of the stars). *The freedom* of his movements and *their fidelity* are founded in a singular splendor. If the one diminishes, the other will be challenged. *Boldness* and *security* prevail over it upon their tranquil and triumphant wings. Boldness does not pull it along, and security does not hold it in thrall. Both of them make the same movements, departing from the same point, going to the same goal. The powers that seem divided here below make for peace upon the heights.
>
> The great contemplative is blinded by an excess of light. His lips are closed by the immensity because it rebels in the face of explanations. Ordinary things can be spoken; extraordinary things can only be stammered. These stammered expressions seem eager to die in the shadow and in the silence where they had been conceived.[38]

It is not useless to bring this to an end by saying how the sense of mystery of which we have spoken was altered in pagan antiquity. There remains, in this alteration, even something profound.

---

[37] See again, *ST* I, q. 23, a. 5, corp. and ad 3.

[38] Ernest Hello, in Jan van Rusbrock, *Rusbrock l'admirabile: oevres choisis*, x–xi. [Tr. note: Fr. Garrigou-Lagrange has slightly paraphrased parts of this quotation from Hello.]

The Riddle of the Sphinx

The writer whom we have cited has written regarding the secrets that the pagan world has altered in transmitting them:

> Among the secrets that antiquity reveals, de Maistre[39] could have counted the sphinx.

> The sphinx is a monster who proposes the *riddle* (or, *enigma*) *of destiny*: It is necessary to divine the riddle or to be devoured by the monster. What could be more preposterous? However, what could be more profound if men knew how to read!

> *To divine*! In human language, this word has a truly singular status, for the thing that it expresses does not seem to be at man's disposal.[40] And yet, for man it is a matter of importance that makes him tremble. In order to accomplish this thing, there is not a foreknown process; and yet, nobody can express the regret to which he who does not accomplish it is exposed. . . .

> Life combines together persons and things: the good, the bad, the mediocre, the very good, the very bad, the sublime, the hideous; all of these jostle among each other on the roads of life (and seem to come together by chance). . . . We live upon appearances. A multitude of veils (e.g., timidity, dissimulation, ignorance) hide the realities. Men do not speak their secrets; they keep their uniform.

> The man who would see from his window a very populous road would be terrified if he were to reflect upon the magnificent or awful realities that pass before him without speaking their name—profoundly disguised, covered, dissimulated. . . .

---

[39] [Tr. note: Joseph de Maistre (1753–1821) was a French political philosopher best known for his conservative defense of authority against the excesses of Continental European Enlightenment political ideals.]

[40] Certain efficacious aids of God do not seem to be further at our disposal.

Yet, the dread of this unspeaking, intelligent spectator of the crowd would grow if he would say to himself, "My life depends, perhaps, upon one of the men who passes by here, under my very eyes." . . . However, if he is there, by what sign can he be recognized?

Everything warns the man who may need to divine, and there is no rule for divining well. Whence—the sphinx.

The spectacle of things that it is necessary to divine and that one cannot divine led antiquity to the edge of an abyss, and the abyss has drawn its prey. This abyss—it is *fatalism*. On the edge of fatalism, leaning over the chasm, the sphinx stands, with an attitude at once mysterious and terrible.

If fatalism were true, all questions would be insoluble, and the only appropriate response to them would be despair.

However, in general, the questions that seem to call for a despairing response are questions that are posed poorly, and the despairing responses often are *as superficial as their seeming profundity*.[41]

Throughout all time, there is in this world *an unknown* to be brought to light—an X, indeed a great X that defies the resources of algebra.

The ancient sphinx wished that there would not be a response.

There is a response, and we can slay the sphinx.

How are we to divine?

---

[41] This could be said of many of the theories proposed by modern idealism, for example, that of Fichte, when he deduces the consequences of Kantianism.

A poor man approaches and asks for hospitality!

Perhaps, he is an angel of the Lord!

But, also, perhaps he is an assassin!

Therefore, how are we to divine? Must we make an effort of thought, an astonishing act of intelligence?

No, see now the secret.

To divine—it is to love. (He who loves, he who has the highest of the virtues, charity, love for God and neighbor—this man also has the seven gifts of the Holy Spirit, the gifts of wisdom, knowledge, understanding, counsel, which, despite the obscurity of faith, allow him to penetrate and taste that which he must grasp in the mystery of things and in the mystery of God.)[42]

Left to itself, the intellect embarks upon an ocean of thoughts. The problem of life stands before it, and if the compass's needle has lost its *knowledge for finding the north*, if the compass is distracted, the intellect very easily can arrive, in practice, at doubt; in theory, at fatalism.

The ancient sphinx—it is the impotent intellect, arriving at despair and rushing toward death.

Love knows better its path. In practice, it arrives at the light; in theory, at justice.

This recompense, conferred upon him who divines, refused to him who does not divine . . . contains a supreme justice—*a*

---

[42] We have added these parentheses, in conformity with the doctrine exposited by St. Thomas in *ST* I-II, q. 68, a. 5. The seven gifts of the Holy Spirit are connected in charity, which unites us to the Holy Spirit.

justice that is superior to the justice that speaks its rules. (It is the secret corrupted [*altéré*] by the myth of the sphinx.)

He who divines is repaid, for he who divines is he who loves.— He who does not divine is not repaid, for he who does not divine is he who does not love.

He who loves grandeur and he who loves the forsaken, *will recognize grandeur, if grandeur is there.*[43]

Such is the good Samaritan toward the greatly afflicted, who are sometimes vilified by those who ought to aid them. We do not excuse ourselves for the length of this citation. These pages from Ernest Hello recall certain reflections of de Maistre; they show that he had the sense of mystery to a high degree.

The Response of the Lord

This expression, "He who divines is he who loves," brings to mind what the author of *The Imitation of Christ* says in chapter 25 of book I with regard to the mystery of predestination about which we have spoken. On this subject, he counsels the person who is worried about this subject to act as though he were predestined—to love God and his neighbor. Thus, the soul recovers peace and finds, in practice, the answer to the riddle: "If you were to know what you ought to hope, what would you do? *Do now what you would then do, and you will enjoy peace.*"

Calvin and Jansen, on the contrary, fell into the abyss of fatalism, over the edge of which the sphinx stands. They did not find the answer to the riddle, for they wanted to make a theology without love. Calvin,

---

[43] Ernest Hello, *L'homme: la vie—la science—l'art*, 7th ed. (Paris: Perrin, 1903), 1.14 (pp. 120–23). This last remark is one of the highest applications of the principle often cited by St. Thomas (see *ST* I-II, q. 58, a. 5): "Qualis unusquisque est, talis finis videtur ei (As a given man is, so does the end seem to him)." He who is magnanimous will recognize magnanimity under vilifications and the worst trials.

above all, has distorted the *principle of predilection*. He has rendered this principle irreconcilable with the other principle: *God never commands the impossible.* He has completely disfigured the love of God in saying that God decides to inflict punishment (i.e., the subtraction of grace) before the foreknowledge of fault. In this, there is no longer justice but, instead, a cruelty that is irreconcilable with mercy.

How different is the contemplation of this mystery in chapter 58 of the third book of *The Imitation of Christ*? (Lest it be overcome, theology ought to be brought to completion here in contemplation.):

> Jesus Christ: Son, see thou dispute not of high matters, nor of the hidden judgments of God: why this man is left thus, and this other is raised to so great a grace, or why this person is so much afflicted and that other so highly exalted.
>
> These things are above the reach of man, neither can any reason or discourse penetrate into the judgments of God.
>
> When, therefore, the enemy suggests to thee such things as these, or thou hearest curious men inquiring into them, answer with the Prophet: "Thou art just, O Lord: and thy judgment is right" (Ps 118[119]:137)....
>
> In like manner do not inquire nor dispute concerning the merits of the saints.... I am He who made all the saints; I gave them grace; I have brought them to glory. I know the merits of each of them; I have prevented them with blessings of My sweetness (Ps 20[21]:4). I foreknew My beloved ones before the creation; I chose them out of the world; they were not beforehand to choose Me (John 15:16).
>
> I called them by My grace, and drew them by My mercy; I led them safe through many temptations. I imparted to them extraordinary comforts, I gave them perseverance, I have crowned their patience.

I know the first and the last: I embrace them all with an inestimable love. I am to be praised in all My saints (Ps 67[68]: 36); I am to be blessed above all things (Dan 3:52) and to be honored in every one of them whom I have thus gloriously magnified and eternally chosen, without any foregoing merits of their own. . . .

They are all one through the bond of love; they have the same sentiments, the same will, and all mutually love one another (John 17:21).

And yet, which is much higher, they all love Me more than themselves and their own merits. For being elevated above themselves, and drawn out of the love of themselves, they are wholly absorbed in the love of Me, in whom also they rest by an eternal enjoyment.

Nor is there anything which can divert them from Me, or depress them; for being full of the eternal truth, they burn with the fire of charity that cannot be extinguished.

Rejoice you that are humble, and be glad that you are poor, for yours is the Kingdom of God (Matt 5:3): yet so, if you walk in truth.[44]

---

[44] *The Imitation of Christ* 3.58. [Tr. note: Text taken from Thomas à Kempis, *The Imitation of Christ*, trans. Richard Challoner (New York: Benziger Brothers, 1926), 318–23.]

Chapter 7

The Created Pure Spirit, and Its Limits

O NE CANNOT FORM A COMPLETE IDEA of what was the sense of mystery in a theologian like St. Thomas without calling to mind the idea he had of the created pure spirit, of its nature, of its knowledge, of its will, and of the life of grace found in it. This is what the holy Doctor exposits in his treatise on the angels. It is important to note this, for there is a significant amount of obscurity that exists for us and not for the angels, given that our intellects are the very last in the order of created intellects.

In order to give a brief sketch of this part of St. Thomas's doctrine from the perspective that we are taking, it seems best to allow the angel himself to speak about what constitutes his natural life and his supernatural life, in particular concerning the object of his natural knowledge and concerning that which exceeds it.

* * *

Our existence is certified for you—so, speaks the Angel to us—by Scripture in numerous places in both the Old and the New Testament, in particular with regard to the birth of the Savior, His agony in the garden of Gethsemane, His Resurrection, and in His Ascension. Without us, the hierarchy of created beings would be truncated and too abruptly cut short. The prophet Daniel says that, transported in spirit among us, he saw that there are "ten thousand times a hundred thousand in the presence of God."[1] He wished to say that we are as innumerable as the stars in the sky. Count, if you can, the stars; think of those that are, as it were, forgotten in the nebulas; having done this, believe still that you have not reached the number of the angels. It costs the Most High nothing to multiply the most excellent and the most beautiful things, as the sun multiplies its rays and the bird multiplies the most beautiful notes of its song. If Jerusalem, Athens, and Rome contain a profusion of splendors, for all the stronger reason is there a profusion of splendor at the summit of creation where God reigns in the "splendor of his saints."

Among this ever so numerous throng of pure spirits, the highest of hierarchies is that of the great contemplative angels who remain always in the presence of God, at the highest degree of the unitive life. Next come those who are ministers of the Most High in the general governing of the world, and finally there are the angels who simply execute the orders of God, as are the invisible guardians of men, communities, and nations.[2]

We have all been freely created by God at the time when He willed it, and He has given us at one and the same time our spiritual and immortal nature as well as the Divine grace that, like a supernatural graft, makes us participate in His intimate life.[3] We had to journey but an instant in faith, obedience, and love. Those among us who were faithful passed from infused faith to the supernatural and immediate vision of the Divine Essence. However, those of us who, through pride

---

[1] Dan 7:10. [Tr. note: Or, as one finds in other translations, ten thousand times ten thousand.]

[2] See *ST* I, q. 108.

[3] See *ST* I, q. 62, aa. 1–3. [Tr. note: Note well the distinction of the angel being created in grace but not in beatitude. Based upon texts such as q. 62, a. 1, later Thomists would hold that the angel is sufficient by its own powers for its own natural beatitude, though not for its supernatural beatitude. In a very insightful essay, Jacques Maritain (who was a very faithful follower of the Dominican Thomistic commentators, especially John of St. Thomas) questions this point *as regards the angel's natural ordination to God Himself.* On this topic, even if the reader does not agree with Maritain, much insight would be gained by pondering the matters explained in Jacques Maritain, *The Sin of the Angel*, trans. William L. Rossner (Westminster, MD: Newman Press, 1959).]

and disobedience, were unfaithful, have been lost forever.[4] Redemption is impossible for them, for the angelic intellect, being absolutely intuitive and not discursive like your human intellect, cannot revoke the decision that it has made. This decision is either holy or perverse, but once it is made, it remains as such forever. Because of the perfection of our knowledge, our free choice participates in the immutability of the free choice made by God.[5]

The Nature of the Created Pure Spirit

Our nature is absolutely spiritual; there is no matter in us; only our essence [*nature*],[6] which has received existence, is really distinct from its existence.[7] None of us can say, "*I am* existence, truth, and life." *NONE of us IS his own existence*. God alone is "He Who Is"; only Christ was able to say, "I am the Truth and the Life."

Given that none of us is his own existence, *none of us is his own activity* [*agir*]; for, activity follows upon being, and the mode of acting [*agir*] follows upon the mode of being. Our nature (or, essence) is only *a real capacity for existence*; hence, it is really distinct both from our intellect, which is a faculty, *a real capacity for intellection*, and also from our will, *a real capacity for willing*.[8] Therefore, none of us is Being Itself, nor Thought Itself, nor Love Itself. In this sense, all creatures are *equally small* before God; between each one of them and the Most High, there is an infinite distance, and one of them is superior to another only *in ratione finiti* [from the perspective of the finite order].

---

[4] See *ST* I, q. 62, aa. 4 and 5; q. 63, aa. 4–6.

[5] See *ST* I, q. 64, a. 2. Angelic intuition, which directs the angel's choice and concerns— not successively but, instead, simultaneously—everything that touches upon the decision to be made. This is why the decision is irrevocable and cannot be changed by some later consideration. *Liberum arbitrium angeli est flexibile ad utrumque oppositorum ante electionem, sed non post* [The free choice of the angel can be turned to both opposed things before the choice is made, but not after].

[6] [Tr. note: The more standard "essence" is used. Fr. Garrigou-Lagrange expresses them interchangeably in the next paragraph as well.]

[7] See *ST* I, q. 50, a. 2, ad 3; q. 54, aa. 1 and 2.

[8] See *ST* I, q. 54, a. 3.

Although our essence is really distinct from its existence (and, therefore, infinitely distant from God), it has the nobility of *being purely spiritual* and, thus, is absolutely incorruptible (or, immortal).

From this, it follows that there cannot be two angels in the same species, for *only matter* (capable of this given quantity rather than some other quantity) *can multiply a specific form* (or, nature) in such a way as to constitute numerous individuals of the same species. Two drops of water, so perfectly similar though they be, are *two* because they are constituted by two distinct parts of matter; thus also for two twins. The created pure spirit is a pure, substantial form; therefore, there cannot be two angels of the same species. If it were so, they would be completely indiscernible (i.e., identical). Thus, whiteness would be unique if it were not *received* in a material subject, i.e., if it were to subsist as a pure quality.[9] Created pure spirits are wholly specifically distinct, far more than are the seven colors of the rainbow.

The Object of the Natural Knowledge of a Pure Spirit

What is the proper object of our intellect?

The object of every intellect is intelligible being. The *proper* object of the Divine Intellect is the Divine Intelligible, the Divine Essence.

The *proper* object of the angelic intellect is *our own essence*, where, naturally, as in a mirror, we know God. The proper object of your human intellect is the intelligible nature of sensible things.[10]

This is why the human intellect is the last and *the weakest of intellects*, having as its proportionate object, *the least of intelligibles*, the intelligible being of sensible things, as the very weak eye of the owl sees only at dusk or before dawn. This is why your intellect needs the senses

---

[9] [Tr. note: The point is a thought experiment of sorts used by St. Thomas on occasion. Whiteness, wholly of itself, does not differentiate itself into *this* or *that* whiteness. For such differentiation, a subsistent subject would be needed, itself individuated by matter.]

[10] See *ST* I, q. 12, a. 4.

in order to know its object in the shade of the sensible.[11] Your natural knowledge, no matter how perfect it may become, remains as though in the twilight.

Although your ideas are *abstracted* from sensible things (where, as though in a mirror, your intellect knows spiritual things), *our ideas* are in no way the fruit of abstraction for us; instead, they are a *participation in the Divine Ideas*, in the *Active Ideas* by which God is the cause of things.[12] Both extramental things and our ideas representing those things to us are derived from these Divine Ideas, these Eternal Exemplars. And as the Divine Ideas represent not only the universal character of things but also that which is singular and concrete in them, so too our angelic ideas are *concrete universals* that represent not only natures but also individuals, not only the lily [i.e., the nature of the lily] but also the lilies [i.e., as individuals], not only man but also men in their very singularity.[13]

Each of our ideas of things that are inferior to us is thus a kind of intelligible panorama that represents to us immense regions corresponding to numerous human sciences.

From this fact, it follows that our knowledge is in no way *discursive*; it is very superior to reasoning, for we intuitively[14] see the singulars in the universal and the conclusions in the principles.[15]

Similarly, in order to judge, we do not need to compose (or, unite)

---

[11] *ST* I, q. 76, a. 5.

[12] [Tr. note: For some help on this, see the insightful, if somewhat idiosyncratic, reading of John Deely on these matters, following John of St. Thomas, in "The Semiosis of Angels," *The Thomist* 68, no. 2 (2004): 205–58.]

[13] [Tr. note: In addition to Fr. Garrigou-Lagrange's treatment of the topic of the Divine Ideas in his commentary on the *Summa*, see the recent work of Gregory Doolan, *Aquinas on the Divine Ideas as Exemplar Causes* (Washington, DC: Catholic University of America Press, 2011).]

[14] [Tr. note: On this topic, see note 31 in the second chapter of this section. However, some important qualifications need to be made regarding intuitive knowledge in the angels, given that they are not abstractive in their primary mode of conceptualization. See the insightful remarks in Yves Simon, *An Introduction to the Metaphysics of Knowledge*, trans. Vukan Kuic and Richard J. Thompson (New York: Fordham University Press, 1990), 85n1. See also Jacques Maritain, *Bergsonian Philosophy and Thomism*, trans. Mabelle L. Andison and J. Gordon Andison (New York: Philosophical Library, 1955), 150–58; and Deely, "The Semiosis of Angels."]

[15] *ST* I, q. 58, a. 3.

ideas or to separate them—as you need to do.[16] Our intellectual intuition permits us to attain immediately, with a given nature, its properties (e.g., with the nature of man, his various properties); and we also see the contingent existence of a given man inasmuch as this existence derives from the Divine Ideas according to the free will of God.

Why do we not need to reason as do you? It is because of the vigor of our intellect, which enables us to attain at one and the same time the created spiritual order and the sensible from on high in the spiritual. In contrast, your intellect, due to its weakness, cannot attain at one and the same time the intelligible abstracted from the sensible and, in this inferior mirror, the higher things.

From this, it follows that we cannot be deceived regarding that which is (and is not) suitable to the *very nature* of things. Our natural knowledge thus attains all the workings of the universe, which are in relation with one another. What we cannot attain are the mysteries of grace, future contingents, and the secrets of hearts. I will explain soon why this is the case.

Finally, the superior angels, due to the very vigor of their intellects, know, by *very few ideas, immense regions of the intelligible world* that inferior angels attain only by more numerous ideas and by multiple, successive thoughts. The succession of these thoughts does not have continuous time (like that marked out by the solar hour) for its measure; instead, it has for its measure *discrete time*, in which one instant represents a thought and the following instant represents another. One instant of our angelic time can thus correspond to ten, fifty, or more years in your time, depending on whether we stop more or less at a given thought.

However, while *our time* may be superior to yours, it is infinitely distant from the *unique instant of immobile eternity* that is the measure of the Divine Life. However, participated eternity is the measure of the Beatific Vision by which we see supernaturally God immediately (as He sees Himself) and love Him (as He loves Himself). There, at the summit of our intelligence and that of all the saints, there is no more mutability, no more succession.

---

[16] Ibid., a. 4.

The Limits of the Natural Knowledge of the Pure Spirit

By our natural powers, we know God as the proper and unique Cause of our being—each of us according to a unique, active virtuality of the Divine Being. However, this knowledge remains abstract, for there is not an intuitive knowledge of God without grace.

The Deity (i.e., God's intimate life) absolutely exceeds our natural knowledge. By our natural powers, we know much better than does man that God is Being Itself, Wisdom Itself, Love Itself, Mercy Itself, Justice Itself, and Sovereign Freedom. However we cannot grasp by our natural powers how all these absolute perfections are *identified without being destroyed in the eminence of the Deity*—that is, in the intimate life of the Most High. This is so because our natural powers of knowledge grasp God only in the *mirror of our nature*. That is, we know Him in an ever so inadequate effect. Yes, in this effect, there is indeed a participation in being, intelligence, and will. However, there is not a *participation in the Deity*. We have received this superior nobility only by *grace*, which is really and essentially distinct from our nature.

Just as our natural knowledge cannot attain unto the intimate life of God, no more can it attain unto *sanctifying grace*, which is of a wholly supernatural order and of a supernaturality far superior to that of a miracle that might, of itself, be naturally knowable. The mysteries of grace absolutely exceed the natural knowledge of even the most elevated angels.

By way of our natural powers, we cannot know with absolute certitude if a given man is in a state of grace. Likewise, we cannot know the degree of charity he has attained. Still, the demons themselves perfectly know the miracles that confirm faith.

We have other limits as well. So long as God does not wish to manifest them to us, we cannot know His free decrees relative to the future, even in respect to *future contingents* of the natural order: for example, when the end of the physical world and the laws that currently govern it will be.

Moreover, there are things already existing that escape us—*the secrets of hearts*. We see with great clarity the body, the soul, the latter's faculties (whether superior or inferior), and the degree of science and acquired virtues that are in a given man. We see his exterior acts and the agitation of his sensibility. However, *the free act* of his will escapes our vision, inasmuch as that free act remains *absolutely immanent* and is not manifested externally by a word or a gesture. This secret of the heart is indeed *not necessarily linked to any working of the world.* It is not linked to any of the pieces of the universe that we have indeed perfectly known. Your will itself has only a contingent relation with this interior act, which it can—while remaining the same—revoke or transform.[17]

This is not known except by God alone and by each of you, for God alone produces in you and with you this *free act* and its *free mode.* He alone is able to produce it with you, just as He alone was able to give you a will ordered to the universal good. The order of agents corresponds to the order of ends. Only the most universal Cause can move from within a free will ordered to the universal good (and, thus, to the Supreme Good). So long as you do not wish to manifest them to us, these purely interior free acts are the secret of God and of you; it is one of the grandeurs of the hidden life and of the mystery that is found in it.

* * *

With regard to ourselves, we know ourselves immediately. Our intellectual faculty emanates from our dazzling essence at one and the same time as from its subject and its object.[18] Our absolute immateriality makes

---

[17] See *ST* I, q. 57, a. 4. See also the commentary made on this by John of St. Thomas.

[18] [Tr. note: That is, the angelic intellect emanates from the angelic essence as a quality emanates from its substance (i.e., the subject in which it inheres); simultaneously, its very first object is that same essence, which is already intelligible. The situation is quite different for the human intellect. It does indeed emanate from our substantial essence as from its subject. However, its first object is the quiddity of material things, not our substantial essence. We win our way to self-knowledge step by step and only indirectly. The topic of self-knowledge in Aquinas is a very interesting and difficult issue. See Réginald Garrigou-Lagrange, "Utrum mens seipsam per essentiam cognoscat, an per aliquam speciem," *Angelicum* 5 (1928): 37–54. A translation of this article is anticipated in a future volume by Emmaus Academic. Also, for a survey on the current state of discussions of this matter, see the detailed study in Therese Scarpelli Cory, *Aquinas on Human Self-Knowledge* (Cambridge: Cambridge University Press, 2013).]

it that we are immediately intelligible for ourselves in act. However, we do need to express ourselves to ourselves in an interior word, an accidental mode of our thinking, which is itself an accident in our spiritual substance. God alone is *Being Itself* of Itself ever *known* and not merely knowable.[19] He is Eternally Self-Subsistent Thought—*Ipsum intelligere subsistens*—a pure, eternally subsistent intellectual flash.

We see the world of bodies such as it evolves through time, as it derives from the *active ideas* of God. Thus, in virtue of a pre-established harmony, the clock marches with the same step as do the stars. Our idea of sensible beings remains immobile in the specific types that they express, although it only successively represents the individuals as they progressively appear in time. The past remains engraved in us, recorded in these determinations, unless we have not given attention to a given fact that, thus, does not leave the aforementioned trace. As regards the future, we can conjecture it by examining secondary causes; however, God alone can see it in His decrees, for second causes do not contain all that there is. In created freedom—indeed, even in matter—there is an *indetermination* that does not permit us to foresee with utter certainty. We must await the instant of the appearance of the contingent fact and its certitude. For us, like you, there is a double obscurity—that from below (due to the indetermination of matter) and that from on high, for if, by grace, we see the Divine Essence immediately, we do not, however, have a comprehensive view of it. We do not know God in the fullness of His intelligible depths; we do not attain the infinite multitude of possible things, and we know not what in the future depends upon God's free decrees, for they are not manifest to us. However, we do know that God is the Author of every good and that nothing would be better than something else if it were not more loved by God. This is the very foundation of humility. We know as well that no evil happens

---

[19] [Tr. note: That is, for its initial specification of intellection, the angel does not need an *impressed* species. Being *intelligible in act* already, his own essence functions as that specifying intelligibility for intellection. However, this essence, while *intelligible in act*, is not *actually intellected*. For that, the angel must express himself to himself. That is why he needs a *verbum/conceptus/species expressa intellecta*. Only in God is knowledge so interior and simple that He is at once intelligible in act and known in act. On this, see Simon, *An Introduction to the Metaphysics of Knowledge*, 73–84 (esp. 82–83n46).]

unless God has permitted it for the sake of some superior good—though, we cannot always say precisely what this superior good may be.

Our will follows our intellect. We love God seen face-to-face with a love that is utterly spontaneous, though it is not free—*with a love that is superior to freedom*—for we are invincibly ravished by the vision of Infinite Goodness. Sin is no longer possible for us. Our beatitude consists in seeing God and loving Him; and it is an ever new joy for us to make Him known and loved.

*   *   *

Thus can the angel speak concerning the life of a pure spirit and of its limits.

This brief sketch of the life of the created pure spirit shows us what remains mysterious for us without it being obscure for the angel. For us, there is a notable amount of obscurity deriving from the fact that our intellect is the *least of created intellects*, to which corresponds, as its proper object, *the least of intelligibles*, the intelligible being of sensible things.[20] It is in this ever so inferior mirror that we know spiritual things here below. It is why we define them *negatively* as *immaterial*—in order to speak of pure spirit, we are obliged to speak of matter, at least by denying it. We also define them *relative* to sensible realities, saying that a given spirit is elevated, extensive, penetrating, subtle, or luminous—making allusions to the dimensions of space or to certain properties of bodies.

In contrast to this state of affairs, the created pure spirit knows spiritual realities immediately; and, in them, the created pure spirit knows, from on high, sensible beings, which it must conceive as being *nonspiritual*, as we conceive spirit as being *nonmaterial*.

By this, we see that the part of mystery (or, obscurity) is greater for us than it is for the created pure spirit. However, the created pure spirit certainly has *the sense of mystery* more than we; for, this sense is the characteristic of superior intellects. The higher such intellects are elevated, the better do they see the transcendence of the intimate life of

---

[20] See *ST* I, q. 76, a. 5.

God and the sovereignty of His Freedom. Much better than we do, the angel knows that no intellect that has ever been created (or ever could be created) can, *by its own natural knowledge,* demonstrate the possibility (or the intrinsic nonrepugnance) of the mysteries of the Trinity, of the Incarnation, of eternal life, or of our elevation to the life of grace. *Possibilitas horum mysteriorum nec probatur, nec improbatur, sed suadetur* [The possibility of these mysteries is neither proven nor disproven; it is only suggested persuasively].

The angel sees better than we do that, if someone demonstrates the nonrepugnance of the Trinity, that same person demonstrates at the same time Its existence, for the Trinity is not something contingent but, instead, something necessary.

The angel sees better than we do that the argument of the suitability [of the Beatific Vision], taken from the natural desire to see God, does not rigorously demonstrate the possibility of this ESSENTIALLY SUPERNATURAL (and not only contingent, like a mere free choice in the natural order) *mystery that is eternal life.* The angel sees better than we do that such an argument from suitability is something of admirable grandeur, that it can always be deepened, and that it tends, at the limit, toward evident knowledge [*une évidence*]. And better than we does the angel see that this evidence, which is found *at the limit,* is not that of a demonstration, but that of the Beatific Vision.

The sides of the polygon, inscribed within the circumference of the circle, can be ever multiplied, but never will it be reduced to being a point; never will the polygon be the circumference. Never will it be the case that reasons of suitability concerning supernatural mysteries will be demonstrations of them. These are sublime probabilities, above the sphere of the demonstrable; they allow one to approach from a distance (along with infused contemplation, which remains in the order of faith) that which will be the *wholly supernatural evidence* found in the Vision of the Divine Essence.

Chapter 8

The Spiritual Chiaroscuro

HAVING SPOKEN OF THE SENSE OF MYSTERY in the intellectual order, it is appropriate for us to close by considering it in relation to the life of the soul. Often, there is a spiritual chiaroscuro in the interior life. This chiaroscuro can be disconcerting for us when we do not arrive at distinguishing (as is necessary) the superior obscurity of certain ways of Providence from the inferior sort of obscurity arriving from sin, error, or bodily troubles (from the slightest to the gravest), which are often quite difficult to understand well.

Let us first recall that each of our free acts contains a mystery: if it is good and salutary, it contains the mystery of grace; if it is evil, it contains the mystery of the Divine permission of evil in view of a superior good, which often still remains hidden. Now, in the concrete reality of life, there is not a single deliberate act that remains indifferent.[1]

As the ridge formed at the crest of a hill separates every drop of water, making every drop proceed to the left or the right of this line, so too could one say that each of our deliberate acts, due to the fact that it is either posited or not posited for a good end, leads either to the left or the right of the line separating good from evil. And who can precisely measure the consequences of each of his words and each of his acts? Here, we find something very mysterious immediately next to something that is very clear. It is clear that every deliberate act (considered in its concrete reality) is either morally good or morally

---

[1] See *ST* I-II, q. 18, a. 9.

evil—if not by reason of its object (which can be indifferent), at least by reason of its end. We must always act for a good end in whatever we do, even in the diversions that we undertake for the sake of refreshing our powers so that we can continue our work. If we deviate from this path, we begin to lose ourselves—and what will be the consequences for doing this?

To this obscurity is added that of certain tests that we undergo. Already we see this in the natural order, where, for example, it is not rare that a real intellectual or moral superiority is accompanied by some great misfortune. Perhaps one recalls the exile and poverty of Aristides the just, the death of Socrates, the captivity of Vercingetorix (who was strangled by Caesar's order), the disgrace of Christopher Columbus, the complete deafness by which the musical genius of Beethoven was overcome. Infirmity sometimes comes to afflict man in that which is precisely his glory. Thus, it is necessary for him to have a true magnanimity, a true grandeur of soul.

However, above all else, the spiritual chiaroscuro stands out in the supernatural life of the soul, particularly in the two crises often studied by great spiritual authors—the crises that are called the passive purification of the senses and the passive purification of the spirit. We have spoken of these at length elsewhere.[2] We will speak here only about the aspects of the question that pertain to our immediate concerns.

The Chiaroscuro of the Night of the Senses

One of the great imperfections found in beginners in the spiritual life is the unconscious self-seeking that can happen in work and prayer. It is the natural willingness to be carried toward that which validates ourselves, for example within study and exterior activity; likewise, it is expressed in the interior life as a kind of spiritual "sensuality," an immoderate desire for sensible consolations and spiritual pride.

Now, in order to purify the soul, God deprives it of these conso-

---

[2]   See Réginald Garrigou-Lagrange, *The Love of God and the Cross of Jesus*, trans. Sr. Jeanne Marie (St. Louis, MO: B. Herder, 1948), 2:3–195.

lations and this ease in which it lingers and that it abuses. The soul finds only *aridity and dryness* in prayer, especially in meditative prayer [*oraison*]. Nothing that is offered for meditation in the books that it once loved now attracts it any longer. It has the impression of being in the shadows, and a coldness penetrates it, as though the sun that illuminates and warms the spirit was now withdrawn.

The soul can poorly withstand this test, fall into spiritual sloth, and remain a tepid or retarded soul that exteriorizes itself in order to forget the emptiness that it finds within itself.

However, if, on the contrary, it successfully passes through this crisis of prolonged dryness, one sees that it ordinarily maintains a *recollection concerning God, fear* of not serving Him, and *lively desire of loving Him.* Then, a third sign appears in it: with the dryness and the fear of not serving God well enough, there comes *an inability to meditate* in a way that is discursive and, instead, an inclination to have in meditation [*oraison*] *a loving regard for God* in order to be spiritually nourished by Him, His Truth, and His Goodness.

Whence comes this? St. John of the Cross explains it:

> Whence comes—he asks himself—the inability to meditate, as had been its custom, by having recourse to the sense of imagination? The effort remains without result. *The reason for this is that God now begins to communicate Himself no longer through the senses*, as before, by means of discursive reasoning, which evoked and classified knowledge heretofore. Instead, *He now communicates Himself by means of pure spirit*, which knows not reason's discursive chains and is the place where God communicates Himself *in an act of simple contemplation.*[3]

Thus, the aridity of sensibility and the difficulty of applying oneself to discursive meditation arise from the fact that grace takes on a new, purely spiritual form without repercussions upon our sense powers, [a form] superior to the discourse of reason, which uses imagination.

At first, the soul believes that light and consolation have been

---

[3]   St. John of the Cross, *Dark Night of the Soul* 1.9.

removed from it, that it enters into an obscure night. However, in reality, it receives here an *infused, superior light.* "This passive purification of the senses is common; it is produced in a great number of beginners," if they are truly generous.[4] According to St. John of the Cross, this marks the entrance into the illuminative way, for he then adds: "The proficients (or, advanced) are found in *the illuminative way; this is where God nourishes and strengthens the soul by means of infused contemplation.*"[5]

In this obscure passage from an inferior form of light to another that is more spiritual, there are often two concomitant tests: temptations against the virtues of chastity and patience, which are seated in the sensibility, so that the soul may be steeled by a generous resistance; and exterior difficulties, contradictions, and trials permitted by God so that we may do the good not from a natural willingness in us for seeking ourselves but, instead, for Him, in ever asking for His assistance.[6] If one passes through this crisis well, it is like a second conversion that calls to mind that of Peter during the dark night of the Passion.[7] Thus does one arrive at a superior form of light, at a spiritual life more disengaged from the senses. Here, one truly is nourished by the mysteries of salvation—the mystery of the Redemptive Incarnation, the Sacrifice of the

---

[4]　Ibid. 1.8.

[5]　Ibid. 1.14.

[6]　We see a very striking case of this spiritual chiaroscuro in the life of the foundress of the Redemptoristines, Bl. Marie-Céleste Crostarosa, recently published by the Redemptorist, Fr. Jean Baptiste Favre. In the midst of unbelievable hardships, Our Lord said to her: "My spouse, it is me, not a demon. Everything that is done to you in relation to this work, I will consider it as though it were done to me. Hope in me and be assured that you will see it established. . . . You know how much I was scorned. . . . I passed my existence amidst humiliations, the hidden life, and scorn. Thus it was that I glorified my Father, established the foundations of my Church, and remedied the evils of men's pride. . . . Take no account of the favorable judgment of men, for I love you with a perfect love, and dispose all things for your greatest good." In this ever so beautiful life, the chapter entitled "Un direction divine" is one of incontestable grandeur.

　　[Tr. note: A translation of the work can be found in Jean Baptiste Favre, *A Great Mystic of the Eighteenth Century: The Ven. Sister Mary Celeste Crostarosa*, trans. Anonymous Redemptoristine of the Convent of Chudleigh (London: A. Ousley, 1935).]

[7]　[Tr. note: For a more extended reflection on the themes of the conversions of the spiritual life, see Fr. Garrigou-Lagrange's *The Three Conversions in the Spiritual Life.*]

Mass, communion, the indwelling of the Holy Trinity in us, and eternal life. One begins to know them in a manner that depends less upon the senses, in a manner that is less bookish; in a saintly manner, one is familiarized with them in seeing the supernatural radiance of infinite Goodness in them. Then, the intimate conversation that man has with himself tends, indeed, to become a conversation with God.

*   *   *

Then, the intellect of the proficients is submitted to God. If they are faithful, He gives them, no longer, strictly speaking, sensible consolations as in the spiritual age that precede the night of the senses, but instead gives a *greater abundance of light* in prayer and in action, as well as *lively desires* for His Glory and for the salvation of souls. Thus, the proficients experience a rather great readiness for prayer and acting for the good of their neighbors.

However, it is not rare that, through an unconscious pride, the soul takes pleasure in this great readiness; it tends to forget that this is a gift of God, taking pleasure in it with a self-satisfaction, which is in no way fitting to someone who adores God in spirit and in truth. Here, we find an unconscious concern with oneself that makes one lose one's purity of intention and perfect righteousness. In this state, one is too certain of oneself, one gives too much importance to oneself, one prefers oneself to others, one does not take care regarding one's own weakness. Practically speaking, one forgets that God alone is great. This is a sign that *the very depths of the soul* are not yet purified—indeed, that they are far from it. St. John of the Cross has well noted these defects of those who are advanced in the spiritual life, noting well their spiritual or intellectual pride, which sometimes leads them to deviate altogether.[8]

From this comes the necessity, as he says, "Of the strong lye of the purification of the spirit," in order to clean the very depths and foundation of the superior faculties.

---

[8]   See St. John of the Cross, *Dark Night of the Soul* 2.2.

The Chiaroscuro of the Night of the Spirit

Here, there is a new spiritual chiaroscuro, one that is more striking and that, during a period of crisis, if it is borne well, becomes a transformation of the soul so as to introduce it into the unitive way of the perfect.

Here, the soul seems to enter into an even darker night. It appears utterly shorn—not only of sensible consolations but also *of its lights* concerning the mysteries of salvation, *of its ardent desires, of the readiness* for praying and acting in which it delighted with a secret pride, thus preferring itself to others. It is a time of *great aridity*, not only sensible aridity but also *spiritual aridity* during prayer [*oraison*]. And it is not rare that great temptations arise, no longer precisely against chastity and patience, but against the virtues of the most elevated part of the soul—against faith, hope, and charity both toward neighbor and even toward God, who seems cruel to test souls in such a crucible through such a state of soul. Thus, it is necessary *to believe* in His love for us.

God, who never commands the impossible, gives great graces if the soul for its part does not resist them and lets itself be led by Him. In the midst of these interior difficulties, which often are augmented by external distractions and obstacles, the generous soul performs often-heroic acts of faith, as well as acts of confidence in God and love of Him. Under the light of the gifts of the Holy Spirit, we then see in powerful relief (despite the obscurity of the night) *the First Revealing Truth* (the motive of infused faith), *the Merciful Help of God* (the motive for hope), and the *Infinite Goodness of God* (the primary object of charity). In the night of the spirit, these are like three stars of highest grandeur that enable one to advance while *the very depths of the soul* are purified.

The servant of God thought he was entering into a profound night in which he was bereft of all his lights. In reality, this impression arises from a spiritual light that is even more elevated and more intense, that illuminates the soul to the point of dazzling it with regard to its indigence and its poverty and by the infinite grandeur of God. St. John Vianney saw so clearly the full ideal of the priest that he believed himself to be so very distant from it. More and more did he discover the immense needs of innumerable souls who addressed themselves to him, and he asked himself how he should respond to them. Thus, he prostrated himself before the tabernacle, like a small dog at the feet of its master.

Here, in the night of the spirit, there is a profound transformation of the soul. It calls to mind the transformation that Pentecost effected upon the Apostles. "The soul receives a new manner of considering things. The light and grace of the Holy Spirit being very different from the perceptions of the senses . . . and also from the common manner of understanding things, . . . the soul thus thinks itself to be walking outside of itself."[9]

Thus, the soul is introduced into the perfect, unitive way, where *it knows God*, present within it, *in a way that is quasi-experiential* and nearly continuous. Instead of unconsciously considering oneself and bringing everything back to a relation with oneself, the soul now brings everything back to God. It no longer contemplates Him in the mirror of sensible things, nor even in that of the mysteries of Christ's life. The soul now contemplates God in Himself. In the penumbra of faith, it contemplates *the Divine Goodness* from Whom proceeds all that is good, a little like how we see the diffused light that illuminates from on high all things. This contemplation, greatly superior to discursive reasoning, brings to mind a kind of circular movement or the flight of the eagle that loves to make its path many times in the same circle in the heights of the sky.[10]

Thus, the servant of God truly becomes "an adorer in spirit and in truth." He has peace, the tranquility of order; he can give it to others, and he thus arrives at bringing peace to the most tormented of souls. It is the fruit of the cross of the spirit at the end of the dark night, in this superior sort of light, where the soul feels more and more that which is the *intimate life of God*, far above all the analogical concepts that we can form concerning Him and that represent Him very imperfectly (as we have said, somewhat like the small squares of a mosaic representing a human face). Thus, the soul feels experientially that, in this intimate life of God, there are identified (without being destroyed) Infinite Wisdom, Love, Justice, Mercy, and Sovereign Freedom. Thus,

---

[9]   St. John of the Cross, *Dark Night* 2.9.

[10]   See *ST* II-II, q. 180, a. 6.

with a new light, the mystery of predestination is illuminated, along with the truth that every good, whether natural or supernatural, comes from God.

Finally, the Passion of the Savior appears in a new light. The soul discovers in the Passion, next to the obscurity of the greatest of crimes (indeed, of hell-inspired deicide), an incomparable splendor—the splendor that definitively illuminated the good thief and the centurion and the splendor that captivated the Virgin Mary, St. John, and the holy women. Above the obscurity from below (i.e., that of sin and death), there appears ever more and more the grandeur of the mystery of the Redemption, which contains the entire history of the world. The spiritual chiaroscuro, in which the soul must continue to walk until the end of its travels, is expressed in an ever better manner for it in this expression of the Savior, an expression that the soul tastes and more deeply understands: "Qui sequitur me non ambulat in tenebris, sed habebit lumen vitae" ("He who follows me will not walk in darkness, but will have the light of life") (John 8:12).